CW01091578

STRONG WOMEN

THE CLARENDON LECTURES
IN ENGLISH 2007

STRONG WOMEN

Life, Text, and Territory

1347–1645

DAVID WALLACE

OXFORD
UNIVERSITY PRESS

OXFORD
UNIVERSITY PRESS

Great Clarendon Street, Oxford, OX2 6DP,
United Kingdom

Oxford University Press is a department of the University of Oxford.
It furthers the University's objective of excellence in research, scholarship,
and education by publishing worldwide. Oxford is a registered trade mark of
Oxford University Press in the UK and in certain other countries

Published in the United States of America by Oxford University Press
198 Madison Avenue, New York, NY 10016, United States of America

British Library Cataloguing in Publication Data
Data available

ISBN 978-0-19-954171-3

For our mothers

Acknowledgements

This book has slowly developed from a series of Clarendon lectures, given at Oxford in October 2007; I am grateful to Andrew McNeillie, Sally Mapstone, and Vincent Gillespie for facilitation and warm hospitality. It incorporates some material from the 2005 Matthews lecture (Birkbeck, University of London); thanks here are due to Anthony Bale, Carol Barwick, Ruth Clydesdale, Vanessa Harding, Thomas Healy, and Sally Ledger. Jacqueline Baker of Oxford University Press showed great patience and understanding as this project evolved into book form. Further thanks are due to Ariane Petit and Jenny Townshend, and to Kay Clement for copy-editing and Christine Shuttleworth for indexing.

I began teaching courses on premodern women on moving to the University of Pennsylvania in 1996; my greatest debt is to those who studied and argued with me, showed me the way (and occasionally the door). Many of these women are now colleagues, friends, and professors of literature; thanks, then, to Holly Barbaccia, Rachel Buurma, Urvashi Chakravarty, Clare Costley, Jane Degenhardt, Jennifer Higginbotham, Rosemary O'Neill, Maria Cristina Santos Pangilinan, Genelle Geertz-Robinson, Robbie Glenn, Marissa Greenberg, Stephanie A.V. G. Kamath, Michelle Karnes, Jessica Rosenfeld, Veronica Schanoes, Stella Singer, Jamie Taylor, Suzanne Webster; Ian Cornelius and Jon Hsy; Aryn Klich, Sara Gorman, Erica Machulak, Maxine Mendoza, Sara Murphy, Brooke Palmieri, Bethany Wong; and, more recently, Tekla Bude, Elizabeth Churchill, Megan Cook, Kara Gaston, Emily Gerstell, Caroline Henze-Gongola, C. J. Jones, Sierra Lomuto, Marissa Nicosia, Chelsea Pomponio, Courtney Rydel, Elizaveta Strakhov, Marie Turner, Bronwyn Wallace, and Alex Devine. Lana Schwebel (1971–2007), the first graduate student who worked with me at Penn, was a *mulier fortis* indeed; her memory lives on in all that we do.

I am grateful to friends and colleagues who read parts of this work at various stages, including Rita Copeland, C. J. Jones, Melissa Sanchez, Paul Strohm, and Nancy Warren, and to audiences at Adelaide, Belfast,

Cambridge, Canterbury, Chicago, Cleveland, Edinburgh, Florence, Germantown, Kalamazoo, New York, Rochester, Swansea, and Villanova. Colleagues at Penn in Comparative Literature, English, Italian Studies, Religion, Romance Languages, and Women's Studies have provided both tough criticism and abundant proof that we are, embarrassingly, America's happiest campus. Some responsibility for this lies with Rebecca Bushnell, Ann Matter, and Ralph Rosen, our deans in Arts and Sciences; thanks for understanding and support in tough times. The Penn med/Ren seminar, based in the English department, shapes and informs every aspect of this book. My understanding of literary periodization has been sharpened by the brilliance of Margreta de Grazia, and of Jennifer Summit (Stanford). Only in finishing this project can I see how the pioneering History of Material Texts seminar—led at Penn, week in and week out, by Peter Stallybrass and Roger Chartier—has reformed my *modus agendi*. Daniel Traister, prince of bookfinder-librarians, must never retire; John Pollack, Cathy Henderson (Harry Ransom Centre, Austin, Texas) and David Sutton (University of Reading Library) have offered invaluable advice on matters of copyright. Friendships sustained through the weekly coffee klatsch at St Patrick's, Philadelphia, enrich my life; thanks here to Yvonne Cook, Commander Andrea Lemon, Soo-Jin Ridgell, Mary Stanulis, and Joan and Joe Tedesco. Members of the Philadelphia Reevaluation Counseling communities help me stay connected and thinking; special thanks to Milly Lilly, Rachel Gazda, Patti Hoyt, Marcy Morgan, Ellen Deacon, and Nancy Sleator for holding my manly feet to the fire. I owe most to Cynthia Fowler: counsellor, friend, engineer.

A book about women's *lives* cannot but be inspired and instructed by the lives and writings of friends; and so I would like to recognize Crystal Bartolovich, Ardis Butterfield, Terry Castle, Jacky and Tricia Clarke, Helen Cooper, Mary Erler, Elaine Freedgood, Barbara Hanawalt, Claire Harman, Ann Hutchison, Ann Rosalind Jones, Kathryn Kerby-Fulton, Clare Lees, Sheila Lindenbaum, Ania Loomba, Heather Love, Claire MacDonald, Darielle Mason, Jenna Mead, Elena Moses, Caroline New, Miri Rubin, Diane Shisk, Emily Steiner, Sophie Steiner, Stephanie Trigg, Susan Williams, and Nicolette Zeeman; Robin Kirkpatrick, Gordon McMullan, Bill Sherman, Paul Strohm, and Colin Thubron. My work on Mary Ward would not have been possible, simply put, without the support, generosity, and very considerable practical assistance of Christina Kenworthy-Browne CJ, Gemma Simmonds CJ, and the late

Gregory Kirkus CJ. Paul Quinn, producer of our BBC Radio 3 documentary on Margery Kempe's 1433 journey, taught me much about finding locations and asking the right questions; our path from King's Lynn to Gdańsk and back was illuminated by Kate Parker, John Arnold, Eamon Duffy, Agnieszka Błewicz, Zbigniew Borcowski, Jerzy Litwin, Beata Możejko, Jerzy and Justyna Limon, Cornelia Oefelein, Sandra Lowerre, Stuart Jenks, Peter Johanek, A. C. Spearing, Pamela Robinson, Vincent Gillespie, and Prunella Scales. I learned much from involvement in Primavera Productions' staging of *The Tragedy of Mariam* in the Nag's Head, Islington, on 2 July 2007; and thanks to the Anglican Benedictines of Burford Priory, Oxfordshire, who provided access to their building (before selling up and moving on in 2008).

My greatest debt of all, accumulated over thirty years and counting, is to Rita Copeland. During the last year, especially, we have grown closer in attending to our extraordinary mothers: to Lilian Beryl Lucetta Wallace who, having recovered rapidly from hip surgery, soon resumed driving and has just won silverware again with Wessex Ladies; and to Evelyn Goldin Copeland, who was playing Chopin at her piano (before the eyes of an astonished visiting rabbi) just days before her death at Brith Shalom, Philadelphia, on 6 February 2010, aged 95. These two women, born far apart, came to love and respect each other perfectly; to them, and to the spirit of their friendship, this book is dedicated.

All photographs are my own, with the following exceptions, for which acknowledgment is made: (3) *America*, Bibliothèque Nationale, Paris, France/ Giraudon/ The Bridgeman Art Library; (5) 'Jeanne d'Angleterre', the estate of George (György) Buday (1907–1990), as yet untraced; (10, 11, 13, 14) artwork and architecture at Gdańsk photographed by Alicja Sobecka; (16–17) King John's Cup, photographed by David Wallace with the permission of the Borough Council of King's Lynn and West Norfolk; (20–24) *Painted Life*, Geistliches Zentrum Maria Ward, Augsburg and Foto Tanner, Nesselwang, Germany.

Contents

List of Illustrations

Introduction

> Here begynnyth a schort tretys and a comfortabyl for synful wrec-
> chys, wherein thei may have gret solas and comfort.
>
> Margery Kempe

L iterature is the truest history. Historians compile data to fashion an
account that is uniquely their own, told in their own voice. Literary scholars, however, must give way to voices from the past; the premodern speaker awaits her turn on the page. But women wait less
hopefully than men. It takes a *strong woman*,[1] this book will argue, to

1. A *mulier fortis*, in the biblical tradition of Proverbs 31, a series of instructions by the
queen-mother to her son Lemuel. Her advice on administering justice, perhaps first
framed in a northern Arabian tribal context, modulates into an acrostic poem in praise
of strong female qualities at verse 10, rendered thus by Vulgate: 'ALEPH: Mulierem
fortem quis inveniet procul et de ultimis finibus pretium eis' (*Liber Proverbiorum*, in
Biblia Sacra iuxta Vulgatam Versionem, ed. Robert Weber, 2 vols (Stuttgart:Württembergische
Bibelanstalt, 1969), 31.10; *The Oxford Bible Commentary*, ed. John Barton and John
Muddiman (Oxford: Oxford University Press, 2001), p. 422a-b). Recent biblical translations, such as the New Jerusalem or the New English, speak of 'a capable woman',
evoking a domesticated sub-heroine from a Barbara Pym novel rather than the formi-
dable *mulier fortis* of Jerome. The 1609 Douay Bible, the first rendition of the Old
Testament for English post-Reformation Catholics, translates as follows: 'A valiant
woman who shall finde? far, and from the utmost borders is the price of her' (*The Holie
Bible faithfully translated into English out of the authentical Latin*, tr. Cardinal William Allen,
Gregory Martin, and Richard Bristow, 2 vols (Douai: The English College, 1609),
Proverbs 31.10).The woman of Proverbs 31, Claudia V. Camp argues, 'is not simply the
maintainer of a household but the source of its identity'; 'in fact', she continues, 'the
female image in Proverbs 31 defines not only the home itself but also indicates the
proper character of the public domain' (*Wisdom and the Feminine in the Book of Proverbs*
(Sheffield:Almond, 1985), p. 92).The *strong women* of Proverbs excited much commentary and illustration in pre-Reformation Europe: see, for example, Barbara Newman,
Sister of Wisdom: St Hildegard's Theology of the Feminine (Aldershot: Scolar Press, 1987),
esp. pp. 42, 73–6.

secure bookish remembrance in future times; to see her life becoming a *life*. Even the strongest of women—such as Christine de Pizan, or Isabella Whitney—can, for many generations, disappear. Women might be remembered through their offspring—although childbirth can prove fatal, and children change names, or (especially young women) live far away. Written afterlife, for premodern women, seemed a remote prospect: for textual memorialization was chiefly a masculine practise, intended for male subjects. And yet women have always wondered what will become of them, and the memory of them, once their lives end. Here, for example, a female memoirist of our own time attempts to preserve some record of her youthful affair, as an ingénue graduate student, with 'the Professor':

At some point my mixed-up memories of her and much else might simply *expire*: like coupons for a defunct rug-cleaning service or an old take-out menu lying in the dry leaves of my porch. Then might a lesson be said to be learned: *I'll be expiring myself, of course—no doubt soon enough. After a while no one will remember either of us.*[2]

The comic-edged bleakness here owes something to the nondescript landscapes in which this 'writing' unfolds: from 'SoCal strip-mall stupor' (p. 168) to 'one of the big Midwestern state schools' (p. 194), 'my new (and strange) Grain Belt home' (p. 203). This young protagonist suffers intensely, like her premodern forebears.[3] Part of this suffering, as mediated by the older female author, lies in thinking that the very banality of her surroundings might muffle or swallow up or epitomize her *life*. Quite different in tone, although similarly absorbed with memorialization, is Christa Wolf's short novel *Nachdenken über Christa T.* With the austere beauty of a graveside metaphysical poet, Wolf meditates on how a vibrant, idiosyncratic woman—like and unlike the author—might be recalled.[4] Her *Versuch* or attempt orients itself, in its opening paragraph, between textual traces, the fact of the grave, and the challenge of location:

2. Terry Castle, 'The Professor', in *The Professor and Other Writings* (New York: Harper Collins, 2010), 153–340 (p. 202).
3. The puritanism of the all-female communities glimpsed throughout 'The Professor', rendered with great comic *brio*, is unnerving by any standard, modern or premodern.
4. Peter Böthig cannot resist proposing the elfin-featured Christa Tabbert (1929–1963), Wolf's friend since school days, as the model for Christa T.: see *Christa Wolf: Eine Biografie in Bildern und Texten*, ed. Böthig (Munich: Luchterhand, 2004), p. 73 (and photograph).

Nachdenken, ihr nach - denken. Dem *Versuch, man selbst zu sein.* So steht es in ihren Tagebüchern, die uns geblieben sind, auf den losen Blättern der Manuskripte, die man aufgefunden hat, zwischen den Zeilen der Briefe, die ich kenne. Die mich gelehrt haben, daß ich meine Erinnerung an sie, Christa T., vergessen muß. Die Farbe der Erinnerung trügt.
So müssen wir sie verloren geben?
Denn ich fühle, sie schwindet. Auf ihrem Dorffriedhof liegt sie unter den beiden Sanddornsträuchern, tot neben Toten. Was hat sie zu suchen? Ein Meter Erde über sich, dann der mecklenburgische Himmel...[5]

The quest for her: in the thought of her. And of *the attempt to be oneself.* She speaks of this in her diaries, which we have, on the loose manuscript pages that have been found, and between the lines of those letters of hers that are known to me. I must forget my memory of Christa T.—that is what these documents have taught me. Memory puts a deceptive colour on things.
But must we give her up for lost?
I feel that she is disappearing. There she lies, in her village cemetery, beneath the two buckthorn bushes, dead among the dead. What is she doing there? Six feet of earth on top of her, and the Mecklenburg sky above...[6]

Such 'thinking back' or 'afterthought' (*Nach – denken*: Wolf pointedly splits her verb) was both alluring and dangerous in the German Democratic Republic in the 1960s and 70s: a place where anything but *collective* memorializing was *de facto* unprogressive, retrograde.[7] And now, amazingly, the very structure that lent *Nachdenken* its thrilling, *aktuell* timeliness (to all who read it in East Germany) has itself collapsed: the wall is down, and east and west—the retro Ossie quaintness of Alexanderplatz, the roaring capitalist excess of Kurfürstendamm—are now the same place, Berlin.

Wolf marked the heady events of 1989 by publishing an autobiographical narrative entitled, instructively, *Was bleibt* (*What Remains*). In the 1960s Wolf had struggled to get *Nachdenken*—a stark challenge to the ontologies of socialist realism—past the state censors: the versions of 1965 and 1967 were rejected, and the book only finally appeared in 1969.[8] In 1990, *Was bleibt*— in which a woman writer fears being spied

5. Christa Wolf, *Nachdenken über Christa T.*, ed. Sonja Hilzinger (Munich: Luchterhand, 1999), p. 11.
6. Christa Wolf, *The Quest for Christa T.*, tr. Christopher Middleton (New York: Farrar, Straus and Giroux, 1970), p. 3.
7. See David Wallace, 'Inside East Germany', *The Tablet*, 231 (1977), pp. 859–60, 884–5.
8. See Gail Finney, *Christa Wolf* (New York: Twayne, 1999), pp. 31–2. It is amusing to observe this novel of so many questions, beginning with 'so müssen wir sie verloren

on by the STASI—got her into trouble again: why had this narrative, composed in 1979, not been published until June 1990?[9] Had not Wolf, the most fêted of all DDR writers, enjoyed an altogether too cosy relationship with the state apparatus? Two aspects of these attacks are worth addressing. First, Wolf clearly hoped that the newly-united Germany of east and west might find a *third way*, rather than see the western capitalist model win out so completely, *über alles*.[10] And second, all her critics were men; Wolf is, above all, the great novelistic explorer and exponent of the first-person female.[11] Christa Wolf knows that she, too, will shortly become subject to *Nachdenken*; or, that the process has already begun.[12]

The four women considered in this book are Dorothea of Montau (1347–1394) and Margery Kempe of Lynn (*c.*1373–*c.*1440); Mary Ward of Yorkshire (1585–1645) and Elizabeth Cary of Drury Lane (*c.*1585–1639). Work of recovery begins, like Wolf's, with textual remains and local geographies: but wide expanses of time divide us from these women. The earliest texts of these *lives* are mostly near-contemporaneous with the women they represent, but their public reappearances have been partial and episodic, with their own complex histories. Dorothea of Montau's *Leben*, for example, comes to us via one early manuscript (messy and incomplete), a first printed edition of 1492, another edition (1863) invested in the Franco-Prussian war, and deployment as both a bulwark against eastern paganism (early in her career) and

geben?' (p. 11), provoking so many questions in its censors: 'Woher ist ein solches Buch des Rückzugs zu erklären?'; 'Weshalb beschriebt die Autorin sie [Christa T.] und dieses ihr Leben?' (*Dokumentation zu Christa Wolf, Nachdenken über Christa T.*, ed. Angela Drescher (Hamburg: Luchterhand, 1991), pp. 36, 47.

9. Christa Wolf, *Was bleibt: Erzählung* (Frankfurt am Main: Luchterhand, 1990); *What Remains and Other Stories*, tr. Heike Schwarzbauer and Rick Takvorian (New York: Farrar, Strauss and Giroux, 1993). The files containing STASI observations of Wolf, it turns out, extend to 42 volumes: see Sonja Hilzinger, *Christa Wolf*, Suhrkampf BasisBiographie, 24 (Frankfurt am Main: Suhrkamp, 2007), p. 53.

10. 'When the cry "We are the people" changed to "We are one people"', says Grace Paley, 'freedom, unemployment, and colonization of East Germany began'.

11. Anna K. Kuhn, 'Rewriting GDR History: The Christa Wolf Controversy', *GDR Bulletin*, 17 (Spring 1991), p. 10; Finney, *Wolf*, p. 10.

12. An article entitled 'Nachdenken über Christa W.' was published as early as 27 March 1969 (by Günter Zehm, in *Die Welt*, a newspaper that he then edited: see now *Wirkungsgeschichte von Christa Wolfs Nachdenken über Christa T.*, ed. Manfred Behn (Königstein: Athenäum, 1978), pp. 38–9).

Bolshevism (in the 1930s); her canonization in 1976 is attended by a polemical scrap that pits Cardinal Ratzinger against Günter Grass. The textual afterlife of the three other women—Margery Kempe, Mary Ward, and Elizabeth Cary—is similarly complex and eventful. Even in yearning to get as close as we possibly can to the lives of these women, then, we must acknowledge that their *lives* (responding to so many complex, posthumous agendas) keep us at bay. For me, the ambition (if not the desire) to speak with the dead—as dreamed by Petrarch, and by Stephen Greenblatt—seems much to ask.[13] But then, as Carolyn Dinshaw argues, 'if we did not already in some sense connect with Margery, we could not even begin to understand or historicize her'.[14] Dinshaw connects with medievals through brilliant *touches*.[15] This book approaches them chiefly through the post-life traces, histories and landscapes, of their *lives*.

Each of these women is a *mulier fortis*, a strong woman: had she been otherwise, her *life* would never have been written. Christa T. first becomes memorable, enrolling herself in the narrative time of first-person memory, by acting egregiously; *Nachdenken*'s opening chapter begins thus:

> Es war der Tag, an dem ich sie Trompeten blasen sah.   (p. 15)

> It was the day on which I saw her blowing a trumpet.   (p. 6)

All four women in this book shock and surprise. Dorothea of Montau whips her body to the consistency of muddy furrows and spends all day in church; only one of her nine children, abandoned at home, survives. Margery Kempe, mother of fourteen, astonishes Norwich by showing up at the cathedral in white robes on Trinity Sunday; her piercing cry, learned at Jerusalem, empties churches. Mary Ward maddens Catholic priests, from London to Rome, by living holily but un-immured; she is thus, according to such men, an Amazon, a chattering hussy, an Apostolic

---

13. 'I began with the desire to speak with the dead': Greenblatt, *Shakespearean Negotiations: Social Energy in Renaissance England* (Berkeley: University of California Press, 1988), p. 1.
14. 'Temporalities', in *Middle English*, ed. Paul Strohm, Oxford Twenty-First Century Approaches to Literature (Oxford: Oxford University Press, 2007), p. 115. See further, on queer kinship, Dinshaw, *Getting Medieval: Sexualities and Communities, Pre- and Postmodern* (Durham, NC: Duke University Press, 1999), p. 158.
15. See *History's Queer Touch: A Forum on Carolyn Dinshaw's Getting Medieval: Sexualities and Communities, Pre- and Postmodern*, ed. Elizabeth A. Castelli, *Journal of the History of Sexuality*, 10.2 (April 2001).

Virago, and a galloping girl. Elizabeth Cary, having left her husband torturing Catholics in Dublin castle, converts to Roman Catholicism in Irish stables in London; her neglect of common civilities and personal dress, according to her more orderly daughters, is legendary. The impulse to pathologize these strong women persists, as teachers can attest, in modern classrooms and critical texts. But part of what makes these women *strong* is their channelling of historical energies: if Margery Kempe is insane (for being Margery Kempe), so too is Henry IV (for murdering Richard II; for burning Lollards).

Each of these women lives, like Christa Wolf, on an edge of historical danger: the strength of character demanded from them, while living, invests their *lives* with something greater than individual personality. Dorothea of Montau lives at the far eastern border of Teutonic Christendom, where the *Drang nach Osten* of Germanic colonial settlement bogs down in the mud. The violence directed at her body—by a succession of male overlords, and by her own hand—speaks to and of this place (and ultimately, I shall argue, of borders as yet unmarked). Margery Kempe seems drawn to the religious hotspots not just of Arundel's England, but of all Europe: she sees the holiest Christian sites of Jerusalem under Muslim escort; she flees Danzig as a Hussite army razes the suburbs. And she maps the extended terrain of the Hundred Years War: the troops that arrest her in 1417 will later burn Joan of Arc. Mary Ward is three when the Spanish Armada sails and comes of age with the gunpowder plot; related to almost all the plotters, she first pursues her religious vocation in the Spanish Netherlands. She is later imprisoned in a Munich cell, with blood-spattered walls, and then shadowed by Vatican spies. Elizabeth Cary, disinherited by her father, is denounced by her husband as a traitor to England. She learns Irish, creates a native Irish cloth industry, and (having converted) kidnaps two of her sons and sends them to Paris for Catholic education; she is interrogated in Star Chamber.

Each of these women lived not for picaresque adventuring (although with Margery one does wonder), but to realize spiritual imperatives; the only *life* of interest to them, should anyone care to remember, was a religious one. Their times of life enabled them to court danger in pursuing highly distinctive models of Catholic practise; through such danger they become *strong women*. Terry Castle would likely not claim such a title: the handle she proposes for herself, in her memoir, is 'Spoiled Avocado Professor of English at Silicon State University' (p. 166).

But if too little historical danger fails to test and define *strong women*, too much makes it impossible to endure: there are periods of history when violence disables rather than nurtures such living, and the writing of such *lives*. A woman may act as a lightning rod for contentious issues (as did Mary Ward, in her apostolate of the streets): but a woman dying violently and arbitrarily, frazzled to a crisp, loses much of her *life* to the perpetrator. Power totalized in a single masculine figure, and his state apparatus, is not friendly to the kind of female *life* writing explored here. For this reason, and for others explored below, this book avoids the English Reformation. Of course, courageous women lived and wrote in those decades; but in crucial ways, their life/*life* was not their own. Consider the last day, and the last speech act, of Anne Boleyn. The precise dating and location shortly to be given suggest that the reader is in for 'a touch of the real'; the violence of this hermeneutic[16] compounds the violence of this scene, namely the judicial murder of an anointed queen.

On the morning of Friday 19 May 1536, Queen Anne Boleyn, kneeling upright, was beheaded on Tower Green by a swordsman from Calais. C. C. Humphreys, billing himself as 'a schoolboy fencing champion and a fight choreographer', affirms that her head sat on her shoulders until raised by the hair: a remark that sparks alternative imaginings of her head flying across the scaffold.[17] To go down that imaginative path—wondering about Anne's last conscious thought—is to retrace Henry's increasing fascination with the *techne* of killing his wife. We might rather then turn to Anne's last speech, given minutes before:

Good christian people, I am come hether to die, for according to the law, and by the law, I am iudged to death, and therefore I will speake nothing against it. I am come hether to accuse no man, nor to speake any thing of that wherof I am accused and condempned to die, but I pray God saue the king, and send him long to raigne ouer you. For a gentiller, or a more merciful Prince was

---

16. For discussion of the phrase 'a touch of the real', as formulated by Catherine Gallagher and Stephen Greenblatt, see Steven Justice, 'Literary History', in *Chaucer: Contemporary Approaches*, ed. Susanna Fein and David Raybin (University Park: Pennsylvania State University Press, 2010), p. 203. 'The anecdote', says Justice, writing of New Historicist method, 'was not experienced as "literary" because it was what held the literary at bay: it counted as the real' (p. 203).

17. C. C. Humphreys, *The French Executioner* (London: Orion, 2002), p. 2, and see further p. 31. Humphrey's book is endorsed as 'an entertaining read—a charming page turner' (David Evans, *Edmonton Journal*) and as 'a rollicking good yarn' (John Daly, *Irish Examiner*).

there neuer, and to me, he was euer a good, a gentle and soueragyne Lord, and
if anye personne will meddle of my cause, I require them to iudge the best,
& thus I take my leaue of the worlde and of you all.

This unhappy leavetaking would seem to capture that crucial moment
of life becoming *life*: a person ceasing to draw breath, at a particular
place and time, assumes textual afterlife. This book does indeed consider how four strong women negotiate this space, this transition. The
first two, living in post-pandemic, pre-Reformation Europe, are linked
by the east–west axis of Hanseatic trade. The second pairing, of exact
contemporaries, lives through the reigns of Elizabeth I, James VI and I,
and Charles I; continually drawn to the same parts of London, they
negotiate a north–south axis of faith that leads to Rome. All four of
these women end their lives, non-violently, as Roman Catholics. Pressures of the Reformation, especially in England, tended to crush—
rather than inform—the lives of strong women: their capacity to
determine their own *lives* (the written accounts we have of them)
appears highly impaired. One has only to think of Elizabeth Barton,
the 'nun of Kent', whose destruction was assured the moment she
doubted Henry's divorcing of Anne Boleyn; or even of Anne Askew,
whose *life* (as mediated and continually interrupted by John Bale, that
awful ambulance chaser) is imperfectly her own.[18] Even the admirable
Katherine Parr and the plucky Princess Elizabeth turn servile in facing
the gale of Henrician reform, or the idiot wind of Henry's paternal
will.[19] The Reformation decades in England, structuring so powerfully
the period paradigms in which we think, hardly allow us to reflect

18. See Nancy Bradley Warren, *Women of God and Arms: Female Spirituality and Political
    Conflict, 1380–1600* (Philadelphia: University of Pennsylvania Press, 2005), pp. 119–38;
    Alan Neame, *The Holy Maid of Kent: The Life of Elizabeth Barton, 1506–1534* (London:
    Hodder and Stoughton, 1971); *The Examinations of Anne Askew*, ed. Elaine V. Beilin
    (New York: Oxford University Press, 1996).
19. For Elizabeth's only known letter to Henry VIII, prefacing her translation of Queen
    Katherine Parr's *Prayers or Meditations*, see Elizabeth I, *Autograph Compositions and
    Foreign Language Originals*, ed. Janel Mueller and Leah S. Marcus (Chicago: University
    of Chicago Press, 2003), pp. 8–9; Elizabeth I, *Collected Works*, ed. Leah S. Marcus, Janel
    Mueller, and Mary Beth Rose (Chicago: University of Chicago Press, 2000), pp. 8–10.
    On Katherine Parr, see James Kelsey McConica, *English Humanists and Reformation
    Politics under Henry VIII and Edward VI* (Oxford: Clarendon Press, 1965), pp. 225–6;
    Janel Mueller, 'Katherine Parr and Her Circle', in *The Oxford Handbook of Tudor
    Literature, 1485–1603*, ed. Mike Pincombe and Cathy Shrank (Oxford: Oxford
    University Press, 2009), p. 229.

upon processes of making female *lives*: their recollection, reviewing, and commitment to writing. The Reformation reorders lives (including those of its students and scholars) according to its own furious, idiosyncratic logic.

But Anne Boleyn cannot be left so heartlessly at the block. Her fate, as we shall see, haunted the imaginings of literate women down the sixteenth and seventeenth centuries;[20] and the vexed relations of life to *life* in her unhappy case offer instructive points of departure. Her final speech could never be her own, from its moment of first articulation: it soon spread through Europe, in various translated and elaborated forms, before assuming a subordinate place within greater textual projects. The version above, for example, appears in the 1563 edition of John Foxe's *Book of Martyrs*, prefaced by the following formula: 'The words of this moost worthy Lady, at the hour of her death were these'.[21] Herald Charles Wriothesley (1508–62) offers a different account in his *Chronicle of England*. Charles—who claimed cousinage with Thomas Wriothesley, the 'lorde Chauncellor' who personally racked Anne Askew[22]—attended both Anne Boleyn's creation as marquis of Pembroke in 1532 and her coronation in 1533.[23] Here is his text of her last speech:

Maisters, I here humblye submitt me to the lawe as the lawe hath judged me, and as for myne offences, I here accuse no man, God knoweth them; I remitt them to God, beseechinge him to have mercy on my sowle, and I beseche Jesu save my sovereigne and maister the Kinge, the most godlye, noble, and gentle Prince that is, and longe to reigne over yow.[24]

20. See Chapter 4 below, pp. 211–17.
21. John Foxe, *Actes and Monuments* (London: John Day, 1563), III, p. 526. This account actually sees Anne die talking: the passage cited above, ending '& thus I take my leaue of the worlde and of you all', continues 'and I hartely desire yow all to pray for me. O Lord haue mercy on me, to God I commende my soule, and then she kneled down, sayinge: To Christ I commend my soule, Iesu receiue my soule diuers times, til that her heade was stricken of' (III, p. 526).
22. '*Anne Askew.* And bycause I laye styll and did not crye, my lorde Chancellour and master Ryche, toke peynes to racke me their owne handes, tyll I was nygh dead' (*Examinations*, ed. Beilin, p. 127). On the relations of Charles to Thomas Wriothesley, see Charles Wriothesley, Windsor Herald, *A Chronicle of England during the Reigns of the Tudors*, ed. William Douglas Hamilton, 2 vols, Camden Society NS 11, 20 (London: Camden Society, 1875–77), I, pp. iii–v.
23. See Gordon Kipling, 'Wriothesley, Charles (1508–1562)', *ODNB* online (2004).
24. Wriothesley, *Chronicle*, ed. Hamilton, I, pp. 41–2.

Some themes are shared by the Foxe and Wriothesley versions of Anne's last speech: her submission to the framework of law; her characterization of Henry as most 'gentle' of princes. But what we have here is the generic scripting of an iconic act: the *langue* of public execution, not the *parole* of personal departure. Alison Weir's recent recreation of Anne's death scene weaves together a great and diverse array of French, Spanish, Portuguese, and English sources.[25] But the denser this quilting of supposedly eyewitness testimony becomes, the greater our sense that Anne's actual words are irretrievably lost. Weir's inability to *leave the scene* leads her, as it leads others, into moments of desperate, almost pornographic, speculation: how the sword might have been designed to channel blood away from its leading, cutting edge; how many seconds (two? thirteen?) might Anne's brain have continued to work, post-decapitation.[26]

Weir's tarrying with the queen here, her unwillingness to let Anne Boleyn give up the ghost, is certainly something with which I can sympathize. Some years ago, I identified Anne's beheading as the effective terminus of Chaucerian courtly rhetoric: that is, the moment at which Chaucer's scripting for eloquent queens—surrogates for Anne of Bohemia, who stood between her subjects and her irascible spouse—becomes historically redundant.[27] Once a king can kill his queen, I reasoned, we lose those possibilities of articulate, wifely mediation that, through centuries of courtly romance, have saved many a 'nekke-boon from iren'.[28] The beheading of Anne Boleyn must traumatize anyone reading forward from medieval English time. But the cure here is not to remain fixated on her scene of departure, and the impossibility of reassembling her last speech, but to *continue* reading forward. Eventually one comes to Henrietta Maria, a queen who again deploys the full range of romance tropes and theatrics to charm and persuade her spouse; when revolution comes around, again, it is the king who perishes, and not the queen.

James Simpson opens the second chapter of *Reform and Cultural Revolution*, the volume of the Oxford English Literary History covering

25. *The Lady in the Tower: The Fall of Anne Boleyn* (New York: Ballantine Books, 2010), pp. 273–87.
26. *Lady in the Tower*, pp. 285–7.
27. See *Chaucerian Polity: Absolutist Lineages and Associational Forms in England and Italy* (Stanford: Stanford University Press, 1997), pp. 383–4.
28. *The Wife of Bath's Tale*, in *The Riverside Chaucer*, ed. Larry D. Benson (Boston: Houghton Mifflin, 1987), 3.906; all references to Chaucer follow this edition.

the period 1350–1547, by describing Lord Protector Somerset's destruction of the cloister on the north side of St Paul's. Lost in the cloister wall's rubble in 1549 is 'the Marchabray, or dance of death, commonly called the dance of Pauls', a painting adorned by 'meters or poesie...translated out of French into English by Iohn Lidgate, Monke of Bury'.[29] Simpson then considers what has been lost, in every sense, by such violent erasure; he does much of this by restoring (in the fullest and most vigorous sense) Lydgate. He also deplores Somerset's razing of a medieval past in raising Somerset House:

> There can be no doubt but that the Duke's practise, conducted within a triumphalist Protestant regime, conforms to the revolutionary model of historical writing. The very act of unearthing the dead, and of dumping a thousand cartloads of their bones on unhallowed ground, itself marked a sharp break with the system by which the community of the living negotiated for the community of the dead.[30]

The *jouissance* of this powerful writing, even in marking the sharpness of historiographical fracture, draws more from the destructive duke than from the medieval dead. This phenomenon of men writing fiercely on the fierce effects of the English Reformation itself has a long history; scholars such as Eamon Duffy, Richard Rex, Diarmid McCullough, and Brian Cummings are only the most recent inheritors of this masculine lineage.[31] The urgency and occasional vehemence of such writing

29. John Stow, *A Survey of London*, as cited in James Simpson, *Reform and Cultural Revolution*, The Oxford English Literary History, 2, *1350–1547* (Oxford: Oxford University Press, 2002), p. 35.
30. Simpson, *Reform and Cultural Revolution*, p. 36. For a disenchanted view of the Wallace–Simpson relationship, see Elizabeth Scala, 'The Gender of Historicism', in *The Post-Historical Middle Ages*, ed. Scala and Sylvia Federico (New York: Palgrave Macmillan, 2009), pp. 205–6.
31. See Eamon Duffy, *The Stripping of the Altars: Traditional Religion in England, 1400–1580*, 2nd edn (New Haven: Yale University Press, 2005); Duffy, *Fires of Faith: Catholic England under Mary Tudor* (New Haven: Yale University Press, 2009); Richard Rex, *Henry VIII and the English Reformation*, 2nd edn (Basingstoke: Palgrave Macmillan, 2006); Diarmid McCullough, *Tudor Church Militant: Edward VI and the Protestant Reformation* (London: Penguin/Allen Lane, 1999); McCullough, *Reformation: Europe's House Divided 1490–1700* (London: Penguin/Allen Lane, 2003); Brian Cummings, *The Literary Culture of the Reformation: Grammar and Grace* (Oxford: Oxford University Press, 2002). See further Cummings, 'Reformed Literature and Literature Reformed', in *The Cambridge History of Medieval English Literature*, ed. David Wallace (Cambridge: Cambridge University Press, 1999), pp. 821–51. This last chapter in a literary history spanning the period 1066–1547 threatens, partly through the fierce brilliance of its writing, to swallow all that precedes it into the Reformation maw, to make the Reformation *fons et origo*: 'it may be no exaggeration to say that it is only with the Reformation that it makes sense to talk of something called "English literature" rather than "literature written in English"' (p. 824).

suggests that everything is being settled *now*, at this revolutionary time; comparatively few women scholars make their home in Reformation Studies. By way of escaping the self-encapsulating decades of this hyper-masculinist Reformation hothouse, then, we might again plot a path to Henrietta Maria. On the Feast of the Immaculate Conception of the Blessed Virgin Mary, 1636, we find this queen of England processing her way to Somerset House: Inigo Jones has built her a Roman Catholic chapel, and it is to be opened with a polyphonic pontifical mass. What had seemed inconceivable in 1549 becomes possible again less than ninety years later; women gather to perform masques centred on their French Catholic queen.[32]

The four principal women of this book died Catholic. Such a simple statement comes fraught with difficulties, evoking once again the turbulent forcefields of Reformation Studies. Our first, earlier pairing of Catholic women, Dorothea of Montau and Margery Kempe, might be thought to dwell unselfconsciously within the universalist claims of their religion: but, as we shall see, they show marked awareness—through travel and local knowledge—of the limits and borders of Catholic faith. For the second pairing, Mary Ward and Elizabeth Cary, the very ambition to live and die Catholic marks them as alien to and within their native polity; yet also intensifies in them a heightened sense of and longing for Englishness. We might thus speak of a plurality of female Catholicisms, sensitive not only to historical variations of practise but to modalities of female Catholicism—especially in the case of Mary Ward—as yet unfulfilled. At any event, it seems inadequate to consider these women as merely *religious*: for the category of *religious*, especially in Medieval Studies, comes too often twinned with implied, ghostly opposition to *secular*—an archaic antithesis which undersells the labile complexities of premodern writing.[33] *Writing*, rather than *religious*

32. See further Chapter 4 below, pp. 220–24. Comparably mind-popping spatial continuity is offered by the site of the English hospice of St Thomas in Rome, home to Margery Kempe in 1414; this became the Venerabile Collegio Inglese, the 'English College' which launched missions to re-Catholicize England; Elizabeth Cary's son Patrick met John Milton here in 1638. See Margaret Harvey, *The English in Rome, 1362–1420: Portrait of an Expatriate Community* (Cambridge: Cambridge University Press, 1999), pp. 1–2, 129–30; Chapter 4 below, p. 245. Continuity of practised space does not, of course, imply timeless identity of belief.
33. On 'the creation of an anthropological profane—that part of human affairs untouched by religion', see Jonathan Sheehan, 'Sacred and Profane: Idolatry, Antiquarianism, and the Polemics of Distinction in the Seventeenth Century', *Past and Present*, 192 (August

writing, seems a helpful point of departure, since those who compose these texts, I shall argue, themselves seem unsure of quite what (generically speaking) they are getting into. The borderline between romance and hagiography, for example, is famously elusive. A travelling woman—these women travel prodigiously—cannot be assured of providential framing *as her journey unfolds*; it is rather something to be hoped for, then written into her *life* at journey's end. Divinity assumes human form (as a feudal lord; as a jealous lover; as a spouse) to astonishing effect: how are we (author, reader, and female protagonist) to reckon with God as both player in the game, and the game's providential arbiter? Each of our four women, identified primarily with vernacular expression while living, maintains complex relations with Latinity in her textual afterlife; performativity and theatricality—marked traits of all four *lives*—merge with liturgical play[34] and sacramental action. And, by way of concluding this brief excursus on life and writing, we might recognize that the handy life/*life* binome, marking a difference between biological being and textual accounting, is itself unreliable: for as Mary Carruthers suggests, much living (especially by religious women) is devoted to imitating exemplary *lives*.[35]

The *lives* explored in this book stand at greatly varying distances from the lives of the women they represent. The hardest case is that of Dorothea of Montau: for her entire literary opus is controlled by the father-confessor who supervised both her enclosure at Marienwerder, and the earliest popularization of her cult. We can be certain of no scrap of *parole* attributed to Dorothea by *Das Leben der Heiligen Dorothea*: the German of that text does not transcribe her native tongue, but rather translates back from the Latin of her priestly confessor. The happiest case is perhaps that of Mary Ward: for here we have *lives*

2006), p. 38. See especially Section IV, 'Sacred and Profane: Human Science Categories' (pp. 60–66), which analyses the reductionist effects of a new social science of religion: 'All the world's people got religion, but it was a religion divorced from the ordinary parts of daily life, bounded in its own regime, distinct from the quotidian' (pp. 65–66).

34. See Katie Normington, *Medieval English Drama: Performance and Spectatorship* (Cambridge: Polity Press, 2009), esp. pp. 17–33.
35. *The Book of Memory: A Study of Memory in Medieval Culture* (Cambridge: Cambridge University Press, 1990), p. 180; see further Carolyn Dinshaw, 'Margery Kempe', in *The Cambridge Companion to Medieval Women's Writing*, ed. Dinshaw and David Wallace (Cambridge: Cambridge University Press, 2003), p. 230; Catherine Sanok, *Her Life Historical: Exemplarity and Female Saints' Lives in Late Medieval England* (Philadelphia: University of Pennsylvania Press, 2007), pp. 12–14.

composed by her closest female companions, autobiographical fragments, and a rich cache of correspondence (much of it autograph).
Elizabeth Cary, too, bequeaths us a *life* buttressed by letters. This *life*—
authored and emended, erased and glossed by her daughters—stages a
powerful agon: for how can you, even as a Benedictine nun, frame
your mother as a saint when you knew her as your mother? Margery
Kempe presents the most complex case of all; we have barely begun to
address the peculiar intimacies of her compositional process. The text
is *hers*, bought and paid for: but without her collaborator, a man of
exceptional literary gifts, there would be no *Book*. What new critical
language might specify its engendering?

Margery Kempe emerged to astonish the world in the 1930s; the
context of incipient European war determined, I shall argue, *what her
Book had to be* at the time of its first appearance. Dorothea of Montau,
too, is a creature of the 1930s; her twinning with Margery (especially
in the mind of Hope Emily Allen) must be read in that context. The
life of Elizabeth Cary only came fully into view in 2001, through the
brilliant editorial work of Heather Wolfe; and the time of Mary Ward
is *now*, or the immediate future. Part of the unfinished business associated with Mary Ward concerns enclosure, or resistance to it: a long-
standing issue for Catholic women, certainly, but of concern for
women of any religious tradition (or none) intent on public life. Since
enclosure, *clausura*, emerges as a major issue in all four chapters it seems
fitting to conclude here with a few preliminary remarks.

Attempts by Catholic clergy to enclose religious women with
greater rigour actually *increased* during the period covered by this book,
1347–1645: just one example of how progress over time for men may
spell the reverse for women.[36] Texts before this period, such as the
highly popular *Dialogus Miracolorum* by Caesarius of Heisterbach
(*c.*1180–1240), do not worry unduly about keeping women behind
walls. Indeed, the tales gathered by the Cistercian Caesarius show
plentiful signs of cross-gendered solidarity: life removed from the

36. The rise of universities, most notably, signaled increasing educational chances for men
and diminishing opportunities for women. No woman in Catholic culture has experienced the creative freedom in matters of music, dance, drama, fashion design, book
production, holistic natural science, public preaching and institutional self-governance
enjoyed by Hildegard of Bingen (1098–1179): see David Wallace, 'Periodizing Women:
Mary Ward (1585–1645) and the Premodern Canon', *Journal of Medieval and Early
Modern Studies*, 36.2 (Spring 2006), p. 401.

world is hard, so why should women carry a heavier variant burden of this sacrifice?[37] Worldly men, however, have long been fascinated by the dynamics of all-female communities; the tighter such enclosure becomes, the more intense the fascination. An obvious example here is *Decameron* 3.1, in which Masetto da Lamporecchio plays the part of a deaf-mute gardener in order to penetrate a community of nuns. But it is as a greater textual complex that the *Decameron* performs the more insidious work of confirming and naturalizing female enclosure. When pandemic plague grips Florence, the whole city (rather than just the cells of enclosed religious) hangs liminally between life and death. Female initiative establishes a new social order in the countryside: seven women and three men constitute a rotating monarchy, with each of the ten to rule for one day. Once the *brigata* returns to Florence, however, the three young men seek further public pleasures, while the women return to their homes ('alle lor case').[38] And in their homes, such women may read Boccaccio: for he writes, he says, for 'ladies with time on their hands'. 'And besides', he adds', 'since none of you goes to study in Athens, or Bologna or Paris, you have need of a lengthier form of address than those who have sharpened their wits with the aid of their studies'.[39] The invention of the novel, or at least of the Euro-novella, thus presents itself as a masculine device to keep education-deprived women off the streets.[40]

A later master of European short fiction, Denis Diderot, seemingly does better in penning his account of a woman inclaustrated against her will in *La Religieuse*. Encyclopaedist Diderot, 'the supreme figure of the Enlightenment',[41] was moved and inspired by the plight of Marguerite Delamarre, a woman seeking to end her life of conventual enclosure at Paris and return to the world. The first half of *La Religieuse*

37. See Caesarius of Heisterbach, *The Dialogue on Miracles*, 2 vols, tr. H. Von E. Scott and C. C. Swinton Bland, intr. G. G. Coulton (London: Routledge, 1929).
38. Boccaccio, *Decameron*, in *Tutte le opere di Giovanni Boccaccio*, ed. Vittore Branca, 10 vols (Milan: Mondadori, 1964–98), IV, p. 958. This is the last phrase of the last day; the 'Conclusione dell'autore' follows.
39. Giovanni Boccaccio, *The Decameron*, tr. G. H. McWilliam, 2nd edn (London: Penguin, 1995), p. 801; *Decameron*, ed. Branca, pp. 962–3.
40. Hence reserving them for private exercise of authorly *lingua*: see David Wallace, *Giovanni Boccaccio: Decameron* (Cambridge: Cambridge University Press, 1991), p. 107.
41. 'Introduction' to Denis Diderot, *The Nun*, tr. and intr. Leonard Tancock, lithographs by Charles Mozley (London: Folio Society, 1972), p. 5; Diderot, *La Religieuse*, ed. Heather Lloyd (London: Bristol Classical Press, 2000).

explores empathetically the life of a young woman perpetually immured against her will. The second half, however, abandons Enlightenment rectitude for lurid imaginings of what transpires between women in hidden circumstances, and what might drive them mad.[42] Diderot did not hurry to publish his text, which circulated among a few male friends.[43] Come the Revolution, however, *La Religieuse* was fêted for exposing the evils of the *ancien régime*; an edition was published in 1796, with translation into German, Italian, and English within a year. *La Religieuse*, much praised as forerunner of Gothic or psychological fiction, forgets the woman whose life first set it in motion.[44] Marguerite Delamarre lost her case for dispensation of vows in 1758 and remained locked up in perpetuity: a life with no true *life*.

Dorothea of Montau traveled to Marienwerder seeking religious enclosure for herself in 1393; she died one year later. Margery Kempe refused to be enclosed in a 'house of stone', in an anchorhold, or locked up at home with her husband; the martyrdom of tending to her elderly and incontinent spouse, following his tumble down the stairs, is clearly not (her *Book* suggests) the life she would have chosen.[45] Elizabeth Cary, mother to four Benedictine nuns, had no desire for either enclosure or rustication (to her native Oxfordshire): she loved living on Drury Lane, one of the busiest and noisiest of English Catholic locales. Mary Ward knew this part of London well, plus

---

42. According to Tancock, 'the evolution of the Superior from a kindly, if somewhat scatterbrained and comic, person to a sinister Lesbian is beautifully graded' (p. 10). Diderot's own sister Angélique died insane as an Ursuline nun at Langres, aged twenty-eight: see Otis Fellows, *Diderot*, 2nd edn (Boston: Twayne, 1989), pp. 15–16, 75–6; Richard Terdiman, *Body and Story: The Ethics and Practise of Theoretical Conflict* (Baltimore: Johns Hopkins University Press, 2005), p. 74.

43. It was published in Diderot's *Correspondance littéraire* in 1783, the year before his death: see Mita Choudhury, *Convents and Nuns in Eighteenth-Century French Politics and Culture* (Ithaca: Cornell University Press, 2004), p. 29.

44. Most literary criticism on *La Religieuse* shows scant interest in the later life of Marguerite Delamarre (for which see Annie Flandreau, 'Du Nouveau sur Marguerite Delamarre et *La Religieuse* de Diderot', *Dix-Huitième Siècle*, 24 (1992), pp. 410–19). Choudhury points out that between 1731 and 1789 only two Parisian nuns, Delamarre and Marie-Michelle Couhé de Lusignan, sought to renounce their vows; there were many more abjurations by men. Delamarre was actually a mature woman in her mid-thirties during her trial and not, like her surrogate Suzanne in *La Religieuse*, a teenage *ingénue*: but *vocation forcée* narratives, for which there was great public appetite, carried their own generic requirements. See *Convents and Nuns*, pp. 99, 123–4.

45. See *The Book of Margery Kempe*, ed. Barry Windeatt (Cambridge: D. S. Brewer, 2004), lines 870 ('hows of ston'), 6007–80. All references follow this edition.

urban spaces from Naples to Bratislava. It was her refusal of enclosure, coupled with her resolution to live as religiously on the streets as any nun in her cloister, which excited papal wrath. *Pastoralis Romanis Pontifici*, which abolished her movement in 1631, was an exceptionally harsh papal bull; Mary Ward's followers could not recognize Mary Ward as founder of her own movement until 1909. On 19 December 2009, however, she was recognized as a woman of 'heroic virtue' by Benedict XVI, and proclaimed 'Venerable'. What will the women of her movement, now spanning five continents, do next? Relief from regimens of enclosure promises more than license to roam in wide-open public spaces. It hopefully entails infiltrating, opening up, the enclosed masculine spaces of Roman Catholic life and governance—for the greater *salute*, health and salvation, of all men, women, and children. Mary Ward's words to sixty Englishwomen in Spanish Flanders, spoken in December 1617 but not published *as* spoken until 2007, sound an anticipatory note:

All looketh uppon you as new beginners of a cours never thought of before; merviling what you entend and what will be the end of you.[46]

---

46. *Mary Ward und ihre Gründung: Die Quellentexte bis 1645*, ed. Ursula Dirmeier CJ, 4 vols, Corpus Catholicorum 45–8 (Münster: Aschendorff Verlag, 2007), I, 363; for more on this 'spech', see Chapter 3 below, pp. 136–9.

I

Borderline Sanctity: Dorothea of Montau, 1347–1394

Exalta Deum Prussia
Pro Dorothea filia

> Hymn, cited in Nieborowski, *Die Selige Dorothea von Preussen*

...you make of your own body your very own kingdom where you
are the tyrant, the absolute dictator

> Hilde Bruch, *The Golden Cage*

wir wissen... nicht, was Dorothea gewollt hat

> Günter Grass, *Der Butt*

Dorothea Swarze was born in 1347 as the seventh of nine children, the youngest of five sisters, at Montau (now Montowy: the territory was designated Polish in 1945). From an early age, Dorothea cultivated extremes of ascetic practise and religious self-discipline. At the age of sixteen, following her eldest brother's initiative, she was married to[1] a swordsmith called Albrecht and then accompanied him forty miles upriver to his hometown of Danzig (now Gdańsk) and settled in that Baltic city.[2] While producing nine children, Dorothea

---

1. 'What is significant for the domestic relation is that women in the family, like serfs in feudal Europe, can both have and be property' (Joan Kelly, *Women, History and Theory* (Chicago: University of Chicago Press, 1984), p. 13).
2. The most reliable guide to such biographical matters is the 1992 Heidelberg dissertation now presented as Petra Hörner, *Dorothea von Montau. Überlieferung—Interpretation; Dorothea und die osteuropäische Mystik* (Frankfurt am Main: Peter Lang, 1993); on her marriage at Montau, see p. 13.

continued haunting churches and dark corners and practised extremes of self-mortification. In her thirty-eighth year, with all but one of her children dead, she went on pilgrimage with husband and daughter to Aachen (Aix-la-Chapelle, the citadel of Charlemagne). On returning to Gdańsk, she reportedly underwent her greatest visionary experience: the physical ripping out of her heart and her reception of a new one.[3] In her thirty-ninth year her husband sold up his possessions and they headed off to Aachen for a second time, hoping to settle permanently: but they returned to Danzig, following a sea voyage fraught with dangers. In 1389, Dorothea journeyed alone to Rome (for the 1390 jubilee); by the time she returned, after Easter 1390, her elderly husband was dead. In 1391 she moved sixty miles south of Danzig (twenty miles south of Montau) to Marienwerder (Polish Kwydyzn) and subjected herself to the spiritual direction of Johannes, a Dominican canon. On 2 May 1393, Dorothea was walled into a cell in Marienwerder cathedral, thus becoming Prussia's first anchoress, *Dorothea von Preußen*. Having survived an exceptionally cold winter, in which she was intensively interrogated by her confessor, Johannes von Marienwerder, she died on 25 June 1394. By 1406, 260 people from all over Prussia had attested to her sanctity, and there were 342 sworn and notarized accounts of miracles and cures.[4] The process of building her case for canonization was masterminded and controlled by Father Johannes. Having composed a series of Latin works,[5] in 1405 he

---

3. See Richard Kieckhefer, *Unquiet Souls: Fourteenth-Century Saints and Their Religious Milieu* (Chicago: University of Chicago Press, 1984), p. 29; Undine Brückner and Regula Forster, 'Die Herzenserneuerung bei Dorothea von Montau, Katharina von Siena und Muhummad', *Oxford German Studies*, 39.2 (2010), a special issue, ed. Almut Suerbaum and Annette Volfing dedicated to Dorothea, pp. 198–212; Annette Volfing, ' "Du bist selben eyn himmel": Textualization and Transformation in the "Life" of Dorothea von Montau', *Oxford German Studies*, 39.2 (2010), pp. 157–8.
4. Siegfried Rühle, 'Dorothea von Montau. Das Lebensbild einer Danziger Bürgerin des XV. Jahrhunderts', *Altpreussiche Forschungen*, 2 (1925), p. 99.
5. John of Marienwerder produced a trilogy of major Latin writings on Dorothea: the *Vita*, c.1398, and two books of visions (*Liber de festis*; *Septililium*); the German *Leben* selects and adapts carefully from these writings. As Karl Helm and Walter Ziesemer argue, 'das Werk ist in der Verdeutschung stark geändert' (*Die Literatur des Deutschen Ritterordens* (Giessen: Wilhelm Schmitz Verlag, 1951), p. 131): Marienwerder is intent, above all, upon fashioning a *life* for wide and popular consumption ('für Laien', p. 131). This means that biographical detail (childhood and marriage, pilgrimages and ascetic practices) is accentuated, whereas inner visions and theological excurses are downplayed. This, I would argue, brings us closer to Dorothea: for whereas Marienwerder employs his own extensive theological training in framing and

released a German text now known as *Das Leben der Heiligen Dorothea* but first printed, in 1492, as *Des Leben der zeligen frawen Dorothee clewsenerynne yn der thumkyrchen czu Marienwerdir des landes czu Prewszen.*[6] Bishops sent forward copies to their parish priests; churchgoers throughout Prussia heard tell of the extraordinary virtues of this great *merterlinne*, or martyr,[7] of the Prussian frontier.

Placing Dorothea

Clarissa W. Atkinson has argued that 'Dorothea of Montau (1347–1394) was the Continental holy woman closest to Margery Kempe in time, place, and spirit'.[8] Hope Emily Allen believed that the influence on Margery might well have been direct; here, as often, we can only regret that the second volume of Allen's great Kempe edition never appeared.[9] Parallels between the lives of Dorothea and Margery are indeed striking. Neither was blessed with the aristocratic pedigree that could win credibility for a female religious in the late Middle Ages (or secure a convent dower). Both inhabited spaces touched and inspired by Bridget of Sweden; both travelled on pilgrimage to Aachen and Rome. Both

smoothing the Latin texts, he is more dependent (as confessor-amanuensis) upon the words of Dorothea in detailing her life. As so often with women, *life and movement through the world* is likelier to be remembered, and to remain their own, than domestic or inclaustrated visions.

6. Such is the title chosen by Max Töppen in 1863; citations follow his edition. See *Dorothea*, ed. Max Töppen, in *Scriptores rerum Prussicarum*, ed. Theodor Hirsch, Max Töppen, and Ernst Strehlke, 5 vols (Leipzig: S. Hirzel, 1861–74), II, pp. 197–350. Töppen edits from the unique surviving manuscript witness of the *Leben* (then Royal Library, Königsberg, Nr. 1128, dated to the beginning of the fifteenth century). This manuscript was reported both mutilated ('sehr verstümmelt') and incomplete; Töppen supplements from the 1492 edition and finds some clarification from the Latin sources (*Dorothea*, ed, Töppen, II, pp. 187–8, 196). On the political significance of Töppen's 1863 edition, see below. Königsberg, founded by the Teutonic Order in 1255, was bombed to ruination in 1944; it was Russified and renamed Kaliningrad in 1946 and remains a Russian exclave. The manuscript is now at Toruń (German Thorn, another settlement with a long history of involvement with the Teutonic Order).

7. Translations follow (with some modifications) Johannes von Marienwerder, *The Life of Dorothea von Montau, a Fourteenth-Century Recluse*, tr. Ute Stargardt, Studies in Women and Religion, 39 (Lewiston, NY: Edwin Mellen Press, 1997).

8. *Mystic and Pilgrim: The Book and the World of Margery Kempe* (Ithaca: Cornell University Press, 1983), p. 179.

9. On Allen's strong personal attachment to Dorothea, see Dinshaw, 'Temporalities', p. 117.

inhabited and travelled through spaces of Hanseatic trade; each sailed along the Baltic coast when overland travel proved exceedingly dangerous. Each was burdened with a husband bent on fathering a large number of children (Dorothea calculated that she lost 360 days of churchgoing eligibility on this score; Margery lost more). Each of these husbands proved slow to die; each husband was finally persuaded to yield to a superior spouse (the Lord). Each woman worried about her sanctity as a non-virgin; each wept prodigiously (accelerating souls through purgatory); each reported elaborate visions involving visits from Jesus, chiefly as a strikingly handsome and well-dressed young man. Each was given to short, enigmatic utterances such as 'it is ful mery in hevyn' (328) and 'ich enkan nicht eygentlich sagen, wi mir was oder wi wol mir was' (2.7: 'I cannot really say how I felt nor how well I felt', p. 87); each was at times thought insane or feared going mad.

It is unlikely to be true, as Günter Grass reports, that 'Prinz Heinrich Derby' bought a gold-plated crossbow from Dorothea's husband, the Danzig swordmaker Albrecht Slichting, which he failed to pay for.[10] It is, however, certain that in the summer of 1392, when Margery was about nineteen, ships fitted out at Lynn carried Bolingbroke to Danzig: having sojourned with the Teutonic Knights, Henry and company intended to fight the pagans east of Prussia.[11] In 1433, Margery sailed to Danzig herself with her German-speaking daughter-in-law and stayed five or six weeks. Between these dates Margery learned something of Danzig and its religious culture from her son, her only known disciple, who had lived and worked in that Hanseatic port. Fanned by the enthusiasm of Atkinson and Allen, then, we approach the reading of *Das Leben der zeligen frawen Dorothee* with considerable anticipation: perhaps it might prove to be a prototypically German *Book of Margery Kempe*; failing that, perhaps 'Dorothee clewserynne' might provide Teutonic cousinage to her fellow recluse and exact contemporary, Julian of Norwich.

Such expectations are soon defeated. Scraps and fragments of clerical and mystical lore do indeed float between these East Anglian and Prussian texts; and it remains entirely possible that Margery Kempe knew of Dorothea's *Leben* before commissioning her own *Book*. But it is the differences between Dorothea of Montau and Margery of Lynn

---

10. *Der Butt: Roman* (Darmstadt: Hermann Luchterhand Verlag, 1997), p. 142; *The Flounder*, tr. Ralph Manheim (Brooklyn, New York: Fawcett Crest, 1979), pp. 117–8.
11. See further Chapter 2 below, p. 102.

that remain arresting, hence mutually clarifying. To grasp this we must commit to *reading* Dorothea's *Leben*: a process upon which much criticism has been loathe to report or to dwell.[12] One soon sees why.

Young body as ploughed field

The central and most defining experience of Dorothea's life, according to the *Leben*, occurred 'in the thirty-ninth year of her life and the tenth year before her death within eight days of the holy day of Candlemas' (2 February: 2.1, p. 77). Before the high altar of the great brick parish church of St Mary's, Danzig, Dorothea senses her old heart being ripped out and a new, hot one ('ein nuwe hitzig hertze') put in its place; this new organ, it is emphasized, really is a hot piece of flesh ('eyn hitzcig stucke fleischis', 2.1). *Das Leben* urges us to understand this heart transplant as a physical, and not merely spiritual, matter ('nicht alleyne geistliche, sundir ouch liplich geschen', 2.1): comparison is made to the sleeping Roman who, thanks to the work of surgeons Cosmas and Damian, awakes to find himself with one white leg and one black (cut from the body of a Moor, recently deceased). All this, however, is narrated at the beginning of Book II of *Das Leben*; our reading should properly begin with the Proem and Book I.

The Proem quickly brings us to a direct question:

Wer hat y gehort oder gelesen, das eyn mensche ym selben mit guten willen y hot also manchveldig manchirley groz bitter und lang liden gemacht, als sy ir gemacht hot an irre synlichkeit?

('Vorrede', p. 197)

Who has ever heard or read of human beings deliberately inflicting upon themselves such a variety of very bitter and lengthy sufferings as she inflicted upon her sensuous nature?

(p. 27)

---

12. A notable recent exception is Simone Haeberli, '*Manchirley groz bitter und lang liden*: Herkunft, Zweck und theologische Rechtfertigung der Leiden Dorotheas von Montau in der deutschen Vita des Johannes Marienwerder', *Oxford German Studies*, 39.2 (2010), pp. 124–37; see further Almut Suerbaum, '"O wie gar wunderlich ist die wibes sterke!"': Discourses of Sex, Gender, and Desire in Johannes Marienwerder's Life of Dorothea von Montau', *Oxford German Studies* 39.2, pp. 182–4.

Part of the strategy of this text is to forge imaginative associations between the *liden* of young Dorothea and the sufferings of the 'heiligen mertireren, di williclich mit vreuden zeu grusamer martir gingen' (p. 199, 'the holy martyrs, who willingly and joyfully confronted cruel martyrdom', pp. 29–30). The stumbling block here, however, is that Dorothea's cruelties are self-inflicted.[13] Marienwerder does point out that Dorothea's body is assaulted both by her own hand *and* by 'usirm herren, der sie vil gemartirt hot' (p. 197, 'Our Lord, who tormented her often', p. 28). But his most characteristic recourse, here as elsewhere in *Das Leben*, is to berate the wavering or resistant reader:

Und dorumme, du vylicher mensche, ader du widersprecher der werk gotis, die dir unbekentlich syn, swig und verstumme.

(p. 198)

Therefore, you beastly person or you who discredits the works of God which are incomprehensible to you, be silent and hold your tongue.

(p. 28)

German here finds two active verbs for keeping the mouth shut where English has none; a little later, Dorothea-doubters are likened to mad dogs devouring themselves with mindless barking ('wutenden hundes, der sich selbin vorzcert mit syme unvornumftigen bellen', p. 198). Book I proper opens with a rousing exhortation:

Hebit uf uwir ougin, negit uwir oren, aller inwoner Prusenlandes, und ouch alle cristgeloubige menschin, seht und vornemit, wi der alde, der ewige got syne gnade in dem lande zcu Prusen vornuwet hot an siner sundirlichen dirnen Dorothea genant.

(1.1)

Lift up your eyes, incline your ears, all inhabitants of Prussia and all believers in Christ. See and hear how the ancient, the eternal God has renewed his grace in the land of Prussia in his special maiden named Dorothea.

(p. 35)

The suggestion of grace *renewed* (*vorneuen*) in this region, rather than simply occurring, suggests a genealogy perhaps stretching back to Adalbert (martyred, as recounted by the Roman *Vita sancti Adalberti*, while attempting to convert the locals in 997). The life of Dorothea,

---

13. 'Die stetigste Quelle ihres Leidens ist Dorothea selbst' (Haeberli, 'Herkunft', p. 126).

Marienwerder tells us, cannot (like the lives of many other saints) be told briefly,

...von groser unwonlicher ubunge, castyunge, lydunge und ungehorter quol, die sie ir selbin anlegite, anzcuhebende vom sibenden jare bis an irs lebindes ende.

(1.1)

...because of the severe, uncommon spiritual exercises, castigations, sufferings, and unheard-of torments she inflicted on herself from her seventh year until the end of her life.

(pp. 35–6)

The age of seven was thought to mark the end of bodily innocence; after that date, a young person might experience sensations and temptations of a fleshly and sexual nature. Dorothea is seen limbering up for this lifelong *agon* even before reaching seven: under her mother's direction she performs serial prostrations; alone at night, she subjects herself to sleep deprivation, stands with her arms in the shape of a crucifix, hangs like a cross on the wall (pushing her fingers into holes, or draping arms over nails). Having reached seven, however, Dorothea suffers an unforeseen bodily assault that marks, as the chapter heading has it, the beginning of her sufferings ('Von der irsten sachen irre lydunge', 1.13):

Do dy seilige Dorothea das sibende jor irs aldirs anhub, do geschach is von vorsumnis, das sy mit sidendem wasser so gar begossen wart, das ir mutir also gros gequelt in grosir mitlydunge sy in eyner wigen dirqueychlen muste.

(1.13)

When the blessed Dorothea was seven years old, carelessness caused her to be scalded all over her body with boiling water to such a degree that her mother, greatly tormented by compassion, had to nurse the child in a cradle.

(p. 44)

In the midst of this trauma, which binds mother and daughter through diverse experiences of pain and mental suffering, Christ appears to offer comfort; the short chapter closes with Dorothea gazing at the starry heavens as her future home. Whereas the vision of 'hot flesh' at the beginning of Book II is framed as a climactic experience, this one seems foundational; it resonates strangely with the image of St John the evangelist boiling alive in a cauldron that Dorothea was to

encounter at Marienwerder many years later.[14] *Das Leben* itself immediately leaps forward to a holy conversation—or monologue—said to
have taken place several weeks after the feast of St Agnes, 1394 (a rather
forced dating: one that strains to keep contact with another mutilated
female saint). Christ here invites Dorothea to accept her status as
Christ's chattel ('du hast wol dirkant, daz das lebin myn was und nicht
dyn', 1.14) while contemplating 'the pain of great wounds that you
have lived since childhood' (p. 45). 'Consider', Christ says,

...how I kept your wounds open, brimful of bitter pain, whose scabs sometimes itched as though they were working alive with gnawing worms. At other
times they delivered such sharp jabs as if they were shot crammed full by sharp
arrows. Sometimes they burned as if ignited by fire. At times they swelled until
they broke open; at still other times they bled freshly and profusely with excru-
ciating pain as though they were indeed fresh and new. During such times your
eyes were so full of bitterness that even when you were asleep they seemed
filled with smoke and soot. Because ever since childhood you endured so many
and such serious wounds, you would have become lame, crooked, and ravaged
by the foulness of your wounds had I not miraculously protected you.

(pp. 43–4)

Betrachte, wi ich dine wundin offen hilt, dirvullet mit bittirn smertzen, in den
zcu stundin di rofe stymete als gnagende wurme, ab sie ir vol weren. Czu stunden
worin in yn so tovende schusse, ab sie vol weren scharfir phile. Etzwen hitzen sy,
ab sie gar vom fuyre entzunt weren. Ynhant swollen sy so hoch, das sy von swol-
ste ufbrochin. Andir wile von goer smerzcen bluten sy so frischlich und milde-
clich, ab sy frisch und nuwe weren. In dem liden worin dine ougin in slofis
zciten so vol bitterkeit, ab sy vol rouchs und romis weren. Du hattist von kind of
so vil und so grose wunden, hette ich dich nicht sundirlich enthalden, du weris
vorleemit und vorkrummit und vortorbin von fulunge diner wunden.

(1.14)

The suggestion, especially in that last German sentence, of willing
submission to physical pain twinned with willing application of it,

14. This Venetian mosaic image, commissioned by Pomesanian bishop Johannes Mönch,
is to be found above the south entrance of the building. St John the evangelist was
said, by *The Golden Legend*, to have been plunged into boiling oil at Rome during the
persecution of Domitian; unharmed by this experience, he was exiled to Patmos. See
Jacobus de Voragine, *The Golden Legend*, tr. William Granger Ryan, 2 vols (Princeton:
Princeton University Press, 1993), I, p. 51. On the influence of the *Legenda Aurea* on
writings associated with the Teutonic Order, see Helm and Ziesemer, *Literatur*, pp.
51–3. On John as a spiritual model in Dorothea's Leben, see Volfing, 'Textualization
and Transformation', pp. 154–8.

looks forward to the woodcut chosen for Jacop Karweysze's 1492 edition of *Das Leben* (the first book printed in Prussia): which sees Dorothea menaced by a shower of 'scarfir phile', sharp arrows. The injunction that the adult Dorothea should think her way back to childhood and the great wounds she suffered has already been plentifully fulfilled by the text. Chapter 5 of Book I told of 'wunden' aggravated by the wearing of a knotty hair shirt; of log pillows and sleepless nights; of crawling on hands and knees; of imaginary bondage coupled with hurlings face-first to the ground. Chapter 6 tells of the tortures of both fasting and forced eating; of remaining hungry at the dinner table or of eating yesterday's leftovers or the 'kleyne visschelyn' (little fishes) passed over by the servants. Chapter 12 sees the newly-wedded Dorothea jabbing her feet with needles to induce festering that (mistaken for frostbite) excuses her from dancing. Forced to the dance floor, she wears shoes and stockings to cover up her self-wounding. Vigorous movement fills her shoes with blood; straw-lined clogs chafe on her scabs and set her bleeding again. Chapter 15, immediately following the call to reflection on such moments quoted above, cycles us back to childhood as we cross (once again) the crucial *limen* of the seventh birthday, signalling the onset of sexual self-awareness. Dorothea is a heroine or conqueror ('heldyne'); the conquered territory (localized with great exactitude) is her own body:

Welche eyne heldyne sy was obir eren lichnam durch gots libe, mag eyn mensche vornemen, und wundirn, wen sie eren lichnam ofte slug mit rutin, pytzen, dystiln, dornswigen und mit hertin knotechtin geysiln vol stichiln. Ouch noch dem sebinden jore vorbrante sy sich uffte mit sedinden wassir, ouch zcu zeiten mit gloynden ysen und burnenden lichten. Czu stunden mit sedinder vettikeit vorserete und wunte sy sich an manchirley gledin als scholdirn, armen, huften, dyen, lendin, knyn, waden und vuzin, und machte mit den vorgenanten gezcoyen eyne wunde bi der andirn von den scholdirn bis da di ermil wantin, und von der huf ufwert, als is di kleyder bedackten, eyne wunde bi der andirn, und glichir wys tate sy daz vorne zcu an ire brust, das ir wunden so dichte bi ein andir worin, ab is eyne wunde wer, ir lip mit castyunge als eyn ackir mit eyme pfluge durchvarn.

(1.15)

What a conqueror she became over her body through God's love anyone may hear and marvel about, for she flagellated her body often with rods, whips, thistles, thorny branches, and with hard, knotty, barbed scourges. Even after her seventh year, she burned herself often with boiling water and from time to time with red hot iron and burning candles. At times she injured and wounded various parts of her body with boiling hot oil, mainly her shoulders, arms, hips, sides, loins, knees, calves and feet. With such devices she inflicted one wound beside the other from her shoulders down to the hems of her sleeves and from the hips upwards as far as her clothes covered the body. And she treated her breast in the same way until all these individual wounds looked like one single big wound and her body resembled a ploughed field.

(p. 46)

Marienwerder continues his account in ever-more harrowing detail, emphasizing again that such practices began 'in the seventh year of her life' (p. 47) and acknowledging, finally, that his account is 'difficult to listen to' ('swer zcu horinde ist'). The next chapter begins by addressing itself directly to the reader ('Gedenke, leser dises capitils'); we are soon summarily requested simply to accept the omnipotence of God ('gloube gots almechtikeit', 1.16). We then hear how Dorothea keeps her wounds 'open and fresh' by pricking and poking at them with stinging nettles, broom twigs, nutshells, and any other hard instruments laying to hand. Such wounds are sometimes submerged in brine; in winter she sits under dripping taps until frozen to the ground. Tinnitus, experienced as the whistling and roaring of a great flock of birds, reminds us of Margery Kempe (2968–71); Margery, however, hears just one bird at a time (a dove, and then a robin), and in her the effect is not induced by extremes of sleep deprivation and self-castigation. All this, Marienwerder summarizes, is to be celebrated as savvy *sacrum commercium* ('wysen koufinschatz'); but all this, he anticipates, may (again) spark readerly resistance:

Swig, du weleger, vylicher, fleischlichir, wollustegir, swachir, vorlosnir, dorftiger mensche, und widersprich nicht, noch entsrofe di wunderwerk gots.

(1.16)

Be silent, you smug, beastly, carnal, sensuous, weak, lost, wretched creature and do not contradict nor condemn the miraculous deeds of God.

(p. 48)

Although there is much to balk at in Marienwerder's text, the rebellious resistance he anticipates in his medieval Prussian readers may differ from what troubles us. We are appalled at violence applied to a tender young body; they may doubt that a *female* could withstand so much— that such a manly heart was encased in womanly flesh ('daz eyn sulch menlich hertze wer in eyns wibes lichnam', 1.16). This last phrase finds an echo in Petrarch's *Seniles* 17.3, where the young heroine is said to possess a manly soul of mature years in her virgin heart ('virilis senilisque animus virgineo latebat in pectore').[15] Correspondences between the Griselde and Dorothea stories have been noted by several readers.[16] Marienwerder's *Leben* is, of course, a clerk's tale: one in which the narrator assumes absolute, Walterian control of the writing process and of its female protagonist. Dorothea, who was unlettered, has scant life outside the text and little voice within it. Marienwerder has her enclosed within the cathedral of which he is canon. She is forbidden to speak to anyone without permission. Marienwerder, as Dyan Elliott has shown, determines the shape of Dorothea's *leben* by employing the extractive processes and privileges of the confessor; and he writes and disseminates the texts.[17] He writes first, moreover, in Latin. His German *life* returns to, rather than originates in, the vernacular; hope thus diminishes of catching particular inflections of Dorothea's tongue.[18] Dorothea is said to love him, on first seeing him at Marienwerder, like no other; her long speeches (which are actually long speeches of Christ, voiced through her) flourish only once she comes under his control. Towards him she must be totally obedient: 'was her dir gebewt', Christ tells her, 'das thu' (2.28); she must similarly obey her two battering spouses (Albrecht and Christ). All things that are to be done in the world will be done without her involvement ('an deine sorge', 3.1). She owns nothing; once dead, the Lord will decide whether she is to be buried naked or clothed ('blos adir gekleyt begraben', 3.3). Once she *has* died, Marienwerder attempts to control all reference to and memory of her: an extraordinary feat, since more than 260 people are called to testify in

15. See J. Burke Severs, '*The Clerk's Tale*', in *Sources and Analogues of Chaucer's Canterbury Tales*, ed. W. F. Bryan and Germaine Dempster (New York: Humanities Press, 1958), p. 302; all quotations from the Latin of Petrarch's Griselde story, *Seniles* 17.3, follow this text. The base text of Severs' edition is Biblioteca Apostolica Vaticana, Rome, MS Vat. Lat. 1666. For an edition based upon Peterhouse, Cambridge, MS 81 (collated with eight other manuscripts), see Thomas J. Farrell, 'The Story of Griselda', in *Sources and Analogues of the Canterbury Tales*, vol. I, ed. Robert M. Correale and Mary Hamel (Cambridge: D.S. Brewer, 2002), pp. 108–29.

16. See Barbara Newman, *From Virile Woman to Woman Christ* (Philadelphia: University of Pennsylvania Press, 1995), p. 115.

17. 'Authorizing a Life: The Collaboration of Dorothea of Montau and John Marienwerder', in *Gendered Voices: Medieval Saints and Their Interpreters*, ed. Catherine M. Mooney (Philadelphia: University of Pennsylvania Press, 1999), pp. 168–91.

18. The only texts said to be transcribed directly from Dorothea, 'von irem munde…geschriben', are collected at the end of the *Septililium* (*c.*1400): see John of Marienwerder, *Septililium Beatae Dorotheae Montoviensis*, ed. Franz Hipler (Brussels: Polleunis, Ceuterick and Lefébure, 1885), pp. 207–37.

the canonization process.[19] And the unquestioning obedience demanded of Dorothea when alive is now expected of the reader: harsh lashings into line ('Swig, du weleger...') anticipate any wobbling of readerly credulity. For Johannes von Marienwerder (but quite differently from Derrida) *il n'y a pas de hors-texte*; readings beyond his terms of reference are figured as disobedient, lily-livered, perhaps heretical.[20]

Peasant colonists and Teutonic Christendom

Dyan Elliott, in her superb account of the Marienwerder–Dorothea relationship, speaks of Dorothea 'being born at Montau into the well-to-do artisan class', and of her becoming 'an exemplar of the contemporary lay penitential movement'.[21] Marienwerder himself presents Dorothea as the first and most brilliant local exemplar of faith values comprehended throughout Christian Europe; and he begins his account of her life by locating her birth:

Dy vorgenante Dorothea ist geborn in eyme dorf, Montow genant, des stichtis Pomezan zcu Prusinlant, von erbarn, gotvorchtigen eldern.

(1.2)

19. Paul Nieborowski, *Die selige Dorothea von Preussen: Ihr Heiligsprechungsprozess und ihre Verehrung bis in unsere Zeiten* (Breslau: OstdeutscheVerlagsanstalt, 1933); see further *Die Akten des Kanonisationsprozesses Dorotheas von Montau von 1394 bis 1521*, ed. Richard Stachnik (Cologne: Böhlau Verlag, 1978), pp. 495–539. Maps 3 and 4, between pp. 498–9, illustrate the extraordinary range of small locales (within tightly-defined geographical limits, east of the Weichsel river that empties out into the Danziger Bucht) from which these witnesses were drawn. As Ute Stargardt remarks, 'her [Dorothea's] biography would command the attention of a sizeable segment of Prussia's rural population' ('Dorothea von Montau, the Language of Love, and Jacop Karweysze, "Goldsmyd"', in *Interpreting Texts from the Middle Ages: The Ring of Words in Medieval Literature*, ed. Ulrich Goebel and David Lee (Lewiston, NY: Edwin Mellen Press, 1994), p. 307).
20. Marienwerder's control and indeed *production* of Dorothea might be seen as a species, or extreme limit case, of the symbolic violence discussed by Pierre Bourdieu in *La domination masculine*: see especially *Masculine Domination*, tr. Richard Nice (Stanford: Stanford University Press, 2001), pp. 33–4; *La domination masculine* (Paris: Seuil, 1998), pp. 39–40. 'Symbolic force', according to Bourdieu, 'is a form of power that is exerted on bodies, directly and as if by magic, without any physical constraint' (p. 38; 'et comme par magie', p. 44). Does the fact that Dorothea makes her own way voluntarily to Marienwerder at Marienwerder, and to his strict regime of enclosure, represent an act of recognition....make her seem the more potent a figure in choosing to embrace a life of violence, symbolic and corporeal, without benefit of magical disguise?
21. Elliott, 'Authorizing a Life', pp. 170, 174.

The above-mentioned Dorothea was born to honourable, God-fearing parents in a village called Montau in the episcopal see of Pomesania in Prussia.

(p. 36)

Marienwerder's ecclesiastical geography offers nothing to explain how Dorothea's father made a living in this part of Prussia; he is simply described as a man of 'erbarn lebens', repeating the bland formula applied to both parents above. Wilhelm Swarze was in fact a newcomer to Montau at the time of Dorothea's birth. Like many other peasants from German, Dutch, and Flemish territories, he was expert in draining and working swampy terrain. Montau, located in the delta of the Vistula and Nogat rivers, was a new settlement much in need of such expertise.[22] Montau attracted peasant colonists to the far borders of Teutonic Christendom by offering them the prospect of (to reprise Marienwerder's phrase) 'erbarn lebens', a life less tied to those labour obligations traditionally exacted upon serfs. Wilhelm Swarze was one of the first to arrive, and he proved very successful. With Dorothea's mother, Agatha (a woman of fierce piety: her fingers were deformed through constant plying of paternoster beads), he fulfilled *the* primary obligation of the successful colonist: namely, the production of a large extended working family (seven children, and some fifty grand-children).[23] Dorothea obediently played her part here, although eight of her nine children died young; the lone survivor, Gertrude, was placed in a convent, aged twelve.[24]

Germanic peoples had been moving east since the time of Charlemagne; from the twelfth century on, the rural economies of central and northeastern Europe were undergoing radical transformation. 'Economic Germanization' in these rural areas was relatively straightforward, since natural features—including climate, topography, and soil—differed little from what was already known. Germanic language and culture flowed in with such settlements, ousting or overwhelming local languages and traditions. *Prussian,* which becomes almost

22. See Michael Burleigh, *Prussian Society and the German Order: An Aristocratic Corporation in Crisis, c.* 1410–1466 (Cambridge: Cambridge University Press, 1984), pp. 28–30.
23. See Herman Aubin, 'The Lands East of the Elbe and German Colonisation Eastwards', in *The Cambridge Economic History of Europe,* vol. 1, *The Agrarian Life of the Middle Ages,* second edition, ed. M. M. Postan (Cambridge: Cambridge University Press, 1966), p. 455; Marienwerder, *Life,* tr. Stargardt, p. 6.
24. A letter from Dorothea 'an irre tachter czum colmen in daz vrouwen closter' survives, full of orthodox, Passion-minded sentiment: see Hörner, *Dorothea,* pp. 320–21.

synonymous with *German*, in fact refers to a Baltic language that is related to Lithuanian and Latvian; by the seventeenth century it had become extinct. The native population certainly declined with the arrival of the Teutonic Order, although it is exaggerated to speak of a 'Prussian genocide'; many Baltic peasants took German names.[25] The peak of German settlement in Prussia was reached in the first half of the fourteenth century; Wilhelm Swarze thus arrives towards the very end of this process. His new family cultivated an area that could not (given its marshy character) be extended much further; it thus established itself at something of an economic frontier.[26]

Wilhelm Swarze was recruited and transported from the Netherlands by Ludolf König, High Master of the Teutonic Knights. The Teutonic Order did more than just complement economic expansion into Prussia by adding military might and religious rationalization; they were themselves deeply invested in pioneering land development and commercial exchange. They thus financed costly processes of moving peasant populations eastward and of sustaining them until the first crops could be harvested; they supplied them with vital infrastructures for colonization, such as mills, dredging equipment, housing, and places of worship.[27] This drive to the east first accompanied, and then substantially replaced, an earlier *Drang nach Osten* by the Knights of the Order of the Hospital of the Blessed Virgin Mary of the German House in Jerusalem (to give the Teutonic Knights their full title). The Virgin Mary, as Robert Bartlett observes, is the least localizable of all the saints: she travels well, equipped with mighty accretions of iconography and tradition

25. See Kristjan Toomaspoeg, *Histoire des Chevaliers Teutoniques* (Paris: Flammarion, 2001), pp. 108–111; William Urban, *The Teutonic Knights: A Military History* (London: Greenhill Books, 2003), pp. 41–6; Burleigh, *Prussian Society*, pp. 32–6. The Prussian population, estimated at 170,000 on the arrival of the Teutonic Knights, declined to *c.*90,000 in 1300 before reaching 140,000 a century later. See further Aubin, 'East of the Elbe', pp. 453–9; S. C. Rowell, 'Baltic Europe', in *The New Cambridge Medieval History, vol. VI, c.*1300–*c.*1415, ed. Michael Jones (Cambridge: Cambridge University Press, 2000), p. 715; Robert Bartlett, *The Making of Europe: Conquest, Colonization and Cultural Change, 950–1350* (London: Allen Lane, 1993), p. 203. A simple catechetical language was produced in Prussian following the Reformation, but to little avail; the last reported Prussian speaker died in 1677 (Bartlett, pp. 203–4).
26. Historical geographers have disproved the notion that this area between the Vistula and Nogat rivers was 'an unsettled swamp' before the coming of Germanic settlers; 'behind a German-sounding placename', Burleigh argues, 'there often lies an earlier Slav settlement' (*Prussian Society*, p. 10).
27. See Rühle, 'Dorothea', pp. 61–2; Aubin, 'East of the Elbe', p. 462.

to sacralize and federate new territories.[28] Members of the Teutonic Order were popularly known as *Marienritter*, Mary's Knights; they generated and consumed a great deal of Marian literature, although the *mulieres fortes* Judith and Hester were also commemorated in verse.[29] Mary figures prominently, for example, in Tilo von Kulm's metrical life of Christ (completed on 8 May 1331); the 'vrowe gut' is beseeched

> Schenken dinen orden vrut,
> Ich mein den rittern, dinen kint,
> Vi von dem duschen huse sint
> Genennet und gemezzen,
> In Pruseland gesezzen.[30]

> To bestow fruit on your Order:
> I mean the knights, your children,
> Who are named and directed
> According to the German house
> And located in Prussia.

The most important locales structuring Dorothea's physical movement and visionary life (Marienburg, Marienwerder, and Danzig's Marienkirche) are dedicated to Mary; Tilo's characterization of the Virgin as a green and fertile plain, and then as a palace,[31] resonates with the landscapes and landmarks of her life in Prussia.

The Domus hospitalis sanctae Mariae Theutonicorum in Jerusalem, or Teutonic Order, had emerged during the Third Crusade (1189–91) when Hohenstaufen rulers were keen to encourage a German-based brotherhood that might better advance their interests than did the Knights Templar or Hospitaller. The founders of the Order were merchants from Bremen and Lübeck.[32] For the first century of their existence, the Teutonic Knights defended the Latin colonies of the region from their castle at Starkenburg (thirty miles inland from Acre).

28. *Making of Europe*, p. 279; see further, on Mary's 'east and west' universalism, Miri Rubin, *Mother of God: A History of the Virgin Mary* (London: Allen Lane, 2009), pp. 169–73.

29. See Mary Ellen Goenner, *Mary-Verse of the Teutonic Knights* (Washington: Catholic University of America Press, 1943); Helm and Ziesemer, *Literatur*, pp. 41–4; and, on Judith and Hester, Edith Feistner, Michael Neecke, and Gisela Vollman-Profe, *Krieg im Visier: Bibelepik und Chronistik im Deutschen Orden als Modell korporativer Identitätsbildung* (Tübingen: Niemeyer, 2007), pp. 49–79.

30. Lines 70–74 as cited in Goenner, *Mary-Verse*, p. 35; my translation.

31. See Goenner, *Mary-Verse*, pp. 41–3.

32. See Burleigh, *Prussian Society*, p. 1.

Figure 1. Marienburg, castrum Mariae, Mary's castle by the Nogat river (Malbork, Poland).

They maintained a second front against Muslims from a stronghold in Armenia; and they took an increasing interest in campaigns against the non-Muslim infidels or 'Saracens' in Prussia and Lithuania.[33] When Acre fell in 1291 the Teutonic Order lost its Palestinian base; crusading and colonizing energies could thus be more exclusively concentrated at and beyond the Prussian frontier.[34] Control of the Vistula, the mighty waterway connecting central Europe to the Baltic at Danzig, proved vital to the conquest of Prussia; it also drew the Teutonic Order to take ever-increasing interest in matters of commerce and long-distance trade. In 1308, when invited to put down a revolt at Danzig, the Order restored order and elected to stay; a fortress was built and Teutonic

33. On the tendency for romance chroniclers, and even the Teutonic Knights themselves, to refer to Prussians and Lithuanians as 'Saracens', see Helen Nicholson, *Love, War and the Grail* (Leiden: Brill, 2001), pp. 89–90. Heinrich von Plauen wrote to Germany seeking aid against the 'Saracen infidels' who were besieging Marienburg: see Urban, *Teutonic Knights*, p. 225. It should be noted that the term 'Saracen' meant 'unChristian', rather than (as Urban suggests, p. 225), 'Moslem'.

34. The *Livländische Reimchronik*, written in some 12,000 lines of Middle High German, narrates events to 1290 and was written just a few years later; its short rhyming couplets represent the oldest *Ordensgeschichte*. See *Livländische Reimchronik*, ed. Leo Meyer (Paderborn: Ferdinand Schöningh, 1876); *The Livonian Rhymed Chronicle*, tr. Jerry C. Smith and William L. Urban (Bloomington: Indiana University, 1977).

(Chelm) law applied. The following year the grand master of the Order transferred his seat from Venice to Marienburg (*castrum Mariae*, 'Mary's castle').[35] This mighty fortress monastery by the Nogat (Figure 1), which dominates the flat and muddy landscape, lies just eight miles from Montau. When young Dorothea marries her ageing 'Albert gladiator' at Montau and then heads north to Danzig she already moves within the orbit of the Teutonic Knights.[36] When she heads south to her final earthly destination, Marienwerder, she feels their influence even more keenly: for Domdechant Johannes, dean of the cathedral, her confessor and author, was also a member of the Teutonic Order.[37] Her day of enclosure was set for 2 May 1393: the feast of the translation of the remains of St Elisabeth of Hungary. The Teutonic Knights were especially devoted to Elisabeth (their second patron); Elisabeth had especially commended the dedication of the Marienritter to Mary. In 1394, the year of Dorothea's death, the Knights at Marienburg had forty-one Latin books in their library and twelve books in German (including part of a German Bible, and 'Hester und Judith in eyme buche').[38]

John of Marienwerder, born in 1343, was educated at the hometown cathedral he would return to more than forty years later. In between he pursued a promising twenty-year career at Prague, advancing to

35. See Eric Christiansen, *The Northern Crusades: The Baltic and the Catholic Frontier, 1100–1525* (London: Macmillan, 1980), pp. 74–8; Rowell, 'Baltic Europe', pp. 712–13; Goenner, *Mary-Verse*, pp. 2–3; Helm and Ziesemer, *Litteratur*, p. 42; Edmund Cieślak and Czesław Biernat, *History of Gdańsk*, tr. Bożenna Blaim and George M. Hyde (Gdańsk: Fundacji Biblioteki Gdańskiej, 1995), pp. 44–53; Terry Jones, *Chaucer's Knight: The Portrait of a Medieval Mercenary*, revised edition (London: Methuen, 1985), pp. 49–56; Burleigh, *Prussian Order*, p. 3.

36. An 'Albert gladiator' appears in Danzig city records at this time; he may or may not be Dorothea's swordmaking husband. See Rühle, 'Lebensbild', p. 69.

37. All cathedral canons in bishoprics within the Teutonic state were required to enter the Order. As Stephen Mossman notes, this does not mean that they closely associated with the Order's hierarchy ('Dorothea von Montau and the Masters of Prague', *Oxford German Studies*, 39.2 (2010), p. 111). But it does suggest the all-encompassing power of the Order in this region. On distinctions in liturgical literacy between Ritter- and Priesterbrüdern within the Teutonic Order, see Anette Löffler, 'Das sogenannte deutschsprachige Stundenbuch', in *Deutschsprachige Literatur des Mittelalters in östlichen Europa*, ed. Ralf G. Päsler and Dietrich Schmidtke (Heidelberg: Universitätsverlag Winter, 2006), pp. 95–106. Löffler gives notice of a Latin breviary amply supplied with German language rubrics for the convenience of sisters of the Order (p. 99).

38. See Goenner, *Mary-Verse*, pp.viii, xii–xiv, and (on Hester) pp. 77–81. Helen Nicholson notes that 'the Military Orders [Hospitallers, Templars, and Teutonic Knights] did not appear in literature as a model of chivalry' (*Love, War, and the Grail*), p. 235.

Magister in the theological faculty in 1380. Further advancement, however, was stymied—perhaps by disputes between Germans and Bohemians, masters of two languages. Hopes for a position at a new university foundation at Kulm (Chełmno),[39] a Hanseatic town ruled by the Teutonic Order, evaporated.[40] He thus returned to Marienwerder in 1386-7; in 1388 he joined the Teutonic Order and was appointed dean of the chapter.[41] Such a position, while locally prestigious and well-remunerated, seems a strange ending for a well-connected Prague master. His fortunes changed, however, on the eve of Corpus Christi, 1391, when a widow arrived begging him to hear her confession. It was not possible for Dorothea of Montau to join the Teutonic Order: but from the moment of her arrival at Marienwerder, and in the narrative progress of Johannes' German *Leben* (read to the Knights at mealtimes), we see her steady absorption into the *Gesamtkunstwerk* of this complex and contradictory organization.

Hovel to palace: Griseldian translation

Perhaps the most consistent feature of Dorothea's *leben* is her extreme and unquestioning obedience to masculine authority. This begins with obedience to her parents and to the brother who contracts her marriage; it continues with the husband who regularly beats her for wifely shortcomings. This is presented as part of her spiritual formation: it is fitting, *Das Leben* says, that she 'receive hard knocks while serving his [the husband's] needs, for well-observed obedience is more pleasing to

39. Kulm, now Polish Chełmno, lies thirty miles south-west of Kwydyzn (Marienwerder). It was transferred from German to Polish sovereignty after World War I, seized back in 1939 (with widespread massacres), and reassigned to Poland in 1945; its oldest surviving building is a Teutonic Order watchtower. Dorothea's only surviving child, her daughter, became a Benedictine nun 'czum colmen' (see note 24 above); 'Culm' is an older German spelling of 'Kulm'.
40. Mossman doubts that Johannes invested any hopes in Kulm; he makes the larger point that the reasons for Johannes' departure from Prague in 1386–7 remain mysterious ('Masters of Prague', p. 112).
41. See Franz Hipler, revised by Hans Westpfahl, 'Johannes Marienwerder, der Beichtvater der seligen Dorothea von Montau', *Zeitschrift für die Geschichte und Altertumskunde Ermlands*, 29 (1954), pp. 6–14, 27–32; Heribert Rossman, 'Johannes Marienwerder OT, ein ostdeutscher Theologe des späten Mittlealters', in *Sacrum Pragense Millennium, 973–1973*, ed. Augustinus Kurt Huber (Königstein: Königsteiner Institut für Kirchen- und Geistesgeschichte der Südetenländer, 1973), pp. 221–33.

God than sacrifices' (2.16; p. 105). Thus when Albrecht punches her on the mouth for failing to prepare his fish supper she smiles at him with her fat lip (2.15; pp. 100–1). When she forgets to buy straw he beats her chest so hard that blood mingles with her saliva; she bears these blows joyfully, 'mit frouden' (2.15; p. 101). When her daughter cries on the road back from Aachen her husband beats her fiercely around the head, appalling all bystanders; Dorothea, although the wounds take years to heal, accepts this cheerfully ('frolich', 2.11; p. 93). The most humiliating moment for Dorothea, as a medieval wife, comes when her husband 'finally took the keys from her and left nothing at all to her authority. He himself went to market to purchase what they needed' (2.15; p. 101). In medieval narrative, control of the keys is the most powerful signifier of domestic rule. For Margery Kempe, recovery of the keys represents definitive return from post-partum depression and self-determining renewal.[42] For Dorothea's *Leben*, surrender of 'die slussel' marks one more step towards the loss of all such personal authority as she enters the anchorhold.[43] Christ, who has figured throughout as a severe and violently-inclined second spouse, makes it clear that Dorothea is entering into a new, more restrictive form of domestic bondage:

Du salt gar czüchtig in der clause seyn, dich nacht und tag fleisen, das du nymand andirs magst behagin den mir! Dir sal seyn als eynem weybe, dy do hot eynen gestrengin hartin man, vor dem sy nimmer dar aus dem hause geen.

(3.3)

You shall live chastely in your cell, busy day and night to please no one but me. You shall live as a wife who has a strict, harsh husband because of whom she never dares to leave the house.

(pp. 150–1)

---

42. Such is the drama that concludes the very first chapter of Margery's *Book* (ed. Windeatt, lines 237–45). Anglo-Saxon England saw the keeping of domestic wealth in chests or storerooms, and the keeping of the keys, as women's work. The seventh-century law code of Aethelbert speaks of 'a free woman in control of the keys' (cited in Daniel Donoghue, *Lady Godiva: A Literary History of the Legend* (Oxford: Blackwell, 2003), p. 22). Barbara Hanawalt notes that medieval funeral effigies sometimes feature women with a key ring (*'Of Good and Ill Repute': Gender and Social Control in Medieval England* (New York: Oxford University Press, 1998), p. 99.

43. The stripping of the household keys from Christina of Markyate, along with 'all her clothes', 'preter camisiam', is similarly symbolically fraught; her father then expels her from the house (*The Life of Christina of Markyate: A Twelfth Century Recluse*, ed. and tr. C. H. Talbot (Oxford: Clarendon Press, 1959), p. 72.

This sounds unpromising. By the end of her short life in the anchorhold, however, Dorothea is to behold a palace of unimaginable splendor where she will marry her magnificent, knightly master. Such heady translation reminds us, once again, of the Griselde story: for Dorothea is a peasant girl marrying way above her station.[44] Unmarried Dorothea, we are told, is a chaste and modest virgin, glistening like a beautiful lily ('als eyne schone lylie glantze sy', 1.21; p. 58). Suitors flock to her, since she is 'sober, moderate, humble, outgoing, gracious, pleasant, and peacable'; she is also skilled in bringing 'disputes...to positive conclusions'.[45] This last suggestion of public virtue, given Dorothea's other-worldliness and liking for dark and obscure places, seems unlikely: it does, however, conform our Prussian heroine to the Griseldian paradigm.[46] Much is made, early on, of Dorothea's distaste (never, of course, voiced aloud) for 'adornments': those 'pins, brooches, hats, garments, and other such items of fashion' that her mother confers upon her (1.11; p. 43). Later on, in the long and lumbering allegory that takes up the latter part of the *Leben*, much is made of how she is 'adorned' ('geczirt'): Christ sets a wedding gown or 'hochczeytcleidt' upon her that makes all virtues gloriously visible (3.26; p. 183). In between, Christ is at pains (like Walter) to rationalize his violence and neglect: 'it was my will that the foundation of your true, constant patience be tempted, tested, and made manifest'.[47]

Stephen Mossman convincingly argues that Marienwerder's Dorothea figuration takes inspiration from Latin female *lives* encountered at Prague.[48] Perhaps Griselde should be added to the list: Petrarch had travelled to Prague and had corresponded with members of the court; *Seniles* 17.3, composed in 1373, circulated widely outside the collection

---

44. Aspirant members of the Teutonic Order were asked, by the presiding member of the Chapter, 'are you a serf?': see Goenner, *Mary-Verse*, p. 12.
45. 'Wen sie waz nuchtirn, messig, demutig, mitsam, gutig, wolgemut, vredesam; zwyvelden ding wante sy jo zcum besten, und dorumme hatte sy vil vrier' (1.21; p. 58).
46. On Griselde's brilliant accomplishments in *res publica* and dispute resolution, see *Epistolae Seniles* 17.3, ed. Severs, pp. 308–9.
47. 'Es was mein wille, das der grunt deyner worn stetin gedult vorsucht, geprüfft und gemerckit worden' (2.25; p. 123); compare *Seniles* 17.3, ed. Severs, p. 328.
48. The most fascinating of these being Elizabeth, wife of a leading Prague citizen, as recounted by Archbishop Jan of Jenštejn's *De bono mortis*: for Latin text and translation from this unedited text, see Mossman, 'Prague Masters', *Appendix* (pp. 121–3).

of letters.[49] Correspondences with the Petrarchan text might be ascribed to Marienwerder's absorption in modalities of Latin prose composition (of which Petrarch was master): particularly the habit of representing rhetorical figures, *ornamenti*, as items of dress or adornment that might make hidden virtues shiningly visible to world-weary eyes.[50] Christ's adornment of Dorothea thus corresponds to Godlike Walter's dressing of Griselde, translated from the peasant hovel, as beautiful and virtuous bride.

Before translating his Dorothea from anchoritic cell to palace wedding, John of Marienwerder emphasizes that she considers herself 'vor eyne asche und vor das allernedirste ding' ('a speck of dirt, the lowest of the low', 3.20; p. 175). She considers herself wicked; she is humiliated by Christ for failing to achieve absolute humility; she strives for *Vernichtung*, self-obliteration.[51] And the Lord tells her that she 'must be more submissive than ever before and must give yourself entirely into the authority of your B and P [spiritual directors]'.[52] It is under this strong authority, within the enclosed space of the anchoritic cell, that Marienwerder performs the crucial *translatio* of Dorothea in the latter part of his or her *Leben*: once again, at the end and beyond the end of her life as at the beginning, she remains under the spatial aegis of the Teutonic Order.[53] Even in Book I, military metaphors had been

---

49. There are some 150 uncollated versions of *Seniles* 17.3 (which circulated independently, as well as part of the collection): see Charlotte C. Morse, 'Exemplary Griselde', *Studies in the Age of Chaucer*, 7 (1985), p. 64. On Petrarch's connections with Prague and its court, see Wallace, *Chaucerian Polity*, pp. 359–60. See further Wallace, '*Letters of Old Age*: Love between Men, Griselda, and Farewell to Letters', in *Petrarch: A Critical Guide to the Complete Works*, ed. Victoria Kirkham and Armando Maggi (Chicago: University of Chicago Press, 2009), pp. 321–30. On Griselda's European-wide diffusion, see now K. P. Clarke, *Chaucer and Italian Textuality* (Oxford: Clarendon Press, 2011).

50. On Walter's preparation of these clothes and ornaments, see *Seniles* 17.3, ed. Severs, pp. 302–4; on Griselde 'subito transformatam' as she puts them on, see p. 306.

51. 'Dy vornichtunge in iren eygenen gedanckin und wortin...' (3.20, p. 175; see this chapter *passim*, pp. 173–5).

52. *Leben* 3.20; p. 174. Johannes refers to himself in *Das Leben* as B, being Dorothea's *Beichtvater* or confessor; P. refers to Johannes Reymann, Dorothea's second confessor and prior of Marienwerder cathedral. On the importance of these two men in the process of textual composition, see Volfing, 'Textualization and Transformation'.

53. Cordelia Heß argues that Dorothea's cult was promoted chiefly by Marienwerder's cathedral canons. These honorary Teutonic Knights took pains to avoid suggesting that Marienwerder might compete with other cultic centres in the Teutonic state, especially Marienburg: see *Heilige machen im spätmittelalterlichen Ostseeraum: Die Kanonisationsprozesse von Birgitta von Schweden, Nikolaus von Linköping und Dorothea von Montau* (Berlin: Akadamie Verlag, 2008), pp. 289–99.

invoked: 'y vestir burg, y vestir storm' ('the stronger the fortress, the greater the assault', 1.20; p. 57). Dorothea's soul is thus a mighty *burg* (like Marienburg), built to withstand ferocious engines of war:

Wol waz di burg der selen Dorothea bevestent mit tyfen grabin der demut, mit vestin muren der sterke des gemutis, mit umlofinder weir der vorsichtikeit, mit hohen turmen der engelhute, mit vil geschossis und schirmunge manchirhande tugunt.

(1.20)

Excellently fortified was the fortress of Dorothea's soul with its deep moat of humility, its solid walls of strength of character; with its surrounding wall of caution, the high towers of angelic protection; with the many assault engines and defense mechanisms of various virtues.

(p. 57)

If Marienwerder is the ground zero of Dorothea's anchoritic enclosure, Marienburg—the great castle fortress, palace, and monastery of the Teutonic Order—figures as her visionary point of arrival. Dressed by female attendants as if she were 'eyns grosin königes dochtir', Dorothea peers out across the endless, flat plane of her native landscape. Finally she espies her bridegroom approaching from afar:

...den allirerwirdigisten, den alliredelsten, und den allirlöbelichsten, der ye uff dem erthreych irscheyn, komen mit eynem groszen gewaldigem here. Dar here was gar wol geschickit und hatte schöne wolgebornen personen, dy sundirlichin worin yrwelt, das sy mit dem brewtegam qwomen.

(3.27)

...the most honourable; the most noble; and the most praiseworthy ever to appear on earth, he arrived with a huge, mighty host. The army was excellently equipped and made up of handsome, well-born men especially selected to accompany the bridegroom.

(pp. 185–6)

Prussian audiences, which included members of the Teutonic Order, could readily visualize Teutonic Knights sweeping across the horizon, bearing Dorothea to their castle; anyone who has stood on that bleakly flat landscape south of Gdańsk knows that there is nowhere to hide. Further anticipated delights in 'the wine cellar of my sweet love', and in 'my secret chamber'[54] might easily be associated with the famed

---

54. See 3.27 (p. 186): 'in eynen weinkellir meyner sussen libe'; 'in meynen heymlichen gadem'.

opulence of well-provisioned, centrally-heated, and richly-wallpapered Marienburg.[55] Such a *translatio*, we are told, 'always took place at the time Dorothea received the holy, gracious sacrament of the true body of Our Lord Jesus Christ' (3.27; p. 186): that is, Dorothea's vertical, eucharistic integration with God is imaginatively associated with lateral transfer from Marienwerder (anchorhold) to Marienburg (Teutonic stronghold). Johannes von Marienwerder labours to sustain this association from this point on to the very end of his text, sometimes at the expense of narrative logic or clarity. The ambitiously climactic palace scene in the penultimate chapter of Book IV sometimes defeats visual imagining: 'the fatted calf, that is I, has been slaughtered', Christ says, 'and a sumptuous feast is prepared'.[56] Finally, however, straightforward allegoresis is served as Dorothea gazes upon 'ir pallas, das ist ire sele' ('her palace, that is her soul', 4.8; p. 245). The elaborate allegory thus ends by envisioning its lateral progression from anchorhold to palace as a homecoming and return to interior space. It thus resonates with the fourth and final lesson that, much earlier in the text, Christ had instructed Dorothea to teach:

Zcuhant wen her di ere gots seht, so vorget ym ane sumenis dye vretikeit des ynren ougin und alle fel dicke und dunne sint denne vortriben von synen ougin. Eyme sogetan menschin sint denne geoffent di rechtin wege, di do geen zcum ewigen leben, di her mag wandirn. Wen her daz tut, so beginnet her wider zcu keren von fremden landen und kerit sich wandirn zcu synes vatir lande.

(2.32)

Upon beholding God's glory, the infection of the inner eye disappears without delay and all blinders, thick or thin, are removed from their eyes immediately. To such seekers the correct paths to eternal life they must travel will then be revealed, and as they do, they will be returning from a foreign country, retracing their steps into their father's land.

(p. 134)

For Dorothea, the 'rechtin weg' or correct path leads to a visionary place very like the palatial fortress of Marienburg that had dominated the horizon of her youth; and yet, of course, she never leaves her

---

55. And with the *Song of Songs*. See further Chapter 2 below, p. 97, and Heinrich Wolfrum, *Die Marienburg: Das Haupthaus des Deutschen Ritterordens und seine Geschichte* (Leer, Ostfriedland: Verlag Gerhard Rautenberg, 1972), p. 29.

56. 'Das vette kalp ist getötit, das ist: ich, und eine grose wirtschafft ist bereitet' (4.8; p. 244).

anchorhold at Marienwerder. The two sites seem connected by an umbilical cord of visionary conceit; it is of course her father confessor, the Teutonic Knight and author of her *Life*, who is (so to speak) in both places at once. Between them, these two locales map a spiritual *Heimat*, a 'vatir lande' to which every German-reading traveller should ultimately return. Dorothea was Prussia's first anchoress; her *Leben* was Prussia's first printed book. It is thoroughly in keeping with the work's internal logic that this account of *Dorothee clewsenerynne yn der thumkyrchen czu Marienwerder des landes czu Prewszen* should have been printed, in 1492, in Marienburg.[57]

Restlessness and martyrdom, territory and work

Pilgrims flocked to Marienwerder following Dorothea's death on 25 June 1394; traffic on her *Todestagen* proved particularly heavy. Her anchorhold is very unlike those we infer from *Ancrene Wisse* and Julian's writings. Such English spaces seem altogether more permeable to the world, more open to initiative and particular vision from within; both these texts or textual complexes open up to geographic or cosmic imaginings (of a network of houses; of a hazelnut) that ease our sense of perennial confinement. The regimen to which Dorothea is subjected by Marienwerder at Marienwerder, as documented by his text, is altogether more severe, claustrophobic, and closed to the world. And yet, at the same time, this airless Prussian space seems entirely crowded out by exterior forces: that which proves intractable on the plane of history struggles to find expression, if not resolution, through the martyring body of Dorothea. This next section explores the interrelated topics of restlessness and martyrdom, territoriality, and economics; I then question quite where (amid such large historical forces) Dorothea wishes to be. Like Moses coming back down the mountain, Marienwerder says, Dorothea bears many signs ('manch czeychen', 3.32; p. 192) of her ecstatic experiences; how, within Marienwerder's text, might such signs of particular pleasure be located and read?

The later Middle Ages, Caroline Walker Bynum has argued, shifts from stasis-like imagining of the afterlife to a more dynamic pursuit of

---

57. The book was printed in the town (beneath the fortress) of Marienburg by goldsmith Jacop Karweysze: see Stargardt, 'Jacop Karweysze', pp. 305, 317–18.

desire: thus each angelic order in Dantean heaven pursues the order that flanks it to the outside.[58] In Marienwerder's *Leben*, however, extreme restlessness seems to power all protagonists—human and divine—rather than the orderly pursuit of desire. *Das Leben*'s fourth and final Book opens by schematizing degrees of love, reportedly following a system taught to Dorothea by the Lord. At the mathematical centre of this scheme—the eighteenth and nineteenth of love's thirty-seven degrees—lie 'ungerwige libe' and 'ungedultige libe': 'restless love' and 'impatient love'. The first of these sees the lovestruck running this way and that, 'hen and her', in search of her beloved (4.1/18; p. 217); the second sees her grow desperate and depressed:

So wirt dy libe unleydelich, addir ir wirt unbehegelich, was ir begeynt, und sy ducket das, das allis, das irer begerunge nicht dynet, das ir das unötcze sey.

(4.1/19)

The result of searching without finding is that love becomes dissatisfied or displeased with everything she encounters, convinced that everything not furthering the fulfillment of her desire is utterly useless.

(p. 217)

Das Leben shows how such restlessness, such oscillation between headlong desire and utter disappointment, dictates Dorothea's movement through space. When visiting strings of churches in search of indulgences, she is questioned by the 'envious spirit' within: why does she need to rush about 'like a fool'? On staying put in one church, however, she hears the same inner voice telling of better spiritual pickings to be had elsewhere (1.20; p. 56). Ambivalence, or contradictory desire, further possesses her in returning from Einsiedeln (Finsterwald, 1.31; p. 70): she leaves, then retraces her steps; leaves again, returns again; leaves again, but returns once more to worship at the Marian chapel. Dorothea is the acknowledged 'driving force' (2.9; p. 90) that sets her family travelling across war-ravaged German territory in search of a superior religious life. They hide out among cows and sheep in churchyards; they are robbed and the husband is beaten; the daughter is threatened with abduction and rape (2.9). Such restless and often impulsive movement is shared throughout the text by the visionary

58. 'Why All the Fuss about the Body? A Medievalist's Perspective', *Critical Inquiry*, 22 (Autumn 1995), pp. 25–7.

Lord she pursues: in the book's penultimate chapter he is seen yet again with his powerful host, 'rushing toward her with great speed' ('mit allem fleys', 4.3.8; p. 245). Such extreme physical energy, consistently expressed in spatial terms, can hardly be contained by the strict bounds of the cloister. Her ravening hunger for the eucharist, that which feeds her visionary life and brings the Lord rushing to her (3.40), finally exceeds the cloister's limits: in receiving the sacrament for what will be the last time, she actually pokes her head out of the window to get it faster (3.40; p. 204).

Insatiable desire to pursue spiritual grace across physical territory proves particularly poignant at this first and only anchorhold on the Prussian frontier. Dorothea's travels before inclaustration always led her westward; traveling east was an option for Teutonic Knights, not for a wife from Montau. In dying, however, Dorothea disposes herself (Marienwerder takes great pains to tell us) into the last of her bodily *czeychen*:

Hy ist ouch czu wissin, das dy keusche, demutige Dorothea hatte sich gelegit andirs do, do sy starbe, wen sy czuvor gelegen hat. Sy hatte ir hopt gekart kegen deme undirgange der sonnen und ire fusse kegin deme uffgange der sonnen, als man dy toden leget.

(3.42)

At this point it is worthwhile to know that as she was dying, the spotless, humble Dorothea positioned herself on her cot differently from the way she ever had before by placing her head towards sunset and her feet towards sunrise, the way the dead are placed in their graves.

(pp. 208–9)

Such alignment, by a soul soon to bequeath a corpse to the world, might be taken simply as a last act of tidy-minded housekeeping. The setting of feet to the east, however, might also signify solidarity with Teutonic Knights (and with those who, like Bolingbroke, *reysed* with them) in their long, eastward march against Lithuanian pagans. At the very end of Book II, in a chapter entitled 'How she was and still is a great martyr' ('Das sy eyne grosze mertelerinne was und ist', 2.38; p. 141), Dorothea is reassured by the Lord that 'you are a great martyr, tormented through and through with spiritual exercises, self-castigations, disciplines, and torments'; when she dies, Marienwerder and Mareinwerder's prior, Johannes Reymann, will bury her 'as a martyr and shall esteem and honor you as such'. The very last chapter of Book

III sees Marienwerder, having discovered Dorothea's corpse, honour this agreement:

Hyrumbe sullen sich mit mir froyen alle wore cristen und den herren der ewigin ere loben und eren, das her dy irwirdige mertelerinne Dorothea hoth gebrocht dohen, do sy nu nymmer darff leydin keynerley leydin, sundir sy hot pur lautir froyde, dy sich nimmer wirt endin!

(3.44)

For these reasons all true Christians must rejoice with me and praise the Lord of eternal glory for having taken the praiseworthy martyr Dorothea where she will never have to endure any suffering whatsoever but enjoy nothing but pure, everlasting delight.

(p. 210)

In the course of her life, Dorothea shed as much blood as any virgin saint in the Golden Legend. The problem remains, however, that she was not, like some of those marching eastwards from Prussia, martyred by pagans: her blood was shed chiefly by her own hand. Marienwerder presses no claims for the sacralizing power of Dorothea's blood: indeed, it is her tears that are most intensively discussed as the most efficacious means of spiritual redemption and (so to speak) menstruation.[59] The bid to have Dorothea acclaimed as the first saint (as well as the first anchoress) of the Prussian frontier badly needs the credentializing support of martyrdom. Ultimately, almost six centuries later, Dorothea *will* be canonized. But her bloody body never perfectly aligns with this process; it is worth pondering what other meanings (what other conflicts) it might assume. Which is to say: we must continue to try and *place* Dorothea's bloody upbringing at Montau and her death at Marienwerder, mindful that (as Noel Castree has it), 'the term place...derives its character, in part, from its willing or unwilling engagement with something "bigger" or "wider" than itself'.[60]

Dorothea of Montau is born into a twofold struggle, directed by the Teutonic Order, for territorial conquest: against Lithuanian pagans, and against the land itself. Christian Europe regarded the first of these

---

59. See especially 3.15 (pp. 165–7). This chapter declares it necessary 'for a human being to cry hotly once a day to wash [small sins] from the soul' (p. 167). On Dorothea's blood: it is worth noting, given the later uses of her text, that no blood-based arguments are made against those beyond the Prussian, Catholic, and German pale.
60. 'Differential geographies: place, indigenous rights and "local" resources', *Political Geography*, 23 (Feb. 2004), p. 138, n. 7.

Figure 2. Knights battling pagans, frieze at Marienburg castle.

struggles, still visible in a frieze above a fireplace at Marienburg castle (Figure 2), with increasing scepticism in the course of Dorothea's lifetime.[61] Polish and Lithuanian crowns united in 1385 to form the Jagiellonian dynasty. Lithuanian Grand Duke Jogaila was baptized Catholic on 15 February 1386, married twelve-year-old Jadwiga, and became king of Poland. This did not stem the *Reisen*: the Teutonic Order, like other colonial powers in later centuries, took pains to emphasize residual and inveterate paganism at its borders.[62] Cultivation and settling of this border territory thus assumes particular strategic importance: land is at once wrested from paganism and (as in the marshy delta region of Montau) reclaimed from nature. Wilhelm Swarze was thus drawn from the Netherlands across Europe by the Teutonic Knights to support such a venture; his daughter, Dorothea, is eventually drafted into associated processes of spiritual and military conquest.

Processes of subduing and improving upon nature continue to breed anxiety and suspicion in and of Roman Catholic cultures: thus, Catholic

61. The provenance of this frieze, which depicts fierce combat with pagans, cannot be known with certainty, given the extensive rebuilding of the castle after World War II.
62. See Jerzy Lukowski and Hubert Zawadzki, *A Concise History of Poland* (Cambridge: Cambridge University Press, 2001), pp. 32–5; Christiansen, *Northern Crusades*, pp. 163–7; Urban, *Teutonic Knights*, pp. 153–94.

politicians, even in England, are suspected of ambivalence on issues such as stem cell research and birth control.[63] Such anxieties have deep historical roots. In *Inferno* 15, where Dante meets his old teacher Brunetto Latini, fire rains from the skies, the earth is barren, and nature runs backwards.[64] This is the circle of the sodomites: a place delimited by a series of walls that compare with those built in Flanders, 'between Wissant and Bruges', to reclaim land otherwise lost to the sea. The marshy desolation of Flemish landscapes, wrested so precariously from or against nature, was also imagined to resist the claims of noble blood: for Bavaria Herald, who travelled to the English court in 1390, the waste land of Flanders ('dat woeste land') could only be redeemed by the healing touch of knightly rule. For Eustace Deschamps, Flanders, 'la terre maudite', bears comparison with Sodom and Gomorrah. Flemish merchants were themselves willing to acknowledge, to their count, that 'Flanders *is* a sterile country, infertile in itself...populated with foreigners, merchants, and others'. Flanders is the imaginative terrain trodden or narrated by Chaucer's Pardoner: a figure who generates wealth from sterile conditions; a man whose ambivalent sexual appearance draws both fascination and impulses to violence from his fellow travellers. Perhaps the ultimate visual equivalents of the arid, disease-ridden, death-dealing landscapes traversed in the *Pardoner's Tale* come in the wasted and fruitless landscapes of Hieronymus Bosch. But Bosch is not an exceptional figure in this part of the world: the Groenige Museum at Bruges, for example, must rate as one of the most harrowing museums in Europe for its various visions of disintegrating human bodies, set within frameworks of severe, retributive justice. Read within this context, the endlessly tortured, near-martyred body of Dorothea Swarze looks less out of place. The connection with Netherlandish landscape, claimed from or against nature, is suggested both by her father's profession and by a telling detail of her *Life*: her body, endlessly cut and castigated, suggests a field ploughed up by a peasant ('als eyn ackir mit eyme pfluge durchvarn', 1.15; cited above). Ambivalences projected onto bodies at one extreme territorial frontier (where the

---

63. These would include Ruth Kelly, Secretary of State for Education and Skills 2004–6, who was suspected by newspapers of unsavoury involvement with the secretive, self-castigating, clerically-directed Opus Dei.

64. For a fuller account of what follows in this paragraph, see David Wallace, *Premodern Places: Calais to Surinam, Chaucer to Aphra Behn* (Oxford: Blackwell, 2004), pp. 90–138.

sea is 'driven back', as Dante has it) here play out at another. Dorothea's physical action is truly ambivalent, in that she is both the plougher and the ploughed; both *kultour* and field. Later in the text, following enclosure at Marienwerder, Dorothea is said to run or fly over the land, in spirit ('sy lif ym geiste obir di lant'); her tears of compassion, watering the world, gather like rain in the furrows ('daz wasser stunde noch in den vorchen', 3.15; pp. 165–6).

The ways in which anxieties over land use, natural limits, economic viability, spiritual fidelity, and geographic borders play out through artwork and psychosomatic practises cannot be mapped with absolute precision: it is enough to suggest that Dorothea's bodily practises and such Netherlandish cultures are, in some ways, isomorphic. This suggestion might be tested comparatively: for the heady complex of anxieties that issues in the breaking or ploughing of human bodies finds little purchase on English territory. Julian of Norwich, it is true, wishes to be taken to the point of death: but there is no sense of her being continuously at war with her body. Margery Kempe at one point bites her own hand so deeply as to leave it permanently marked: but this is presented as part of one manic, postpartum episode from which full recovery is made.[65] Most telling, perhaps, is the fate of the flagellants who came to London from Flanders in 1349. By way of expiating sins and thus lifting the curse of the plague, groups of men processed twice daily around St Paul's and elsewhere, lashing bare backs with needle-sharp scourges. Three times per procession, chronicler Robert of Avesbury tells us, they assumed the shape of a cross on the ground; their bloody fellows would then lash out in stepping over them.[66] All this failed to catch on. Such lack of enthusiasm for self-flagellation (in 1349–50, or in English guild gatherings generally) should not be taken as a perennial trait of English character; but it is difficult not to hear a note of laconic detachment in Walsingham's report of such imported activities in his *Historia Anglicana*:

[1350] In this year penitents arrived in England—noble men of foreign birth, who lashed themselves viciously on their naked bodies until the blood flowed,

65. See *A Revelation of Love*, in *The Writings of Julian of Norwich*, ed. Nicholas Watson and Jacqueline Jenkins (University Park: Penn State University Press, 2006), pp. 63–7, 127–35; *Book of Margery Kempe*, ed. Windeatt, lines 216–17.
66. See Robert of Avesbury, *De Gestis*, as cited in *The Black Death*, ed. and tr. Rosemary Horrox (Manchester: Manchester University Press, 1994), 153–4.

now weeping, now singing (nunc flendo, nunc canendo). However, it was said that they were doing these things ill-advisedly, in that they did not have permission from the apostolic see.[67]

Anxieties over the reclamation of land in Flanders compounded with those attending urban life. Unable to raise sheep on their loamy polders and plains, Flemings imported wool from England and corn from France.[68] They then manufactured textiles through highly complex, urban divisions of labour: once again, it proved necessary to *improve upon nature*, a process productive of exhilaration and guilt (in matters religious and cultural) in equal measure. The Teutonic Order, we have noted, was deeply involved in both land development and international trade; Dorothea moved from the first to the second of these domains in leaving her peasant father in Montau for a swordmaker of Danzig. Marienwerder's *Leben* grapples continuously and sometimes confusedly with issues of economics, labour, and productivity. As a child and young wife, Dorothea is rarely seen to perform the kind of *work* that peasant colonists or urban artisans need: she is forever seeking out dark corners, staring at the stars, or forgetting domestic errands. But a woman of her modest rank cannot claim the *otium* needed for higher forms of contemplation; her spiritual life must therefore be defined as a matter of *work*, 'erbeit und wirkunge'. Marienwerder dedicates an entire chapter to arguing such a case, beginning thus:

Von jugunt uf waz Dorothea vol erbeit und wirkunge; ir werk worn groz, swere, stark, langwernde, moysam, manchirley...

(2.33)

From the time she was a child, Dorothea's life was full of work and activity. Her labours were intense, hard, heavy, full of effort, varied...

(p. 135)

Such work is said to produce great spiritual good, 'groz geistlich gut'. 'Prayers, vigils, fasts, and genuflections' are the outward and visible signs of such labour, although the work ('dy arbeyt') performed internally when tears will not come is said to be much harder. The Lord tells her that she can never work hard enough; she must never rest, day

67. Thomas Walsingham, *Historia Anglicana 1272–1422*, ed. H. T. Riley, 2 vols, Rolls Series (1863–4), I, p. 275 as translated in *Black Death*, ed. Horrox, p. 154.
68. See Wallace, *Premodern Places*, pp. 95–6.

or night. Those wishing to help others acquire spiritual wealth can never slacken or be idle; even wealth already acquired must be worked for to the point of exhaustion. Dorothea has sacrificed herself to *der herre* ('daz du dich mir host williclich geoppirt'): an agreement suggestive of an absolute feudalism shading into slavery. Unwilling workers shall cry ('owe, owe, we, we') and fry:

Di do nu nicht wellen swere burde tragen in der erbeit, di werden schryen in der pyn: Owe, owe, we, we, daz wir nicht habin di burde getragen, dir wir solden habin getragen an libe und an sele.

(2.33)

Those who are unwilling to carry a heavy burden when they should be labouring will wail in purgatory: 'Woe is us that we did not carry the burden that was ours to bear in body and soul'.

(p. 136)

Had Dorothea not wept and laboured ('geweynt und geerbeit') for so many people, the Lord says in closing out this chapter, many would still be licked by purgatorial flames ('burnen in dem vegevuyr'). Such a Lord would be a terrifying and exacting landlord; not every *ackir* or ploughman is as compliant and tireless as Dorothea. Like Griselde, then, Dorothea knows how to work; but like Griselde, too, she discards her peasant weeds on entering the palace. The Marienwerder anchorhold and the Marienburg fortress, I have argued, are imaginatively linked through *Das Leben*; it is thus fitting that Dorothea should enter enclosure at Marienwerder experiencing 'sochende libe', 'languishing love' (3.2), since those thus enamoured 'find it impossible to perform bodily work to earn their living'.[69] Without conceding that Dorothea achieves upward social mobility here, Marienwerder does locate her very precisely in his own spiritual scale: for 'zöchende libe' represents the twenty-fourth of his thirty-seven degrees of divine love (as expounded at the beginning of Book 4). Under his direction, he tacitly suggests, her upward ascent may now be securely mapped and completed.

This moment of the twenty-fourth degree marks a stepping back from or falling out of the world; to grasp this fully, we need to consider Marienwerder's meditation on degree twenty-three, 'unsetige libe', 'insatiable love' (4.1.23; p. 218). Visionary possession of the elusive Lord,

---

69. '[N]icht mag der leyplichin arbeyt gepflegin und leypnarunge irwerben' (3.2; p. 150); it is the Lord who speaks here.

in the dynamics of this chapter, seems very like the tantalizing experience of commodity fetishism. Long craved and pursued, the Lord

...so leet her sich abir finden, begreyffin und kostin, addir nicht lange; sundir wen man wil wenen, das man en habe, szo hot her sich entczogen, dorumbe das her in der sele grössir begerunge, geyrunge und hunger noch im irwecke...

(4.1/23)

...at last allows himself to be found, grasped, and tasted once more. But not for long. On the contrary: even as his seekers think to hold him, they find that he has extricated himself yet again to arouse still more fervent desire, greed, and hunger for him in the soul...

(p. 218)

The endpoint of such a circular process of desire, possession, loss, and reheated desire can only be 'zöchende libe': languishing or debilitating love, the state in which Dorothea finally exchanges the world for the cloister. If the Lord were an amber necklace, the cycle would be much the same (although the Lord can never disappoint): craving defines one object in the universe that will satisfy all desires; possession disappoints, as magic disappears; a new object is sighted that *will* satisfy all desires. Vision is vital to such cyclical processes: for 'the values of commodities', D. Vance Smith writes, 'must be seen, or capable of being seen, in order to be grasped or apprehended, yet they can only be seen in the moment at which they disappear'.[70] Such doubling of religious and consumerist erotics remind us that the Teutonic Knights were not passive overseers of international trade at Danzig (looking down from their castle) but active agents of it. *Business* and *commerce* are medieval words; their original embeddedness in religious discourse continues to inform the mysterious dynamics of capitalist marketing.

What Dorothea wants

Much of *Das Leben der zeligen frawen Dorothee* is taken up by Marienwerder's chronicling and calibration of Dorothea's desires.[71] But what

---

70. *Arts of Possession: The Middle English Household Imaginary* (Minneapolis: University of Minnesota Press, 2003), p. 177.
71. Gisela Vollmann-Profe summarizes the collaboration between Dorothea and Marienwerder as follows: 'Die Inkluse berichtete, Johannes notierte und bearbeitete dann seine Notizen' (Feistner, Neecke, and Vollmann-Profe, *Krieg im Visier*, p. 175). But

signs or traces might be read here of Dorothea herself? Where is her
jouissance? We are several times told, in equivalent medieval language,
that she has no sex drive. Since she began tormenting and castigating
her body before the age of seven, sexual desire ('nature corrupted by
original sin', 1.20; p. 55) fails to develop. Self-castigation is seen not as
a form of sensuality, but as its negation: 'her flesh did not incline towards
sensuality because of the extreme pain (der obirswenkin pyn) to which
she subjected it'; her body is referred to as 'der ezil', 'the donkey' (1.20;
pp. 55-6). Although she gives birth to nine children, Dorothea is said
never to make any demand for conjugal rights (1.24; p. 60). She shows
scant interest in her swarming brood, which features chiefly as an
obstacle to piety: once she has attended to its needs she heads off to
church, generally arriving before the doors have opened for the day's
sacrum commercium (1.25; p. 61). She is sometimes distracted from her
plan of hearing all daily masses by a sign of infant need, such as milk
trickling from her breasts; she must then, to her great annoyance, rush
home (1.25; p. 62). Another sign sends her rapidly homeward from the
churchyard of the great parish church of Gdańsk, dedicated to St Mary,
on a Marian festival; she arrives just in time to prevent four infants
burning to death in a storeroom fire (1.30; p. 69). All such reports come
to us through the mediation of a male author keen to desexualize his
candidate saint. But Dorothea's relative indifference to children is
unexceptional among medieval religious women. Heavy emphasis
upon mother-child bonding, fostered in later Catholic centuries (and
even then, not by all Catholic cultures),[72] is largely foreign to their
spirituality.

as with the case of Margery Kempe and her clerical co-author, the roles and phases
of composition cannot be so neatly distinguished.

72. See Nancy Scheper-Hughes, 'Two Feet Under and a Cardboard Coffin: The Social
Production of Indifference to Child Death', and 'Our Lady of Sorrows: A Political
Economy of the Emotions', Chapters 7 and 9 respectively of her *Death Without
Weeping: The Violence of Everyday Life in Brazil* (Berkeley: University of California
Press, 1992), pp. 268-339, 400-445. On 'maternal basic strangeness' or (a less pejo-
rative term) 'slowness to anthropomorphize the infant', see pp. 412-16. Scheper-
Hughes elsewhere comments that 'the dialectic between fertility and mortality,
reproduction and death, survival and loss, is a powerful one in the lives of most
people living outside or on the periphery of the "modern", industrialized world'
('The Cultural Politics of Child Survival', in *Child Survival: Anthropological
Perspectives on the Treatment and Maltreatment of Children*, ed. Scheper-Hughes
(Dordrecht: D. Reidel, 1987), pp. 1-29 (p. 1)).

John of Marienwerder does acknowledge that the language of Dorothea's mystical love experience remains alien or *barbaricam* to him; he can but frame a Latin text (and a German one derived from the Latin) to contain rather than reproduce Dorothea's barbaric yawp.[73] The most suggestive signs of something like pleasure in his text emanate from those experiences of ecstasy interspersing the endless regimen of self-castigation. Several of these occur in bed; several involve experiences of oblivion that cut across the official texts and scripts of Catholic piety. In one instance, which was to spark accusations of heresy, Dorothea is so transported by her weeping in church that she fails to rise for the elevation of the host (4.3.6; p. 240); in another, she is led—by protracted, bed-ridden ecstasy—to utterly forget her *Pater Noster* and *Creed* (2.25; p. 122). This second example occurs at Rome, following long weeks of abandonment, illness, and debilitation. It might be thought that what Dorothea craves is indeed oblivion: she several times wishes herself dead, and the thirty-seventh degree of love will see her frail body utterly crushed by the Godhead. Her most joyful moments come, it seems, as she is about to slip out of the social frame by assuming the life of a beggar. In Rome she determines to beg for alms. In Finsterwald, convinced that her husband is about to return to Danzig without her, she begins to practise the beggar's (or beghard's) call ('Bread, for the sake of our Lord', 2.12; p. 96). It delights her 'that she should remain there in misery, far from her worldly friends'; she laughs aloud for joy and rehearses her begging call loudly, 'mit lutir stymme'. Can it be, then, that Dorothea yearns for *blos Leben*, mere life,[74] freed from every kind of symbolic (civic, ecclesiastical, textual) determination; freed from the mighty superstructure that Marienwerder builds around her? I would argue *not*, pointing (again) to the places she chooses to inhabit: not just the physical spaces of her tireless journeying, but also those of her flights into beggary. In Rome, she determines to beg *on the steps of St Peter's*

73. '...potius linguam hujus idiomatis fuisse et esse mihi barbaricam': 'Prologus', *Septililium*, I (p. 12); Elliott, 'Dorothea of Montau', p. 185; Walt Whitman, 'Song of Myself', in *Leaves of Grass*, ed. Jerome Loving (Oxford: Oxford University Press, 1990), 52.3-4 (lines 1332–3): 'I too am not a bit tamed, I too am untranslatable,/ I sound my barbaric yawp over the roofs of the world'.
74. See Giorgio Agamben, *Homo Sacer: Sovereign Power and Mere Life*, tr. Daniel Heller-Roazen (Stanford: Stanford University Press, 1998); and see *Das Leben* 3.3, cited above, where Dorothea is told that it lies not in her power even to decide whether she is to be buried naked or clothed ('blos adir gekleyt').

('vor sint Petirs monstir uff der treppen', 2.25; p. 121); in Danzig/ Gdańsk she begs at the main portal of the great Marian parish church of Our Lady (1.29, pp. 67–8; 2.19; p. 109). These are two of the most powerful, symbolically supercharged *limines* of Dorothean Christendom; the anchorhold at Marienwerder, located between life and death, seems their only worthy successor. The poor of Danzig were doubtless happy to see her move there, since her faux-beggary cut into their business.[75] Dorothea loves acting or voguing the part of a beggar: she comes dressed in a threadbare coat and has 'eyme bosin vechellyn' ('a cheap piece of cloth', 1.29; p. 67) for her head by way of disguise; she is, however, recognized. She is so keen to be walled into her cell, Marienwerder tells the canonization inquiry, that she helps the masons lay the bricks.[76] Such individuating, self-dramatizing flashes at key locales might owe much to inspired authorship; but the decision to *move into* such liminal places seems genuinely hers.

Dorothea of Montau is more than the mere object of Marienwerder's hagiographic designs. Her commitment to enclosure is but the last and most momentous of a lifetime's decisions. Her space of enclosure roils, as we have seen, with supercharged affect confined in tight space; the pressures encountered here are at once personal and historical.[77] Which is to say: the forces besieging Dorothea, body and soul, speak at once to her very peculiar personal history and to tensions playing out in places structuring her life: Montau, Marienburg, Danzig, Marienwerder, the Prussian frontier—and even Rome, in time of Hussite rebellion and papal schism. The impulse to pathologize Dorothea seems as misguided as equivalent attempts aimed at Margery Kempe: Margery is no more hysterical than the times, the

---

75. 2.19 emphasizes that Dorothea has no need of the alms for which she begs; the beggars, to her annoyance, argue that they *are* genuinely needy ('durfftig') and resent suffering in the cold to no good effect. This exposes one of the perennial paradoxes of medieval poverty theory: that only those who, like mendicant friars, assume *voluntary* poverty ('willigem armut', 1.19) reap spiritual rewards; the indigent poor make no choice (no sacrifice of will), so their merit is less.

76. See Marienwerder, *Life*, ed. Stargardt, p. 12, n. 13.

77. Amy Hollywood argues that the body of Marie of Oignies, like that of other women from Liège, 'contains (both in the sense of holding and of holding in check) intense cultural conflicts concerning the body and authority'; she later argues that 'although our experiences of loss, limitation, and death are always embedded in the social, and hence in the ethical and political, they are not reducible to these realms' (*Sensible Ecstasy*, pp. 256, 277). Here as elsewhere, she carefully avoids reducing the innerly personal to the material facticity of the historical record.

impossible historical circumstances, of which she forms part.[78] Of course, the impulse to sanctify, too, can be just as suspect. Sanctification is the task to which John of Marienwerder sets himself from the minute he discovers Dorothea's cooling, eastward-pointing corpse in late June, 1394.

Changing places: uses and fortunes of Dorothea

Dorothea of Montau was buried at Marienwerder, three days after her death, during the vigil of Saints Peter and Paul (June 29; 3.43): an auspicious start to the long campaign for her canonization. Miracles and cures at the shrine were systematically accumulated, recorded, and notarized; by 1396, John of Marienwerder had produced the first *Ausgabe* of his Latin *vita*. Marienwerder's prologue urges the Roman papacy to deploy a canonized Dorothea against heresy, exhorting them to

... add this morning star which appeared in far-away Prussia, the furthest hem of the as yet unsewn garment of Christ, to the ecclesiastical starry firmament of saints so that through its light the sad darkness of the Schism... may be lifted and the day of grace and of the true Catholic faith dawn in the hearts of those now separated from the Mother Church.[79]

A more triumphalist tone might speak of Dorothea as a saint at the very edge of Christendom, uniting with those (like the Teutonic Order) shedding blood to extend the seamless garment of 'the true Catholic faith'. But Marienwerder writes in time of schism, division, and doubt. The pope of Rome finds a counterpart in Avignon (the pope of France and Scotland). Hussites are reaching beyond Bohemia, meddling with the territorial disputes of Germans and Poles; and Konrad von Wallenrodt, high master of the Teutonic Order from 1391–3, has been condemned for entertaining Wycliffite ideas.[80] Enthusiasm

---

78. On the impossible circumstances of symbolization in early fifteenth-century England, see Paul Strohm, *England's Empty Throne: Usurpation and the Language of Legitimation, 1399–1422* (New Haven: Yale University Press, 1998); for discussion of male hagiographers 'ventriloquizing their own hysteria through women's bodies', see Hollywood, *Sensible Ecstasy*, pp. 241–57 (p. 247).

79. Marienwerder, *Life*, ed. Stargardt, p. 19. Marienwerder's Latin is cited by Hipler, 'Beichtvater', p. 63.

80. Konrad is almost certainly to be identified with the soul of a great leader, now burning in hell, seen by Dorothea in a vision recorded by the *Liber de festis*: see Ute

for supporting further eastward expansion of the Teutonic Order is waning; Anna, wife of the recently-converted Vytautas of Lithuania, astutely chose to visit the shrine at Marienwerder during a state visit. Reconciliation of the Lithuanian cousins Vytautas (grand duke of Lithuania) and Jogaila (now Władysław II of Poland) in 1409 led to the massive and mythic defeat of the Teutonic Order at Grunwald (or Tannenberg) in 1410.[81] But chances for canonization in time of schism, and especially for a woman, were at any event very slender. After the canonization of St Hedwig in 1267, only two women were canonized before 1460: Bridget of Sweden (d. 1373, canonized 1391) and Catherine of Siena (d. 1380, canonized 1460).[82] Catherine thus had to wait for eighty years; Bridget, the only female schism saint, had her supposedly successful case raked over by two church councils. Jean Gerson, chancellor of the University of Paris, challenged Bridget's canonization with his De probatione spirituum (1415) while treating female mysticism generally with extreme scepticism.[83] The affective extremes of Dorothea, coupled with the inexorable decline of the Teutonic Order, made Marienwerder's Leben an untimely text.[84] Its future will ride on the fortunes of place: those movements of history marked, as Danziger

Stargardt, 'Political and Social Backgrounds of the Canonization of Dorothea von Montau', Mystics Quarterly, 11 (1985), pp. 112–15; Elliott, 'Dorothea of Montau', p. 181. Wallenrodt attempted to block Dorothea's enclosure at Marienwerder. Dorothea supposedly prophesied his death ten days in advance; she later sees him in hell, bound hand and foot, blackened like an Ethiopian, and tortured by the pitchforks of demons.

81. See Stargardt, 'Backgrounds', pp. 109, 118; Urban, Teutonic Knights, pp. 195–229 (esp. pp. 228–9). Legend has it that Bogurodzica, a Marian hymn that is the first known poem in Polish, was sung on the eve of battle on the Polish side. The epic and mythic dimensions of the battle, one of the bloodiest of the Middle Ages, are vividly realized by Aleksander Ford's film of 1960, Krzyżacy (TVP S.A./ Pegaz). A different view is offered by W. von Bülow's chapbook poem Heinrich von Plauen: Des deutschen Ritterordens letzter Held (Leipzig: Verlag für Literatur, Kunst und Musik, 1911). The prose Vorwort begins by noting how, in 1910, many thousands of Polish youths loudly acclaimed the 500th anniversary of the 'Schlacht bei Tannenburg' before proclaiming, chillingly, that that year is over. The poem celebrates Heinrich von Plauen, 'last hero of the Teutonic Order', who defended Marienburg after the battle and went on to become the twenty-seventh grand master.

82. See André Vauchez, Sainthood in the Later Middle Ages, tr. Jean Birrell (Cambridge: Cambridge University Press, 1997), p. 369.

83. See Elliott, 'Dorothea of Montau', p. 190; Vauchez, Sainthood, pp. 269, 409; Hollywood, Sensible Ecstasy, p. 8. We might remember, however, his late-life support of Joan of Arc.

84. Mossman associates the failure of Dorothea's cause with the diaspora of German masters from Prague ('Prague Masters', p. 121).

Günter Grass has it, by mutating names: 'Mein Giotheschants, Gidanie, Gdancyk, Danczik, Dantzig, Danzig, Gdańsk'.[85] Germanic devotion to Dorothea developed in two streams in the fifteenth century: the north chiefly accentuated her *life* (hagiography proving strongest in Prussia), whereas the south (Bavaria, Austria) revered her as *Mystikerin*. In 1486, urged by the high master of the Teutonic Knights, Rome reopened Dorothea's canonization process. Richard Stachnik, Dorothea's greatest scholarly champion after World War II, compiled and meticulously edited over six hundred pages worth of the material generated for her cause between 1394 and 1521.[86] But despite the publication of *Das Leben* as Prussia's first book in 1492, little progress was made; in 1525 the wheels came off as the last high master in Prussia turned Lutheran.[87] In 1544, just a little behind equivalent developments in England, Dorothea's shrine at Marienwerder was destroyed and her cult suppressed. A century later, however, it was revived as part of a Counter-Reformation offensive with Poles, rather than Germans, leading the charge.[88] Dorothea again marks a faith frontier: where Teutonic Germans had once battled with Lithuanian pagans, German Lutherans now eyed Catholic Poles.

Ostmark and *Middlemarch*: George Eliot in Prussia

The nineteenth century sees Dorothea folded into both large-scale histories of Prussia and more local investigations typical of the *Zeitschrift für die Geschichte und Alterthumskunde Ermlands* (first published in 1858) and (since 1865) publications of the *Historischen Verein für Ermland*.[89] Little of this, one might imagine, made its way to England: yet one particularly talented translator of German seems to have brushed imaginatively with the mystic from Montau. The heroine of George

---

85. *Der Butt*, p. 138; *The Flounder*, tr. Manheim, p. 114.
86. See *Akten*, ed. Stachnik.
87. See Hörner, *Dorothea*, p. 107; *Akten*, ed. Stachnik, pp. 544–9; Stargardt, 'Backgrounds', pp. 118–9; Toomaspoeg, *Histoire*, pp. 157–8.
88. Friedrich Szembeck, a Jesuit from Cracow living in Thorn, published three works on Dorothea in Polish between 1627 and 1638; the third of them was translated by Jesuit Adalbert Turschi into Latin: see Hörner, *Dorothea*, p. 111.
89. See Hörner, *Dorothea*, pp. 116–18. Ermland, a district of east Prussia, was designated one of the territorial possessions of the Teutonic Knights in 1243, along with the dioceses of Culm, Pomesanien, and Samland.

Eliot's *Middlemarch* is one Dorothea Brooke (even the surname could pass, aurally, for German). Dorothea, a young woman 'likely to seek martyrdom', has 'strange whims of fasting like a papist'.[90] She falls suddenly to fervent prayer on a brick floor (p. 9); she relishes the pleasure of renouncing pleasures (p. 10); she suffers insomniac struggles (p. 478) and is cruelly treated. Her lifestory is framed by references to a saint who, as a child, seeks 'martyrdom in the country of the Moors' (p. 3); the saga ends with reference to 'Crusaders of old' (p. 832). At the Vatican in Rome, whence she has travelled on a fateful journey, it is remarked that 'she should be dressed as a nun' (p. 189). But she has married a disappointed, clerical, Latin-based scholar:[91] a man whose systematizing pedantry seeks to cage her passionate and impulsive spirit.[92] Later she marries a fiery and romantic Pole called Ladislaw. Like Dorothea of Montau, this English Dorothea disappears into history while living out 'faithfully', as the last sentence of the novel has it, 'a hidden life' (p. 838).

Dwelling, briefly, upon George Eliot's putative familiarity with the Prussian Dorothea helps crystallize a significant moment in Dorothea's strange evolving from borderline mystic to militant German icon. Eliot was a famously accomplished and well-travelled Germanist. In 1849, following her father's death, she spent nine months in Switzerland; her

90. *Middlemarch*, ed. Rosemary Ashton (London: Penguin Classics, 1994), pp. 8, 9; all references follow this edition. My suggestion is that George Eliot, a brilliant Germanist, has experienced an imaginative brush with a text something like Marienwerder's *Leben der zeligen frawen Dorothee* (which compounds with many other models and influences); she is not writing (despite phrases such as 'is it any wonder the cholera has got to Dantzic?', p. 444) a *roman à clef*.

91. Casaubon's famous refusal to learn German (*Middlemarch*, pp. 208, 221) takes on a sad, almost cruel aspect when viewed in the context of George Eliot's German travels: for the kinds of analytical and classificatory skills needed by Casaubon for his epic work of scholarship had been most decisively developed by Germans. The intellectual loneliness of Lydgate, too, is thrown into higher relief when viewed against the posse of scientists and researchers that forms around Lewes and Eliot on their German travels. And his fear of being scooped by 'some plodding fellow of a German' proves—again, almost cruelly—true: see Gisela Argyle, *German Elements in the Fiction of George Eliot, Gissing, and Meredith* (Frankfurt am Main: Peter Lang, 1979), p. 41.

92. On 'the unlikely match' of Dorothea of Montau and John of Marienwerder, a 'union [that] is metaphorically infused with matrimonial imagery', see Elliott, 'Authorizing', p. 168 and passim. On 'Mr. Casaubon, the dessicated walking corpse to whom the ardent Dorothea Brooke is joined in indissoluble wedlock', see A. D. Nuttall, *Dead from the Waist Down: Scholars and Scholarship in Literature and the Popular Imagination* (New Haven: Yale University Press, 2003), pp. 26–71 (p. 26). Nuttall's energetic account shows scant knowledge of Eliot's German reading.

translation of Strauss's *Das Leben Jesu*, a text of some 1,500 pages, was already in print. Following three years' work at the *Westminster Review*, a journal sympathetic to German culture,[93] she saw her translation of Feuerbach's *Das Wesen des Christentums* through the press before accompanying George Henry Lewes to Weimar and Berlin. This extended journey into Prussia,[94] from 20 July 1854 to 13 March 1855, saw Eliot bedding down in her new liaison with Lewes both domestically and academically: for Lewes too was a fine Germanist, always seeking out the scientifically, medically, and philosophically inclined;[95] the couple were to make six more visits to Germany before the end of 1872. Eliot continued to excogitate and compose her English fiction while in German locales: chapters 18–26 of *Adam Bede* were written in Munich in 1858, and the final section of *Middlemarch* at Bad Homburg in the autumn of 1872. Her sojourn at Bad Homburg also included a first foray to a casino, where she saw Lord Byron's grand-niece lose £500: an incident that led to short-term denunciation of gambling (in a letter) but longterm inspiration (in opening *Daniel Deronda*).[96] Her encounter with Dorothea of Montau, by text or in conversation, floats somewhere between systematic study of German, casual inspiration, and historical timeliness.

In 1861, the scholarly trio Theodor Hirsch, Max Töpen, and Ernst Strehlke published the first volume of their *Scriptores Rerum Prussicarum*; the last of the five projected volumes appeared in 1874. The general scope of this series, and its political underpinnings, is suggested by its subtitle: *Die Geschichtsquellen der Preussischen Vorzeit bis zum Untergange der Ordensherrschaft (Historical Sources of Prussian Antiquity, to the Decline of the [Teutonic] Order's Overlordship)*. The first volume begins by

---

93. As Gisela Argyle notes, the *Westminster Review* was in 1846 renamed *The Westminster and Foreign Quarterly Review (German Elements*, p. 12); see further Anthony McCobb, *George Eliot's Knowledge of German Life and Letters* (Salzburg: Institut für Anglistik und Americanistik, 1982), p. 18.

94. For a map of the route, via Leipzig and Berlin, see Gerlinde Röder-Bolton, *George Eliot in Germany, 1854–55: 'Cherished Memories'* (Aldershot: Ashgate, p. 2006), p. xiv.

95. 'Mr Lewes', writes George Eliot to Mrs Congreve from Berlin on 3 April 1870, 'has had a good deal of satisfaction in his visits to labouratories and to the *Charité*, where he is just now gone for the third time to see more varieties of mad people' (John W. Cross, *George Eliot's Life, as Related in Her Letters and Journals*, 3 vols (Edinburgh and London: Blackwood, 1886), III, p. 90).

96. See McCobb, *Knowledge of German*, pp. 44, 72; Gordon S. Haight, *George Eliot: A Biography* (New York: Viking Penguin, 1985), p. 457.

listing subscribers: His Majesty the (newly-crowned) king of Prussia is named first, then the queen, then four princes, then the *Hoch- und Deutsch-Meister des Hohen Deutschen Ritterordens* (*High- and -German-Master of the Noble German Knightly Order*). Societies of a royal, military, juridical, and educational nature are then noted, city by city, in a mapping of terrain that extends from Berent and Berlin to Woinowitz and Zürich (pp. 5–8). The *Vorwort* that follows soon makes clear the general scope of the *Scriptores Rerum Prussicarum*: to conjoin the *Monumenta Germaniae Historica*, our great 'Nationalwerke', with the deep history of those easterly regions of our united fatherland ('östlichen Marken unsers gemeinsamen Vaterlandes'); the outstanding role played by the German knightly orders, noteworthy for extending and defending German culture ('für die Ausbreitung und Vertheidigung deutscher Kultur', p. ix), merits particular emphasis. It is in this context, as part of a monumental work framed by three scholarly champions of the Teutonic Order, that the appearance of Dorothea's German *vita* in volume 2 of *Scriptores Rerum Prussicarum* is to be viewed. From this point on, until her canonization one hundred years later, she becomes a potent icon of and for 'the extension and defense of German culture'.[97]

Das Leben der heiligen Dorothea, edited by Max Töppen from the sole surviving manuscript (supplemented, for missing sections, by the 1492 edition), takes up almost two hundred pages. Published at Leipzig in 1863, a copy had found its way to the British Museum—in handsome, gold-tooled red morocco—by 4 November of that year.[98] George Eliot was acquainted with a number of scholarly German expatriates in London, including Emmanuel Deutsch (employed at the British Museum); her acquisition of German scholarly works—now to be seen at Dr William's Library, Gordon Square—intensified through his influence.[99] Eliot's third trip to Germany with Lewes, begun on 7 June 1866, was disrupted by the Austro–Prussian war; their fourth trip pushed east to Dresden and Berlin (29 July to 1 October 1867). After

97. The Teutonic Order had always, unlike other medieval military orders, recruited men of a single nationality, or tongue: 'the Order was a German creation for Germans' (Burleigh, *Prussian Society*, p. 38).
98. According to the red stamp in BL 9385.i.4, vol. 2, p. 866.
99. See McCobb, *Knowledge of German*, pp. 61, 87. Eliot took Hebrew lessons from Deutsch; her German scholarly works on Judaism form an impressive part of the George Eliot—George Henry Lewes collection at Dr Williams's Library (which moved to its current location in Gordon Square, London, in 1890).

their fifth trip, in 1868, *Middlemarch* episodes began forming in Eliot's mind; their sixth trip, in the Spring of 1870, took them first to Berlin.[100] Here they were much fêted and 'lionized at a great rate'; new acquaintances included the celebrated historian and Prussian academic, Theodor Mommsen. Perhaps most remarkably, they heard Bismarck give a speech at the Reichstag:[101] this less than four months before the outbreak of the Franco–Prussian war, the conflict that was to unify Germany under Wilhelm I of Prussia (dedicatee of the *Scriptores Rerum Prussicarum*), aggrandize German territory, and topple the Second French Empire. On 1 September 1870, back in England, Lewes sent a cheque to alleviate the sufferings of German war victims ('on all accounts the Germans must have the first place'); George Eliot too first identified with the German cause but,[102] as the war and its aftermath unfolded, sympathized more with the French.[103] She began writing her Dorothea story—or, as she calls it, 'Miss Brooke'—in early November.[104] 'Miss Brooke', which subsequently became the opening section of *Middlemarch*, tells of a heroine 'enamoured of intensity and greatness, and rash in embracing whatever seemed to her to have those aspects; likely to seek martyrdom, to make retractions, and then to incur martyrdom after all in a quarter where she had not sought it' (p. 8). 'Miss Brooke', or Miss Bruch, does have a nice Germanic ring to it: suggestive, perhaps, of 'breaking away from, renunciation of (tradition, one's old way of life, etc.)'.[105]

George Eliot began learning Middle High German after her first trip to Germany; her second trip, in 1858, saw her disappointed by Munich

100. See Cross, *George Eliot's Life*, III, p. 82 (19 July 1869), p. 83 (2, 5 August 1869), p. 84 (1 September 1869).
101. See McCobb, *Knowledge of German*, p. 70.
102. 'I am very sorry for the sufferings of the French nation; but I think these sufferings are better for the moral welfare of the people than victory would have been' (25 August, letter to Madame Bodichon, in Cross, *George Eliot's Life*, III, p. 101).
103. See McCobb, *Knowledge of German*, p. 69 (Lewes's letter of 1 September is to Adolf Stahr); Argyle, *German Elements*, p. 36. Eliot's distaste for aspects of Prussian militarism on display at Berlin (as omnipresent royal entourages, or as bellowing in restaurants or swinging swords in the streets) was registered vividly during her first visit to Berlin, in 1855, a year that saw the banning of *Punch* (for parodying the Prussian king): see Röder-Bolton, *In Germany*, p. 148.
104. See Haight, *Biography*, pp. 431–2.
105. *The Oxford–Harrap Standard German–English Dictionary*, ed. Trevor Jones, 4 vols (Oxford: Clarendon Press, 1977), *Bruch*, 1 (b); see further *Missen*, v. tr., 'to be *or* do without (s.o., sth)', *Misbrauchen*.

but driven to ecstasy (and many evocative pages) by the premodern charms of Nürnberg.[106] Her movement through German territory, even in seeking out its medieval delights, is unmistakably modern: for she rides the same rails that were shortly to transform the nature of modern warfare.[107] Her susceptibility to interesting herself in the intense and erratic *Mystikerin,* Dorothea, seems high. And the timeliness of such an encounter is good, given the dramatic rise of Prussian-based German nationalist sentiment. It has been observed that each fresh clash between France and Germany occasions fresh editing or reappropriation of a disputed Ur-text: *La Chanson de Roland,* the military epic in which a Germanic tribal hero does battle in French with pagans at the border.[108] And 'in fact', Howard Bloch argues, 'in Germany by 1875 the publication of primary medieval sources had become a matter of state'.[109] Dorothea emerges in this context as a heroic Germanic borderline figure, set to suffer a martyrdom as memorable as that of Roland in his encounter with paganism. War, or the approach of war, continues to determine what Dorothea's *life* must come to mean.

Patronin Preußens: Nazism and Communism, Ratzinger and Grass

Pressures for canonizing Dorothea of Montau, building again through the later nineteenth century, intensify with developing political and

106. Eliot read *Das Niebelungenlied* and the beast fable *Reinecke Fuchs* (no doubt inspired by Wagner and Goethe, respectively) and Wolfram's *Parzival* (in modern German translation): see McCobb, *Knowledge of German*, p. 44. In her journal for 15 September she writes: 'Reading Chaucer, to study English' (Cross, *Life of George Eliot*, II, p. 378). The extended journal evocation of Nürnberg, as edited by Cross, ends poignantly (viewed from a longer historical perspective) thus: 'it is pleasant to think there is such a place in the world where many people pass peaceful lives'.
107. 'Our view both of Würzburg and Bamberg', she writes in April 1858, came 'as we snatched it from our railway carriage' (Cross, *Life of George Eliot*, II, pp. 15–16).
108. See Sharon Kinoshita ' "Pagans are Wrong and Christians are Right": Alterity, Gender, and Nation in the *Chanson de Roland*', *Journal of Medieval and Early Modern Studies*, 31:1 (2001), pp. 80–81; Hans Ulrich Gumbrecht, ' "Un Souffle d'Allemagne Ayant Passé": Friedrich Dietz, Gaston Paris, and the Genesis of National Philologies', *Romance Philology*, 40 (1986), pp. 1–37. It is always pleasing to note that the best text of *La Chanson de Roland* is actually English, *id est* Anglo-Norman, housed in an English library (Bodleian MS Digby 23, Part 2).
109. '842: The First Document and the Birth of Medieval Studies', in *A New History of French Literature*, ed. Denis Hollier (Cambridge, Mass.: Harvard University Press, 1989),

Figure 3. Dorothea of Montau at prayer, wearing a cloak of the Teutonic Order: frontispiece to Paul Nieborowski, *Die Selige Dorothea von Preussen* (1933).

territorial urgencies in the 1930s. Paul Nieborowski's *Die Selige Dorothea von Preussen*, published by the Ostdeutsche Verlagsanstalt at Breslau in 1933, boasts a *nihil obstat* with supporting ecclesiastical letters
from Danzig, Ermland, and Berlin. Nieborowski's titlepage faces a
'Dorotheenbild' depicting the saint at prayer (Figure 3); her cloak is
emblazoned with the cross, soon to be carried into Poland and points
east, of the Teutonic Order.[110] Nieborowski argues that his collection
of documents, pertaining to Dorothea's canonization process, is
extremely timely:

Denn die Zeiten für Deutschland, für das Christentum, die ganze Zivilisation
Mittel- und Westeuropas sind heute drohender denn je. Der russische
Bolschewismus, der geistig schon zum großen Teil Deutschland und andere
christlichen Länder vergiftet hat, rüstet sich, seine zerstörende Lehre auch mit
Waffengewalt uns zu bringen und aufzuzwingen. Da braucht die deutsche
Christenheit, besonders die der am meisten bedrohnten Ostmark, Ostpreußen,
Westpreußen, Schlesien, eine Schützerin und Fürbitterin, die für sie um Hilfe
zu Gott rufen kann.

(pp. 11-12)

For the times for Germany, for Christendom, for the entire civilization of
middle and western Europe are more threatening today than ever before.
Russian Bolshevism, having already spiritually poisoned the greater part of
Germany and of other Christian countries, readies itself to bring and impose
its ruinous doctrine upon us by force of arms. German Christianity, especially
the most threatened Ostmark,[111] East Prussian, West Prussian, and Silesian
regions, needs a protectress and intercessor who can call God for help on their
behalf.

Nieborowksi goes on to argue the case for Dorothea as 'eine *Heilige
unserer Tage*', with special reference to her 'starke Heimat- und Vaterlandsliebe': her fierce love of homeland and fatherland (p. 13). This

p. 10. 'Medieval specialists around 1870', Bloch argues, 'perceived erudition as a form
of war' (p. 10); the defeat of 1870 inspired the endowment of 250 new chairs of literature and history in France, between 1876–9, based on the German model (p. 11).

110. See Bruce Quarrie, *Hitler's Teutonic Knights: SS Panzers in Action* (Wellingborough:
Patrick Stevens, 1986); this depicts numerous scenes where the Knight's Cross is
awarded for valour. Nieborowski's caption explains that his frontispiece comes from
a painting now 'im jetzigen Haupthaus des Deutschen Ordens'.

111. 'Ostmark' is a nineteenth-century translation of *marchia orientalis* (the medieval
march of the Babenburgs); the term was revived and applied to Austria by the Nazis
after the *Anschluss* of 1938.

affective elision from local place into national territory, from mystical ground zero to nebulous homeland, is embellished further:

Wahrlich, die 'preußische Heilige', die 'Patronin Preußens', wie sie jahrhundertelang genannt wurde, möge uns als Beispeil edelster, glaubensverklärter Heimatliebe voranschweben in einer Zeit, da böswillige Menschen den deutschen Katholiken mangelhafte oder fehlende Vaterlandsliebe vorwarfen.

(p. 13)

Truly, the 'Prussian holywoman', the 'patroness of Prussia' (as she has been known for hundreds of years) may float before us as exemplar of the noblest, faith-transfigured love of homeland: this in a time when evil-disposed men accuse German Catholics of faulty or defective love of the fatherland.

Nieborowski perorates by pleading for non-Catholic German Christians to reconcile themselves with this medieval German saint: for she saw the repulse of 'eastern unChristendom'[112] as the chief purpose of the German *Ostmark*, her native ground; with him they should pray

...daß es wie damals einst wieder von Deutschland heiße:'Ein Gott, ein Volk, ein Glaube!'

(p. 14)

...that Germany may be called again, as it once was, the land of 'one God, one people, one belief!'

This prayer or call to arms echoes, of course, the Nazi's 'ein Reich, ein Volk, ein Führer'; Nieborowski's book, published in September 1933, caps off a year which sees Hitler become chancellor (30 January), the *Reichstag* burned (27 February), Hitler assume dictatorial powers (23 March), and 20,000 books burned in Berlin (10 May). The first shots of World War II were fired in Danzig; on 19 September 1939, Hitler was making a speech in the Artushof, the meeting

---

112. Nieborowski's reference to 'östlichen Unchristentums' in 1933 compares with sentiments expressed by the English Catholic journal *The Month* as late as July 1938: 'Poland, like Hungary, has become one of the Eastern Marches of the Church, one of the countries that has felt the attack of Tartar and Turk from the East, with the added complication of Russians and Swedes. And Poland remains an Eastern March in a very definite sense to-day: it is the bulwark of the West against the advance and influence of the Soviet States' ('The Eastern Marches', a section of 'Editorial Comments', *The Month*, 172 (July 1938), p. 4). *The Month* hopes, by way of Catholic resistance, for the possible 'canonization of St. Andrew Bobola, now considered there as a national patron' (p. 4).

place of medieval merchants. The great castle of Marienburg became a centre for Hitler Youth rallies, broadcast all over Germany; later it functioned as a prisoner of war camp.[113] The 'Teutonic Order' became the highest award bestowed by the Third Reich; one of its ten recipients was Reinhard Heydrich. It therefore seems extraordinary that Nieborowski should get his way: for on 9 January 1976, Dorothea was canonized by Pope Paul VI. The formula applied was *casus exceptus*: confirmation of a cult ongoing 'since time immemorial'.[114] Pressure for this canonization had come chiefly from German Catholics displaced from Prussia in 1945: a process that saw Marienwerder become Kwydyzn and Danzig Gdańsk (thus ending a Teutonic presence that had begun with the Knights in 1308). Dorothea's canonization thus 'recompenses' the final loss of border territory that her father helped Germanize and cultivate. On 17 July 1979, Cardinal Joseph Ratzinger, who in 1943 had been manning anti-aircraft guns to protect the BMW plant north of Munich, preached a sermon in Munich to celebrate Dorothea's elevation.[115] Displaced Danziger Günter Grass, however, was quicker off the mark: Dorothea of Montau appears in his novel *Der Butt* (1977) as wife to the narrator, a.k.a. (for a certain duration of this picaresque text) Albrecht Slichting, swordmaker of Danzig. As such she comes fourth in a succession of female cooks spanning the whole history of this region, from primordial ooze to seventies feminist ferment.

Petra Hörner, who has written the most exhaustive account of Dorothea's *Nachleben*, has denounced *Der Butt* (translated as *The Flounder*) as 'ein verzerrtes und verfälschtes Bild': a distorted and falsified portrait (p. 132). This can hardly be denied: but does John of Marienwerder's *Leben* brings us any closer to flesh and blood Dorothea? Günter Grass, at any event, keeps us within Marienwerder's imaginative ambit: for his ideas of 'High Gothic Lenten cook Dorothea of Montau' (pp. 116, 140)

113. The castle features prominently in *Der Unhold* (1996), Volker Schlöndorff's film adaptation of Michel Tournier's *Le Roi des Aulnes* (1970).
114. 'ab immorabili tempore': see Stargardt, 'Backgrounds', p. 120. An equivalent formula was employed in canonizing Cunegund (died 1033, canonized 1234) and Margaret of Scotland (died 1093, canonized 1249): see Vauchez, *Sainthood*, p. 369.
115. See John L. Allen, Jr., *Cardinal Ratzinger: The Vatican's Enforcer of the Faith* (NY: Continuum, 2000), p. 21; Hörner, *Dorothea*, p. 133. Ratzinger's sermon was later published as 'Die Heilige Dorothea von Montau', in *Christlicher Glaube und Europa. 12 Predigten* (Munich: Erzdiözese München und Freiin, 1981), pp. 31–41.

develop from this very text.[116] As a schoolboy, young Günter was actually instructed by Dorothea's greatest twentieth-century champion, Monsignor Richard Stachnik: a man of courage and character[117] who worked obsessively for Dorothea's canonization, chiefly through his edifying organ *Das Doroteenbote* (1951–1978). Grass actually addresses a fictional letter to Stachnik in *Der Butt*: 'as my Latin teacher', the narrator says, 'you were a failure, but you infected me for good with the Dorothean poison (p. 172; 'mit dem dorotheischen Gift', p. 211). The letter proposes a scurrilous deal: if Stachnik renounces the canonization campaign (a process approaching its climax as Grass writes), the narrator will stop calling Dorothea a witch. Extraordinarily, the octogenarian Monsignor writes back: his own lifelong devotion to Dorothea was just then reaching its climax; the impertinent irruption of his one-time pupil was untimely and distracting.[118] So it is that the thirty-eighth and last volume of *Das Doroteenbote*—the periodical expires as Dorothea is sainted—vigorously denounces *Der Butt*.[119] This strange dialogue of Latin-based scholarship with German fictionmaking actually seems a fitting terminus to six centuries of intensive, male-dominated struggle over Dorothea. And Grass does not lie (for once) in suggesting that Stachnik bit him with the Dorothea bug: for he adheres to the northern tradition of Dorothean reception (and that of the German rather than Latin texts) in emphasizing her life rather than her mysticism.[120]

Grass's particular genius lies in evoking urban and rural geographies, and their changing with time: in particular Danzig and the rural hinterland that gave rise to Dorothea, 'hier in dem nebligen Sumpfland zwischen den Flüssen'.[121] His narrative faithfully adheres to the historically concrete style of the German *Leben* and obligingly fills in those details that *Das Leben* has missed: how, for example, did a Danzig

---

116. That is, from the German *Leben* rather than from one of Marienwerder's Latin texts: see Timothy McFarland, 'The Transformation of Historical Material: The Case of Dorothea von Montau', in *Günter Grass's Der Butt: Sexual Politics and the Male Myth of History* (Oxford: Clarendon Press, 1990), p. 82.

117. Opposition to National Socialism won Monsignor Stacknik some time in the Stutthof *Konzentrationslager*.

118. The *Vorwort* to Stachnik's monumental *Akten des Kanonisationsprozesses Dorotheas von Montau* is dated 25 June 1977 (p. vi); the book was published the following year.

119. See Hörner, *Dorothea*, pp. 130–32; McFarland, 'Transformation', pp. 90–96.

120. See McFarland, 'Transformation', p. 82.

121. *Der Butt*, p. 102 ('[here in] this foggy marshland between rivers', p. 87).

swordmaker find his way to Montau, and how might he have courted young Dorothea? Knowing swordmaking to be 'a trade with a future',[122] his Albrecht Slichting

...kam ja oft nach Montau: unterwegs zur Marienburg durch das (nach den Hungerjahren) neu eingedeichte Land zwischen Nogat und Weichsel.

(p. 148)

...often went to Montau on my way to the Marienburg through the country between the Nogat and the Vistula, which had been freshly diked in (after the famine years).

(p. 123)

Here, as often, Grass joins historical dots: a swordmaker seeks out the Teutonic Knights in their greatest stronghold; newly-diked Montau lies by Marienburg; Albrecht discovers his future bride. Their early courtship, as Grass tells it, moves between farce, horror, and arresting detail:

Auch daß mir das Kind (mittlerweile zehnjährig) eine siebenkettige Geißel mit Silbergriff, in den Perlmut und zu Tränen geschliffener Bernstein eingelegt waren, wie ein Spielzeug abschwatzte (der Abt zu Marienwerder hatte das Werkzeug in Auftrag gegeben) rührte mich eher; denn wie hätte ich ahnen können, daß sich Dorothea nächstens durchs Büßerhemd bis aufs Blut geißelte. Auch ihre ersten Verse—'Jesusliep min geißlin für, das min leip sich smertz erkür'—hielt ich für modisches Geplapper. Erst als die Sechzehnjährige mir angeheiratet und doch nicht meine Frau wurde, ertastete ich, nun zeitweilig im Besitz ihres gleichgültig bleibenden Fleisches, den zernabten Rücken, die immer offenen, schwärenden Wunden.

(p. 149)

And when the child (grown to the age of ten by that time) wheedled me into giving her a seven-chained scourge with a silver handle (inlaid with mother-of-pearl and amber tears) to play with (it had been ordered by the abbot of Marienwerder), my only feeling was one of affectionate amusement; for how was I to guess that Dorothea drew blood night after night by flaying herself through her hair shirt. And her first verses—'Jesu, guide my litel chaine, for my flesh hath chosen pain'—struck me as nothing more than fashionable babble. Only when at sixteen she was married to me yet did not become my wife, did I, in temporary possession of her utterly indifferent flesh, feel the scars on her back and the festering, still-open wounds.

(p. 123)

122. *The Flounder*, tr. Manheim, p. 115 ('ein Beruf mit Zukunft', p. 139).

Grass here vividly reminds us that self-punishment, the wounding of her own flesh, was Dorothea's most singular and consistent form of action. It is what she *did* and what she cared to do: 'for our nine little children, all but one of whom died young' Grass's swordmaker says, 'she had hardly a glance' (pp. 129, 157). Dorothea is a strange feminine icon for modern Catholicism: but since Dorothea was canonized for her *cult* rather than her *life*, the meaning of her life was never up for serious examination in the 1970s; and besides, the life and the cult were essentially one, alike authored by 'the onetime Prague professor of theology and later dean of Marienwerder cathedral' (pp. 169, 207). Since John of Marienwerder 'was too intent on producing a saint for the Teutonic Order'[123], Grass prefers to rely upon 'personal memories': that is, fictive speculation. Yet he himself, at the very end of his fictional letter to Stachnik, embraces his former teacher through acceptance of common defeat: 'wir wissen ja beide nicht, was Dorothea gewollt hat. .'. (p. 211). While neither man 'knows what Dorothea wanted' (p. 172), the letter does suggest what she has come to mean: 'Dorothea was the first woman (in our region) to rebel against the patriarchal tyranny of medieval marriage' (pp. 170, 208–9). To support his case, Grass cites the 'Vorsitzende' or president of the Feminist Tribunal in Berlin: 'Dorothea Swarze wanted freedom for herself. Religion and Jesus were only a means, the one permissible agency through which to press her demand for emancipation and escape from the all-engulfing (penetranten) power of men' (pp. 170–1, p. 209). Such a rationale, which evokes that informing some strains of Margery Kempe criticism, forms part of the satirical running battle Grass conducts with second generation feminism throughout *Der Butt*. Third wave feminism, itself a controversial and contentious strain of writing within Women's Studies, might reclaim Dorothea—or, more savvily, the pleasures of reading her—for its quickly-expanding canon.[124] But for

123. *The Flounder*, tr. Manheim, p. 169 ('eine Heilige für den Deutschritterorden produz-ieren', p. 207).
124. The phrase 'third wave' was apparently first employed by Rebecca Walker in 1992; for a bibliographical survey of this largely anthology-driven phenomenon, see Astrid Henry, *Not My Mother's Sister: Generational Conflict and Third-Wave Feminism* (Bloomington: Indiana University Press, 2004), esp. pp. 23–36. For sceptical, historical, and revisionary critiques, see *Third Wave Feminism: A Critical Exploration*, ed. Stacey Gillis, Gillian Howie, and Rebecca Munford (Basingstoke: Palgrave Macmillan, 2004).

many readers, the castigated and self-wounded body of Dorothea (largely neglected by post-medieval scholarship and criticism) will remain the most troubling and seemingly intractable aspect of her life and legend. With Susan Bordo, we might 'take the psychopathologies that develop within a culture, far from being anomalies or aberrations, to be characteristic expressions *of* that culture; to be, indeed, the crystallization of much that is wrong with it'.[125] Bordo concerns herself chiefly with anorexia, a behavioural trait that (in less spectacular fashion) underlies the self-disciplining of Dorothea, the 'Lenten cook' (as Grass calls her). But Bordo's Foucauldian critique grounds itself in an account of the body conceived 'as an alien force and impediment to the soul' (p. 149) that runs deep and long in western tradition. Dorothea's case, however, seems yet more terrifying than those adduced by Bordo's *Unbearable Weight*. In Hilde Bruch's *The Golden Cage*, one anorectic avers that 'you make of your own body your very own kingdom where you are the tyrant, the absolute dictator'.[126] Dorothea's body is tyrannized from within and without: but can it be accounted (given the violent and dictatorial attentions of confessor, husband, and Lord) a kingdom of her own making? Does her obedience to ecclesiastical authority express more, in intensified form, than the *paradox of doxa*, and subjection to that *domination masculine* to which all women, according to Bourdieu, more or less subscribe?[127]

---

125. *Unbearable Weight: Feminism, Western Culture, and the Body*, tenth anniversary edition (Berkeley: University of California Press, 2003), p. 141; emphasis added. Bordo, alert to ceaseless media imaging of ideal bodily types, urges us 'to take cultural imagery seriously' (p. xxi): an invitation we might apply to premodern girlish fascination with the mechanics and detail of virgin martyrdom. See Wallace, 'Periodizing Women', pp. 415–16.

126. *The Golden Cage: The Enigma of Anorexia Nervosa* (New York: Vintage, 1979), p. 65; Bordo, *Unbearable Weight*, p. 150.

127. 'I have always been astonished', Bourdieu remarks, 'by what might be called the *paradox of doxa*—the fact that the order of the world as we find it . . . is broadly respected' (*Masculine Domination*, tr. Nice, p. 1; *La domination masculine*, p. 7). Ironically, Bourdieu's commitment to demonstrating the power of *doxa* makes him seem, at moments, Marienwerder-like, constructing a prisonhouse or anchorhold of totalized symbolic confinement from which women cannot escape: 'women themselves', he writes, 'apprehend all reality, and in particular the power relations in which they are held, through schemes of thought that are the product of embodiment of those power relations and which are expressed in the founding oppositions of the symbolic order. It follows that their acts of cognition are acts of practical recognition, doxic acceptance, a belief that does not need to be thought and affirmed as such, and which in a sense "makes" the symbolic violence which it undergoes' (pp. 33–4; *Domination masculine*, pp. 39–40). Thus every woman, unknown to her, is a Dorothea.

Frontiers, east and west

The 'psychopathologies' that run through *Das Leben der zeligen frawen Dorothee*, I shall argue by way of conclusion, are locational, testifying to irresolvable tensions and contradictions at a far border of Christendom. Günter Grass, again, offers vital clues and points of departure: perhaps beginning with his own departure from the region in 1945, as Danzig becomes Gdańsk. For in countering Stachnik's canonizing dreams, Grass does not straightforwardly set himself against belated and benighted Teutonic aspirations. He could not, at any event, do this *straightforwardly*, since he had worn the Teutonic cross himself: while seminarian Ratzinger was protecting BMW in Bavaria, schoolboy Grass was manning anti-aircraft guns of his own further east.[128] And, as we learned only in 2006 (seven years after his acceptance of the Nobel prize) he did much more than this as a member of the Waffen-SS.[129] As mythologized by *Die Blechtrommel*, Grass's own cultural and familial identity is split: a Cassubian mother, carrying forward the ancient and pagan traditions of a rural people that survives German and Polish invasion; an uncertain paternity, shared between a German and Pole who play with the mother at the same Danzig cardtable.[130] The mother, conceived on a bleak rural plane, eats herself to death after witnessing horror: a horse's head filled with blood-gorged eels. The *meaning* of this scene, the most unforgettable from both book and film of *The Tin Drum*, is (so far as I can tell) indeterminate; allegoresis is overrun by sheer visual and descriptive revulsion. Artistic finessing is here enabled by the cultural assumption—most deeply rooted, as Bordo again observes—that women are *too much*.[131] *The Tin Drum*'s true heroine

128. Michael Hollington, *Günter Grass: The Writer in a Pluralist Society* (London: Marion Boyars, 1980), p. 6.

129. See *Beim Häuten der Zwiebel* (Göttingen, 2006): 'ein wort ruft das andere. Schulden und Schuld' (p. 36; 'one word evokes the other: *Schulden, Schuld,* debts, guilt' (*Peeling the Onion,* tr. Michael Henry Heim (London: Harvill Secker, 2007), p. 28). The Nobel prize committee declined to rescind the award; Lech Wałęsa called upon Grass to relinquish his honorary citizenship of Gdańsk: see *Ein Buch, Ein Bekenntnis: Die Debatte um Günter Grass'* Beim Häuten der Zwiebel (Göttingen: Steidl, 2007), pp. 12, 15. A cartoon in *Focus* on 21 August 2006 suggests that, for his next book-promoting PR stunt, Grass should reveal his membership in the STASI.

130. *Die Blechtrommel: Roman* (Darmstadt: Luchterhand, 1959); *The Tin Drum*, tr. Ralph Manheim (London: Secker and Warburg, 1970); *Die Blechtrommel,* directed by Volker Schlöndorff (West Germany, France, Poland, Yugoslavia, 1979), 144 minutes.

131. See *Unbearable Weight*, pp. 160–63.

dies because she eats too much; Dorothea whips her way towards oblivion while eating too little. In either case, bloating or starving, the full force of cultural and familial tensions that prove irresolvable is borne by the female body.

Pressures bearing down upon Dorothea of Montau, the first female recluse at the Prussian frontier, are, we have seen, many and complex: they include psychic unease at 'reclaiming' or improving upon nature (carried eastward from the Low Countries); the crusading and commercial ambitions of the Teutonic Order; the career anxieties of one particular knight; a split between mind or *Geist* and body that can only end (at the thirty-seventh degree) with the final destruction of the human frame. One further source of tension, as experienced at Marienburg, Montau, and Marienwerder, needs to be addressed: the sheer vastness of the Eurasian landmass that the Teutonic Order presumes to conquer. Fear of this unknown territory is as old as Ovid; the folly of *seriously* setting out to conquer it as recent as Napoleon and Hitler. The imperative to expand Christendom ever eastward in this region, following the failure of the Middle Eastern Crusades, was only relieved by discovery of a new border: a new way, it seemed, to get east. This is not my argument, but Richard Hakluyt's. The second edition of Hakluyt's *Principall Navigations, Voiages and Discoveries of the English Nation* celebrates Henry of Derby, 'afterward king of England', for his journeys 'into Prussia & Lithuania, with a briefe remembrance of his valiant exploits against the infidels there'.[132] Following brief mention of 'Tho[mas] of Woodstock his trauel into Pruis', Hakluyt salutes 'the learned, wittie, and profound Geoffrey Chaucer [who], vnder the person of his knight, doeth iudicially and like a cunning Cosmographer, make report of the long voiages and woorthy exploits of our English Nobles, Knights, & Gentlemen, to the Northren, and to other partes of the world in his dayes' (p. 8). Later in his volume, Hakluyt prints 'verses of Geoffrey Chaucer in the knights Prologue', ending at line 66 with the Knight fighting 'Heathen in Turkie'. The principal subject of Hakluyt's *Navigations* is the inexorable drive of the English nation into the Americas (a task unaccomplished as Hakluyt writes); this probing of an eastern limit prologues and pedigrees subsequent westward conquest.[133]

132. *Voyages, Navigations, Traffiques, and Discoueries of the English Nation*, 3 vols (London: George Bishop, Ralf Newberie, and Robert Barker, 1598–1600), vol. I, 'A Preface to the Reader', unpaginated, 8th page.
133. See Wallace, *Premodern Places*, p. 121.

Chaucer's Knight is a cunning choice: for his tale begins with conquest and triumphant return to the imperial centre—Athens—with enslaved enemies. These are Amazons, proud rulers of 'the regne of Femenye' (1.866), embodiments of all men hope and fear to find in that vast Eurasian plain.

Such ambivalences travel with Columbus as he sails from the medievalized Canaries, site of a Norman conquest and a major Marian cult, to 'new Canaries' further west;[134] and they attend discovery of the great continental landmass with two medieval names, 'Terra de Vera Cruz' and 'Brazil'. The 'Land of the True Cross' imagines medieval crusading tradition extending itself westward; the colour *bresil*, as worn by the hero of Chrétien de Troyes's *Perceval le Gallois*, is a red that 'stands for the customary medieval color of desire'.[135] Natives of these new European borderlands are found to be in acute need of severe rational regulation; the continent itself is often portrayed as a naked female form.[136] Slavery, which intensifies selective aspects of medieval serf–lord relations, supplies a westward flow of labour to the new Christian frontier; and again at this *limen*, in the face of a new but similarly vast and unknowable continental landmass, anxieties play out. Plantation settlements, located between the sea and impenetrable savannah, evolve strange new forms of borderline enclosure; female bodies, again, bear the marks of ambivalence and pressurized control. William Blake's engraving of a female slave being whipped in Surinam[137] seems a long way from Dorothea's Prussian martyrdom; but it is not *so* far as to forbid contemplation in a shared geopolitical frame.

The image of New World encounter that has excited most commentary over the last thirty years is *America*, as engraved by Theodor and Phillipe Galle from an original drawing by Jan van der Straet.[138]

---

134. See Wallace, *Premodern Places*, pp. 203–38.
135. Roland Greene, *Unrequited Conquests: Love and Empire in the Colonial Americas* (Chicago: University of Chicago Press, 1999), p. 86; see further pp. 20–1, 80–86, 112–15.
136. See Peter Hulme's discussion of Jan van den Straet's engraving *America* (c.1600) in his *Colonial Encounters: Europe and the Native Caribbean 1492–1797* (London: Methuen, 1986). Representation of the 'new' continent as a naked female form evidences 'an anxiety [that] concerns the relationship between European, native and land...the classic colonial triangle' (p. 1).
137. See Wallace, *Premodern Places*, pp. 270–73 and figure 28.
138. For fine independent analysis and a conspectus of critical views, see Michelle R. Warren, *History on the Edge: Excalibur and the Borders of Britain 1100–1300* (Minneapolis: University of Minnesota Press, 2000), pp. 245–51.

Figure 4. *America*, engraved by Theodor and Phillipe Galle after a drawing by
Jan van der Straet (Giovanni Stradano). Bibliothèque Nationale, Paris.

This records Amerigo Vespucci *inventing* or coming across the new
continent, figured as a near-naked female indigene, at its extreme eastern border. Jan van der Straet was a Fleming, born in Bruges, who
flourished in Florence as Johannes Stradanus; his engravers and print-
ers were based in Antwerp. His original drawing for *America* upholds
the *east is west* principle in eccentric fashion: for in order to have his
drawing (c. 1575) engraved, van der Straet must anticipate reversed
polarities; the word *AMERICA* proceeding from Amerigo's mouth
towards the reclining figure, in the drawing, thus emerges as mirrored
backwards.[139] This word actually disappears from the engraved form: it
is replaced by a bottom caption, 'America', that speaks of Amerigo
*re*peating or *re*discovering America ('Americen Americus retexit': see
Figure 4). Her name is his feminized; 'henceforth' (to complete the

---

139. See José Rabasa, *Inventing A-m-e-r-i-c-a* (Norman: University of Oklahoma Press,
     1993), pp. 23–5 and figure 1; see further Hulme, *Colonial Encounters*, pp. 1–9.

captional citation), 'once he spoke, she was always awake'. Commentators have noted the many ways in which this scene conflates known and unknown elements (animals, foliage, ornaments), vectoring strange simultaneities of medieval and futuristic time. The four crosses on Vespucci's banner, for example, are to be associated with the Southern Cross, 'never seen' (according to Dante, as cited and illustrated later in van der Straet's *Nova reperta*) 'except by *la prima gente*'.[140] The banner, sword, and astrolabe with which Amerigo confronts *America* are standard accoutrements of medieval crusading, warfare, and science: activities that remind us, again, of Marienwerder's encounter with Dorothea, *clewsenerynne* of the far eastern border. Such comparisons, teased out a little, prove as compelling as they are unlikely. Anchoresses like Dorothea live in an enclosed space, typically with a bed and three windows. *America*, too, is structurally enclosed: two trees support her hammock, while the third functions perspectivally to suggest enclosure while opening lines of sight to specific scenes beyond. Vespucci, like Marienwerder, stations himself immediately outside this enclosed space, looking in. Both men possess instruments of Christian warfare and scientific measurement (Marienwerder, an inquisitorial knight under the Teutonic banner, subjects Dorothea's body and soul to thirty-seven degrees of calibration) with which to perform surveillance and interrogation; they then mediate texts and impressions of this female barbarian—at once *their* particular creature and a more abstract claim to territory—to their masculine, Latinate worlds. The structured tree space, like an anchorhold, has three openings: one, at her back, to native sources of supply (the service window); one for dialogue with the world (Vespucci and Marienwerder); and one through which to view cannibalistic rites. The fact that the female anchoress views the Christian cannibalism of the mass through her interior window represents the strangest congruence between these border scenes; suggests, perhaps, that the kinds of interrogation, fabrication, projection, and control rehearsed by Marienwerder and his clerical kind carry forward, half-acknowledged, to 'inquisitions of curiosity' at borders further west.[141]

140. The plate *ASTROLABIVM* in Jan van der Straet's *Nova reperta* features Dante contemplating the Southern Cross and cites *Purgatorio* 1.23–7. See further Rabasa, *A-m-e-r-i-c-a*, pp. 31–2; *Giovanni Stradano e Dante*, ed. Corrado Gizzi (Milano: Electa, 1994).
141. The phrase 'inquisitions of curiosity' is from Michel de Certeau, *The Writing of History*, tr. Tom Conley (New York: Columbia University Press, 1988), p. 234.

Pope Benedict XVI, early on in his career, wrote a book called
Die Christliche Brüderlichkeit; values of Christian brotherhood perhaps shaped his appreciation of Dorothea, the anchoress coached so
painstakingly towards sainthood by the Teutonic Order. The celebratory sermon preached by the future pontiff on Dorothea's canonization was subsequently published in a volume called *Christlicher
Glaube und Europa*; the authoritarianism and violence visited upon
Dorothea by three masculine hands (the husband, the confessor, the
Lord) would thus seem integral to Josef Ratzinger's idea of 'Christian Belief and Europe'.[142] More than forty years later, as Prefect for
the Doctrine of the Faith, Cardinal Ratzinger took a strong stand
against admitting Turkey to the EU on the grounds that Turkey had
always been 'in permanent contrast to Europe'.[143] On 12 September
2006, just one day after the five year anniversary of 9/11, Pope Benedict floated the notion—drawing from a medieval Byzantine
emperor—of the intrinsic violence of Islam. This reiterates a long-
established habit, famously exemplified by Jacob Burckhardt, of
characterizing barbarities endemic to western societies as Islamic
imports.[144] In his earlier remarks *contra* Turkey, then-Cardinal Ratzinger conceded that the Ottoman empire once stretched almost to
Vienna, but argued that it was never European because it was always
invasive. Quite what the Christian brotherhood of the Teutonic
Order was up to, in Palestine and Prussia, awaits papal clarification.[145] It remains extraordinarily difficult to *read* Dorothea of Montau: to seek, as Günther Grass has it, 'was Dorothea wollte'. But we
can at least counter Josef Ratzinger's notion of an authentically European *inside* and *outside* by studying the religious history from which he

142. See *Die Christliche Brüderlichkeit* (Munich: Kösel Verlag, 1960), translated as *The
      Meaning of Christian Brotherhood* (San Francisco: Ignatius Press, 1993); 'Die Heilige
      Dorothea'.
143. Interview with *Le Figaro* as reported by *CWNews.com*, Paris, 11 August 2004; see
      further *Aljazeera.net*, same day. See also *www.ratzingerfanclub.com*.
144. See Wallace, *Chaucerian Polity*, pp. 55–60.
145. But see, *à propos* the long genealogy of these mounted Teutonic monks, Ratzinger's
      comment that 'as a pre-political and supra-political force, monasticism was also
      the harbinger of ever welcome and necessary rebirths of civilization and culture'
      (Joseph Ratzinger, 'The Spiritual Roots of Europe: Yesterday, Today, and
      Tomorrow', in Ratzinger and Marcello Pera, *Without Roots: The West, Relativism,
      Christianity, Islam*, foreword by George Wiegel, tr. Michael F. Moore (New York:
      Basic Books, 2007), p. 56.

supposedly draws.[146] And we can counter his championing of Dorothea as a Christian patroness keeping barbarism at bay with a different proposition: that the 'psychopathologies' incubated in her cell and in her cult have a long and powerful afterlife within and beyond European borders.

The Teutonic Order lives on today, in attenuated form. Headquartered in Austria, it enjoys papal recognition, although there are only twenty fully-professed and celibate 'knights'; there is even a Calvinist branch in Holland.[147] Visitors to Gdańsk can visit the house of Albrecht and Dorothea Slichting, although it has been rebuilt in Flemish Renaissance style. Old Danzig, flattened by British, American, and Russian bombardments (in that order), was reconstructed by Poles who omitted anything too redolent of Prussian style. The city is still much visited by German tourists; some leave bearing calendars entitled 'Danzig: Stadt meiner Träume'. At Marienburg, now Malbork and a UNESCO World Heritage Centre, most foreign visitors are German: here you can view arrowheads left by the Teutonic Knights and bear away souvenir axes made of balsawood. You can tag on to a tour group, which might see (as I did) a Polish local dressed up in Teutonic guise pointing out highlights to a visiting general and Malbork's mayor.[148] Kwydyzn gets fewer visitors; Montowy fewer still. Such changes only accentuate the difficulty of reading *for* Dorothea in John of Marienwerder's text. In the end, perhaps, *Das Leben*'s most arresting moment remains its sighting of Dorothea at the porch of Danzig's huge parish church, the site of her greatest flesh-ripping revelation. Dorothea

---

146. 'Europe, Joseph Ratzinger writes', declares George Wiegel, 'has become hollowed out from within, paralyzed in its culture and its public life by a "failure of the circulatory system". And the results of that hollowing-out are most evident in the unprecedented ways in which Europe is depopulating itself. Generation after generation of below-replacement-level birthrates have created a demographic vacuum which, like all other vacuums in nature, is not remaining unfilled: the vacuum is being filled by transplanted populations whose presence in Europe is a challenge to Europe's identity' ('Foreword' to Ratzinger and Pera, *Without Roots*, pp. viii–ix). Such dimwit mediation of Ratzinger's more nuanced discussion of European *inside* and *outside* thus spells danger for non-Christian Europeans.

147. Most of the Order's members are actually women: uniquely among Catholic Orders, and ironically from the long perspective of this essay, these sisters are set under the authority of a masculine head.

148. On the ruin of Marienburg in 1945 and its subsequent reconstruction see Wolfrum, *Die Marienburg*, pp. 39–40 and plates following.

dresses beggar-like, but is no beggar; aspiring to pass unnoticed, she assumes the most prominent liminal space in town. The only space of greater potency, after this, is the anchorhold: that life-and-death threshold entered voluntarily by Dorothea on 2 May 1393. Her transcendent power, down through the centuries, comes from living anchorism at a disputed frontier (conjoining Christian and 'Saracen', Teuton and Lithuanian, Catholic and Lutheran, fascist and communist, German and Pole, pope and novelist). Her most obsessive scrutineers—editors and calibrators, detractors and champions—have all been (one cannot help but notice) men.[149] Can it be that Dorothea fulfills so perfectly the logic of *domination masculine* that she draws it to destruction? In this, and in her impeccable devotion to *doxa*, she does finally emerge as the German–Polish cousin that Hope Emily Allen dreamed of finding for Margery Kempe.

149. I thus join a line of succession extending from Marienwerder and his premodern followers to Nieborowski and Stachnik, Grass and Ratzinger, and Richard Kieckhefer ('who in 1984', Ute Stargardt observes, 'introduced Dorothea to American readers in *Unquiet Souls*': *Life*, tr. Stargardt, p. 1) while acknowledging the influence of Stargardt herself, and of Petra Hörner.

2

Anchoritic Damsel: Margery Kempe of Lynn, *c*.1373–*c*.1440

Dorothea of Montau's cult, we have noted, was revived in the 1930s as a bulwark against Bolshevism; her subsequent canonization was derided by Günter Grass and applauded, from his Munich pulpit, by Cardinal Ratzinger. The *Book of Margery Kempe* is also very much a text of the 1930s: it was, in fact, first identified in 1934, *the* greatest year of the century for English Medieval Studies. So many of our current lines of interpreting Margery's *Book* originate from the 1930s and early 40s: the period from first notice of discovery in *The Times* to reviews of the modernized version of 1936 and of the Early English Text Society edition, Original Series 212, in 1940. Virginia Woolf, writing on 27 June 1940, could not 'conceive that there will be a 27 June 1941'.[1] Dr Mabel Day, EETS Secretary, proofread the scholarly edition of Margery's *Book* in air raid shelters; the context of European war, and approach to war, powerfully influenced what *The Book of Margery Kempe had to be*. Part of this story concerns changing attitudes by English intellectuals towards *Germany*: the terrain, physical and intellectual, travelled so passionately by George Eliot and her late-Victorian peers. Part of it concerns terms such as *hysteria* and *neurosis*, freely applied to both Margery and Dorothea, which were just finding their feet in the 1930s. As with Dorothea, Margery's critics sought both to save and pathologize their heroine; such conflicted impulses epiphenomenalize, I will argue, anxieties of the times (the 1930s, and also the 1430s).

---

1. 'We pour to the edge of a precipice . . . & then? I cant conceive that there will be a 27 June 1941' [*Thursday 27 June*], *The Diary of Virginia Woolf*, ed. Anne Olivier Bell, assisted by Andrew McNeillie, 5 vols (London: Hogarth Press, 1977–84), V, p. 299. The entry for Friday 14 June opens with 'Paris is in the hands of the Germans' (V, p. 296). Woolf drowned herself in the tidal River Ouse on 28 March 1941.

Figure 5. The River Great Ouse at King's Lynn.

I cannot help but notice, as a male reader, the *Book of Margery Kempe* drawing generative power from the death of men. Further difficulties arise from genre trouble: Books I and II are just not the same, generically speaking. The later part of this chapter, in this book dedicated to life and *life*, text and territory, sticks with Book II. This brings us to Danzig, the city still ruled (in 1433) by those Teutonic Knights who controlled Dorothea's textual afterlife; it brings us to Wilsnack and Aachen, major sites of pilgrimage; and it also brings us, crucially, to London. Book II, especially its traversing of Germanic terrain, stuck in the craw of the earliest, prewar criticism; had it been discovered sixty years earlier, in the age of *Middlemarch*, things might have been different.[2] But interwar criticism, foundational to the emergence and first reading of Margery's text, took an unnuanced view (quite understandable, historically speaking) of Margery's *Duchelond*; here, and now, we may dwell a little longer in Germanic locales. The effort will be worthwhile, I hope, since the travelling and sojourning of Book II led directly to composition of what Hope Emily Allen was first to call *The Book of Margery Kempe*.

Medieval Studies in 1934: hidden women

The other great medieval discovery of 1934, made in the warden's bedroom at Winchester College, was the manuscript of Malory's *Morte*

2. On English Victorian enthusiasm for German life and letters, and for travelling through Germanic territories, see Chapter 1 above, pp. 39–44.

Darthur, a moment worth dwelling on, since it opens pertinent themes of national identity and of occluded female lives. When the *Morte's* appearance was prematurely splashed in *The Daily Telegraph*, its finder—Moberly librarian Walter Oakeshott—found himself soon doorstepped by an ambitious academic. This, Oakeshott recalled, was during 'the great biennial pagan festival in Winchester College life, the two day cricket match against Eton'.[3] From insistent ringing of the doorbell, Oakeshott deduced the presence of 'a powerful will...behind the thumb'. This 'small, but insistent figure', demanding that 'he MUST see the manuscript AT ONCE', was Eugène Vinaver.[4] He had been born Yevgeny Maksimovich into a cultured Jewish family at St Petersburg. His father, a member of the first national Duma, fled from the Bolsheviks and took ship at Sebastopol, with Yevgeny, in 1919; Vladimir Nabokov and his father travelled with them. Having studied Malory's French sources with Joseph Bédier at Paris, Eugène Vinaver became professor of French at Manchester (home to the only Caxton Malory in Britain); he remained a French citizen all his life.[5] There was some resistance at Winchester to ceding editorship of the Malory to Vinaver. English candidates were mooted, including T. E. Lawrence (who had campaigned with Malory in his saddlebags, and who designed a chivalric device—featuring three golden camels—memorializing Wyckhamists who fell in Arabia).[6] Sir Frederick Kenyon, director of the British Museum, urged Oakeshott to assert 'discoverer's rights' and edit the manuscript himself.[7] But Oakeshott, an admirable man, argued

3. W. F. Oakeshott, 'The Finding of the Manuscript', in *Essays on Malory*, ed. J. A. W. Bennett (Oxford: Clarendon Press, 1963), pp. 1–6; private correspondence. See further M. H. Keen, 'Oakeshott, Sir Walter Fraser (1903–1987)', *ODNB* 41, 322a–323a. Oakeshott became master of the Skinners' Company (see further below) and vice-chancellor of the University of Oxford (1962–4).
4. Oakeshott hams up the English idyll aspects of his encounter with Vinaver to the very end: 'Eventually he withdrew, expostulating, and I retired and sank bank exhausted in a deck-chair, listened to the click of the bat, and meditated on the forthcoming strawberries and cream' (private correspondence, pp. 15–16). Vinaver gives his own account of the Winchester visit, which involved a frantic search around the cricketing boundary for Sir Frederick Kenyon, in a letter to Kenneth Sisam dated 30 June 1934 (Oxford University Press Archives, 917.16).
5. See Philip E. Bennett, 'Vinaver, Eugène [Yevgeny Maksimovich Vinaver] (1899–1979)', *ODNB* 56, 528a–529a; Elizabeth Vinaver, 'Eugène Vinaver', in *The Winawer Saga*, ed. Herman Marjan Winawer (London: H. M. Winawer, 1994), pp. 166–70.
6. Correspondence on this matter, with the design outlined by Lawrence, is to be found at Winchester College.
7. Kenyon was himself a Winchester College scholar (1875–82); he retired as British Museum director in 1930, becoming yet more prolific as a scholar: see H. I. Bell, 'Kenyon, Frederick George (1863–1952)', *ODNB* 31, 341a–343a.

that Vinaver was best qualified for the job, and the *Morte* was sent to Manchester. Having obtained the necessary rotographs, Vinaver entrusted the transcribing and typing work to a teenage convent girl with whom he holidayed in 1938: Sonia Brownell. Sonia was set up in a flat on the Euston Road, London, and paid three pounds a week; Eugène popped down by train on Friday nights to see how things were going. Sonia, according to an especially evocative description, 'had luxuriant pale gold hair, the colouring of a pink and white tea-rose, and the kind of shapely, deep-breasted, full-hipped figure that would have looked well in close-fitting Pre-Raphaelite green velvet'.[8] Known as the Euston Road Venus, Sonia was painted by all leading members of the fledging Slade School of Art. She later lived between London and Paris, befriending Marguerite Duras, Jacques Lacan, Georges Bataille, Maurice Merleau-Ponty, and especially Albert Camus, whom she described as 'the Galahad of the left-wing intellectuals'; she also became one of the greatest, and always semi-occluded, literary editors of her age.[9] When Vinaver's edition on the *Morte* appeared in 1947 her work lay far in the past. She was about to marry George and thus take up another burden of literary custodianship—which eventually killed her—as Mrs Sonia Orwell.

In turning to Margery Kempe, it might be supposed that the woman half-occluded here is Hope Emily Allen. But the truly equivalent figure to Sonia Orwell in this editing process is not Allen, but Ruth Meech: for as Sonia worked from rotographs of Malory in the Euston Road, so Ruth worked from rotographs of Kempe in Ann Arbor, Michigan. Like Vinaver, Sanford Meech was too busy to perform this labour himself: he worked by day on the *Middle English Dictionary*, reviewing transcriptions of the *Morte* made by his wife, Ruth Meech, each night after supper. It was from Ruth Meech's text that the first popular edition of *The Book of Margery Kempe* was prepared by the manuscript's owner, Lieutenant-Colonel William Erdeswick Ignatius Butler-Bowdon, DSO. Raymond Wilson Chambers, Quain Professor of English at University College, London, was chosen to write the 'Introduction' to the 1936 popular edition; Butler-Bowdon wrote the 'Editor's Note' (which acknowledges Sanford, but not Ruth, Meech). The scholar who had identified the manuscript, however, was Hope Emily Allen.

8. Hilary Spurling, *The Girl from the Fiction Department: A Portrait of Sonia Orwell* (London: Hamish Hamilton, 2002), p. 25.
9. Spurling, *Fiction Department*, pp. 74–81, and (for Camus) p. 85.

It is by now a notorious fact of Middle English scholarship that Hope Emily Allen does not appear on the title page of the EETS *Margery Kempe* as volume editor: she is credited with a 'Prefatory Note', and again gets second billing to Sanford Brown Meech as co-author of the 'Notes and Appendices'. Her career may be measured by its first and last notices in the London *Times*. On Monday 18 November 1929, Allen features as the winner of the £100 Crawshay prize, 'awarded annually to a woman of any nationality for a work, critical or historical, on any subject connected with English literature'; on Tuesday 19 July 1960, her death is briefly noted. Her obituary records her education at Bryn Mawr and at Radcliffe College, and her work for the Oneida Community of upstate New York (where she grew up); it does not, however, credit her with identifying *The Book of Margery Kempe*. By 1934, Allen, just past fifty, was an experienced and well-published medievalist (with particular expertise on Richard Rolle and the *Ancrene Wisse*); since 1921 she had lived, like George Eliot before her, at Cheyne Walk, SW 10.[10] She was lucky that Butler-Bowdon brought his manuscript to the Victoria and Albert Museum during the summer of 1934: for the usual suspect English palaeographers, M. R. James and Dom Roger Huddleston, were unavailable, presumably on holiday; the third choice, Evelyn Underhill, happened to be the English cousin of Allen's mother.[11] When drafted in, Allen was able to associate the mystery manuscript with short extracts published by Henry Pepwell in 1521. Pepwell had identified Margery Kempe as an 'Ancress of Lynn'; her words thus feature in a volume edited by Edmund G. Gardner, well known to Allen, called *The Cell of Self-Knowledge*.[12] In seeking a collaborator for the work of editing, Allen quickly thought of Sanford Meech, a young Yale Ph.D. working as an assistant at Ann Arbor on the *MED*. She wrote to Meech, assuring him that she would work to seek

10. See John C. Hirsh, *Hope Emily Allen: Medieval Scholarship and Feminism* (Norman, Oklahoma: Pilgrim Books, 1988), p. 60. Other past residents of this illustrious London street include Thomas Carlyle, Whistler, and Turner.

11. See Hirsh, *Allen*, pp. 3, 113–14; Dinshaw, 'Temporalities', p. 116.

12. See *The Cell of Self-Knowledge: Seven Early English Mystical Treatises Printed by Henry Pepwell in 1521*, ed. Edmund G. Gardner (London: Chatto and Windus, 1910), pp. 49–59. The 1521 redaction had first been published as a free-standing work by Wynkyn de Worde in 1501 with the colophon 'Here begynneth a shorte treatyse of contemplacyon taught by oure lorde Ihesu cryste, or taken out of the boke of Margerie kempe of lynne': see Allyson Foster, 'A Short Treatise of Contemplacyon: The Book of Margery Kempe in its Early Print Contexts', in *A Companion to The Book of Margery Kempe*, ed. John H. Arnold and Katherine J. Lewis (Cambridge: D. S. Brewer, 2004), p. 95.

approval from the EETS. This offer, according to John Hirsh, was 'the single greatest misjudgment of her career'.[13]

And so a senior female scholar, Hope Emily Allen, gradually loses top billing to a twenty-something dictionary assistant consistently referred to as 'Professor' Meech: a man who cosies up to Butler-Bowdon and wins the support of the EETS board as editor. This is a painful and by now pretty familiar story, and there is no happy ending.[14] Allen sells her half-share of the Cheyne Walk house as war intensifies, returning to America on 6 September 1939. She never completes her projected EETS volume of commentary on *The Book of Margery Kempe* and she never returns to England; her remaining twenty years see her publish fewer than twenty pages. Allen might seem something of a rube, as Americans might say, to be so comprehensively blindsided by Meech: especially since she fought so hard for their right to co-author this EETS volume *as* Americans. But it is through this fight that we first glimpse what *The Book of Margery Kempe* will have to be in its first modernized appearance in 1936, and in its scholarly garb of 1940: that is, a text exemplifying *national character*. Margery Kempe is *huge* in this period; her *Book* quite overshadows the discoveries being made at Mound 1, Sutton Hoo, in the spring and summer of 1939.[15]

Margery Kempe, 1936–41: an English Joan of Arc

R. W. Chambers, in his 'Introduction' to the 1936 'modern version' of *Margery Kempe*, acclaims the text's importance as follows: 'it is our first extant prose narrative in English on a large scale: original, not translated, not a mere succession of Chronicle entries, but a continuous

---

13. *Allen*, p. 113.
14. Except perhaps in HEA's dedicated work for the Oneida community and her increasing interest in the history of the Oneida tribe. See further Dinshaw, 'Temporalities', pp. 116–20.
15. *The Times* dedicates no editorial space to the Sutton Hoo finds; column inches address matters of treasure trove, the rights of private property, and of access to the site. The first letter to the *Times* on the matter, by Guy Maynard, curator of the Ipswich Corporation Museum (9 August 1939, issue 48379, p. 13, col. F), is headed 'ANGLO-SAXON SHIP BURIAL': an excavation *too* deep into the English past in the context of incipient war with Germany. The grave goods, moved to London in August 1939, spent the war in a tunnel off the Aldwych tube. The last notice in the *Times* of Sutton Hoo appears on 23 February 1940; nothing more is heard until 27 February 1948. See further *The Sutton Hoo Ship Burial: A Provisional Guide*, ed. T. D. Kendrick (London:

biography'.[16] Kempe's *Book* must have come to Chambers as a white
dove from the void, a near-miraculous response to his clarion call of
1932: 'Probably there are few better tests', Chambers had then written,
'of a people having reached and maintained its place among nations
than this power of writing stirring prose in its own tongue'.[17] This
remark occurs in Chambers' most influential book, published by EETS
with great fanfare as something of an institutional mission statement.[18]
It has a treatise-like title: *On the Continuity of English Prose from Alfred
to More and his School*. He goes on to quote from an essay, published in
Dublin in 1913, by way of accentuating how good prose confirms, in
effect, a people's readiness for empire:

> Poetry is a wind that bloweth where it listeth: a barbaric people may have
> great poetry, they cannot have great prose. Prose is an institution, part of the
> equipment of a civilization, part of its heritable wealth, like its laws, or its
> system of schooling, or its tradition of skilled craftsmanship.[19]

Two of the vital stepping stones in Chambers' vision of English continuity were *Ancrene Riwle* and the prose of Richard Rolle: texts in
which Hope Emily Allen was perhaps *the* preeminent published
expert.[20] In negotiating over a series of *Ancrene Riwle* editions that
she was keen for EETS to publish, Allen perceived that Chambers, a
member of the EETS council, was 'too intent on assigning British

British Museum, 1947), pp. 9–11; Angela Care Evans, *The Sutton Hoo Ship Burial*,
revised edition (London: British Museum Press, 1994), pp. 9–22; Martin Carver, 'The
Future of Sutton Hoo', in *Voyage to the Other World: The Legacy of Sutton Hoo*, ed.
Calvin B. Kendall and Peter S. Wells (Minneapolis: University of Minnesota Press,
1992), pp. 183–200.

16. *The Book of Margery Kempe 1436: A Modern Version*, tr. W. Butler-Bowdon, with an
    introduction by R. W. Chambers (London: Jonathan Cape, 1936), p. 3.

17. R. W. Chambers, *On the Continuity of English Prose from Alfred to More and his School*
    (London: EETS, 1932), p. lviii.

18. This volume was published by EETS by way of celebrating the centenary of its own
    somewhat mythical origins in 1832 ('Prefatory Note', p. iii; this 'Note' ends by affirming
    that 'the work of the Early English Text Society is far from being completed', p. xi).

19. Chambers here quotes (p. lviii) from J. S. Phillimore, 'Blessed Thomas More and the
    Arrest of Humanism in England', *Dublin Review*, 153 (1913), p. 8.

20. See especially 'Survival of Religious Prose: The *Ancrene Riwle*', section VIII of
    Chambers, *Continuity*, pp. xc–c ('It may be asked…where does the continuity of
    English prose come in?…The continuity of English prose is to be found in the ser-
    mon and in every kind of devotional treatise', p. xc). On Rolle, see pp. ci–ciii ('Rolle's
    date, his style and his popularity give him a supreme place in the history of English
    prose', p. ci). Chambers acknowledges Allen's expertise in both authors: see *Continuity*,
    pp. xcix–c, cii, cix. Chambers plays up the influence of Rolle and the *Riwle* by way of
    deemphasizing that of Wycliffe and Wycliffite writing (pp. cvii–cviii).

editors...and passing over good American ones'.[21] Allen reminded Chambers of the sterling work already being done by American editors, supported by the American Council of Learned Societies; she also enlisted the support of American scholarly heavyweights such as Chaucer editor F. N. Robinson. Her dedication to Anglo–American bilateralism, from which young Meech was richly to benefit, extended to thoughts about the popular edition: the first publisher with whom she corresponded was the Anglo–American at Faber and Faber. Even Margery Kempe's coming out party to a wider public was conceived and staged by Allen as an Anglo–American event: as Meech was reading a paper to the 1934 MLA convention in Philadelphia, which Allen had written, English readers were reading Allen's letter to the London *Times* of 27 December.[22]

The plan for a modernized Margery, to precede the scholarly edition, was cordially supported by Hope Emily Allen.[23] In attempting to sell Kempe's *Book* to the widest possible public, her 1934 letter to the *Times* sets terms of reception—and of critical contradiction—that have been with us ever since. Margery's text, Allen says in plain language, 'is found to be crammed with highly interesting narratives of real life'. Some of its spiritual passages are highly elevated, but others 'highly fanatical'. Allen's own upbringing in the millenarian Oneida community made her wary of religious excess; this perhaps coloured her view of Kempe's more exuberant medieval moments.[24] 'She had been mad', she continues, 'after the birth of her first child, and a neurotic strain ran through her religious life; religious feeling brought on excessive weeping, which brought her evil-thinking wherever she went'. Such behaviour would have made her less than popular with a pilgrim band, such as that of the *Canterbury Tales*: 'continual talk of religion and incessant tears', Allen argues, 'made her a most unwelcome travelling companion'.

21. Hirsh, *Allen*, p. 115.
22. See Hirsh, *Allen*, pp. 116–118; *Times*, Thursday 27 December 1934, p. 15, issue 46946, Letters to the Editor, col. b.
23. See Hirsh, *Allen*, p. 114.
24. The first community was settled on a farm just outside Oneida, New York, by John Humphrey Noyes in March 1848. Noyes believed that Christ had returned to earth *c*.70 CE. In pursuit of 'holy community', his followers needed to seek committee approval—not marriage—for sexual relations. HEA's only sibling, Grosvenor Noyes Allen, was conceived in this way; his parents were directed to separate for becoming too attached to him. HEA herself was born after the breakup of the community (when her parents ended their enforced separation and married). See Hirsh, *Allen*, pp. 1–3.

And yet, she continues, 'she emerges from her story as a woman of great character and force'. Allen attempts to resolve such contradictions in Kempe—between neurosis and fanaticism on the one hand, and *mulier fortis* character on the other—by extending or reinterpreting her motherhood: 'Margery Kempe brings to life', Allen says, 'not only famous persons of the early fifteenth century, but also humble ones, at home and abroad'. Such celebration of Kempe as only begetter of a whole new narrative world recurs through the earliest reviews: present-day concerns with masculine co-creation of her text—with A. C. Spearing as the bad angel of the debate—do not trouble a 1930s world concerned, preeminently, with English character.[25] And yet we might say that Kempe pays a high price to *become* such a character: the requisite procedure, in 1936, is lobotomy. Which is to say: those religious passages deemed neurotic or fanatical—or, as Butler-Bowdon puts it, 'wearisome'—are actually excised from the narrative sequence of the *Book* and collected in an appendix, in smaller type.[26]

On 29 December 1934, two days after the publication of Allen's letter, the *Times* publishes a short note from the Rev. Dundas Harford: a sometime vicar of St Stephen's, Norwich, styling himself 'one who succeeded [Richard] Caister in that vicarage just 500 years later (1402 to 1901)'.[27] Such continuity in English culture, which would have pleased R. W. Chambers, impels him to urge others 'to encourage Miss Allen to arrange for the publication of a popular edition of Dame Margery Kempe's

---

25. 'So far there has been little more than sub-Bakhtinian babble about "voices"', remarks Spearing; 'our understanding', he continues, 'would surely be improved by an experimental envisaging of *The Book of Margery Kempe* as *The Book of Robert Spryngolde about Margery Kempe*' ('Margery Kempe', in *A Companion to Middle English Prose*, ed. A. S. G. Edwards (Cambridge: D. S. Brewer, 2004), p. 93). Broader critical principles informing Spearing's approach may be gleaned from his *Textual Subjectivity: The Encoding of Subjectivity in Medieval Narratives and Lyrics* (Oxford: Oxford University Press, 2005). The strongest statement of Kempe's status 'as a writer', with specific authorial strategies, is Lynn Staley, *Margery Kempe's Dissenting Fictions* (University Park: Pennsylvania State University Press, 1994), p. 39.

26. 'Except to those particularly interested in it, the great amount of mystical matter would probably prove wearisome. Certain chapters, entirely devoted to that subject, have therefore been removed from the body of the book and printed as an appendix. This arrangement does not affect the sequence' ('Editor's Note', in *Book*, ed. Butler-Bowdon, p. 16). Ironically, as Karma Lochrie points out, much later (scholarly) writing has criticized Kempe's *Book* for being too concerned with 'life', too autobiographical, at the expense of spirituality and mysticism (*Margery Kempe and Translations of the Flesh* (Philadelphia: University of Pennsylvania Press, 1991), p. 226).

27. *Times*, Saturday 29 December 1934, issue 46948, p. 6, Letters to the Editor, col. c. The letter begins: 'The letter of Miss Emily Hope Allen, the noted authority upon

writing'. Butler-Bowdon also honours centennial continuity in entitling his eagerly-awaited text of 1936 *The Book of Margery Kempe 1436*; it is accorded both a review and a leader in the *Times* of 30 September (issue 47493, p. 13). The editorial appears in column e, and the review begins at the top of column g.[28] Like the top of column f next door, the review has three headlines; it is instructive to read across from f to g headlines, as the layout clearly invites us to do, by way of testing the political temperature *of* 30 September 1936: 'HOUSE OF LORDS REFORM', 'MARGERY KEMPE'S OWN STORY'; 'SOCIALIST PLANS', 'THE FIRST ENGLISH AUTOBIOGRAPHY'; 'THE ELECTORATE AND REVOLUTION', 'A LIBRARY DISCOVERY'. The text of column f is a letter from Lord Selbourne, of 14 Buckingham Palace Gardens, warning of the dire consequences of a Socialist electoral victory: 'They will abolish the Second Chamber altogether. They will in effect reduce the House of Commons to a debating society. Rule and legislation will be by orders in Council, directed by a small junta of Socialist dictators'.[29] Meanwhile, in column g, the book reviewer has Butler-Bowdon tell of Margery Kempe's longterm sojourn in his family seat of Pleasington Old Hall, Lancashire.[30] 'It may be remembered', Butler-Bowdon boldly begins, 'that we are a Catholic family'. It is a sign of the times that Socialists, rather than Catholics, are to be seen as the enemies within. Margery is described as a 'wandering evangelist', espousing views 'frequently marked . . . by an intense fanaticism . . . But not all is fanaticism', the review continues: 'the story for the most part has a charming simplicity of expression and is packed with pictures of medieval life and character'. Over in column e, the *Times* editorial judges the discovery of Kempe in an English country house to be 'more unexpected and more important than the discovery of the "Morte d'Arthur" at Winchester': a remarkable assertion, since in late 1936 one might think

Richard Rolle of Hampole, in *The Times* of December 27 must be of profound interest to all who care for the story of middle-English mysticism'.

28. This review announces, beneath the three headlines, that the *Book 'will be published on October 9 by Mr. Jonathan Cape, by whose permission the following article based on the text is published'*.

29. On the 'fashion for catastrophism' in this period, see Richard Overy, *The Morbid Age: Britain Between the Wars* (London: Allen Lane, 2009), p. 20.

30. The column g review extends to p. 14, col. a. Some extracts from Margery's interrogation before the archbishop at York are cited, prefaced with the following remark: 'Some passages are worthy to be set beside the spirited replies of St Joan'.

that the trope of Arthur's return in England's hour of need might commend itself to journalism. But the return of Kempe is a triumph of English: a vindication of Chambers' views on the *continuity* of language,[31] and a rebuff to new-fangled historiographical theorists who, after Nietzsche, were proposing *cyclical* models of imperial rise and decline.[32] Kempe further provides a powerful expression of Englishness from a part of the country that, so Chambers says, was precocious in forgetting its French.[33] Pilgrims like Chaucer's might have found her 'maddening': but none can doubt Kempe's 'whole-hearted candour', and this (so the editorial ends) 'will make of MARGERY KEMPE a well-known medieval character'. Kempe thus discovers herself as a creature both exotic and familiar, strange but speaking our language; and Norfolk stands in for locales both geographically eccentric and essentially English. In 1936, Margery Kempe, as the windows rattle on Buckingham Palace Road, is the perfect colonial subject.

Since T. S. Eliot, at Faber and Faber, could not be enthused about Margery Kempe it fell to Jonathan Cape to publish and promote the modernized edition. This they do with great vigour, making Margery the star turn of their advertising campaign for the 1936 Christmas season. Cape first buys space for Margery on the front page of the *TLS* on 10 October.[34] She holds her place in Cape's first-page *TLS* panel until 7 November, drops out on the 14th, but then returns triumphantly for the 21 November 'Christmas Books' number. On her first appearance, 10 October, she gets top billing, immediately above *the* absolute icon of period Englishness: A. E. Housman.[35]

31. 'No one who knows PROFESSOR R. W. CHAMBERS'S views about the English prose that went underground after the Conquest, to struggle to the surface again in the fourteenth century, but can imagine his delight in this very remarkable specimen, the first extant biography in the English tongue' (*Times*, Wednesday 30 September 1936, issue 47493, col. e).

32. Most famously, Oswald Spengler, whose two-volume *The Decline of the West* was published in English (translated from the German) in 1926–8 and, after him, Arnold Toynbee: see Overy, *Morbid Age*, pp. 28–49.

33. 'But Norfolk, says DR. CHAMBERS in his introduction to COLONEL BUTLER-BOWDON'S edition, was notorious for ignorance of French'.

34. The front page of the *TLS* features three columns throughout 1936; all other pages are of four columns.

35. See *The Times Literary Supplement*, Saturday 10 October 1936, issue 1810, col. a. The advertising panel begins with a tie-in to the sister paper: '*The TIMES of September 30th devoted a leader, in addition to a two column article, to The Book of Margery Kempe. A detailed advertisement of this book will be found on page 3 within*'. The volume advertised immediately below this is *More Poems* by A. E. Housman.

Readers are directed to the *Times* leader and article of 30 September
and to a further 'advertisement' within. This quarter-page *TLS* panel
excerpts from the *Times* review, emphasizing Margery Kempe as 'an
extraordinary and indomitable woman', whose 'whole-hearted candour… sent her tramping in old age through an enemy's country'
(p. 799, c-d). It is a bit of a stretch to describe Book II's journey from
Danzig to Aachen as a tramp through enemy territory: but the
unnamed referent here is clearly Germany. Six pages deeper in the
same *TLS* issue we find yet another review of Margery's *Book*: a full,
two column one. And again, it proves instructive to look to the next
column over. This advertises a book, called *Retreat from Armageddon*,
that begins by asking: 'What shall we do when the next world-war
breaks out?'[36]

The 10 October *TLS* review appears under the headline:'AMONG
THE ENGLISH CLASSICS'.[37] The rationale for this bold statement
is saved until the final paragraph: Kempe 'was a great character, and
her book—it is not too early to say this—is an English classic, while
Juliana's… is a book of English devotions only, though sublime'. England, late in 1936, needs an archetypically English character, whose
mode of 'spiritual autobiography' directly feeds 'the fictional method
of "Robinson Crusoe" and "Moll Flanders"'. Kempe's *Book* thus provides 'one more instance of the continuity of literary forms': the
Chambers principle, projecting ever further forward. And yet, again, it
must be said that Margery is complex and strange: she 'wrote a prose
of remarkable nervousness and simplicity'. That is a remarkable col-
location: did the *TLS* mean to print 'nervelessness and simplicity'
(words that would seem to fit better together)? Or perhaps 'nervousness and simplicity' nods at *hysteria* and *neurosis,* those fashionable
terms, in the depths of this 'great character'? And perhaps this strange
yoking looks back to another, that of fanaticism and poetry, made

---

36. The book advertised, by Muriel Jaeger, seems to propose a course of action based
    upon confused recollection of the *Decameron*:'A party of friends retreat into the Welsh
    mountains, determined while the world falls in ruins to entertain themselves as once
    did certain young ladies and gentlemen of Naples when the plague was devastating
    the city' (p. 805, col. d).
37. A second headline, in a slightly smaller type, follows immediately: 'THE
    AUTOBIOGRAPHY OF MARGERY KEMPE' (p. 805, a–b). The category of *auto-
    biography* is applied to Kempe's *Book* from the very start, with little inhibition.

earlier in the review, where Margery is characterized as 'a fanatic in action, but almost every word of her speech is poetry'. Almost all the early reviews, I would suggest, are haunted by a recent French triumph: the canonization of Joan of Arc in 1920. *Saint Joan* had conquered London in 1925, with Sybil Thorndike breathing life into George Bernard Shaw's greatest heroine; Shaw won the Nobel Prize the following year.[38]

So could Margery Kempe, as a native creature of the 1430s, be billed as an English Joan of Arc? The longing for such a Joan intensified through the war. The *TLS* for 13 December 1941 (nine months after the EETS Kempe edition was reviewed) features a woodcut on its front page entitled 'Jeanne d'Angleterre' (Figure 6): a Joan who is a uniformed English servicewoman at prayer.[39] The idea that Margery Kempe might be associated with *la pucelle* was actually first planted by Hope Emily Allen, in her 1934 letter of discovery to the *Times*: the newly-recovered Margery Kempe, she argues, 'may be placed beside her contemporaries who were also mystics—St Bridget of Sweden, St Catherine of Siena, and St Joan of Arc' (p. 15, col. b). Modern criticism has much to say about Bridget and Catherine as Kempe's near-contemporaries, but next to nothing about Joan of Arc. But the *TLS* review of 10 October 1936 happily invokes comparisons with Joan even while celebrating Kempe's freedom from French contamination: 'The happy fact that Norfolk was notorious for ignorance of French', it argues,

has given us an English fifteenth-century character whose speech and reaction to circumstance are as vivid and original as those of St Joan herself. Whether Margery is canonized remains to be seen; if she is, we shall have a very national saint, one of Chaucer's company, less sib to the Prioress than to the Wife of Bath.

(p. 805, cols. b−c)

---

38. See *Saint Joan: A Chronicle Play in Six Scenes, and an Epilogue*, in *The Complete Plays of Bernard Shaw* (London: Constable, 1931), pp. 963–1009. The first performance of *Saint Joan* was given at the Garrick Theater, New York, on 28 December 1923; the play opened at the New Theatre, London, on 26 March 1925 (with Sybil Thorndike as St Joan). Shaw's winning of the Nobel Prize in 1926 'was generally seen as a tribute to the author of *Saint Joan*' (Leonée Ormond, *St Joan by George Bernard Shaw* (London: Macmillan, 1986), p. 4).

39. This image attaches to no review or commentary; the image says it all for an English audience of 1941. The artist, George (György) Buday, was born in Hungary in 1907 and died in Coulsden, Surrey, in 1990.

Figure 6. 'Jeanne d'Angleterre', front cover of *Times Literary Supplement*, 13 December 1941; woodcut by George (György) Buday, 1907–1990.

Three issues later in 1936, *TLS* again makes reference to Joan of Arc, this time in the concluding sentence of a three column review.[40] The book in question here, by Étienne du Castel, concerns yet another female writer: Christine de Pizan, whose last known poem celebrates the as-yet unde- feated Joan of Arc. This review portrays autobiography as a female vice: 'Like most authoresses', it says of Christine de Pizan, 'she was wont, what- ever subject she took in hand, to drop into autobiography—in the middle of a political allegory or a moral disquisition, suddenly we come on pas- sages of plaintive reminiscence'.[41] There *is* a perennial risk, in considering women's *life* writing, of making a woman's life the subject (rather than the topics that she chooses to write about). But the *TLS* reviewer shows bad faith in pinning this on Christine as a female vice, since what the review delivers *is* Christine's life: a splendid and colourful account of it. A delight- ful miniature of Christine teaching her son, set like a jewel in the middle of the review, is reproduced from British Museum (as was) MS Harley 4431. Christine de Pizan seems set fair to take flight in the English popu- lar imagination; perhaps de Castel's book, with its twenty-four manu- script illustrations, will be translated. But in 1936 this will not happen. Margery Kempe is the woman of this particular year; her newly- modernized *Book* features on the front cover of this very issue. It may be, then, that Margery's powerfully orchestrated reemergence through the Christmas season of 1936 helps retard Christine de Pizan's popular recep- tion in England for more than forty years.[42]

Hysteria, foreign influence, pathologization

Rather than dwelling upon a Frenchwoman who acclaimed Joan of Arc, then, English culture attempts to frame Margery Kempe as Joan's

40. *TLS*, Saturday 31 October, issue 1813, p. 880, cols b–d. November's edition of *The Aryan Path*, a periodical, is advertised at the bottom of col. a; among the articles pur- veyed is Oswald Garrison Villard, 'Dark Men as Cannon Fodder'.
41. Col. b. The book reviewed here is Étienne du Castel, *Ma Grand-Mère Christine de Pizan* (Paris: Hachette, 1936). See further Françoise du Castel, *Damoiselle Christine de Pizan: Veuve de Madame Étienne de Castel, 1364–1431* (Paris: Éditions A., et J. Picard, 1972), a volume which makes reference to sixteen manuscripts found in English libraries and which also features illuminations from BL Harley 4431. Neither of these books were translated into English.
42. For a fine account of how Joan of Arc's life and legend influenced English reception of Christine de Pizan in the fifteenth and sixteenth centuries, see Warren, *Women of God and Arms*, pp. 58–77, 106.

English equivalent: an unlikely process that colours reception of Allen and Meech's EETS edition of 1940. The lengthy *TLS* review, published on 8 March 1941, concludes with the following words: 'Margery, with a difference, may serve as our St. Joan. Her ghost will walk St. Margaret's, Lynn *in saecula saeculorum*'.[43] The review had opened with words of rapture: 'At last the incredible creature is available in the Norfolk speech. If first editions of EETS publications ever attain to the dignity of record auction prices, the issue of No. 212 (with the addenda slip) should become a collector's item of some importance' (p. 111 col. a). Margery now lives, the review continues, 'as vividly as St. Joan or the Pastons for us today' (p. 111a). But thankfully, says the reviewer, 'she had no intention of exposing herself to the charge brought against St. Joan; she made a point of consulting prelates as to her revelations' (p. 111b). English common sense instincts thus save Margery, and yet her *hysteria*, as ever, demands address:[44] what can be its sources? The attempt to answer this itself provokes an outburst that might, itself, seem hysterical; it is worth quoting at some length. Sanity and true Englishness, for this *TLS* reviewer, lie in native originality; trouble thus begins with Hope Emily Allen's learned footnotes:

> Miss Allen, while admitting that Margery's originality seems indisputable, has made, and will continue to make, a very strong case for hints drawn from the Danzig burgess's wife, Bl. Dorothea of Prussia, and other Dominican [*sic*] women mystics in Germany by the redoubtable Lynn bourgeoise. This cannot be helped. Margery stayed in Danzig and her son (whom Miss Joan Wake supposes to have been her first amanuensis) settled there ... It was not just the *Vita Germanica*[:] St Bridget was a useful hauberk, no doubt likewise St Mary d'Oignies; but the authoress who could put into the Deity's mouth a phrase like 'Thou shalt be eaten and gnawn of the people of the world as any rat gnaweth the stockfish' needed no reinforcement from oversea. Professor Meech has no note ascribing this phrase to any known mystical or even proverbial source. Long may it remain the coinage of a fifteenth-century Norfolk woman!

> (p. 111b)

The question of *hysteria* is then directly posed at the beginning of the next section of the review, under the heading 'HER VISIONS':

---

43. *TLS*, 8 March 1941, no 2040, pp. 111, a–d; 120 a (p. 120a).
44. On the extraordinary, newfound authority of the terms *hysteria* and *neurosis* in English cultural discourse of the 1930s, see Overy, *Morbid Age*, *passim* and esp. pp. 136–74.

Again, it matters little, except to neurologists and persons who rejoice in tracing literary works to physical causes, whether Margery, through hysteria, became a mirror of influences to which she had been subject.

(p. 111b)

To succumb to foreign influences, especially German ones like Dorothea of Montau, is to be hysterical:[45] the Margery Kempe that England needs, in March 1941, is a self-made native of Norfolk. This reviewer's anxieties are, of course understandable: England stands alone; the United States of Kempe's two American editors has yet to enter the war.[46] The question of *in-fluence*, the flowing in of external forces that affect behaviour, is newly problematic. The most influential study of *influence* in this period, of what the *TLS* reviewer terms 'tracing literary works to physical causes', is also American: a study of Coleridge, by Harvard professor John Livingston Lowes, called *The Road to Xanadu*.[47] England, *au contraire*, generates what might be termed 'anti-influence' criticism: most famously exemplified, perhaps, by C. S. Lewis's essay, published in Oxford in 1932, entitled 'What Chaucer Really Did to *Il Filostrato*'.[48] Even the title of this highly influential piece is instructive: you have to *do things* to

---

45. Early attempts to expose a wider English public to psychoanalytic ideas were fraught with anxieties concerning national character and national interest. The first series of talks devoted by the BBC to psychoanalysis, broadcast in the autumn of 1935, had many restrictions placed upon them; some 'had to be cut because they touched on issues of foreign policy' (Overy, *Morbid Age*, p. 166).

46. Signs of the times are again provided by the advertising that surrounds reviews of Kempe. The two titles advertised by Cambridge University Press in the bottom half of p. 111d (*TLS*, 8 March 1941) are as follows: *The Social Policy of Nazi Germany*; *The Ideas and Ideals of the British Empire*. Virginia Woolf committed suicide less than three weeks later (28 March, 1941). The *TLS* 'Epitaph' of 12 April 1941 is remarkably sympathetic, viewing Woolf's writing (and perhaps her desperate act, at this desperate time) as integral to contemporary experience ('part of us'). It opens thus: 'Between one great war and another the work of Virginia Woolf has been begun and ended. We cannot look back on it yet, for it is part of us and of our day—of our tormented day, for no moment of which, since 1914, has there been any comforting sense of stability' (175a–d [p. 175a]). The entry of the US into the war on 7 December 1941 passes almost entirely without notice in the *TLS*; attention remains inwardly focused, with discussion of 'Englishism'.

47. John Livingston Lowes, *The Road to Xanadu: A Study in the Ways of the Imagination* (Boston: Houghton Mifflin, 1927). This book, republished in 1959 by Vintage (and in England by Constable) proved highly influential down to the 1970s; *experience* was then invoked as a category foundational to literary criticism on both sides of the Atlantic. Lowes' penultimate chapter addresses opium addiction; his last is entitled 'Imagination Creatrix'.

48. *Essays and Studies* 17 (1932), 56–75.

a foreign source, the suggestion is, before it does things to you—or, in football parlance, get your retaliation in first. Chaucer finds much in Boccaccio that, so Lewis says, '"would never do"': Boccaccio's 'strutting Latinisms' exemplify 'that Latin spirit which in all ages (except perhaps our own) has made the Englishman a little uncomfortable' (p. 68). Lewis then rallies to defend core Englishness from oversexed contemporaries, much as Chaucer had resisted or 'medievalized' Boccaccio. In an extraordinary final paragraph, cut from modern anthologies, Lewis assaults the 'popular corporation swimming-baths of Dr Marie Stopes', by which he means birth control clinics, and 'the teeming marshlands of the late D. H. Lawrence' (p. 75). Against such modern depravities, and by way of ending the essay, he quotes lines from that protective touchstone of English literary tradition: *Beowulf*.

C. S. Lewis was actually an Ulsterman who became an Englishman; after 1918 he crossed the English Channel only once.[49] But he knew Flanders and northern France from his days of trench warfare. In the years of Margery Kempe's reemergence, from 1934 to 1941, this same part of Europe returned to haunt English imagining. It might be said, paradoxically, that the very emphasis upon Kempe's untutored Englishness bespeaks awareness of this greater European context: for should England be invaded, the language of Margery might *really* be lost. Even the constant references to Joan of Arc, which might seem quaint, testify to habits of historical thinking from which we, the new moderns, can learn. Consider this from the long *TLS* review of 1941:

> The great fire that burnt Lynn's Guild Hall, when the snow fell on her intercession at St Margaret's, was on 23 January, 1429. Her husband and son probably died two years later, the year Joan of Arc's burning.

> (p. 111d)

This imaginative leap from snow in Lynn to fire in Rouen is not gratuitous: for England and northern France formed a single theatre of military and political operations that directly affected burgers of Lynn such as Margery Kempe. In the spring of 1417, for example, Kempe hopes to go on pilgrimage to Santiago de Compostella but must cool her heels for six weeks at Bristol: 'in-as-mech', she explains, 'as ther were non Englisch schepys that myth seylen thedyr, for thei wer arestyd

---

49. See J. A. W. Bennett, rev. Emma Plaskitt, 'Lewis, Clive Staples (1898–1963)', *ODNB* 33, p. 595b.

and takyn up for the Kyng' (3525–7, a reference to Henry V's second expedition to France). In the autumn of the same year, Kempe is arrested in attempting to cross the River Humber by troops of the duke of Bedford. They repute her to be the 'the grettest Loller in al this cuntre, er abowte London eythyr' (4318–19); the duke is offering one hundred pounds for her capture. As she is led into Hessle, near Hull, women come running out of their houses, brandishing their distaffs, crying: 'Brennyth this fals herytyk!' (4326). John, duke of Bedford, was lieutenant of England during Henry V's absence in France. Henry died in 1422 and Bedford became regent of France until 1433; Joan of Arc was arrested and burned under his watch. Bedford knighted the five-year-old Henry VI at Westminster in 1426 and oversaw his coronation at Notre-Dame, Paris, in 1431. Joan of Arc was burned in the market-place of Rouen on 30 May 1431; Bedford died in the castle at Rouen four years later.[50] Margery Kempe, threatened with burning on several occasions, survived. Despite the best efforts of her earliest reviewers, she is not nowadays acclaimed as an English Joan of Arc. But on the cross-Channel terrain patrolled by Bedford and his soldiery—and by John Lydgate, for that matter—the wife of Lynn did figure on a common scale of religio-political nuisance with the maid of Orléans.

If the hysterics read into Margery Kempe in the 1930s are grounded in fear of the foreign, of the un-English, what then do we make of the 1430s—and of our own time? Current pathologizings of Kempe ground themselves in internalized mental health oppression: that is, a readiness to denounce certain behaviours as aberrant that bespeaks, by its very speed, anxious apprehension of being the abjected *object*, rather than sovereign subject, of such definitional processes. My appeal here is to the classroom. Anyone teaching *The Book of Margery Kempe* sees, sooner or later, Kempe isolated as a woman in need of treatment: young people donning the white coat to turn prescriptions and diag-noses beamed at them—of Ritalin, Prozac, and ADHD—back upon the head of an old medieval woman, behaving badly.[51] The key term

50. See Jenny Stratford, 'John, duke of Bedford (1389–1435)', *ODNB* 30, 183b–190a; Kelly DeVries, *Joan of Arc: A Military Leader* (Thrupp: Sutton, 1999), p. 185; Françoise Meltzer, *For Fear of the Fire: Joan of Arc and the Limits of Subjectivity* (Chicago: University of Chicago Press, 2001), pp. 188–211.

51. Some of these issues were addressed by 'Mysticism and Mental Health', a session sponsored by the Society for Medieval Feminist Scholarship, Medieval Institute, Kalamazoo, May 1999; my observations are of classroom experience in the USA.

here is *isolate*: for through such pathologizing, scant attention is paid to that greater religio-political culture of which Margery Kempe forms part. Even the briefest sketch of that Lancastrian culture sees it living on edge, its poets and apologists, as Paul Strohm has shown, desperately squaring the circle of illegitimacy and bad faith.[52] The murdered monarch upon whom the new dynasty founds itself haunts the kingdom until his bones are translated to Westminster. A monarch who swore on the sacrament not to seize power burns those who doubt the sacrament's efficacy; a monarch who adopts English for his coronation bans English renditions of religious texts. Part of the fun of Margery's *Book* is to see her antagonize the officialdom of Lancastrian England, driving them mad, by realizing the full measure of their own sponsored imperatives: fully experiencing the pain, à la Nicholas Love, of Christ crucified; contradicting a cleric to proclaim that Jesus lives.

What Margery wants

It is time to turn the question that Günter Grass posed of Dorothea of Montau—what does Dorothea *want?*—to Margery Kempe. In Dorothea's case, considering her lifelong regimen of self-inflicted pain, and her ultimate enclosure as an anchoress, we might say: to fulfill a peculiarly personal and decidedly physical *jouissance* through religion; and this might provide a reasonable starting point for Margery, too. What, then, blocks the path to joy? Margaret Cavendish, duchess of Newcastle, concludes her *True Relation of My Birth, Breeding, and Life* (1656) by worrying that her name might be lost beneath that of her husband (should he outlive her).[53] Husbands living too

---

52. 'Because they are inevitably and complexly enmeshed and entrammeled, the texts of Lancastrian succession can never quite complete or finish themselves. They cannot withdraw themselves from a meaning-making process which continually (in spite of contrary resolve) replenishes alternative understanding' (*England's Empty Throne*, p. 214: these are the book's concluding words).

53. 'Lest after-Ages should mistake', Cavendish ends her *Life* by affirming that 'I was daughter to one Master *Lucas* of *St Johns* neer *Colchester* in *Essex*, second Wife to the Lord Marquis of *Newcastle*, for my Lord having had two Wives, I might easily have been mistaken, especially if I should dye, and my Lord Marry again' (*A True Relation of My Birth, Breeding, and Life*, in *Paper Bodies: A Margaret Cavendish Reader*, ed. Sylvia Bowerbank and Sara Mendelson (Peterborough, Ontario: Broadview, 2000), 41–63 (p. 63). Cavendish was twenty-two when, as Margaret Lucas, she married William Cavendish in Paris in 1645. He was thirty years older, but her fear of being outlived

long also proved problematic for Dorothea of Montau and Margery Kempe: but for them, as medieval women of devout Catholic faith, the problem was more acute. Childcare impeded devotion, and wifehood generated the lowest rate of spiritual return: just thirty fold by clerical reckoning, as opposed to sixty for widows, and one hundred for virgins.[54] The name that Margery took pride in was Brunham, that of her birth: the 'worschyp of hir kynrede' (268) exceeded that of her husband, John Kempe. Margery's *Book* depicts John Kempe as an admirable man who sticks with her through thick and thin when all others run away. But he is clearly a nuisance, and he lives too long. He has no intention of stopping at fourteen pregnancies, and he fails to grasp that his very presence *as* husband testifies to the imperfection of Margery's spiritual state. When he falls down the stairs as an old man, Margery must be sent for (since they no longer live together). If her husband should die, her neighbours say, Margery should hang for murder (6022–4). Margery prays that he might live, but just for one year: the minimal span of time that might exculpate her through statute of limitations. The old man lives on for years, turns childish, and shits himself by the fire or at table, wherever he happens to be ('he wolde sparyn no place', 6071–2). Book II records his death, appended to that of Margery's son-turned-disciple, in detached and perfunctory fashion: 'in schort tyme aftyr, the fadyr of the sayd persone folwyd the sone the wey whech every man must gon' (7568–9).

From her first irruption into modern consciousness, as we have seen, Margery Kempe has been continuously associated with, likened to, Chaucer's Wife of Bath. Chaucer's Wife ends her *Tale* by wishing death to husbands three times in five lines: may wives be given grace to 'overbyde' or outlive those they wed; may those who disobey their wives have shortened lives; and may old and angry, tightfisted husbands die soon of plague (3.1260–4). Chaucer here projects an anxiety that is

proved prophetic: she died at fifty, and her husband lived on to be eighty-three. He liked to exercise his hand in her writings: several songs and speeches of Cavendish's most famous play, *The Convent of Pleasure*, are 'Written by my Lord Duke' (see *Paper Bodies*, 97–135 (pp. 122, 123, 129–31)).

54. Such is the famous calculus of Conrad of Heisterbach, *Dialogus Miraculorum*: 'Wherefore from the same seed which falls from the hand of the sower into good soil *some bring forth thirty fold some sixty, and some a hundred*' (*Matthew* 13.5). The first is due to the married, the second to continent widows, the third to virgins' (*The Dialogue on Miracles*, 2 vols, tr. H. Von E. Scott and C. C. Swinton Bland, intr. G. G. Coulton (London: Routledge, 1929), II, pp. 81–2).

particularly masculine-English: for laws of inheritance were (by contemporary European standards) especially favourable to women in
England.[55] The two signature episodes of the *Book of Margery Kempe*—
which establish what it is that Margery likes to do—are triggered by the
death of men. In 1413, Margery's father dies; within a matter of months
she is off to the Holy Land and Rome.[56] Twenty years later, with her
husband finally buried, she sails to Danzig. What Margery likes to do is
travel, and it is travel that brings her both spiritual authority and textual
inspiration. In forty of the first fifty-five chapters of her *Book*, she travels. For the rest of Book I, associated with a decade of ill health, she lives
at Lynn, expending the cultural capital of a pilgrim returned from Jerusalem, Rome, and Santiago de Compostella.[57] In Book II she suddenly,
unexpectedly, travels again; the conclusion of this second episode segues
seamlessly into the actual composing of the *Book*.

   After Book II, the *Book of Margery Kempe* presents us with prayers,
habitually offered by Margery for 'many yerys' (8337). Towards the very
end, she claims that her efficacy in prayer is grounded upon travel:
'I have ben', she urges her 'Lord' to remember, 'in that holy stede
[place] there thi body was qwik and ded and crucified for mannys
synne' (8523–4). This *I have been*, invoking her personal presence in
Jerusalem, is every bit as proud and exultant (in a good way) as the
equivalent phrase at the opening of the *Paradiso*: 'Nel ciel che più della
sua luce prende', says Dante, 'fu' io' ('High in that sphere which takes
from Him most light / I was—I was!').[58] Chaucer mocks Dante, none
too obliquely, for such a pronouncement: there is nobody in *this* country, he says, who has been to either hell or heaven.[59] Margery Kempe's
very first visionary attestation, made to the burgers of Lynn, is much

55. As compared, for example, with late medieval Florence: see Christiane Klapisch-
    Zuber, *Women, Family, and Ritual in Renaissance Italy*, tr. Linda Cochrane (Chicago:
    University of Chicago Press, 1985), pp. 214–15.
56. Meech and Allen date the death of John Brunham, Margery's father, to some time
    between 19 December 1412 and 16 October 1413. (*The Book of Margery Kempe*, ed.
    Sanford Brown Meech and Hope Emily Allen, EETS OS 212 (Oxford: Oxford
    University Press for EETS, 1940, p. 361).
57. In chapter 84 of Book I Margery travels to visit the nuns of Denny. In chapter 63,
    characteristically, she *refuses* to travel (when advised by her friends to skip town and
    hence to avoid local hostility).
58. Dante, *Paradiso*, tr. and ed. Robin Kirkpatrick (London: Penguin, 2007), I, 4–5 (pp. 2–3).
59. 'But natheles, yet wot I wel also / That ther nis noon dwellyng in this contree / That
    eyther hath in hevene or helle ybe' (*The Legend of Good Women*, F 4–6).

the same as Dante's: 'it is ful mery in hevyn!' (328, 339). And it is greeted with a blast of English scepticism comparable to Chaucer's: *how would you know? You've not been there, no more than we have* ('Ye know it not and ye have not be ther no more than we', 342–3). And yet once returned from Jerusalem, equipped with the spiritual gift she picked up there—her great, roaring cry—Margery *can* talk of Jerusalem, the earthly pointing post to Chaucer's 'Jerusalem celestial'.[60] Spiritual authority thus accrues through distance travelled. And yet, as the early reviews love to tell us, Margery Kempe receives short shrift as a pilgrim: for her fellow travellers, she is just *too* serious. What is the nature or origin of this seriousness? 'Most parish clergy', Eamon Duffy reminds us, 'were in fact farmers, like their people grubbing out a living from the land, their boots just as clogged with dung, their minds just as preoccupied with the state of the weather or the price of corn, their values and beliefs very much those of their parishioners'.[61] For more than the basics, 'one went to specialists' (p. 101): a process exemplified by Margery's book, which (Duffy continues) 'shows her seeking spiritual guidance from Carmelites, Franciscans, Dominicans, even from the woman hermit Julian of Norwich, but only exceptionally from the clergy in local churches' (pp. 101–2). At the very beginning of her *Book*, we do indeed find Margery seeking out 'worsheful clerkys, bothe archebysshopys and byshoppys, doctowrs of dyvynyte and bachelors also'; and she seeks out 'ankrys', to show them 'hyr maner of levyng' (67–9). And the most famous anchoritic personage consulted was, indeed, Julian of Norwich.

Two months after the modernized *Kempe* of 1936 had been reviewed and editorialized in the *Times*, Hope Emily Allen wrote in to share an encounter.[62] Edmund G. Gardner, who had presented Kempe as an anchoress in his *Cell of Self-Knowledge*, was terminally ill in 1934, the summer of discovery.[63] But he was able to see the Kempe manuscript in South Kensington, and to have Allen read him 'some of the most exciting chapters', including 'the interview between Dame Julian of

---

60. *The Parson's Prologue, CT* 10.51.
61. *Faith of Our Fathers: Reflections on Catholic Tradition* (London: Continuum, 2004), p. 100.
62. *The Times*, Tuesday 24 November 1936, issue 47540, p. 15, col. f; letter to the editor.
63. 'The general reader of English mysticism has known Margery Kempe for a generation through the reprint of Early Modern English extracts by Professor Edmund Gardner, "that beloved and saintly scholar whom we have recently lost", as Professor Chambers calls him in the introduction to the new volume' (p. 15, col. f).

Norwich and Margery'.[64] This meeting between Norfolk women—a
favourite from the very beginning—is of definitional, as well as senti-
mental, importance. Margery shares her 'revelacyons' with Julian
because she 'was expert in swech thyngys and good cownsel cowd
yevyn' (1341–2). Over 'many days' (1380–81), Julian schools Margery in
the nature of contradiction, on the efficacy of tears, and on the clean
split between faith in God and the language of the world: 'settyth al
yowr trust in God', Julian says, 'and feryth [fear] not the langage of the
world, for the mor despite, schame, and repref that ye have in the
world, the mor is yowr meryte in the sygth of God' (1373–6). This
clarifies, I think, Margery's particular choice of difficult vocation. She
assumes the seriousness of the enclosed and stable religious, the anchoress, yet passes through regions that reward her with 'despite, schame,
and repref'.[65] She at once elects to renounce the world, and to journey
through it; she wants to travel.

Margery and the fair maid of Dansk

In the early spring of 1433, Margery Kempe limped her way out of
Lynn to visit 'Danske in Duchelond' (7784): the city now known to us
as Polish Gdańsk. Margery, a grandmother and mother of fourteen
children, was considered 'a woman in grete age' by her neighbours
(7697): yet she travelled on and returned to tell the tale, some sixteen
months later, in what is now Book II of *The Book of Margery Kempe*.
Recent researches, building upon the pioneering annotations of Hope
Emily Allen, have given us much clearer understanding of the culture
in which Margery grew up: of her father being five times mayor of
Lynn and alderman of the Trinity Guild, the preeminent merchant
body; of his being commissioned by the crown to finance a diplomatic
mission to Prussia in 1385; of his involvement 'in international trade,
local politics, royal service and merchant banking, all aspects of which',

64. In which 'he said he felt that Julian spoke as St. Catherine would have spoken' (p. 15,
col. f).
65. 'I wold thow wer closyd in an hows of stone', cries one exasperated monk of
Canterbury (870). It is not clear what he has in mind: an anchorhold, a prison, or
worse. All he knows is that stone walls would prevent Margery Kempe from travelling in his direction.

Kate Parker says, 'were run from his home in Lynn'.[66] 'Dansk in Duchelond' lies some thousand miles from here: or as Margery puts it, 'beyowndyn the see' (7504), a place to be reached without modern assurances of time, latitude and longitude, weather reports, and navigational equipment.

Readers have noticed that Book II seems markedly different in mood and *modus agendi* from Book I.[67] Long years separate the travels and adventures of Book I, packed for the most part into the intense period 1413–18, from their commitment to writing: like Julian of Norwich, Margery has some twenty years in which to marinate intense experience in prayerful reflection. The writing of Book II, however, comes very much sooner after the *aventure* of its living out; and it observes a temporality more ordered and sequenced than the more random recollections of Book I.[68] This forward drive of Book II is thus much more akin to the narrativity of romance than to the more static forms of contemplative literature; the trajectory of Book II in fact models a basic structure of romance, what Susan Wittig termed (in the structuralist 1970s) the 'exile-and-return motifeme'.[69]

---

66. 'Lynn and the Making of a Mystic', in *Companion*, ed. Arnold and Lewis, pp. 56–7, 60. On John Kempe's professional connections with Danzig, Lübeck, Stralsund, and other ports, see Anthony Goodman, *Margery Kempe and Her World* (London: Longman, 2002), p. 65.

67. Barry Windeatt has recently argued that the element missing from most critical considerations of the *Book*, as a whole, is *prayer*. This is undoubtedly true: it is more exciting to contemplate Margery confounding clerics than it is to dwell on her soulful, private meditations. It is less true, however, for Book II than for Book I. See Windeatt, 'Introduction: Reading and Re-reading *The Book of Margery Kempe*', in *Companion*, ed. Arnold and Lewis, esp. pp. 7ff.

68. And travelling is no longer the *means* of bringing us to miraculous sites, but the miracle itself. At Aachen, in Book II's return journey, we might anticipate some prayerful reflection upon the four great relics of cloth that were housed there. What we get at Aachen, however, is curt reference to 'owr Ladys smokke and other holy reliqwiis' (7999), glimpsed as it were *en passant*; the truly memorable drama of travelling Aakunward unfolds as Margery sits by the side of the road amidst a group of naked poor folk, picking at lice (7983–94).

69. *Stylistic and Narrative Structures in the Middle English Romances* (Austin: University of Texas Press, 1978), p. 183. The Middle English prose *Three Kings of Cologne*, a text whose genre Julia Boffey cannily resists defining, melds travel writing and romance exotica with articulation of familiar biblical scenes: another complex work to set by *The Book of Margery Kempe*. As Boffey notes, this text was popular with women readers; Margery very likely stopped at Cologne en route to Aachen in 1433. See Boffey, '"Many grete myraclys…in divers contrys of the eest": The Reading and Circulation of the Middle English Prose *Three Kings of Cologne*', in *Medieval Women: Texts and Contexts in Late Medieval Britain: Essays for Felicity Riddy*, ed. Jocelyn Wogan-Browne, Rosalynn Voaden, Arlyn Diamond, Ann Hutchison, Carol M. Meale, and Lesley Johnson (Turnhout: Brepols, 2000), p. 47.

The great journey or quest of Book II sets in motion with Margery sitting one day at Lynn in 'a chapel of owr Lady', thinking of her son, her daughter-in-law, and their 'fayr mayde-child' (their baby girl) in far-off Danzig (7494–7). She feels 'desyr' to see them: and immediately, the text tells us, 'it was answeryd to hir mende that sche schulde seen hem alle er than sche deyid' (7499–7502). Eventually, the son, wife, and daughter at Dansk board ship for England: but such a tempest springs up that they decide to leave 'her childe in Pruce wyth her frendys' (7554). So Margery's 'felynge' that 'sche schulde seen *hem alle* er than sche deyid' (emphasis added) is *almost* fulfilled when son and daughter-in-law arrive at Lynn: but not entirely, since the 'fayr mayde-childe' stays behind. So unless Margery herself crosses the sea, the truth of her inner voice remains incomplete. The 'fayr mayde-child' thus functions rather like the little Indian boy in *A Midsommer nights dreame*: as a small-part player (with no speeches at all) who, nonetheless, catalyzes the plot. It is entirely typical of Margery that on getting to Dansk, she tells us nothing of the 'fayr mayde-child': Margery is interested in baby boys, not little girls, since only boys can remind her of the baby Jesus.

Margery and Bridget: old mothers and fleshly sons

Supplementary inspiration for Book II's travelling comes from Margery's lifelong devotion to Bridget of Sweden.[70] Margery three times mentions 'Bride's book', and while in Rome in 1414 sought out Bridget's serving maid and spent time in Bridget's deathchamber (3118–3131). Bridget had died in 1373, shortly after completing her momentous pilgrimage from Rome to Jerusalem and back; she was then in her seventieth year. 'Bride's book' is some version of the *Liber Celestis*.[71] One of the Middle English

---

70. Margery's desire to emulate Bridget sometimes blossoms into outright competition: as in the 'how do you like me now' moment in Book I where the communion wafer flutters like the wings of a dove: 'My dowtyr Bryde', Jesus tells Margery, 'say [saw] me never in this wyse' (1523). Margery's pilgrimage to Jerusalem in 1414, once she gets to Jaffa, tracks the itinerary taken by the aged Bridget before her; even her move of *nearly* falling of her ass, through sheer religious ecstasy, imitates Bridget ('in poynt to a fallyn of hir asse', 2188; *The Book of Margery Kempe*, ed. Meech and Allen, p. 289 (67/23)).

71. Bridget of Sweden's *Liber Celestis* records some 700 revelations prepared for the canonization process set up in 1377. At least seven English versions of parts of the book survive in fifteenth-century manuscripts, including two major translations (both British Library manuscripts). On legends of Bridget in England, see Sanok, *Life Historical*, p. 125.

translations, BL Claudius Bi, also contains a brief *Life*, in which Bridget pleads old age and poor health against Christ's command that she should travel: 'she bigan to excuse hir bi sekenes and elde. Than saide Criste, "I made thee in thi kinde: I shall strenthe the. I sall lede and bringe the againe to this place"'. [72] This injunction repeats in Book VII of the Middle English *Liber Celestis*: 'Crist bad the spouse that sho suld wende to Jerusalem, and that sho suld not lete for elde [hold back for old age]'. [73] Book VII of the *Liber Celestis* is the only text in the Bridgetine corpus that unfolds, like Margery's second Book, in chronological sequence. [74] It tells how Bridget's son, Charles, dies when the party reaches the court of the infamous Queen Giovanna at Naples. Bridget worries over the destiny, the journey now taken, of her son; she envisions the Virgin Mary and a fiend battling for custody of his eternal soul. [75] The devil-advocate, in the BL Claudius manuscript, is sure of his rights, since Charles 'assented to worldli pride and fleshli likinge' (p. 478, ll. 9–10): yet all this is washed away by the plentiful tears of Bridget, his mother. [76]

72. 'A Life of St Bridget', in *The Liber Celestis of St Bridget of Sweden*, ed. Roger Ellis, vol. I (Text), EETS, 291 (Oxford: Oxford University Press for EETS, 1987), p. 5 (lines 15–17).

73. *Liber Celestis*, ed. Ellis, p. 475 (lines 4–5).

74. See *Birgitta of Sweden: Life and Selected Revelations*, ed. Marguerite Tjader Harris, tr. Albert Ryle Kezel (New York: Paulist Press, 1989), p. 279. The *Liber Celestis*, prepared just six years after Bridget's death for the canonization process, gives a rather sanitized and depersonalized account of this itinerary; the Middle English texts present it through some dense layers of editorializing and Swedish–Latin, Latin–Swedish translation. It is nonetheless possible to get some sense of an eventful journey

75. The Latin text gives us the remarkable revelation of the Virgin Mary appearing to Bridget, describing how she stood by Charles as he died: 'I acted like a woman standing by another woman', she says, 'who is giving birth, in order that she might help the infant, lest it die in the flow of blood or suffocate in that narrow place through which an infant exits': 'Feci quidem sicut mulier alteri mulieri parienti astans, vt iuuaret infantem, ne ex fluxu sanguinis moreretur et ne in illo arto spacio, per quod exiret infans, suffocaretur, cauens eciam, ne infantis hostes, qui in eadem domo essent, ipsum interficere possent' (Sancta Birgitta, *Revelaciones*, Lib.VII, ed. Birger Bergh (Uppsala: Almqvist & Wiksells Boktryckeri, 1967),VII, 13,2; *Selected Revelations*, ed. Harris, p. 181). There are thus three female bodies at this death scene: Bridget, nursing her son, the Blessed Virgin as midwife, and the feminized, dying body of Charles himself. This birthing/dying scene is somewhat muffled in the Middle English Claudius manuscript.

76. The devil is outraged; in the Latin he cries 'O, quam maledicta est illa scrofa seu porca mater eius… What a cursed sow his mother, the she-pig, is, who has a belly so expansive that so much water was poured into her with the result that her belly's every space was filled with liquid for tears!' (*Revelaciones*, ed. Bergh, VII, 13, 72; *Selected Revelations*, ed. Harris, p. 187).

Bridget's anxiety about the 'fleshli likinge' that nearly damned her
son may be better understood if we turn to supplementary materials
that did not make it into the official *Liber Celestis*, or that feature only
as an *additio*. It seems that Bridget's son *did* enjoy something of a liaison
with Queen Giovanna at Naples that scandalized his mother: there are
reports of his kissing Giovanna on the lips, and of Giovanna planning
to keep him as her fourth husband (once she had rid herself of the
third). Happily, Charles falls sick and dies within fifteen days; his mother
nurses him stoically to death.[77] Bridget gives Giovanna fourteen pieces
of advice on how to mend her ways; there follows a vision of a woman
all spattered with semen and mud. 'This woman', we are told, 'is a
monkey that sniffs at its own stinking posterior'.[78]

Thus St Bridget of Sweden. At this point we might turn back to
Margery Kempe and the beginnings of *her* old age journey.[79] The
opening motif of Book II concerns Margery's relations with a 'tal yong
man' (7438), *her* wayward and lascivious son, the merchant at Dansk: he
who lives with 'hys clothys...al daggyd and hys langage al vanyte'
(7510–11); who winds up with his face 'ful of whelys and bloberys, as
it had ben a lepyr' (7461). At first accursed by his mother, he turns to
her for help *in extremis*; she, 'not foryeytyng the frute of hir wombe',
launches a mighty 'meditacyon' that leaves him 'clene delyveryd of the
sekenes' (7487–90). In the very next chapter, however, he rises sick
from Margery's Sunday lunchtable; he dies one month later. Margery
is immediately assured—or assures us—that '"He schal comyn hom in
safte"—not only into this dedly lond, but also into the lond of levyng
men, wher deth schal nevyr aperyn' (7566–7). Margery's very next
lines then brutally dispatch John Kempe, her husband, chief hindrance
to her own religious ambitions (7568–9). Suddenly, Margery of Lynn
finds herself, as a widow of spiritual and prophetic inclinations, much
closer than ever before to Bridget of Sweden.

77. See Bridget Morris, *St Birgitta of Sweden* (Woodbridge, Suffolk: The Boydell Press,
    1999), pp. 122–6.
78. In the *additio* to the *Liber Celestis*: 'Videbatur domina stare in camisia respersa sper-
    mate et luto et audita est vox:"Hec est symia fetencia posteriora..."'(*Revelaciones*, ed.
    Bergh,VII, 11, 23; *Selected Revelations*, ed. Harris, p. 175).
79. Margery is described in Book II as 'a woman in grete age' (7697) and as 'abowtyn iii
    scor yer of age' (7880): this figure might be applied rather loosely, since for St Augustine
    as for many other medievals old age began at sixty. See Shulamith Shahar, *Growing Old
    in the Middle Ages*, tr. Jael Lotan (London: Routledge, 1997), pp. 13, 29.

Parallels between what is effectively the last book of Bridget's *Liber* and Margery's second Book are striking: each sees an elderly widow of religious life and infirm health launched into one last epical journey while preoccupied with the recent death of a son dogged by 'worldli pride and fleshli likinge'. But whereas elderly Bridget travelled with confessors, translators, editors, anchoresses, handmaidens, chaplains, and even an English knight,[80] old Margery travels alone, or with anyone who will have her. Part of the allure of Dansk might thus have been Margery's hope of finding the kind of spiritual and actual *famiglia* which surrounded Bridget: for the son returned from Danzig was the only true family convert that Margery Kempe ever made. This Germanized son, perhaps the first scribe of Margery's book,[81] could have fuelled Margery's Bridgetine enthusiasms and, as we shall see, fixed Dansk in her mind as a special Bridgetine destination.

Margery at sea: heroine, merchant, vicar of God

Margery's route to embarking at Ipswich is a slippery one. The understanding is that as 'eldmodyr' or mother-in-law, she should accompany her widowed Danskian daughter-in-law through the 'strawnge cuntre' (7600) of East Anglia and see her safely aboard; she should then return to Lynn. In preparing for her Jerusalem voyage of 1414, Margery had ordered her affairs properly: the parish priest announced her departure from the pulpit, inviting anyone to settle debts (1939–46). Now she slips out of town with a half-formed plan that is fully concealed from her confessor and spiritual director, Robert Spryngolde.[82] Even *Margery*

80. The large group which set out from Rome with the sick and septuagenarian Bridget on 25 November 1371 included three of her children (Katarina, Birger, and Charles); her two confessors (who also translated her Swedish into Latin); her future editor-in-chief, Alphonse of Jaen; two Spanish anchoresses, called Elvira and Praxedis, who probably doubled as Bridget's handmaids; two Swedish chaplains; and (joining on at Cyprus), the Franciscan confessor to the queen of Cyprus and Sir William Williamson, the English knight. It is perfectly possible that the handmaid ('Seynt Brydys mayden', 3118) interviewed by Margery at Rome formed part of this group. See Morris, *St Birgitta*, pp. 122, 129; *Liber Celestis*, ed. Ellis, pp. x–xi.
81. See lines 164–8.
82. This plan gathers support from a sermon heard in a village near Walsingham: 'Yyf God be wyth us, ho schal be ageyn us?' (7652, a refrain that harmonizes sweetly with the words of Jesus, playing in Margery's head at 7641: 'Yf I be wyth the, ho schal ben ageyns the?'). The answer to the 'who' here, of course, is Robert Spryngolde, Margery's priest–confessor.

has doubts, but Jesus says ('to hir thowt'): 'I am *abovyn* thy gostly fader' (7633; emphasis added). This is a strong claim: that the Jesus inside Margery's head overrules the father–confessor outside it. Her leaving thus suggests semi-sanctioned exile or romantic flight, rather than orderly departure; [83] some of her neighbours, back in Lynn, think they have seen the last of her:

> Sum seyd it was a womanys witte and a gret foly, for the lofe of hir dowtyr-in-lawe, to put hirself, a woman in gret age, to perellys of the see, and for to gon into a strawnge cuntre wher sche had not ben beforn, ne not wist how sche schulde com ageyn.
>
> (7696–9)

Meanwhile, back in the boat, Margery and company head rapidly into trouble. At first there is fair-weather sailing, but by Palm Sunday the shipmates fear the worst. 'The tempestys weryn so grevows and hedows', Margery insists, that

> ...thei myth not rewlyn ne governe her schip. Thei cowde no bettyr chefsyawns than comenden hemself and her schip to the governawns of owr Lord; thei left her craft and her cunnyng and leet owr Lord dryvyn hem wher he wolde.
>
> (7713–17)

These lines are worth considering in some detail, since their combining of mercantile and romance, nautical and religious vocabularies speaks to the complexity of this representational space, namely the ship bearing our heroine to Dansk. Men attempt to govern their ship; but such efforts fail, and all is left to 'the governawns of the Lord'. A *governour* of a ship, in Middle English, is the steersman (as in the Latin *gubernator*); without the 'craft and...cunnyng' of steersmanship, Margery is in a rudderless boat. She thus keeps figurative company with

---

83. Margery finds a Franciscan at Norwich who validates her reasons for departure (7675–7), but doubts remain. The *Book* finesses ambivalences attending Margery's departure in a highly literary way, namely through amplification of a trope familiar from Chaucer, 'diverse folk diversely they seyde': see (for example) *CT* 1.3857. The first of the three response groups, in lines 7695–7706, shows a clear grasp of the perils awaiting Margery. The second and third subgroups of 'the pepil' are more sympathetic, but it is notable that this canvassing of views does not extend to Robert Spyngolde, vicar of St Margaret's Lynn, Margery's father–confessor and perhaps her scribe (the man who will *write* the *Book of Margery Kempe*). It is further worth noting that the *Book* here describes, in summarizing local reaction to Margery's absence, something that Margery herself could not have known: see Spearing, 'Margery Kempe', p. 92 and, on literary troping, p. 93.

the heroine of Chaucer's *Man of Law's Tale*, who, 'sent to straunge nacioun' (2.268), finds herself floating 'in a ship al steerelees' (2.439). God, the Man of Law never tires of telling us, is her steersman as 'Sche dryveth forth into oure ocean / Thurghout oure wilde see' (2.505–6). Chaucer and the Kempe-author play here with the reciprocal identification of ships with churches and churches with ships: a church has a nave, with a wooden-beamed roof sometimes shaped to evoke a *navis*, or ship; and a ship, on the high seas, becomes a church.[84] On the high seas, the frail wooden vessel of your ship is your only hope of salvation. In sailing 'oure wilde see', then, medieval travellers knew themselves liminally suspended between life and death.[85] Anchoresses, such as those at Lynn and Norwich, lived intensively and continuously in this place; they had been walled up with the service of the burial of the dead. The cell of an anchoress was generally attached to the church's nave; *Ancrene Wisse* likens Holy Church to a ship that 'must anchor on the anchoress'.[86] It is fascinating to recall, with Roberta Krug, how powerfully metaphorics of turbulent sea travel figure in the famed dialogue between Julian and Margery, two women of Norfolk.[87]

Old age is another life-and-death threshold. Bridget of Sweden's late prophecies and dicta, like Hildegard of Bingen's before her, acquired exceptional charismatic authority in being delivered as she travelled in old age. So too, I would suggest, does Margery's address to God, delivered in the extremis of Book II, Chapter 3. The *Book* is rather

84. Medieval paintings of the Ship of the Church or of Noah's ark may feature a church spire: see V. A. Kolve, *Chaucer and the Imagery of Narrative: The First Five Canterbury Tales* (London: Edward Arnold, 1984), pp. 315, 317. On the rudderless ship motif, see Helen Cooper, *The English Romance in Time: Transforming Motifs from Geoffrey of Monmouth to the Death of Shakespeare* (Oxford: Oxford University Press, 2004), pp. 106–36. On the motif of *deus gubernator*, see Sebastian I. Sobecki, *The Sea and Medieval English Literature* (Cambridge: D.S. Brewer, 2008), p. 138.
85. Thomas of Woodstock, duke of Gloucester, was commissioned by his nephew Richard II to negotiate with the grand master of the Teutonic Order in Prussia in 1391. His vessels, encountering violent storms, touched on the coasts of Denmark, Norway, and Scotland before making it back to Tynemouth; Gloucester, happy to have survived, returned home to Pleshy. See *Expeditions to Prussia and the Holy Land made by Henry Earl of Derby (afterwards King Henry IV) in the Years 1390–1 and 1392–3. Being the Accounts kept by his Treasurer during two years*, ed. Lucy Toulmin Smith (London: Camden Society, 1894), pp. xv–xvi.
86. *Ancrene Wisse*, tr. Hugh White (London: Penguin, 1993), Part III (p. 70).
87. See 'Margery Kempe', in *The Cambridge Companion to Medieval English Literature 1100–1500*, ed. Larry Scanlon (Cambridge: Cambridge University Press, 2009), p. 225.

cagey about the status of this utterance: is it public or private? We are first told that Margery 'cryid to owr Lord for mercy and preservyng of hir and alle hir felaschep'; yet we are then immediately told that she 'thowt' the address 'in hir mende' (7718–21). Such caginess may stem from anxieties about women preaching in churches. At York in 1417, Margery had been forced to defend herself: 'I preche not, ser; I come in no pulpytt' (4213). The ship may have no pulpit, but it seems sufficiently church-like to prompt caution in the *Book* (even though, of course, we all *hear* Margery's speech, as readers and auditors, as if it were delivered aloud). But we should notice that Margery does not actually *preach* in this chapter: she does something much more radical. She begins her address by speaking to God of herself and her personal safety: 'for thi lofe *I* cam hedyr, and *thu* hast oftyntymes behite *me* that *I* schulde neveyr perischen neithyr on land ne in water' (7721–2; emphases added). By the end, however, her first-person pronouns have switched from singular to plural: 'Help and socowr *us*, Lord, er that *we* perischyn er dispeyryn, for <*we*> may not long enduryn this sorw that *we* ben in' (7737–9). Through this subtle shift, Margery presumes to mediate for the entire ship's company; she has become their representative or *vicar* in addressing God; she assumes a priestly function. And, 'blyssyd mote God ben', her prayers are answered: fair weather returns, and 'in schort time aftyr her schip was drevyn into Norwey coost', just in time for Easter (7759–60).

In Norway, most of the ship's company visit a local church to see the raising of the cross. For their confession and absolution, however, they return to the ship. The text is punctiliously clear about this: 'thei weren howseyled *wythinne* the schip, alle that longed *to* the schip' (7762–3, emphasis added). Once again, the ship becomes church-like for this *particular felaweship* of East Anglians and Danskers. They set sail again, and a good wind 'drof hem hom into Duchelond' (7774). The 'maistyr' or captain of the ship treats Margery well: he is 'as tendyr to hir as sche had ben his modyr' (7778). And so Margery Kempe, who began her journey to Dansk as something of an exilic Jonah figure, ends it as Mary: mother to the Lord who is Himself 'mayster' of her ship, her church. This last analogy seems a little forced, but it is Margery who makes it: that is, she calls Christ her 'Maistyr' for the first and only time in her entire *Book*. This comes as part of a firm bid for closure, for final justification of willful travelling, as the epical sea journey comes to an end:

Sche went at the biddyng of owr Lord, and therefor hyr Maistyr, whech bad hir gone, purveyid for hir so that sche ferd as wel as any of hir felawschep, worschep and preysyng be to owr Lord therfor.[88]

(7780–3)

The description of the journey to Dansk, then, assumes a highly-wrought *literary* character, analogizing ship to church and church to ship through complex figural and typological strategies.[89] I am not suggesting that this ship *becomes* purely a sacred vessel at any point of textual imagining; it is always a merchant ship, plying a familiar Hanseatic route. I would further suggest that the *Book*'s imagining remains perennially mercantile even when contemplating matters of religion. If we look back at lines 7713–17 we find, at the moment of abandoning the ship to 'the governaunce of owr Lord', an evocation of mercantile practise:'thei cowde no bettyr chef-syawns'. *Chevisaunce,* in later medieval contexts, is applied to the raising or borrowing of money. The merchant of Chaucer's *Shipman's Tale* travels to Paris to 'make a chevyssaunce' and thus pay a debt; and Margery, at London in Book II chapter 9, will hide her face with a kerchief until she can make 'sum chefsyawns' and replace her worn out travelling clothes (8184). To *don chevisaunce,* however, can also mean to make atonement for sins.[90] Such movement between commercial and religious lexicons is one of the most striking features of late medieval European literatures.[91] Margery renounces 'the world' with considerable fanfare as she turns to religious life.[92] But commercial consciousness cannot be renounced: it supplies the categories she thinks through; it is integral to her very being. Even her perennial instinct to form *felaweshipe* while journeying speaks to both worlds. She seeks out those who would travel her roads to religious sites of pilgrimage; but above all, she seeks out those of her own *nacyon.*[93]

88. Our editor Barry Windeatt ends this sentence with an exclamation mark. The addition of exclamation marks here and elsewhere, in the *Book of Margery Kempe* as in other texts, adds tonal colour that is difficult to control (with considerable hermeneutic consequences). We seem to need something between the modern exclamation mark (which often seems over-emphatic) and, as in medieval manuscripts, its absence.
89. Some of these draw attention from the manuscript's annotators:'notas' appear at some of the most sensitive points that we have considered.
90. See *Middle English Dictionary,* 1 (b).
91. See further Rosemary O'Neill, *Accounting for Salvation in Middle English Literature,* Ph.D. Dissertation (2009), University of Pennsylvania; David Wallace, *Chaucerian Polity,* esp. pp. 182–211.
92. Or with a series of fanfares: see for example lines 38–55, 153–6, 318–23.
93. Her great gift of 'comownycacyon and good wordys' would, after all, be largely wasted on foreigners (4213–4).

Margery in Dansk

The sea passage that sees Margery Kempe 'drevyn'(7760) forth from
England,[94] then, is a symbolically supercharged episode sounding many
literary registers all at once: romantic, hagiographical, mercantile.[95] It
brings us to Dansk: a place where Margery spent five or six weeks and
where, so she tells us, she was very popular (7785). The symbolic
overdetermination of *this* extraordinary city can hardly be exaggerated.
Shipyard workers were murdered here in 1970, giving rise to Solidarity,
to sanctification by a Polish pope, and ultimately (so the Solidarity
Museum says) to the fall of the Berlin Wall. It is where World War II
started on 1 September 1939; it is, Napoleon thought in 1807, the key
to the conquest of Europe.[96] Its greatest novelist, we have noted, is
Günter Grass; myth-making, one of Gdańsk's most vigorous activities,
endures today in the very layout of the streets. Postwar rebuilding was
quickly undertaken as part of a heroic effort that saw Germans move
out of Danzig and Poles move in. The Main Town was reconstructed
in the period style of Gdańsk's greatest cultural and economic glory;
red brick medieval Gothic or Prussian styles thus lost out to white-
facaded Flemish Renaissance neoclassicism. The lines of reconstructed

94. Talk of 'driving forth' returns us to romance register: we think of Chaucer's Troilus,
    who at the end of Book I 'dryveth forth his aventure' (1.1092). But Chaucer's
    Custance, we have noted, 'dryveth forth' in her rudderless boat. Margery finds herself
    in a similar predicament; her ship's company abandons its 'craft' and 'cunnyng' and lets
    God 'dryvyn hem where he will'. At this point, Margery seems more like saintly
    Custance than pagan Troilus, the errant knight. But Troilus, too, is in a rudderless boat;
    his true *aventure* or errancy, from the viewpoint of the end of the text, concerns eter-
    nal salvation.
95. Every medieval merchant engaged in perilous business, committing himself or herself
    to the great unknown: 'Us moste putte oure good in aventure', another Chaucerian
    speaker says, continuing: 'A marchant, pardee, may not ay endure, / Trusteth me wel,
    in his prosperitee. / Somtyme his good is drowned in the see, / And somtyme comth
    it sauf unto the lond' (*CT* 8.946–50). This sense of merchants adventuring all, espe-
    cially those working outside the wool staple, was keenly felt in these days before joint
    stock companies. Like pilgrims, they sought *felaweshipe* or *hanse* with those of their
    own *nacyoun*; like Margery in Dansk, they were glad to come 'sauf unto the lond'. See
    further Eleanora Mary Carus-Wilson, *Medieval Merchant Venturers: Collected Studies*
    (London: Methuen, 1954), pp. 143–4.
96. The sedimented complexity of Gdańsk is reflected in the very history of its name, as
    recorded by Günter Grass: 'My Giotheschants, Gidanie, Gdańcyk, Danczik, Dantzig,
    Danzig, Gdańsk: you were a bone of contention from the very first' (*The Flounder*,
    p. 114; and see Chapter 1 above, p. 39).

Figure 7. Looking north down the Motława river, Gdańsk, towards the site of the Teutonic castle.

houses often align imperfectly with the original foundations; there is a thus a civilized civil war in Gdańsk between muddy-booted archaeologists, academic historians, and property developers.[97] So long as we remember never to absolutely believe what we are seeing in Gdańsk, however, we may risk contemplating some images.

97. Archaeology in such a deeply-layered city yields, by any urban standards, an extraordinary wealth of finds. At the Old Shipyard dig, for example, they have recovered 11,000 medieval metal artefacts from a 7,300 square metre plot. One would expect to see a lot of nails from a shipyard, but 3,000 of these finds are classed as 'exhibition quality'. These include numerous pilgrim badges, combs, coins, Swiss army penknives (or medieval equivalents), plus shoes, drawings on leather, and money pouches. The same site has yielded 200,000 pottery fragments and 68,000 animal bones. The Polish Maritime Museum, built on the site of the granaries, has an English coin from the reign of King Canute. The dig by the great parish church of St Mary has uncovered long rows of butchers' shops from the fourteenth century, right under the church walls. The excavation site at the Teutonic Castle is to become a sort of rival to the Yorvik Experience at York: Teut's World, perhaps. Such entrepreneurial vigour and imagination flourishes throughout Gdańsk: a continuation rather than negation of the urban and mercantile culture that took in Margery Kempe in 1433.

The first (Figure 7) looks north down the Mottlau (Polish Motława) river from the bridge by Green Gate. Green Gate, to our left, leads directly to Langer Markt and Langgasse, the most important civic thoroughfare of the Main Town.[98] Seven gothic watergates line the quayside of the Mottlau: the first signs of the extraordinary measures taken for protecting the city. The most prominent feature here is the famous Żuraw, the huge medieval crane.[99] Immediately beyond it appear the distant tops of more modern cranes: these mark the site of the famous Gdańsk shipyard. The feature that I would like to concentrate on, however, is that stretch of (orange) wall to the right of the cranes, just disappearing behind the large ship (the Sołdek). This wall survives from the fortifications of the castle of the Teutonic Knights. The castle controls entry to the city and the port rather like the Tower of London protects, or overlooks, London. The Teutonic castle was the first grand structure seen by Margery Kempe and company in 1433; officials and knight-brothers of the Teutonic Order were the first to enter her boat, seeking *Pfundzoll* and *Phahlgeld*.[100] In 1454, the Teutonic castle would be torn down by rebellious townspeople. Very little of it survives today: the townpeople of Dansk were extremely keen *not* to leave the Teutonic castle as a noble ruin in 1454, but rather to remove it from the skyline and to recycle its materials into city architecture. Archaeologist Zbigniew Borcowskí thus has very little to show at his excavation site of the Teutonic castle. This he defends as an example of 'negative archaeology': that is, the near-total absence of material sometimes speaks as eloquently as its abundance.

The Teutonic Order, that controlled Dorothea of Montau's afterlife and had dominated Danzig since 1308, took ever-increasing interest in matters of trade. Marienburg (Figure 1), its mighty fortress thirty-six

---

98. Pilgrims might be accommodated on the Granary Island, immediately over our right shoulder (as we look), but Margery Kempe had family and would thus likely enter at Green Gate.
99. Records speak of a wooden crane in the port from 1367; this one was rebuilt in 1442 (between two massive, round brick towers; you can see one) and again after 1945. The crane is operated by two sets of treadmills, worked by humans as in some hellish gymnasium; it can load and unload very heavy cargo and also step or lower the masts of ships.
100. Poundage and moorage taxes: see Burleigh, *Prussian Society*, pp. 106–7. The port records for this period do not, unfortunately, survive; they pick up in the later fifteenth century.

miles to the southeast, oversaw the whole Vistula delta from the west
bank of the Nogat and hence all goods trafficking down from the
interior of Poland for export to the west.[101] Crusades against eastern
infidels, such as the Lithuanians, continued; with the passage of time,
however, such efforts seemed less and less convincing. The impressive,
fourteenth-century fireplace frieze of Teutonic Knights fighting pagans
(Figure 2) is currently in a recreation room at Marienburg, the place
where knights met *after* their three meals a day. This seems appropriate:
for by the 1430s, crusading knighthood seemed chiefly a matter of
recreational reminiscence. The grand master's bedroom has underfloor
central heating, and next door a room with paintings of *trompe l'oeil*
curtains and of gorgeous green-stemmed flowers, with orange blossoms;
it looks like something from the Brighton Pavilion. One grand master,
Konrad von Jungingen, kept pet monkeys: there were complaints that
they damaged the wall paintings.[102]

The keeping of monkeys speaks, *inter alia*, to significant involvement
in international trade. *The Libelle of English Polycye*, a remarkable poem
about seaborne commerce from the 1430s,[103] speaks of the great galleys
of Venice and Florence exporting

> Apes and japes and marmusettes tayled,
> Nifles, trifles, that litell have availed.   (348–9)

This poet clearly disapproves of such frivolous imports: 'chaffare that is
wastable', he calls them (352). The 'commoditees of Pruse and Hyghe
Duchemenne and Esterlinges' are much more to his liking, since they
are useful: bowstaves and wooden boards; pitch and tar.[104] The

101. The Vistula connects the Carpathian foothills and Cracow with Gdańsk; Cracow
    connects with further major trading routes (from southern Europe and the Near
    East). See Francis W. Carter, *Trade and Urban Development in Poland: An Economic
    Geography of Cracow, from its Origins to 1795* (Cambridge: Cambridge University Press,
    1994), pp. 1, 6, 139 and figure 30.
102. Site visit; conversation with Agnieszka Błewicż (Muzeum Zamkowe w Malborku).
103. The poem survives in two editions (nineteen manuscripts), dated 1436–8 and
    1437–41 (with further revised versions of the second edition): see *The Libelle of
    Englyshe Polycye: a poem (attributed to A. Molyneux) on the use of sea-power, 1436*, ed. Sir
    George Frederic Warner (Oxford: Clarendon, 1926), pp. lii–lvi as updated, corrected,
    and augmented by Carol M. Meale, '*The Libelle of Englyshe Polyshe* and Mercantile
    Literary Culture in Late-Medieval London', in *London and Europe in the Later Middle
    Ages*, ed. Julia Boffey and Pamela King (London: Centre for Medieval and Renaissance
    Studies, Queen Mary and Westfield College, University of London, 1995), pp. 206–8,
    219–226, and 'Appendix' (listing all known manuscripts, pp. 226–8).
104. *Libelle*, ed. Warner, rubric (p. 15) and lines 308–9.

transporting of timber and pitch was obviously dangerous, although for marine archaeologists at Gdańsk it proves a blessing: fire melts the pitch, and the pitch preserves everything onboard (at the bottom of the ocean) including whole cloves of garlic.[105] A kind of tree emerges from this trade: elements of the Polish phrase 'Z Prus' (from Prussia) meld together to give us *spruce*.[106] By Margery Kempe's day, and indeed before, England had largely exhausted the primary growth forest that was best for bows or shipbuilding; timber was thus floated down the Vistula from deep within the Polish interior.[107] Maurice Postan remarked that medieval trade from the 'north and north east' of continental Europe evokes 'none of that romance which clings to the trade of Southern Europe. The latter', he continues, 'brought to western Europe exotic goods of every kind: pepper, ginger and other spices... silks, brocades and tapestries, sweet wines, oranges, raisins, figs, and almonds'.[108] He has a point: it is difficult to think of romance heroines in Middle English texts floating in with Baltic timber; the Mediterranean seems home to the luxuriously fantastical and exotic. But the Baltic merchants who took Mediterranean-based luxuries *to* their native region might have taken a more romantic view of their own enterprise and *aventure*.

It would be misleading to posit straightforward *opposition* between Hanseatic merchants and Teutonic Knights at Dansk: each was deeply involved in the business of the other. The Knights actually oversaw the design and building of the Rechtstadt or Main Town (Głowne Miasto), the city district of Danzig that was the heart of its trading and civic life. The charter was granted in 1343; the process of building was technically demanding, since city buildings essentially floated on driven-pillar

---

105. Site visit and conversation with historian Prof. Jerzy Litwin, director of the Polish Maritime Museum, Gdańsk; see further Litwin, 'Boat and Ship Archaeology in Poland', in *Down the River to the Sea: Eighth International Symposium on Boat and Ship Archaeology, Gdańsk, 1997*, ed. Litwin (Gdańsk: Polish Maritime Museum, 2000), p. 8.
106. *Spruce* sometimes designates the territory of Prussia and sometimes wood originating from that region: see *MED, Spruce*. In MS BL Egerton 2726, *CT* 1.54 (cited in text below) reads 'Aboue all nacions in Spruce'.
107. See Carter, *Trade and Urban Development*, p. 139.
108. 'The Trade of Medieval Europe: The North', in *The Cambridge Economic History of Europe*, vol. II, *Trade and History in the Middle Ages*, 2nd edn, ed. M. M. Postan and Edward Miller (Cambridge: Cambridge University Press, 1987), p. 168.

foundations (in this 'Venice of the north').[109] These monks cultivated a particularly intense devotion to the Virgin Mary that the town clearly shared; *and* there were fewer than fifty of them in the castle. This last detail seems especially remarkable: how might so few knights maintain control over a city of more than 10,000? A message from the Teutonic castle in Dansk could reach the Marienburg fortress, thirty-six miles away, in about an hour (through a series of relays across satellite castles).[110] There was also an express postal service.[111] But Teutonic Knights maintained control at Dansk chiefly through ideological means: that is, through visual signs that might interpellate and intimidate a population; through those cultural fragments that still might be read in the city today.

One of the most impressive of these lies at the heart of the city's massive parish church, Dorothea of Montau's favourite haunt.[112] Red brick St Mary's (Kościół Mariacki) may first be glimpsed through one of the gates along the quayside (Figure 8); it is noticeable how very close this and all the major civic structures at Danzig are to the waterfront. Within this Marienkirke, in the east wall of the chancel, we find the chapel of St Hedwig (Jadwiga, Figure 9). The altarpiece was produced by a local ateliér, *c.*1430; the wall paintings, uncovered in 1988, were whitewashed over during the Reformation. Before this chapel lies a gravestone; its Gothic tablet reads in Latin 'Here rest the honourable men Konrad Letzkau and Arnold Hecht, proconsols of the city of Dansk, who departed this world the Monday after Palm Sunday in the year of our Lord 1411'.[113] On 15 July 1410, the seemingly-invincible Teutonic Knights had been defeated by the combined forces of Poland

109. Governance was complex and peculiar: Dansk in some ways seems like an Italian city state of the Trecento, governed by a mercantile elite—except that a regime of militarized monks is peering permanently over its walls. On the 1343 charter, see Cieślak and Biernat, *History of Gdańsk*, pp. 50–53.
110. It would then take about five days for the force from Marienberg to arrive.
111. On this 'uniquely rational postal system', see Burleigh, *Prussian Society*, p. 47.
112. St Mary's, still one of the biggest brick-built churches in the world, was constructed in three phases, from 1343–1502. The second phase, which remodelled the original small basilica into an aisled hall with transepts, was completed in 1447. See Stanisław Bogdanowicz, *The Basilica of St. Mary's Church in Gdańsk* (Dülmen: Edition Laumann, 1995), pp. 7–11; Jasper Tilbury and Paweł Turnau, *Blue Guide to Poland* (London: A & C Black, 2000), pp. 316–17.
113. Bogdanowicz, *St. Mary's*, p. 97; see further Cieślak and Biernat, *History of Gdańsk*, pp. 75–8; Burleigh, *Prussian Society*, p. 110.

Figure 8. View of Marienkirche (Kościół Mariacki) from the quayside, Gdańsk.

and Lithuania at the battle of Grunwald.[114] The citizens of Dansk, thinking the power of the Knights to be broken, swore allegiance to the Polish king. Henry von Plauen, brother of the Teutonic Knights' grand master, invited a delegation from the city up to the castle at Danzig to talk things over; on 6 April 1411, the two mayors were murdered. In 1433, this murder of mayors was just over twenty years old;

114. Jan Hus sent a congratulatory letter to the king of Poland; the victory at Grunwald is strongly associated with a revival of Slavic fortunes. See Franz Heinrich Hieronymus Valentin Lützow, *The Hussite Wars* (London: J. M. Dent, 1914), p. 2; see further Chapter 1 above, p. 38. Grunwald was known to Germans as Tannenberg; the victory of the Germans over the Russians in August 1914 (fought near Allenstein) was referred to as Tannenberg by way of historical recompense.

Figure 9. Chapel of St Hedwig (Jadwiga), Marienkirche, *c.*1430.

the Teutonic Knights would survive at Danzig for another twenty-one years. The gravestone in St Mary's is thus *the* most poignant reminder of the defining civic and political tension at Danzig at the time of Margery's visit; her father, we have noted, was five times mayor of Lynn.

Forty years earlier, the heroic ethos of the Prussian knights had still (just about) been alive. Chaucer's Knight, in the *General Prologue* of the *Canterbury Tales*, had been one of hundreds from all Europe passing this way, en route to *reysing* in Russe (note the Germanic verb) and smiting Lithuanians 'in Lettow':

> Ful ofte tyme he hadde the bord bigonne
> Aboven alle naciouns in Pruce.   (53–4)

The black-clad knight of *The Book of the Duchess*, taken to be a John of Gaunt surrogate, commends his lady for *not* sending men 'to Pruyse, and into Tartarye' in search of 'worshyp': that is, to the territory of the Teutonic Knights, and to the vast Eurasian landmass beyond their borders.[115] But there was quite a rush to Prussia in the early 1390s. In mid-February 1391, Henry Percy, Clifford, and Beaumont received permission from Richard II to cross the sea, since 'they were keen to see foreign regions'.[116] Gaunt's son, Henry of Derby, twice travelled 'to Pruyse' in the 1390s and was entertained at the 'bord' of the Teutonic castle in Dansk. Margery Kempe, who sometimes seems like a medieval Zelig, knew about this: for in 1392, at about the time she was marrying John Kempe, the three ships that carried Henry of Derby and company to Dansk were being fitted out and provisioned at Lynn.[117] Her tumultuous sea passage to Dansk in 1433 thus retraces the route taken some forty years before by the future Henry IV, father to the great hero of Agincourt. The bows bent by the English *at* Agincourt were likely made of Polish wood, brought from Pruce to England in boats travelling in the opposite direction.[118]

Scenes of chivalry at Dansk were difficult to avoid, even within churches. Statues of the Blessed Virgin and Jesus were plentiful and affectively appealing; this same parish church of St Mary's contains some notable and beautiful examples. There is the intriguing statue of a woman holding two children: this is St Anne, holding Jesus and Mary (who is clasping a book, Figure 10).[119] There is an exceptionally

115. *Book of the Duchess*, 1025, 1032. MS Bodley 638 reads 'To sprewse' (1025). On 'Tartarye', see David Wallace, *Premodern Places*, pp. 121–2, 188–94; Terry Jones, *Chaucer's Knight*, p. 38.
116. '[O]btenta a rege licentia transierunt mare affectantes visere exteras regiones' (Ranulph Higden, *Polychronicon*, ed. Churchill Babington (vols 1–2) and Joseph R. Lumby (vols 3–9), Rolls Series (London: Longman etc., 1865–86), IX, Appendix, p. 246. Gower is sceptical about the motivations for such knightly travel to 'Espruce et Tartarie': 'Le cause dont tu vas ne say' (*Mirour de l'Omme*, 23893–6, in John Gower, *Complete Works*, ed. G. C. Macaulay, 4 vols (Oxford: Clarendon Press, 1899–1902), lines 23893–6 (and see further 23897–988). On British knights in Prussia in this period (Scots had a difficult time, since they did not follow the Roman pope), see Dietrich Sandberger, *Studien über das Rittertum in England, vornehmlich während des 14. Jahrhunderts* (Berlin: Verlag Dr. Emil Ebering, 1937), esp. pp. 233–41.
117. See *Expeditions to Prussia*, ed. Toulmin Smith, pp. xlviii, 157, 270, 278. Derby arrived at Dansk on 10 August 1392 and stayed until 25 August; he stayed there about fifteen or sixteen days on his return journey in September (pp. liii, lxxii) that preceded his pilgrimage to Jerusalem. Some eighty men (including seven minstrels) are recorded as sailing from Lynn; including those unrecorded, living at their master's expense, the number embarked is thought to be around 300 (pp. li–ii, xcvi–vii, cx).
118. A point made by M. M. Postan, *Medieval Trade and Finance* (Cambridge: Cambridge University Press, 1973), p. 98.
119. Miri Rubin tells me that such statues of St Anne holding Jesus and Mary are not unusual in this part of central Europe; another appears in the Ship of the Church painting, discussed below.

Figure 10. St Anne, supporting Mary and Jesus, Marienkirche.

Figure 11. Pietà in white limestone, Marienkirche, c.1410.

expressive *pietà* in white limestone from c. 1410 (Figure 11).[120] The chapel of the brotherhood of St George, in the north transept, contains

120. This pairing, slightly larger than lifesize, was formerly in the Sacristy, but is now in St Reinhold's chapel (by the west porch). It is associated with the 'Beautiful Madonna of Gdańsk', now in St Anna's chapel: this latter pairing of Mary with Jesus (here as a baby reaching for an apple) is also in white limestone (c.1420–5); its current heavy paintwork dates from the baroque period. See Willi Drost, *Die Marienkirche in Danzig und ihre Kunstschätze* (Stuttgart: W. Kohlhammer Verlag, 1963), pp. 90–91, 129–31; Bogdanowicz, *St Mary's*, pp. 66–9, 72–6.

an altarpiece (c.1435) whose locally-painted wings enclose five sections of 'capricious and elegant' English alabaster.[121] Immediately to the left, we find a sculptural group depicting St George and the dragon (Figure 12). St George, England's patron saint, is busily preserving female chastity under threat: a topic close to the heart of the sixty-year-old Margery.[122] The young woman in this sculptural group is identified (at the church and in the artbooks) as a Margaret,[123] since St Margaret's identifying sign was a dragon. English medieval people identified with their patron saints; it meant much to Margery that her parish church in Lynn was dedicated to Margaret; she is pleased to tell us that the relics at Aachen are displayed 'on Seynt Margaretys Day' (8000). This sculpture is worth dwelling on for a moment, not because the young girl in the blonde braid *is* a Margaret (she is not), but because it offers further clues to the peculiar culture of Dansk. One peculiarity is that St George, patron of this elite mercantile guild, is also chief patron of the Teutonic Order.

The sculptural group and the painted background both date from c.1403, which is when a chapel of the St George brotherhood is first recorded in the Marienkirke.[124] They illustrate a scene from the *Golden*

---

121. See Drost, *Marienkirche*, p. 133; see further Bogdanowicz, *St Mary's*, pp. 82–3. One of these 'kapriziös und elegant' English alabasters is an Annunciation: a somewhat startled Mary, turning from her book, sees a baby Jesus figure flying from the mouth of a crowned and bearded God the Father, heading right for her head (plate 133; Drost dates the alabasters to the beginning of the fifteenth century). Another grouping of five English alabasters, dedicated to the life of St John the Baptist and dated c.1420–30, is to be found in this church: see Drost, *Marienkirche*, p. 129. Such English alabaster was exported all over Europe, 'from Iceland to Portugal' (E. M. Carus-Wilson, 'The Overseas Trade of Bristol', in *Studies in English Trade in the Fifteenth Century*, ed. Eileen Power and M. M. Postan (London: George Routledge, 1933), p. 187). Some of it, transported by an English pilgrim, can still be seen at Compostella; the ensembles at Gdańsk represent especially impressive examples of artistic cooperation at the time of Margery's visit.

122. Fearing defilement, Margery in Book II prefers to go to bed 'with a woman er tweyn' (8118).

123. See Bogdanowicz, *St. Mary's*, p. 81; Drost, *Marienkirche*, p. 133; informational material in St Mary's also identifies the princess under threat as a Margareta. The confusion here is with St Margaret of Antioch, who has a God-given vision of her enemy in dragon-like form. The visionary dragon is vanquished by her making the sign of the cross: see Jacobus de Voragine, *The Golden Legend*, tr. Ryan, I, p. 368–70.

124. This according to Paul Simson, the great German Jewish historian of Gdańsk: see Simson, *Der Artushof in Danzig und seine Brüderschaften, die Banken* (Danzig: T. Bertling, 1900), p. 15. Bogdanowicz, *St. Mary's*, dates the group c.1400 and attributes it to a Gdańsk workshop (*St. Mary's*, p. 81).

Figure 12. St George, the princess, and the plague-bearing dragon, Marienkirche, *c.*1403.

Legend, a text written *c.*1260 and disseminated right across Europe.[125] St George confronts a plague-bearing dragon that has arisen from deep waters. The unflappable princess wears a girdle: at a crucial point in the narrative, George commands her to throw it around the dragon's neck. The dragon is thus pacified and follows the princess, the text says, 'like a little dog on a leash' (I, p. 239): this perhaps accounts for his rather disappointing, lizard-like proportions. For the merchants of Dansk, this scene was especially appropriate. Firstly, the idea of a saint killing a plague-bearing beast that lurks in deep waters was especially appealing to a seaport like Gdańsk; the great pandemic of 1348–9 spread primarily through seaborne traffic. Secondly, George is a wonderfully chivalric saint; his damsel-rescuing and beast-slaying overlap with more secular exploits of medieval romance. And thirdly, George is a *genuine* crusader, one who operates on the borders of Christendom: one whose

125. See Jacobus de Voragine, *Golden Legend*, tr. Granger, p. xiii; and see Chapter 1 above, p. 8.

exploits might implicitly critique the more recent record of the Teutonic Knights.[126]

Margery Kempe had ample opportunity to see motifs of St George
outside as well as inside churches in Dansk: the St George's brotherhood was the most exclusive and *worshipful* (in English terms) of all the
city's merchant guilds, setting fashions and practices for all others to
follow. Members of this elite mercantile brotherhood gathered at the
Artushof, the court of King Arthur. It might seem surprising to find
Baltic merchants imagining themselves as knights of the Round Table,
but there were in fact equivalent Arthur's courts all the way along the
Hanseatic trade routes, from Stralsund to Riga.[127] The Arthur's court at
Dansk had been established at the same site since the mid-fourteenth
century, namely just east of the Town Hall on the Long Market, the
Main Town's central thoroughfare.[128] The mercantile brotherhood of
St George attempted to keep Arthur's court, and the right to tourney
at it, as an elite affair:[129] but it was unable to prevent other guilds from
sharing space in the Artushof. These newcomers drew members from
lower social echelons; new statutes of 1421 suggest considerable widening of membership.[130] Eventually, the elite brothers of St George
decamped from Arthur's court to their own Georgshalle by Golden
Gate.[131] What we see here, then, are distinct uses and phases of chivalric

126. 'With the help of Christ I have conquered Palestine', he cries, 'but now I have left
    all that to serve the God of heaven more freely' (I, p. 240). The end of the *Golden
    Legend* account sees St George appearing to Crusaders on their way to Jerusalem,
    wearing his white armour with the red cross. 'Thus reassured', the *Legend* says, 'the
    army took the city and slaughtered the Saracens' (I, p. 242).
127. See Alina Szpakiewicz, *The Artus Court*, tr. Danuta Gumowska (Gdańsk: Museum of
    the History of Gdańsk, 1996), p. 7; Margaret Schlauch, 'King Arthur in the Baltic
    Towns', *Bulletin Bibliographique de la Société Internationale Arthurienne*, 11 (1959), p. 75.
128. In 1358 the Artushof is referred to as the 'curia sancti Georgii'; in 1379, the city's
    oldest treasury account book refers to it as a 'theatrum'; annals of 1421 speak of a
    'Basilica Regis Arturi'. See Simson, *Artushof*, pp. 15, 17, 13.
129. Members were expected to live up to the highest knightly standards, upholding a
    code of honour that was laid out in detail; statutes of 1414 attempt to enforce strin-
    gent qualifications for membership. See Simson, *Artushof*, pp. 23, 28.
130. The expansion of manufacturing and trade in Danzig in the fourteenth century saw
    increasing numbers of guilds establish themselves in the Main Town (smiths, coopers,
    pursemakers... perhaps as many as twenty). Other craftsmen, such as ropemakers, cloth
    shearers, and tinsmiths, strained to organize their activities in guild-like structures. Some
    1032 craftsmen are listed in a document naming those who opposed and overthrew the
    Town Council in 1416. See Cieślak and Biernat, *History of Gdańsk*, pp. 54–5.
131. The Court of the Fraternity of St George was built between 1487 and 1494 as a
    shooting gallery for these merchant patricians; they did, however, return to the
    Artushof for special occasions

culture. Firstly, a merchant patriciate develops forms of knightly behaviour and display that challenge the Teutonic Order's monopoly of honour: the *aventure* of mercantile life may also be *Ehewurdig*, honourable.[132] Secondly, merchants and townspeople lower down the social scale aspire to chivalry: to share in its trappings and ceremonies and romance; to find benchspace for themselves in the court of King Arthur. Such progression, from elite origins to more popular emulation of chivalric ideals, seems not a bad summary of the history of romance in fifteenth-century England: a history in which English merchant families play significant roles.[133]

A rather obscene English fabliau from the mid-sixteenth-century shows impressive knowledge of the workings of Dansk: 'upon a tyme', it begins,

it fortuned in the worthy Cytye of Danswyke that two yonge marchauntes went walkyng together to warde a place called artus gardyn, whych stoode in the market place ...[134]

The tale of adultery that follows depends precisely on the mechanisms of Arthur's court: for as the court's clock beats the hours, an adulterous wife of Danzig knows exactly where her husband will be. This takes us back to the world of the 1421 statutes. If your husband is an alderman, one of the 'olderlude', you know just how long he will be boozing.[135] It is clear that the elite standards of St George's guild have slipped a bit

132. Teutonic Knight John of Marienwerder, in attempting to embellish Dorothea of Montau's lineage, suggests that her father (a translated peasant colonist) is a man of 'erbarn lebens': see Chapter 1 above, p. 12.

133. For precocious meditation on 'the interpenetration of culture between merchant class and gentry', see Sylvia L. Thrupp, *The Merchant Class of Medieval London (1300– 1500)* (Ann Arbor: University of Michigan Press, 1948), p. 249.

134. Text follows Margaret Schlauch, 'A Sixteenth-Century English Satirical Tale about Gdańsk', *Kwartalnik Neofilologiczny*, 4 (1957), 95–120 (p. 116). The tale forms part of *The deceyte of women. To the instruction and ensample of all men, yonge and olde, newly corrected* (London: Abraham Vele, *c.*1560). The copy from which Schlauch edits, BL C.20.C.31, is a second edition (identical in text to that of Robert Copland, *c.*1550). The woodcut frontispiece shows Aristotle ridden by his mistress (knotted whip in hand). The exempla of female deception run from Eve to a rich merchant of Hainault, deceived by his wife. The tale from Dansk (18th in the sequence) is one of the best localized. The word 'fockynge' appears in the denouement of the tale (underlined in the BL copy): this is a relatively early adaptation of the term *fuck*, more common in Scots writing than English in the earlier sixteenth century.

135. 'Item dat de olderlude up dem haue nicht lenger sitten sollen denne to tuelffenne de clocken up den auendt' (Simson, *Artushof*, p. 311)

by the 1420s: there are regulations against unregulated round dancing and the inviting of women to sup in the wine cellar. In the 1430s, the Artushof was evidently a vital civic and social space for locals and aliens alike. It was expected that foreign merchants should visit Arthur's court;[136] locals could discuss sea damages inflicted by the English; citizens and common traders met on a daily basis.[137]

There is little doubt that the idea of an Arthurian Court spread from, and was thought to have spread from, England. A Danzig rhyming chronicler of 1569 actually says that Arthur, 'an der Ostsee wol bekannt', founded the court and garden at Dansk himself: a fanciful claim, but we must remember that the Artushof was by then antique.[138]

In 1344, Edward III had summoned knights and wealthy citizens of London to a great joust at Windsor; here, at an elaborate ceremony, he promised to renew King Arthur's Round Table and to build a great room for 300 knights. Following interruptions forced by war with France, Edward in 1348 founded St George's Chapel, Windsor, associated with the Order of the Garter.[139] This, then, is the conflated model that quickly spread itself along both trade and military routes, from Thorn to Elbing and Danzig. English residents at Dansk, some of whom brought over their families and acquired shops and houses, would have encouraged such exportation.[140] The vigour of this

136. See Simson, *Artushof*, p. 26.

137. In 1435, it was announced at the court that those who had suffered sea damages from the Dutch, Zeelanders, or English should report to the town hall next door. In the same year, a Danziger informed Prince William of Braunschweig of the extraordinary mixing of citizens and officials with common traders at the Artushof; this, he tells the prince, is a daily occurrence ('tegelich gewonlich ist': Simson, *Artushof*, p. 25).

138. For the rhyming chronicle by Johann Hasentöter, published at Königsberg in 1569, see Simson, *Artushof*, p. 13.

139. See Richard Barber, 'The Round Table Feast of 1344', in Julian Munby, Richard Barber, and Richard Brown, *Edward III's Round Table at Westminster: The House of the Round Table and the Windsor Festival of 1344* (Woodbridge: Boydell Press, 2007), pp. 38–43; Stephanie Trigg, 'The Vulgar History of the Order of the Garter', in *Reading the Medieval in Early Modern England*, ed. Gordon McMullan and David Matthews (Cambridge: Cambridge University Press, 2007), pp. 91–105. Ironically, English and Teutonic knights ended up squabbling over the banner of St George; in 1364 and again in 1392, the Teutonic Order insisted on their exclusive right to bear it on their own territory and in *reysas* conducted in their name. See *Expeditions to Prussia*, ed. Toulmin Smith, p. l.

140. English resident representatives at Dansk, known as 'liggers', resumed penetration of Prussia after the settlement of 1388; they dominated trade in English cloth and took some part in local trade. By 1391 the community of the English nation, subject to terms dictated by the grand master of the Teutonic Order, elected its own governor and oversaw its own affairs. See Postan, *Medieval Trade*, pp. 251–2; Carus-Wilson, *Merchant Venturers*, pp. xvi–ii.

English-originated culture at Dansk in 1433, however, is poignant: for one great phase of English Arthurianism has ended (expiring perhaps with the 'Hon y soit' that ends *Sir Gawain and the Green Knight*); and the next has yet to begin. This new beginning comes with Malory's *Morte Darthur*, published by a man who honed his craft in Hanseatic cities before moving to London. William Caxton's 1485 publication of Malory happily coincides with the accession of Henry Tudor, a monarch who Christens his son and heir 'Arthur'.[141] It also coincides with presentation of London merchants to the new monarch, Henry VII, as 'the Merchants Adventurers, citizens of the city of London'. The phrase 'merchants adventurers' is not much heard before this date; after this date the petitioning merchants are referred to in the city's books simply as 'Merchants Adventurers'.[142] This confluence of revived Arthurianism with mercantile adventurism suggests the kind of cultural self-imagining kept alive in Dansk throughout the fifteenth century: following the catastrophic Wars of the Roses, we might say, lighter and more profitable forms of *aventure*, at once knightly and mercantile, can be exported back to their country of origin.[143]

The *Book of Margery Kempe*, I have suggested, is not to be categorized a priori as a religious treatise, a pious *vita*, but rather as a text negotiating and absorbing various genres and values (hagiographic, mercantile, and romantic). With this in mind, let us return to Arthur's Court. The facade of Dwór Artusa has been remodelled in the style of Netherlandic mannerism (*c.* 1616–17), but the rear of the building retains its early

141. Malory's *Morte*, reprinted five times after its first publication, is 'one of the very few of the works first printed by Caxton [in 1485] that retained its hold on the reading public in the following centuries'; the fact that there are so few surviving copies of editions by Caxton and de Worde (1498, 1529) suggests—to A. S. G. Edwards—that it was 'literally read to destruction' ('The Reception of Malory's *Morte Darthur*', in *A Companion to Malory*, ed. Elizabeth Archibald and Edwards (Cambridge: D. S. Brewer, 1996), pp. 241, 243).

142. See Carus-Wilson, *Merchant Venturers*, pp. xxvi, xxvii; Patrick McGrath, *The Merchant Venturers of Bristol* (Bristol: Society of the Merchant Venturers of the City of Bristol, 1975), pp. ix, 1–9.

143. The great publisher of matters Arthurian, William Caxton, had himself been governor of the Merchant Adventurers abroad for almost a decade: see Anne F. Sutton, 'Caxton was a Mercer: His Social Milieu and Friends', in *England in the Fifteenth Century: Proceedings of the 1992 Harlaxton Symposium*, ed. Nicholas Rogers (Stamford: Paul Watkins, 1994), p. 118. Caxton learned the art of printing at Cologne in 1471–2; on the statue of King Arthur in the Hall of the Hanseatic League in the city's Rathaus, see below, p. 121.

Figure 13. Arthur's Court (Dwór Artusa), Gdańsk, rear view (early fifteenth century style).

fifteenth-century gothic style (Figure 13).[144] The interior restoration features benches and decorated arcades of brotherhoods such as the St Christopher, the St Reginald, the Sailors', and the Three Kings. Models of ships hang from the ceiling; such ships were often awarded as prizes in chivalric competitions. In the first arcade of the east wall there is now a painting, c.1568, distemper on wood, by an unknown artist (Figure 14).[145] The city in the background here, top left, is clearly

144. It is pictured on a day dedicated to protests against dictatorial politics in neighbouring Belarus.
145. Only a narrow strip of the original survived the war; the rest is reconstructed.

Figure 14. *The Ship of the Church*, painting on wood *c.*1568, Arthur's Court, Gdańsk.

Danzig; and the ship depicted here is an actual trading vessel of the period.[146] The figures on the ship are religious: military martyrs keep watch front and rear; the Trinity appears amidships, with that distinctive St Anne (holding Jesus and Mary) just below them. Some saints, such as the St Christopher, forge links with the brotherhoods of Arthur's court. This painting is called *The Ship of the Church*. What we see here is that circularity in imagining between mercantile, seagoing, and religious registers that is evident throughout Gdańsk, a city built on water. Ship-shaped pilgrim badges are often found here; golden vessels presented to churches for containing and pouring holy oils are often fashioned *as* vessels, that is, as ships in the shape of a jug. Even in Solidarity Square, such circularity persists: for before the main gate of the shipyard, we find three high crosses where long-armed anchors take the place of Christ and the two thieves. It is thus remarkable how well the first sea journey of *The Book of Margery Kempe*, Book II,

146. Experts reckon it to be a French ship, captured (by the grace of God) by Danskers.

sustains such imagining: for as we have seen, Margery's ship assumes, without ever losing its *commercial* character, church-like status in leading her forth on her great, old-age *aventure*.

The great opening sea journey of Book II arrives triumphantly at its promised destination: but Margery is in no hurry to repeat the experience. And so she is trapped: 'afrayd on the see as sche came thedirward', she cannot travel by land ('for ther was werr in the cuntre that sche shulde passyn by', 7796–8). The solution comes in two parts: first, she meets a man set on pilgrimage to Wilsnack; and second, she encounters 'a marchaunt of Lynne', her hometown, who helps find shipping (7821) and resolves political difficulties. These difficulties see Margery detained at Dansk at the pleasure of the Teutonic Order:

And than myth sche han no leve to gon owt of that lond, for sche was an Englisch woman, and so had sche gret vexacyon and meche lettyng [hinderance] er sche myth getyn leve of on of the heerys of Pruce for to gon thens.

(7817–20)

There are two possible reasons why Margery might be in trouble here with the Prussian 'heerys' (her unique usage of this Germanic term)[147] as 'an Englisch woman'. Firstly, at the time of her visit thousands of Hussites, allied with the king of Poland, are mobilizing against the Teutonic Order; they will head for the Vistula, burning down the fortress at its mouth and even, perhaps, the hospital of St James in the Old Town.[148] In April 1433, while Margery was in Dansk, the grand master was urging the city council to take defensive measures.[149] The townspeople

---

147. This phrase, 'heerys of Pruce', might be considered as a counter-example to the phrasings compiled by Spearing as suggestive of Spryngold's (rather than Kempe's) usage: for only somebody who had actually lived in Danzig for a month, and negotiated with the Teutonic Order, is likely to have remembered it.

148. See Andrej Zbierski, 'The Maritime Fortress of Wisłoujście as seen in the Complex Research by the Department of Archaeology of IHKM PAN and the Central Maritime Museum', in *Wisłoujście Fortress: History, Present, Future* (Gdańsk: Muzeum Historii Miasta Gdańska, 2000), pp. 35–6; Lützow, *Hussite Wars*, p. 314. The Hussite army went on to organize equestrian games and jousting at the edge of the Baltic: see F. M. Bartoš, *The Hussite Revolution 1424–1437*, tr. John M. Klassen (Boulder: East European Monographs, 1986), p. 104.

149. The townspeople were requested to supply thirty armoured carts or wagons, each equipped with four to five crossbowmen, flammable projectiles and hand-held weapons, as well as heavy chains to tie the carts together. See *Historia Gdańska*, ed. Edmunda Cieślak, 5 vols, incomplete (Gdańsk: Wydawnictwo Morskie, 1978–), pp. 566–72; I thank Fr. Adam Szarszewski and Sebastian Sobecki for help here.

were unwilling to involve themselves in military manoeuvres; the Teutonic Order again appealed to orthodox Crusaders for help, but (as Eric
Christiansen succinctly puts it) 'nobody came'.[150] English Lollards had
made common cause with the Hussites; Peter Payne was one of their
most active advocates.[151] Margery had earlier been interrogated as a
potential Lollard, and travelling women famously disseminated Lollard
texts and ideas.[152] Might she thus be seen in Dansk in 1433, plotting to
travel eastward into German territory, as a Hussite sympathizer or even
provocateur? The other potential cause of Margery's 'lettynge' or hin-
derance at Dansk concerns matters of Hanseatic trade. English merchants had long been pressing for privileges equivalent there to those
enjoyed by Danzigers at the German Steelyard in London; they wanted,
in effect, 'a "Hanse" of their own'.[153] This Danzig was loathe to concede:
from the evidence of the war waging with France out west, the English
were inveterate empire-builders; a regularized bridgehead at Dansk
might serve for further economic incursions down the Vistula or along
the coast.[154] In December 1428, however, the Teutonic high master
granted the English the right to elect a governor to rule over their
members, their *nation*. But following further disputes in both London
and Dansk, a period of supreme tension was reached: 'the Prussians',
Postan writes, 'began to behave as if the day of reckoning had come at
last'.[155] English goods were seized by the high master, and ancient claims
revived. All this was going on, at the highest peak of mutual tension, at
the time of Margery's visit.

We thus have two possible causes of Margery's difficulties at Dansk
in 1433: being taken for a Lollard or Hussite sympathizer; being associated with the English mercantile *nation*. On my offering her the

---

150. See Christiansen, *Northern Crusades*:'nobody came ... the knights of Catholic Europe
stayed at home' (pp. 242–3).
151. See Bartoš, *Hussite Revolution*, *passim*.
152. See Rita Copeland, 'Why Women Can't Read: Medieval Hermeneutics, Statutory
Law, and the Lollard Heresy Trials', in *Representing Women: Law, Literature, and
Feminism*, ed. Susan Sage Heinzelman and Zipporah Batshaw Wiseman (Durham:
Duke University Press, 1994), p. 271.
153. Postan, *Medieval Trade*, p. 255.
154. See Postan, 'Northern Europe', pp. 300–301.
155. *Medieval Trade*, p. 260; see further T. H. Lloyd, *England and the German Hanse, 1157–1611*
(Cambridge: Cambridge University Press, 1991), pp. 136–7.

opportunity to pick one, Professor Beata Możejko of the University of Gdańsk replied with a polite Polish version of the famous Bill Clinton formula: 'it's the economy, stupid'.

Option two, then.[156] It was not until 1437 that these extreme trade tensions were resolved; the treaty of that year was, Postan says, 'an undoubted English triumph': the right to enter, settle, and trade in Prussia was guaranteed as never before.[157] Things did not, however, improve for the English; in fact, they got much worse. The chief factor here was civil war: those Wars of the Roses that broke out sixteen years (to the day) after Margery Kempe's last appearance in city records.[158] It is ironic to think that while Arthurian and chivalric culture was being kept alive by the burghers and Teutons of Dansk, the actual knightly inhabitants of Arthur's isle were fighting one another towards extinction. Arthur, we have noted, would return to Britain in the form of bookish recreation, purveyed by a Hanseatic printer, in 1485. By then the victory of the Hanse in the Baltic would be complete. Margery Kempe's visit to Dansk thus comes at a cuspish moment in the fortunes of her *nacioun*; a moment that is quickly lost.[159]

Margery, Bridget, and Dorothea in Dansk

There were two holy wives, subjects of lengthy canonization processes, for Margery to contemplate in Dansk; the first of these was Bridget of

---

156. This is not to deny that overland passage in late spring 1433 might have proved extremely hazardous, especially for 'an Englisch woman' departing from Dansk with an accent that might be mistaken for German.

157. *Medieval Trade*, p. 264.

158. That is, 22 May 1455 (Battle of First St Albans); Margery Kempe is first mentioned as a member of the Trinity Guild at Lynn on 22 May 1439.

159. Władysław Jagiełło, king of Poland and grand prince of Lithuania, died on 31 May 1434 (reportedly from a chill caught while listening to nightingales); his successors waged war with the Teutonic Knights until 1466. Political conditions thus also changed rapidly after 1433. See O. Halecki, 'Problems of the New Monarchy: Jagiełło and Vitold, 1400–34', in *The Cambridge History of Poland: From the Origins to Sobieski (to 1696)*, ed. W. F. Reddaway, J. H. Penson, O. Halecki, and R. Dybowski (Cambridge: Cambridge University Press, 1950), p. 230; A. Bruce Boswell, 'Jagiełło's Successors: The Thirteen Years' War with the Knights, 1434–66', in *History of Poland*, ed. Reddaway et al., pp. 232–49; Lukowski and Zawadzki, *Concise History of Poland*, pp. 38–9.

Figure 15. Churches of St Catherine (left) and St Bridget (right), Gdańsk.

Sweden. On 23 July 1373, following that epical, old-age pilgrimage to Jerusalem, Bridget died in Rome. Her corpse, carried slowly back to Sweden, rested awhile in Dansk (Figure 15: St Bridget's church is on the right, St Catherine's on the left) while her daughter Catherine mounted an excoriating attack on the Teutonic Order.[160] A strangely hybrid religious institution subsequently evolved at Dansk, promoted by Konrad von Jungingen (that high master of the Teutonic Order whose monkeys damaged wall paintings). This was a community of pious female penitents, so-called Magdalenes, supervised by Bridgetines imported from Sweden and following a liturgical rite laid down

160. Catherine thus continued her mother's fierce critique of the Order (for whom she predicted a bleak future). See Arno Mentzel-Reuters, 'Das pomesanische Domkapitel als literarisches Zentrum: Der Fall des Prager Magisters Johannes Marienwerder', in *Deutschsprachige Literatur des Mittelalters in östlichen Europa*, ed. Ralf G. Päsler and Dietrich Schmidtke (Heidelberg: Universitätsverlag Winter, 2006), p. 171. Mentzel-Reuters suggests that Bridget's hostility, plus friendly relations between the Danzig *Birgittenkloster* and the Polish king Jagiełło, in effect created an opening for Teutonic Order sponsorship of a local female saint (p. 171).

by the Teutonic Order.[161] Such a heady brew would have attracted Margery Kempe, one imagines, like a wasp to the honeypot. Her son, we have noted, had fallen into 'the synne of letchery' at Danzig, ending up with 'his face ... full of pimples and pustules, as if he had been a leper' (7460–61). These Magdalenes at Danzig, now under Bridgetine supervision, had served the sexual needs of a busy port population

Figure 16. Watermill on the Radunia canal, Gdańsk, c.1350.

161. Relics from Wadstena were brought over in 1397, the same year in which the Bridgetine cloister received papal recognition. Relations between Bridgetines and Magdalenes remained difficult throughout the fifteenth century. See Willi Drost and Franz Swoboda, *Kunstdenkmäler der Stadt Danzig*, vol. 5, *St. Trinitatis, St. Peter und Paul, St Bartholomäi, St. Barbara, St. Elisabeth, Heilig Geist, Englische Kapelle, St. Brigitten* (Stuttgart: W. Kohlhammer Verlag, 1972), pp. 179–80. St Bridget's church became associated with Solidarity and today serves as something of a shrine to that movement; a small community of Bridgetines endures at Oliwa (just north of Gdańsk). Oliwa, site of a famous Cistercian monastery founded in 1186, was sacked by Hussites in 1433. A Bristolian tells how, c.17 June 1433, monks from a nearby monastery (probably Oliwa) took refuge in Danzig: see Goodman, *Margery Kempe*, p. 159.

before (like Margery's son) finding religion. To cap it all, the church co-dedicated to Mary Magdalene and St Bridget lay just across the street from a massive watermill (Figure 16): a poignant reminder of Margery's own failed, worldly past as a miller, a profession she stuck at until (her *Book* says) 'the hey mercy of our Lord Jhesu Cryst...kallyd hir fro the pride and vanyte of the wretthyd world' (316–17).[162] This mill is now a mall, as in shopping mall.

The other wife, widow, and holywoman for Margery to contemplate at Dansk was, of course, Dorothea of Montau. The two women have much in common: illiteracy, prodigious motherhood, widowhood, mercantile connections, Hanseatic-based travel, prodigious weeping, Bridget-emulation, and husbands who will not die. Dorothea's German *Life*, published in 1405, was widely disseminated through parishes, and St Mary's at Dansk—the structure that utterly dominates the city—was strongly associated with Dorothea.[163] But the differences between them are stark. Dorothea, from first to last, from birth to death and beyond, is a creature of the Teutonic Order. She is given to extreme masochism and self-wounding; she was unconditionally obedient to masculine authority (her brother, her husband, her father confessor, her God). Dorothea's mother tongue is German, although the German of her *Leben* is translated back from her father confessor's Latin; we strain to catch her language, her *parole*. And yet the Teutonic Order was keen to promote her cult by encouraging personal reminiscences, and by spreading the legend of her life at parish level. It thus seems likely that in seeking news of Bridget at Dansk, as she did at Rome, Margery heard talk of Dorothea. She may not have remembered much of the Latin theology with which Marienwerder surrounds and encloses Dorothea; but she would, as a pious adjunct to an Anglo–Prussian family, have welcomed tales of Dorothea's *life*. And such stories may have encouraged her—as a widowed mother of mercantile origins, lacking Bridget's aristocratic pedigree—to contemplate herself, her own *life,* as a suitable subject for dictation. Confidence that a woman of her *estate* might merit textual memorialization—a

162. Dating from the mid fourteenth century, this mill became the largest of its kind in Europe: eighteen waterwheels ground 200 tonnes of grain per day. It lies on the Radunia canal, built by the Teutonic Order in the 1330s; it brought the Order handsome profits. See Tilbury and Turnau, *Blue Guide*, p. 323; Cieślak and Biernat, *History of Gdańsk*, pp. 55–6; Burleigh, *Prussian Society*, p. 102.

163. See Chapter 1 above, pp. 35–6.

confidence, I shall argue, soon to be confirmed in London—may prove to have been the greatest legacy of her 1433 voyage to Dansk.

A pilgrim anchoress: Margery in Wilsnack, and *Aachenward*

It is not untypical of Margery that her chief preoccupation in Dansk becomes, after a month or so, how to leave. She soon falls out with her daughter-in-law, and although she remains highly popular and contented (7790) her voices change their tune: God now says, *get out of town*. Much bustle suggests that Hussites, bellicose Lollards, will soon be at the gates; but 'the heerys of Pruce' are loathe to let her leave. Happily, however, Margery meets a man set on pilgrimage to Wilsnack, *and* a man from her hometown, Lynn, who arranges shipping to Stralsund. And so now, but only now, she can be located within pilgrimage structure: she travels first to Wilsnack, and then on to Aachen.[164] One senses her first Carthusian readers, in the later fifteenth century, breathing a sigh of relief. By way of celebration, perhaps, one of them draws two marginal illustrations: a wafer by the Wilsnack section, and a smock for Aachen.[165]

Wilsnack, today, is a truly dismal hamlet in old East German territory, some seventy miles northwest of Berlin. It once ranked behind only Jerusalem, Rome, and Santiago, places that Margery had already seen, in numbers of pilgrim visitors; some of these have left exotic offerings, such as whale bones, and an ostrich egg. The cult was of recent invention. In 1383 Heinrich von Bülow, a knight at war with the bishop of Havelberg, had burned down the church at Wilsnack. Three hosts were found on the altar, miraculously untoasted, each with

---

164. 'It may be', says Caroline M. Barron laconically of the 1433 journey, 'that Margery did not set out as a pilgrim but turned herself in to one as her travels developed' ('Pilgrim Souls: Margery Kempe and other Women Pilgrims', Confraternity of Saint James Occasional Paper no. 6 (London: Confraternity of St James, 2004), p. 9).

165. Both of these images correspond to pilgrim badges from Aachen and Wilsnack that were brought back to England: see Brian Spencer, *Pilgrim Souvenirs and Secular Badges*, Medieval Finds from Excavations in London, 7 (London: Stationery Office, 1998), pp. 258b–260a, 266b–267a. The Wilsnack badge consists of three roundels representing the three wafers, with scenes of the Flagellation, Crucifixion, and Resurrection depicted upon them (figure 263b); an example of this pilgrim sign has been found at King's Lynn (p. 266b).

a spot that the bishop adjudged to be the blood of Christ. The Holy
Blood of Wilsnack was always a controversial cult, and the Carthusian
illustrator of Margery's *Book* acts quite boldly in placing three red dots
on the round 'O' of his marginal wafer, signifying blood.[166] Margery
reports two miracles at Wilsnack: that of the blood, and that of her
travelling to see it. 'It was gret merveyl and miracle', she says,

> that a woman dysewsyd of goyng, and also abowtyn iii scor yer of age, schuld
> enduryn cotidianly to kepyn hir jurney and hir pase with a man fryke
> [energetic: her travelling companion from Danzig] and lusty to gon.
>
> (7879–82)

A tall man with a weapon, ready to fight, emerges from a wood (but
they pass him by); women of the country appear to cheer her along.
'Thus what with wel and with woo', her *Book* says,

> thorw the help of owr Lord, sche was browt to Wilsnak and saw that precyows
> blood which be myracle cam owt of the blissful sacrament of the awtere.
>
> (7899–7902)

The miracles of her travel and the eucharistic wafer thus fuse to
become a single and indivisible source of wonder. As she journeys on
'to-Akun-ward' (7904), still securely within pilgrimage structure, it is
instructive (as ever) to consider what Margery chooses to tell us, and
what she leaves out. We hear nothing of Havelberg and Cologne, both
on the pilgrim route, but we do hear (again) of the sacrament of the
altar, and of fleas. Havelberg, twelve miles south of Wilsnack, is where
the Holy Blood money was spent. Profits from Wilsnack that flowed to
the bishops at Havelberg helped fund a magnificent cathedral choir
screen.[167] This features sculptural figures of arresting pathos and beauty
but also, on the altar side, ugly, anti-Semitic caricatures: blood miracle
at Wilsnack thus translates to blood libel just down the road. At

---

166. See Carolyn Walker Bynum, *Wonderful Blood: Theology and Practise in Late Medieval
    Northern Germany and Beyond* (Philadelphia: University of Pennsylvania Press, 2006),
    pp. 25–45; *Ev. Kirche St. Nikolai, Bad Wilsnack* (Regensburg: Verlag Schnell & Steiner,
    1994). A commission to investigate the Wilsnack cult was established by the arch-
    bishop of Prague in 1403. Clergy of Bohemia were subsequently required to preach
    against it once a month; Jan Hus, a member of the commission, wrote the first trea-
    tise *contra*. The bishop of Verden had Wilsnack badges ripped from the hats of return-
    ing pilgrims. See Bynum, *Wonderful Blood*, p. 26.
167. See Harald Wildhagen and Torsten Buchholz, *Der Lettner im Dom zu Havelberg*
    (Halle–Zürich: Verlag Janos Stekovics, 1995).

Cologne, pilgrims might visit the magnificent shrine of the most famous seekers after Christ: the Magi, whose travels and translations inspire the Middle English prose of *The Three Kings of Cologne*.[168] The Hansasaal, built upon a vanished Jewish quarter, again testifies how Hanseatic merchants kept King Arthur alive as his legend faded in England: its sculptural scheme of the Nine Worthies, which Caxton certainly knew, has Arthur as the eighth worthy and Charlemagne as the ninth. This revisionary sequencing, following Augustinian teleology rather than temporal order, honours the great Christian emperor across the Rhine at Aachen. Charlemagne's magnificent gilded shrine at Aachen,[169] his new Rome, is just one more thing that Margery Kempe chooses not to remember.

What Margery does recall, from the Wilsnack to Aachen route, is an encounter with 'the preciows sacrament' that brings her just the kind of 'despite, schame, and repref' that Julian had in mind. Any anchoress might routinely experience this vision from her churchside window: a sighting of the 'blissful sacrament' during the octave of Corpus Christi. It is the labour and penance of travelling, however, that renders this sudden apparition of Jesus, under the form of bread, so compelling to Margery Kempe. She is being treated badly by her travelling companions, a monk and some merchants, before she sees the host 'in a cristal' in a wayside church; afterwards, when the sight of it makes her weep and sob 'wonder sor', they abandon her entirely. Kempe now experiences the perils and terrors of the solitary traveller: 'The night fel upon [hyr]', the *Book* says with eloquent simplicity, 'and sche was ryth hevy, for sche was alone' (7957–8). In her lodgings, German priests goad her for being an 'Englisch sterte', an Englishwoman with a tail. At night, fearing rape, she beds down with maidservants: but she is too scared to

---

168. *The Three Kings of Cologne: An Early English Translation of the Historia Trium Regum by John of Hildesheim*, ed. C. Horstmann, EETS OS 85 (London: EETS, 1886). Horstmann denotes the Magi 'the most popular saints of Christendom' (p. xv). The prophecy of Balaam concerning the incarnation was conserved by hilltop dwellers in India (with spies set against Israelites and Romans). When Acre grew famous in 1200, the diadem of Melchior was brought from India (since lost in the destruction of the Knights Templar), plus books about the three kings in Hebrew and Chaldean ('afterwarde translate into frennshe', p. 10). See further Hugh Mountney, *The Three Holy Kings of Cologne: How They Journeyed to Cologne and Their Veneration in England* (Leominster: Gracewing, 2003).

169. See Ernst Günther Grimme, *Der Aachener Domschatz* (Düsseldorf: Verlag L. Schwann, 1972), p. viii (a photograph of the shrine and attendant treasures from 1864).

sleep, 'for dred of defiling' (7968). Next day she falls in with 'a company of powr folk' (7978) who are bound for Aachen; between towns her travelling companions strip off their clothes and sit naked, picking themselves for fleas. Through such interaction, 'thorw hir comownyng', Kempe herself picks up 'part of her [their] vermyn and was betyn and stongyn ful evyl both day and nyght' (7990–1); and thus they come to Aachen. An anchoress, *Ancrene Wisse* says, does perpetual penance up there with Christ on the cross. Margery Kempe, whose superabundant love of Christ precipitates her persecution and privation, lives out her equivalent penance on the road.

Kempe's arrival at Aachen is a miracle of timing: the four cloth relics have been shown only once every seven years, for ten days, in a sequence running like clockwork from the first year of exposition (1349) to the 92nd (1–10 June, 2007). Dorothea of Montau visited Aachen in 1384, the sixth year, and Margery arrives for the twelfth in 1433. But she makes no claims for the providentiality of such timing and pays scant attention to the relics. 'Owr Ladys smokke' (7999) is noted, and this inspires the marginal Carthusian doodle. But nothing is said of the other cloth relics that this city, with its thriving cloth industry, has to offer: *the* swaddling-clothes of Jesus; the cloth which received John the Baptist's head; and the loincloth worn by Christ on the cross. We also get nothing of the experience of sharing all this with thousands of fellow pilgrims, no sense of solidarity in belief. What matters for Kempe are one-on-one encounters with Jesus: even in a crowd, Kempe seeks the singular and exclusive experience of an anchoress in her cell.[170]

The worshipful woman of London

Even before viewing the relics at Aachen, Kempe is laying plans to return to England with 'a worschepful woman' of London, a widow who has come to 'worschepen the holy relikys' (8002–3). But 'the worschepful woman' (8009) slips out of town, leaving Margery to hobble along behind two 'men of London' (8016) and a friar: 'sche was

170. The chapters cut from the 1936 edition, and then relegated to an Appendix in smaller type, are *all* private dialogues between Christ and Margery (Book I, chapters 5, 14, 22, 35–6, 64–6, 77, 84, 86–88; plus 'The Proem' and 'Her Method of Prayer').

to agyd and to weyke to holdyn foot with hem. Sche ran and lept as fast as sche myth tyl hir myghtys failyd' (8043-5). Finally she catches up with the 'worschepful woman of London' (8069), but the 'worschepful woman' (8080) cruelly rebuffs her: "'I wyl nat medelyn with the"' (8082). This *rebuke* (8083) leaves Margery in greater 'diswer and hevynes', doubt and depression, than at any time since she left England. Why does this cut so deep? The epithet *worschepful* is used eight times of this 'woman of London' (8151); her company is something deeply craved by Margery Kempe of Lynn. The *Middle English Dictionary*, which reached *W* seventy years after Hope Emily Allen worked for it, finds *worship* to be one of its most complex terms.[171] Texts adduced for definition sprawl from religion to chivalry to mayoral decrees: from Englished Bibles to Malory to London Letterbooks. As a worshipful woman of *London*, Margery's object of desire would likeliest have belonged to the aldermanic elite, or have boasted impressive guild connections.[172] It is touching that the epithet 'worschepful' finally falls away, as the 'woman of London' (8158) pukes and vomits her way from Calais to Dover, with Margery in dutiful attendance.[173] And it is striking that when Margery herself reaches London she is taken in, and treated well, by other 'worschepful' women of London (8216, 8219).

Margery Kempe lurked in London, it seems, for almost a year; as Hope Emily Allen suggests, her 'long sojourns in London' are very much worth pondering.[174] This last known London residency, between the late summers of 1433 and 1434, occupies an historical micro-period that falls between Henry VI's return from Paris and the end of minority

171. See *Middle English Dictionary*, ed. Robert Lewis, Part W.8 (University of Michigan, 2001), *worship* (pp. 900b–905b). Allen began work for the Early Modern Dictionary Project at the University of Michigan in 1931: see Hirsh, *Allen*, p. 99.

172. On Chaucer's gentle satirization of this London class, see Jill Mann, *Chaucer and Medieval Estates Satire* (Cambridge: Cambridge University Press, 1973), pp. 103–5. 'This portrait', writes Mann (alluding to lines 1.374–8, which tell of guildsmen's wives liking 'to ben ycleped "madam"', to take precedence at vigils and to 'have a mantel roialliche ybore'), 'illustrates the nature of social "worthiness". But we shall be missing Chaucer's point if we merely contrast it with moral "worthiness" and criticise the pilgrims on this basis' (p. 105).

173. More touching still is Margery's denial of *Schadenfreude* here: she helps and comforts the vomiting widow 'for owr Lordys love and be charite—other cawse had sche non!' (8160–61; the editorial addition of an exclamation mark is again, as with all editorial work, questionable).

174. This in a letter to Mabel Day, EETS secretary, explaining (lack of) progress on volume 2 (6 April, 1944, as cited in Hirsh, *Allen*, p. 135). Allen was herself, as noted above, a long-term resident of London.

rule, in 1432, and the Duke Humphrey's pointless *chevauchée* through Flanders in 1436. The first of these events marks the end of Lydgate's career as Lancastrian propagandist; the second inspired anti-Fleming riots in London *and* the *Humfroidos*, quite possibly the worst Latin poem ever written.[175] But what of writing in London itself? Henry Lovelich, skinner and citizen of London, merits no mention in *ODNB*, or its electronic avatar. But before 1435, he wrote and dedicated two works of Middle English verse—some 50,000 words—to Henry Barton, sheriff of London and twice lord mayor. The hero of Lovelich's *Merlin* is conceived when the devil defiles his mother at night.[176] Merlin's mother does penance for her nocturnal rape; Merlin derives his extraordinary abilities from her love and piety.[177] Perhaps Lovelich's *History of the Holy Grail*, translated from a French text very like Bodleian, Douce 178,[178] might have been more to Margery's liking.[179] Its opening, now lost, meditates on the fragility of textual transmission: on how a precious, God-given book is read, then lost, then found again in Norway; of how Christ appears to command that the book be copied into another book.[180] The surviving English portion begins by describing all those sights and locales of Jerusalem that certain English pilgrims knew so well; it ends by explaining that the book's rendering 'Into Owre Modris tonge' (51.527) will make it better understood

175. See Maura Nolan, *John Lydgate and the Making of Public Culture* (Cambridge: Cambridge University Press, 2005), p. 19; Wallace, *Premodern Places*, pp. 117–18, 136–7.
176. 'To this goode maiden wente he anon, / and redy hym made that dede to don, / and on hire he engendred, as I ʒow telle, / a merveillous child ful schortly and snelle' (Herry [Henry] Lovelich, *Merlin*, ed. Ernst A. Kock, EETS ES 93, 112, OS 185 (London: Oxford University Press for EETS, 1904–32), lines 603–6.
177. Merlin speaks: 'And also it is owre lordis wille / that bothe wit & memorye j schal have there–tylle / on his behalve, more thane a naturel man/ jn this erththe knoweth other kan, / for the love of my modir so dere, / that hire penaunce fulfilde here, / that the Goodman ʒaf hire jn charge/ (sche it fulfylde bothe fully and large); / that so be vertu of hire goodnesse / God graunttyd me ʒit more largesse: / to knowen thynges that weren comenge, / J sey the justice, with–owten lesynge' (1475–86).
178. Michelle Warren reports identifying 'Lovelich's source as a book of the same content and form as Bodleian, Douce MS 178'; the spaces provided for images, the chapter initials and the double-column layout of Lovelich's text, uniquely preserved as Cambridge, Corpus Christi MS 80, 'mirror exactly the structure of Bodleian, Douce MS 178' ('Translation', in *Middle English*, ed. Strohm, pp. 55, 57).
179. Herry Lonelich [Henry Lovelich], *The History of the Holy Grail*, ed. Frederick J. Furnivall, EETS ES 20, 24, 28, 30, 95 Part I (London: N. Trübner for EETS, 1874–1905).
180. See the French text, edited from BL Bibl. Reg. xiv E3, provided in Lovelich, *Grail*, ed. Furnivall, Part I (EETS ES 20), pp. 1–100.

than Latin or French. Roger Dalrymple has noticed[181] how Lovelich imagines his readers walking through his literary landscape:

> Now Furthermore let us now Walke,
> And of kyng Claryown let vs now talke.   (17.429–30)

In transitioning between his *Grail* and *Merlin* sections, Lovelich figures his own book-making as a journey in progress, asking us to 'bede' Mary with 'an Ave', so that

> This processe the bettere I myhte procede,
> And bringen this book to A Good Ende.   (51.536–7)

Henry Lovelich, wrote Hope Emily Allen, was a London skinner with King's Lynn connections. When Margery Kempe's father died, and there were some legal problems over inheritance, he stood as mainprise for Margery's brother. Two other Londoners joined him, plus his stepson: a Norfolk man who married a rich Lynn widow with property opposite St Margaret's church. Henry Barton, dedicatee of Lovelich's verse, was also a skinner; he also had links to Lynn. Margery Kempe's father-in-law was a skinner.[182] Lovelich's *Merlin* and *Grail* were not warmly reviewed by either Allen or Dorothy Kempe, in her EETS volume of 1905: 'his version of the famous episodes', writes Kempe, 'may be commended with the rest of his voluminous and incoherent ramblings, to a merciful oblivion'.[183] But this desire to narrate 'famous episodes'[184] should be connected

---

181. '"Evele knowen 3e Merlyne, in certeyn": Henry Lovelich's *Merlin*', in *Medieval Insular Romance*, ed. Judith Weiss, Jennifer Fellows, and Morgan Dickson (Cambridge: D.S. Brewer, 2000), p. 158.

182. Allen adumbrates these skinner associations and connections in her letter to Mabel Day of 6 April 1944: see Hirsh, *Allen*, p. 135. Allen further observes that 'the skinners were a Corpus Christi Guild'; both John Brunhams (junior and senior), plus John and Simon Kempe, 'were brethren of the prestigious Corpus Christi Gild' at Lynn (Goodman, *Kempe*, p. 50). Barton's will of 1435 names 'Henrico *Loveliche* cive et *pellipario* London' as a close associate (cited in Dalyrmple, 'Lovelich's *Merlin*', p. 156).

183. Dorothy Kempe, *The Legend of the Holy Grail, its Sources, Character, and Development. The Introduction to, and Part V of, Henry Lovelich's Verse 'History of the Holy Grail'*, EETS ES 95 (London: N. Trübner for EETS, 1905), p. vi. Allen, in the letter to Mabel Day of 6 April 1944, notes that 'EETS has in print several dull volumes' of Lovelich's work (Hirsh, *Allen*, p. 135).

184. The handling of certain episodes in the *Merlin*, such as the sword-in-the-stone pulling, assumes a communal character foreign to the French original. The 'Ensemble' (7131) declares that 'ho so wolde, scholde hit asaye' (7135); when 250 nobles are

with *the* most significant development in London writing at this period: the transition from monastic and chivalric-based history to chronicles written by the merchant class. The best-known name associated with these new chroniclers, William Gregory, was a skinner supplying ermine, marten, and squirrel pelts to the royal household; he was active for the Skinners' Company from 1427, served as sheriff of London from 1436–7 and as mayor in 1451–2; he was alderman for Cordwainer ward for more than twenty-five years.[185] Thomas Nashe, writing in the sixteenth century, was dismissive of these 'poore latinlesse Authors': 'lay Chronigraphers', he calls them, with trochaic inversions that would please R. S. Thomas, 'that write of nothing but the Mayors and Sheriefs and the deare yeere, and the great Frost'.[186] Antonia Gransden is more appreciative: 'at no time since the Anglo-Saxon period', she writes, speaking of the fifteenth century, 'had the vernacular chronicle achieved such importance'.[187] Hundreds, perhaps thousands, of these texts were written; by the 1430s, London chronicles were approaching their peak of production.[188] Their outlook is London-centric, but not (as in the 1930s) insularist: indeed, they frequently flit across the Channel, connecting events at home and abroad. One account of 1430, for example, moves directly from the capture of 'a woman…whiche was called

unsuccessful, 'alle other in fere / of communes, of power men, that weren there' have a go (7149–50). 'That the common and poor try at all', Warren remarks, 'is a remarkable innovation from the French' ('Translation', pp. 56–7).

185. Elspeth Veale, 'Gregory, William (d. 1467)', *ODNB* 23, 685a–b.
186. *Pierce Penilesse His Supplication to the Divell* (1592), in *The Works of Thomas Nashe*, ed. Ronald B. McKerrow, with corrections and supplementary notes by F. P. Wilson, 5 vols (Oxford: Basil Blackwell, 1958), I, 137–245 (I, p. 194). Such authors, Nashe continues, 'want the wings of choise words to fly to heauen, which we haue: they cannot sweeten a discourse, or wrest admiration from men reading, as we can reporting the meanest accident… For my part, I do challenge no praise of learning to my selfe, yet haue I worne a gowne in the Vniversitie…' (I, pp. 194–5). See further R. S. Thomas, *Poems of R. S. Thomas* (Fayetteville: University of Arkansas Press, 1985).
187. Antonia Gransden, *Historical Writing in England, II: c. 1307 to the Early Sixteenth Century* (Ithaca: Cornell University Press, 1982), p. 220. Gransden points out that the *Brut* and London chronicles of the fifteenth century have common features because the former borrow directly from the latter (pp. 221–2).
188. 'We have forty-four extant manuscripts…We may presume that hundreds, perhaps thousands, were written' (Mary-Rose McLaren, *The London Chronicles of the Fifteenth Century: A Revolution in English Writing* (Cambridge: D.S. Brewer, 2002), p. 98). 1440, for McLaren, is to be seen as 'the peak of London chronicle writing' (p. 150).

lapucell de Dieu', Joan of Arc, to the burning of 'Richard hunden a wolle pakker' at Tower Hill.[189]

If we ask what Margery actually does in London during the long and frosty winter of 1434, her *Book* returns the answer: meditates upon the iniquities of textual circulation.[190] The text in question is a saying that has taken London by storm: '"A, thu fals flesch, thu schalt no good meat eaten!"' (8188). On first arriving in the city, Margery peers out at London like a woman in hiding: she wears a kerchief over her face, not wishing to be recognized until she acquires decent clothes. But the 'fals flesche' taunt is still thrown at her by 'sum dissolute personys, supposing it was Mar. Kempe of Lynn' (8185–6). This really burns her up, as she tells us at some length:

The forseyd wordys wer nevyr of hir spekyng, neythyr of God ne of good man, thow so wer that it wer leyd to hir, and sche many tymys and in many placys had gret repref therby. Thei [those words] wer fowndyn of the devyl, fadyr of lesyngys, favowryd, maynteynd, and born forth of hys membrys, fals invyows [envious] pepil, havyng indignacyon at hir vertuows levyng, not of powyr to hyndryn hir but thorw her [their] fals tungys. Ther was nevyr man ne woman that evyr myth prevyn [prove] that sche seyd swech wordys, but evyr thei madyn other lyars her autorys, seying in excusyng of hemself that other men telde hem so. On this maner wer thes fals wordys fowndyn thorw the develys suggestion.

(8189–8200)

And Margery is not done: she goes on to tell how the 'fals flesch' one-liner 'sprong into a maner of proverbe ayen hir' (8211), and how she finally faces it down at a dinner party thrown by a 'worschepful woman' (8219): '"I am that same persone to whom thes wordys ben arectyd [attributed]"' (8240–41). She works off some frustration by moving

189. Bradford, West Yorkshire Archives MS 32D86/42 as edited in McLaren, *London Chronicles*, 156–226 (p. 204). McLaren notes that fifteen of the twenty-three extant London chronicles covering this period make reference to the capture and death of Joan of Arc (p. 85); these events are part of London history.

190. According to the London chronicle preserved as Bradford, West Yorkshire Archives MS 32D86/42, there was 'a gret frost and a strong' in 1434 that lasted for more than eleven weeks (ed. McLaren, p. 206). See further the Chronicle preserved in BL Cotton Cleopatra C IV: 'in this same yere began a grete frost that began on Seynt Andrewys day and duryd vnto seynt Valentyn, and grete snowe with all, that grete multitude of Byrdes and fowlys dyed ffor honger' (*Chronicles of London*, ed. Charles Lethbridge Kingsford (Oxford: Clarendon Press, 1905), pp. 117–52 (p. 137)).

through London, denouncing 'boldly and mytily' all those who would
swear, curse, tell lies or wear fancy clothes in her presence; she then
goes upriver to Sheen to seek pardon from St Bridget of Sweden. And
then, finally, she heads back to Lynn to face the music before Robert
Spryngolde, her father confessor. She gets a righteous earful, but her
Book's closure is as sweet and complacent as the Wife of Bath's 'After
that day we hadden never debate' (3.822):

He yaf hir ful scharp wordys, for sche was hys obediencer and had takyn upon
hir swech a jurne wythowtyn hys wetyng [knowing]. Therfor he was mevyd
the mor ageyn hir, but owr Lord halpe hir so that sche had as good love of hym
and of other frendys aftyr as sche had beforn, worschepyd be God. Amen.

(8332–6)

The worshipful woman of Lynn

This ending is also, of course, her beginning: once reconciled with
Spryngolde, Margery addresses the making of her text. R. W. Chambers, in introducing the 1936 Kempe edition, gives no space to London
chroniclers: for Chambers, the continuities of English prose are almost
exclusively religious.[191] But if nothing else, I am suggesting, it is the
right confidently assumed by London skinners and aldermen to tell
their story—in a form previously reserved for monks and knights—
that grounds the extraordinary, indeed utterly unprecedented, confidence of *The Book of Margery Kempe*.[192] And if the skinner Lovelich

191. Chamber's valuation of the prose of 'the City Fathers' may be gauged from his characterization of an address by the Brewers to Henry V: 'Their English has very much
the air of a parvenu pressing into society where he is ill at ease' (*On the Continuity of
English Prose from Alfred to More*, p. cxvi). It is perhaps worth remembering, as later
dramatists and prose writers remembered, that Thomas More made his political
reputation by working within London mercantile and artisanal milieux. In his
'Introduction' to the 1936 'modern version', Chambers hails Kempe's *Book* as 'our
first extant prose narrative in English on a large scale: original, not translated, not a
mere succession of Chronicle entries, but a continuous biography' (ed. Butler-
Bowdon, p. 3).

192. The authorship of particular London chronicles remains very hard to determine;
their aim was to produce a common history, commonly recorded (see McLaren,
London Chronicles, p. 47). So while Margery is, I believe, energized and emboldened
by 'the appearance of the London chronicles *en masse* in the early fifteenth century'
(McLaren, p. 145), the individualist stamp of her chronicling—in this context of her
social peers—itself emerges as something all the more remarkable.

dared commit Merlin and the Grail to English, so Margery might share the miracle of her own life and travels. She chooses to work with a literate man of considerable religious education. But her *Book*'s propensity to wander into romance register can hardly be missed. In chapter 12 of Book I, Kempe has herself addressed as 'damsel': 'a form of address to a burgess's wife', says the EETS glossary, 'probably unparalleled in printed Middle English literature' (p. 393a). And on several occasions, Kempe pairs up the wearing of *hayr* and *haburgon* as equivalent forms of penance: that is, the hairshirt worn by dedicated religious, and the hauberk of chainmail worn by a knight.[193] All this perhaps subtends the most brilliant assessment made by a reviewer in 1936: 'her book is a kind of Froissart of the civil life'. The reviewer here—of immaculate Catholic credentials,[194] but possessing an eye for worldly detail and a taste for travel—is Graham Greene.[195] This invitation to view Margery's *Book* as composite generic object finds a splendid correlative in a cup at King's Lynn's town museum (Figure 17). This cup is beautifully enamelled with colourful scenes of ladies and gentlemen hawking and hunting (Figure 18); trappings added later, however, contrive to make it seem more like a chalice.[196] It is worth noting, finally, that Margery's last public act sees her follow in her father's footsteps (Figure 19). On 13 April 1438, Margery joins the Trinity Guild, *the* elite institution for the laity of Lynn; the writing of her Book II begins fifteen days later.

193. See *Book*, ed. Windeatt, ch. 11, lines 732–3; ch. 35, lines 2919–20; Kenneth Hodges, 'Wounded Masculinity: Injury and Gender in Sir Thomas Malory's *Le Morte Darthur*', *Studies in Philology*, 106.1 (2009), p. 15.

194. See *Articles of Faith: The Collected Tablet Journalism of Graham Greene*, ed. Ian Thomson (Oxford: Signal Books, 2006).

195. Graham Greene's review in *The Morning Post*, as cited in George Burns, 'Margery Kempe Reviewed', *The Month*, vol. 171 (March, 1938), p. 239. The notion that Kempe might be considered as a sort of English Froissart again directs attention back to the London chronicles.

196. The fashions of hunting dress, which provoke comparisons with Jehan de Grise's illustrations of the *Romance of Alexander* (1338–42), suggest a date in the second quarter of the fourteenth century; the cup is first mentioned in the *Hall Book of King's Lynn* in 1548 among items of plate delivered to the mayor. The cup is known as 'King John's cup'; the Trinity guild of Lynn (of which John Brunham—five times mayor of Lynn— and, ultimately, his daughter Margery were members) recognized King John as one of its founders. The Trinity guild possessed three silver gilt enamelled cups in 1421: see John Cherry, 'King John's Cup', in *King's Lynn and the Fens: Medieval Art, Architecture and Archaeology*, ed. John McNeill, The British Archaeological Association Conference Transactions, 31 (2008) (Leeds: Maney, 2008), pp. 4, 5, 13, 15.

Figure 17. King John's Cup, silver and enamel, second quarter of the fourteenth century, Town Museum, King's Lynn.

Julian of Norwich, the anchoress, did not counsel Margery Kempe to renounce the world: she advised her not to fear 'the langage of the world'. Although her father's death helped realize her vocation to travel, Margery never renounced the *worschepe* that she felt was his due, and hers,[197] as a member of the town elite, or *potenciores*.[198] She expected

---

197. Kempe, as Spearing observes, early on dresses ostentatiously to uphold the *worschyp* of her kin (268) and to be the more *worshepd* (262) by the burgers of Lynn ('Margery Kempe', p. 91). But the term endures and flourishes, remarkably, to the end of the text; and reference has already been made to 'owyr mercyful Lord Crist Jhesu, evyr to be trostyd, worshypd be hys name' (224–5).

198. As daughter of John Brunham, Anthony Goodman argues, Margery is positioned 'as born into the highest rank of the *potenciores*, part of the tightly knit network of

Figure 18. King John's Cup, detail of enamelled lid.

Figure 19. View of the guildhall, with the great window of the Trinity Guild, from the churchyard of St Margaret's, King's Lynn.

'worschepful' women in and of London to recognize her as their peer; and she shared the new-found confidence in literary self-representation of that London milieu. In travelling the world, rather than withdrawing from it, Margery has adventures that tend to the picaresque; the self-inspired journey of Book II, which begins by defying ecclesiastical authority, struggles to frame itself as conventional religious *life*. And yet Margery's core spiritual experience, one-on-one encounters with Jesus, shows a narrowed-down seriousness normally associated with enclosed female religious.[199] The term *mixed life*, associated with Hilton, seems too milktoast a term for the ferocious, contradictory energies of Margery's *Book*: the question of 'was Margery gewollt hat' turns out every bit as complex and intense as it was for Dorothea of Montau.[200] My chapter title's characterization of Margery Kempe as *anchoritic damsel* bids only to acknowledge, and not to resolve, the mysterious forcefields of her text. Her wonderful *Book* remains as elusive today as it did to her first, astonished readers in the 1930s. *Anchoritic damsel* does, however, gesture across the Reformation divide to the third *strong woman* in this book: a woman who believed that the sanctity and devotion of female religious enclosure might indeed be carried to the world, the 'holy Amazon' of Yorkshire, Mary Ward.

wealthy merchants who controlled the government' (*Margery Kempe and Her World*, p. 48). John Brunham served as mayor of Lynn in 1370, 1377, 1378, 1385, and 1391 and as MP for the borough in 1365, 1368, 1380, 1383, and 1384 (*World*, p. 49).

199. Yoko Wada dates seven of the surviving seventeen *Ancrene Wisse* manuscripts (in English, French, and Latin) to the fourteenth century, and two to the fifteenth; Hope Emily Allen was the first to trace the diffusion of *Ancrene Wisse*'s influence through the fourteenth and fifteenth centuries. Margery may be counted among that select group of laypersons (the few, the proud) who aspired to the seriousness of a solitary religious; yet her text (I am suggesting) also bespeaks pride in the lineage, romance, and *modus agendi* of mercantile life. See Wada, 'What is *Ancrene Wisse*', in *A Companion to Ancrene Wisse*, ed. Wada (Cambridge: D.S. Brewer, 2003), pp. 1–2; Vincent Gillespie, 'Vernacular Books of Religion', in *Book Production and Publishing in Britain, 1375–1475* (Cambridge: Cambridge University Press, 1989), pp. 319–21; Hope Emily Allen, 'Some Fourteenth Century Borrowings from *Ancrene Riwle*', *Modern Language Review*, 18 (1923), pp. 1–8; Allen, 'Further Borrowings from *Ancrene Riwle*', *MLR* 24 (1929), pp. 1–15; Catherine Innes-Parker, 'The Legacy of *Ancrene Wisse*: Translations, Adaptations, Influences, and Audience', with Special Attention to Women Readers', in *Companion*, ed. Wada, 145–73 (pp. 146–7, 155–65); Nicholas Watson, '*Ancrene Wisse*, Religious Reform, and the Late Middle Ages', in *Companion*, ed. Wada, 197–226 (pp. 216–222); Cate Gunn, *Ancrene Wisse: From Pastoral Literature to Vernacular Spirituality* (Cardiff: University of Wales Press, 2008), pp. 175–89.

200. For an interpretation of Margery's experience through the Hiltonian category of *mixed life*, see Naoë Kukita Yoshikawa, *Margery Kempe's Meditations: The Context of Medieval Devotional Literature, Liturgy, and Iconography* (Cardiff: University of Wales Press, 2007), pp. 120–33; on 'was Dorothea gewollt hat', see Chapter 1 above (p. 51).

3

Holy Amazon: Mary Ward of Yorkshire, 1585–1645

She had a most devine art in making this Life happy...it was ordinary to say her Presence made each place a court.

The Briefe Relation

She ys yonge, good dyatte will much help.

Mary Ward to Frances Bruxesby, 7 May 1637

Venerable Mary Ward, a native of this land whose pioneering vision of apostolic religious life for women has borne so much fruit.

Benedict XVI, 17 September 2010

Mary Ward was a strong woman: her closest followers referred to her as *mulier fortis,* the kind of woman celebrated by *Proverbs* 31.[1] Born and buried in Yorkshire, she loved her native country with rare passion: but her reach and appeal were, and are, global. She herself travelled (mostly walked) as far east as Bratislava, to the edge of Turkish domains, and as far south as Naples. Germany remained a heartland

---

1. The texts followed here are *Mary Ward und ihre Gründung: Die Quellentexte bis 1645,* ed. Ursula Dirmeier CJ, 4 vols, Corpus Catholicorum 45–8 (Münster: Aschendorff Verlag, 2007); *Mary Ward (1585–1645): A Briefe Relation...with Autobiographical Fragments and a Selection of Letters,* ed. Christina Kenworthy-Browne CJ (Woodbridge: Boydell Press for the Catholic Record Society, 2008). I follow Kenworthy-Browne for the *Briefe Relation* (with page numbers) and Dirmeier for all else (with volume, page). There are marked variations of spelling within and between texts (attesting, perhaps, to women living between languages in England and continental Europe). The *Briefe Relation* (or *English Life*) favours capitalization of substantives in Germanic fashion; the three St-Omer addresses capitalize very little (not even *god*). I follow original spellings and capitalizations but make occasional

of her movement, and later Ireland, but subsequent expansion followed the sealanes of the British Empire; Canada and South Africa, India and Australia remain strongholds. By 1900, 70,000 girls were being educated in 200 schools by some 6,000 of her followers. And yet none of these might acknowledge her by name; not until 1909 did the Vatican permit her to be recognized as founder of her own movement.[2] What could explain such clerical *animus,* sustained over hundreds of years? Firstly, Mary Ward had defied a papal bull: when *Pastoralis Romanis Pontifici* was published in 1631, abolishing her movement, Mary (for complex reasons) thought that it might be ignored. But secondly, and most significantly, she believed in the right of religious women *not* to be immured or enclosed, but to conduct an apostolate of the streets. She also affirmed the salvific power of female society *and* a woman's right (and duty, to herself) to pursue aloneness with God. But it was clearly the practise of sending religious women to the streets that most unnerved Rome. Here again, geography proves crucial: the southern European men who dominated the *curia* at Rome were simply not prepared for, lacked the cultural literacy to read, this *femina ex aquilone.* For it is clear that Mary Ward's thinking about individual and collective female mission is grounded in, and perennially returns to, her formative years among the persecuted Catholics of England.

Pastoralis Romanis Pontifici is an exceptionally harsh and weighty bull.[3] But it was not until the 1980s that Mary Ward's followers, on first being given access to the key Vatican archives, realized quite how strongly

---

light amendments of punctuation. Translations are mine unless otherwise indicated; I make a few textual emendations [in square brackets]. In its final paragraph, the *Italian Life* affirms that 'we may fittingly acclaim her with that title Mulierem fortem, which she, so to speak, made her own during her childhood' (IV, 145). The phrase 'Mulierem fortem' occurs in *The English Life,* p. 87; the phrase then repeats ('In this quality of Mulieris fortis, whatsoever seemed great in this world, whither in point of honnour, fame, Ritches, or pleasure, was meane and of noe value with her', p. 87). On *mulier fortis,* see above, p. xv, n. 1.

2. Retha M. Warnicke, *Women of the English Renaissance and Reformation* (Westport, Conn.: Greenwood Press, 1983), p. 177; Pamela Ellis, '"They are but Women": Mary Ward, 1585–1645', in *Women, Gender, and Radical Religion in Early Modern Europe,* ed. Sylvia Brown (Leiden: Brill, 2007), p. 261.

3. For a translation, see Margaret Mary Littlehales CJ, *Mary Ward: Pilgrim and Mystic, 1585–1645* (Tunbridge Wells: Burns and Oates, 1998), pp. 253–7; for a photograph, see José Maria Javierre, with Maria de Pablo-Romero IBVM, *La Jesuitessa Mary Ward: Mujer rebelde que rompió moldes en la Europa del XVII* (Madrid: Libros Libres, 2002), p. 491.

Urban VIII had set himself against Ward's movement.[4] These revelations would have surprised her, since this pope seemed always to show great, one might say *courtly*, solicitude towards her. Pope Urban was indeed a cultured man. As plain Maffeo Barberini, before his election, he had written poetry in both Latin and Italian, favouring a Petrarchan idealizing and affirming of women (rather than new currents of baroque misogyny, associated with Giovanni Battista Marino); he also favoured his nephew's wife, Anna Colonna, as the subject of a literary cult.[5] He plainly felt Mary Ward's celebrated personal *charism* during the years that he detained her at Rome. At the same time, however, he set himself determinedly to wreck all that she had presumed to build. Dawning realization of all this drove women in Mary Ward's movement to pointed comparisons with papal treatment of her fellow revolutionary and fellow prisoner of Urban VIII, Galileo Galilei (1564–1642):[6] surely the time for rehabilitation had come? In early October 2009, over a thousand women converged on Rome to celebrate the 400th anniversary of Mary Ward's Institute; Benedict XVI, sweeping by in his popemobile, saw a huge banner reading *Mary Ward: Santa Presto*.

Margery Kempe erupted into public consciousness as World War II loomed over England; Mary Ward's moment is *now*. Before 2007, not one sentence of the early Mary Ward *lives* and autobiographical fragments (in English, Italian, and French) was available as originally written, and her marvellous cache of correspondence remained under lock and key at Schloss Nymphenburg, Munich (birthplace of mad King Ludwig of Bavaria; home to a house of her order). Now, however, all is revealed in five magnificent volumes.[7] It thus becomes possible, for

---

4. See Immolata Wetter CJ, *Mary Ward under the Shadow of the Inquisition*, tr. Bernadette Ganne CJ and Patricia Harriss CJ (Oxford: Way Books, 2006); this book first appeared in German in 2003.

5. See Virginia Cox, *Women's Writing in Italy, 1400–1650* (Baltimore: Johns Hopkins University Press, 2008), pp. 166–95 (a section entitled 'The Rebirth of Misogyny in Seicento Italy').

6. See Littlehales, *Mary Ward*, pp. 132–133. Immolata Wetter CJ finds Pope John Paul II's assessment of relations between Rome and the astronomer applicable to those with Mary Ward: 'una tragica incomprensione reciproca' (*Maria Ward: Misverständnisse und Klärung* (Augsburg: Augsburger Universität, 1993), p. 13).

7. See note 1 above. Half a century earlier, Jesuit scholar Josef Grisar, in a volume published by Rome's Gregorian University, provided a full critical study and edition of the texts written to Rome in 1622 by eight different men, or groups of men, intent on suppressing the 'Englishen Fräulein': see *Die ersten Anklagen in Rom gegen das Institut Maria Wards, 1622* (Roma: Pontificia Università Gregoriana, 1959).

the first time, to follow the *life* of Yorkshire's *mulier fortis* through (and this is a rarity, for premodern Catholic women's writing) a female-mediated textual corpus. We will see a process of slow, individual discernment (*how* should I live?) expanding rapidly into a women's movement that galvanizes Europe. Half of Europe—what might be termed the imperial, or Ghibelline, sphere—is charmed and convinced. The other, papal or Guelf, is (we have noted) unnerved. On 19 December 2009, however, Mary Ward was proclaimed a woman of 'heroic virtue'[8] by Benedict XVI and awarded the title 'Venerable'. It may seem puzzling to see the current uptick in Mary's fortunes unfolding on the watch of a pope considered conservative, even by Vatican standards: but he is a northern European, German rather than Italian.[9] And, as he remarked in London on 17 September 2010, 'I myself as a young boy was taught by the "English Ladies" and I owe them a deep debt of gratitude'.[10] It seems miraculous, from the long perspective of this chapter, to witness a successor of Urban VIII thanking God 'for the life and work of the Venerable Mary Ward, a native of this land whose pioneering vision of apostolic religious life for women has borne so much fruit'.[11]

Merviling what you entend: Mary Ward *in medias res*

In December 1617, Mary Ward, in her early thirties, delivered a series of three addresses to some sixty women at St-Omer in Spanish Flanders, thirty miles inland from Calais. These women were English Roman Catholics who had been inspired and drawn by Mary Ward to a way of life never before seen: 'you are spectakells to god, angells and men', she tells them: 'it is certaine that god has looked uppon you,

8. 'Le virtù eroiche' of nine others were acknowledged on the same day, including Pius XII and John Paul II; Mary Ward is acknowledged as 'Fondatrice dell'Istituto delle Suore della Beata Maria Vergine, oggi Congregazione di Gesù' (Seraphin.Vatican.va/news, 19 December 2009).
9. And he was, as a Bavarian schoolboy, educated by the Englische Fräulein.
10. Pope Benedict XVI, Address to Teachers and Religious, Chapel of St Mary's College, Twickenham, Friday 17 September 2010 <http://www.thepapalvisit.org.uk>. Young Josef Ratzinger was indeed taught by the 'Englische Fräulein' of Mary Ward as a Bavarian schoolboy.
11. Twickenham address <http://www.thepapalvisit.org.uk>.

as he never looked uppon any'; 'all looketh uppon you', she continues, 'as new beginners of a cours never thought of before; merviling what you entend and what will be the end of you'.[12] What they intend, as religious women, is to bond affectionately[13] as a female society and to live with the probity of enclosed religious, but not to be enclosed. Pressure for religious women to accept strict enclosure had been growing since Boniface VIII, Dante's least favourite pope, had slipped an edict into a bull in 1298 and called it *Periculoso*. This, it was argued, represented no more than the enforcement of prior legislation. This was quite spurious: neither the Benedictine nor Augustinian rules mention perpetual *clausura*; a watertight convent could hardly perform those acts of hospitality and almsgiving that these rules do require.[14] Efforts were made, in Mary Ward's native Yorkshire as elsewhere in Britain and Ireland, to enforce the new regime in the early fourteenth century: but local bishops soon gave up, and religious houses again became permeable to their local communities.[15] The Counter-Reformational Council of Trent, however, showed renewed determination to enforce *Periculoso*; Pius V passed more stringent measures yet in 1566 with *Circa Pastoralis*.[16] This bull came just eleven years after *Cum nimis absurdum*, the canon requiring the enclosure of

12. *Mary Ward*, ed. Dirmeier, I, 363.
13. According to *A Briefe Relation*, Mary Ward's last words to her gathered followers at Heworth were "'I comend unto you the practise of your vocation that it be constant, efficacious, and affectionate", which last word came with a particular accent, after which embracing each, spake noe more' (ed. Kenworthy-Browne, p. 73).
14. See Francesca Medioli, 'An Unequal Law: The Enforcement of *Clausura* Before and After the Council of Trent', in *Women in Renaissance and Early Modern Europe*, ed. Christine Meek (Dublin: Four Courts Press, 2000), pp. 138–9, 145; Elizabeth Makowski, *Canon Law and Cloistered Women: Periculoso and its Commentators, 1298–1545* (Washington DC: Catholic University of America Press, 1997).
15. Nuns in Yorkshire were soon allowed one visit per year to friends and family again, and then two; lodgers could be readmitted to help impoverished convents; recreations and relaxations were (Archbishop Melton decreed in 1318) to be encouraged. See John Tillotson, 'Visitation and Reform of the Yorkshire Nunneries in the Fourteenth Centuries', *Northern History*, 30 (1994), pp. 10–11. On the local permeability of nunneries, see Nancy Bradley Warren, *Spiritual Economies: Female Monasticism in Later Medieval England* (Philadelphia: University of Pennsylvania Press, 2001).
16. See Medioli, 'Unequal Law', pp. 138–9, 144–52; Claire Walker, *Gender and Politics in Early Modern Europe: English Convents in France and the Low Countries* (Basingstoke: Palgrave Macmillan, 2003), pp. 45–54.

the ghetto at Rome across the river from the Vatican; Jews, like nuns, were locked in at night.[17]

Ironically, the harsh imagining of women's religious enclosure on English Renaissance stages, as in *A Midsommer nights dreame* and *Measure for Measure*, owes much to Counter-Reformation practise and little to English monastic tradition.[18] But resistance to enclosure, as staged at St-Omer in 1617, was a bold step, and Mary Ward knew that men, male clerics, were sceptical. A prominent Jesuit at Rome, she tells us, opined that the itinerant women of her movement might enjoy some esteem 'while they are in ther fervour, but fervour will decay, and when all is done they are but wemen'.[19]

This dismissive one-liner becomes the starting point of Mary Ward's first address to the women at St-Omer: 'I would know what you all thinke', she asks them, 'he meant by this spech of his "But women"'. 'Veritas Domini manet in aeternum', she quotes at them: 'the verity of our Lorde remaneth forever. It is not veritas hominum, verity of men, nor veritie of weomen, but veritas Domini, and this veritie wemen may have, as well as men. If we fayle, it is for want of this verity and not because we are weomen' (I, 358). In discovering and holding fast to *verity* or truth, Mary Ward insists, women must look to themselves: for the Jesuit fathers esteemed so highly by Catholic women back in England may not be there *ad infinitum*; women must work out their own salvation. 'Hertofore we have ben told by men we *must* belewe; it is

---

17. The opening of *Cum nimis absurdum* (1555) reads as follows: 'it is profoundly absurd and intolerable that the Jews, who are bound by their guilt to perpetual servitude, should show themselves ungrateful towards Christians' (as cited in Roberto Bonfil, *Jewish Life in Renaissance Italy*, tr. Anthony Oldcorn (Berkeley: University of California Press, 1994), p. 67. The bull anticipates the mass conversion of the Jews (Bonfil, p. 67), a notion recently revived, by a prayer in a rite, by Benedict XVI. On Sunday, 17 January 2010, Benedict, the second pope known to enter a Jewish house of worship, followed his predecessor, John Paul II, to the main synagogue at Rome (within the former ghetto, across the Tiber from the Vatican). This came one month after his advancement of Pius XII towards canonization (see above); a thousand Roman Jews were deported during the Nazi occupation of 1943.

18. See David Wallace, 'Nuns', in *Cultural Reformations: Medieval and Renaissance in Literary History*, ed. Brian Cummings and James Simpson (Oxford: Oxford University Press, 2010), p. 519.

19. I, 357. The Jesuit in question here is Yorkshireman Michael Freeman (1578–1642); ordained priest in Rome in 1603, he held positions at the English College, St-Omer (1617–18, 1621) and at York (1623–34); he died at Durham. See Thomas M. McCoog SJ, *English and Welsh Jesuits 1555–1650*, 2 vols, continuous pagination, Catholic Record Society Publications (Records Series), 74–5 (CRS, 1994–5), pp. 177–8.

true we must, but lett us be wise, and know *what* we are to belive, and what not, and not to be made to thinke that we can doe nothing'.[20] Each of these religious women, we might say, must be her own Jesuit. This statement might seem egregious: except that what Mary Ward has in mind *is* a movement or Institute of women that is to be based upon the Jesuit constitutions.

For twelve years or so after this inspirational gathering at St-Omer, Mary Ward's Institute goes from strength to strength: educational and apostolic work is performed, to great acclaim from local populations, at Bratislava (Pressburg), Cologne, Liège, London, Munich, Naples, Perugia, Prague, Rome, St-Omer, Trèves (Trier, Treviso), and Vienna. In 1631, however, *Pastoralis Romanis Pontifici* poleaxes her movement; it was to quash equivalent initiatives by women for generations to come. 'By the Bull', the English *Briefe Relation* tells us, 'she saw not onely, as it were, a period to her further Labours in what was dearer to her then than life, but such a ruine of her passed Labours, the losse of so many houses put into a being by her so great Labours and paynes'.[21] English Catholic fathers were now unwilling to stump up dowry money that would help fund Mary's Institute. Back in England, 'in the last yeares of her Life', Mary Ward could see 'many seeming occasions occurring, wherby God might singularly be served, our Course of Life subsist and needy soules holpen, and all this unfactable for want of money, great Losses having been caused by the Bull' (p. 92). Her course of life might thus seem disastrous. As a good, Latin-literate etymologist, however, Mary might argue that her life was no *dis-astre*, a malignancy of stars and planets: for we must, she says in her second St-Omer address, 'make our benefits of all things that happen as cumming from the hand of god, for the scripture sayeth a sparrow falleth to the ground, but by the spetiall providence of god . . . I verily thinke', she continues, 'it is the best and easiest way to vertue to take everie thing, be it never so little, as from god' (I, 361). This was perhaps easy to say in 1617: but the remarkable thing about Mary Ward is that she continues to say it and mean it after 1631 and for the rest of her life. Such serene faith in Providence must have been hard to sustain for her closest associates, doubly exiled from England and Rome, in

---

20. I, 359; emphases added.
21. *Briefe Relation*, p. 77; see further p. 80 ('the totall destruction of 30 or more years Labours').

composing her *life*. Generically, they sometimes seem caught between *hagiography* and *romance*—especially when telling of a heroine who, from her earliest days, is romanced by a God whose intentions are obscure; who is absolute in his demands, and tactically ruthless.

If Mary Ward is indeed to advance from her new-found Venerability 'towards beatification and eventual canonization', as a current website proclaims, then her *life* might read differently again: for her long game of trust in Providence would indeed turn out to be, for her followers, *veritas Domini*.[22]

The earliest surviving biographical notices of Mary Ward were written by her younger sister, Barbara, between 1619 and 1624.[23] The *Briefe Relation* or *English Life* of Mary Ward was written soon after her death at Heworth, just outside York, in 1645; it was likely complete by the time her surviving companions left for Paris in 1650.[24] Mary Poyntz is now recognized as principal author, with the assistance of Winefrid Wigmore. Wigmore translated the *English Life* into French some time before dying at Paris in 1657; and there is a version in German dating from the early eighteenth century.[25] In what follows I refer chiefly to the *English Life* (*Briefe Relation*), but with supplementation from the *Italian Life*, a text associated with Mary Poyntz's sojourn in Rome as third chief superior of the Institute from 1654 to 1662.[26] An Italian autobiographical fragment, written by Mary Ward herself, covers the

22. Mary Ward, as we will see, was a great believer in prayer to saints; at what point, for her followers, might she become a figure not to be prayed for, but prayed to? The website in question is *www.ibvm.org* (accessed January 2010).

23. For these three fragments, see *Mary Ward*, ed. Dirmeier, IV, 1–3. Barbara, born in 1592, joined Mary at Saint-Omer and accompanied her to Rome (where she died, in 1623): see Henriette Peters CJ, *Mary Ward: A World in Contemplation*, tr. Helen Butterworth CJ (Leominster: Gracewing, 1995), p. 313.

24. The earliest surviving manuscript of the *Briefe Relation,* dated 1716, has been at the Bar Convent, York, since 1988. There is one other manuscript, closely related and known as the Hammersmith/Manchester manuscript; the nineteenth-century copy at York is based chiefly on this manuscript. See *Mary Ward*, ed. Kenworthy-Browne, pp. 1–2.

25. The two surviving French manuscripts, now both at York, date from the seventeenth century; the German manuscript is associated with Bamberg (a house founded from Augsburg in 1717). See *Mary Ward*, ed. Kenworthy-Browne, p. 2.

26. Mary Poyntz has herself been suggested as author. Dirmeier observes that the author, not a native Italian, was clearly a long-standing associate of Mary Ward who was witness to her last days (IV, 100; for the text see IV, 100–145). The Italian text freely reworks the English original, cutting and summarizing quite drastically but adding details that might pique the interest of Italian readers; 'Charakterisierung' of Urban VIII (as Dirmeier delicately puts it) is restrained (IV, 100).

years 1600 to 1609.[27] There is also the rich cache of letters in Munich, many of them autograph. Some are written in lemon juice, a notable sign (according to Thomas Middleton's *A Game at Chess*) of Jesuit influence.[28] Also in Germany is an extraordinary sequence of fifty large oil paintings, known as *Das Gemalte Leben*, or *The Painted Life*: these were commissioned once the indefatigable Mary Poyntz had moved from Rome to found the house at Augsburg in 1662; they are as yet little studied, and are thought to be the work of five different hands.[29] Domenicus a Jesu Maria, a celebrated Spanish discalced Carmelite, warned Mary Ward's closest followers not 'to lett her Life and Example passe without note, not onely for our owne, but others their profit' (pp. 29–30). Mary Ward's life was thus being drawn to memory by her intimates even as she continued to live it.[30]

English country house education

Mary Ward spent more than half her life, and most of her adult years, in continental Europe; her letters show marked macaronic or inter-lingual tendencies. But her first twenty-one years were spent in England; this formative time, spent chiefly in country houses, suggests some parallels with the formative experiences of other well-educated Tudor and Stuart Englishwomen. Most of them, to a greater or lesser extent, lived *between* Catholic and Anglican terms of reference. Mary Sidney, like

27. This is thought to date from the time of Mary's first sojourn in Rome, between 1624–6: see *Mary Ward*, ed. Dirmeier, I, 31–49, and for a translation *Mary Ward*, ed. Kenworthy-Browne, pp. 121–40.

28. See *A Game at Chess*, ed. R. C. Bald (Cambridge: Cambridge University Press, 1929): 'The Jesuite has writ this with juice of lemmans sure / It must bee held closse to the fire of Purgatorie / Er't can be read' (I.i.335–37). As Middleton suggests, writing in lemon juice remains invisible until held to the fire. A large number of these letters in Mary Ward's hand survive at Nymphenburg: see Mary C. E. Chambers IBVM, *The Life of Mary Ward*, ed. H. J. Coleridge SJ, 2 vols. (London: Burnes and Oates, 1882–5), II, p. 351. For a letter written by Mary from London in this medium, see Littlehales, *Mary Ward*, p. 233 (illus. 17).

29. See Immolata Wetter CJ, *Tenth Letter of Instruction* (Institute circulation), i–x, as cited in Jennifer J. Cameron IBVM, *A Dangerous Innovator* (Strathfield, New South Wales: St Pauls, 2000), p. 254. Access to the complete series of the paintings on several sites is now an easy Google (Ward Painted Life). For transcriptions of the German panel texts that appear in each of the fifty paintings, see *Mary Ward*, ed. Dirmeier, IV, 296–304.

30. We often find them noting little remarks made by Mary Ward, rather like the 'sayings of Jesus' that form the core of the Gospel accounts.

Anglo-Saxon nuns before her, contemplated psalms at Wilton; she waited out a planned invasion there in 1588 as learned noblewomen had waited in 1066. Mary Ward's exact contemporary, Elizabeth Cary (née Tanfield), was growing up Protestant in a house formerly occupied by Augustinian hospitallers.[31] Aemelia Lanyer, daughter of an Italian musician, was to pen the first country house poem before 1611 at Cookham, a royal manor formerly controlled by Cirencester Abbey; her poem floats curiously between Anglican and Catholic terms of reference.[32] In 1645, the year that Mary Ward and Aemelia Lanyer died, Elizabeth and Jane Cavendish composed *The Concealed Fansyes* at Welbeck (a sometime abbey of Premonstratensian canons, founded by Thomas de Cuckney in 1140). At two points in the play, the sisters actually enter as nuns, or as the ghosts of two nuns, dressed in 'white sheet of Innocence', and regretting the general state of 'sadness' in which they dwell.[33] Welbeck had hosted a Catholic queen as recently as 1642, when Henrietta Maria was received by the earl of Newcastle and then escorted to the king at Oxford. Upon his return in 1660, following years of Parisian exile, Newcastle brought Margaret Cavendish with him: the self-styled 'She-Anchoret'[34] authoress of con-

31. See further Ch. 4 below.
32. See 'The Description of Cooke-ham', *Salve Deus Rex Judaeorum*, in *The Poems of Aemelia Lanyer*, ed. Susanne Woods (New York: Oxford University Press, 1993), pp. 128–38. Woods characterizes *Salve Deus*, which culminates with the 'Cooke-ham' section, as 'this unapologetic creation of a community of good women for whom another woman is the spokesperson and commemorator' (p. xxxi).
33. *The Concealed Fansyes*, in *Renaissance Drama by Women: Texts and Documents*, ed. S. P. Cerasano and Marion Wynne-Davies (London: Routledge, 1996), 5.2.13. Citations follow this modernized edition; for an original spelling version, see Nathan Comfort Starr, '*The Concealed Fancies*: A Play by Lady Elizabeth Cavendish and Lady Elizabeth Brackley', *Publications of the Modern Language Association*, 46 (1931), pp. 802–38. The stage direction at the beginning of 5.2, cut by Cerasano and Wynne-Davis, is '*Enter the 2 Nunns mallencholly speakeing to one another*' (830); before 4.1.44 the direction, also cut, is '*Luceny the Nunn sings*' (824). Both editions are based upon Oxford, Bodleian Library, MS Rawlinson Poet. 16.
34. Cavendish wrote a novella with this title; she also, as Jennifer Summit observes, expressed the fantasy (in her autobiography) of 'enclosing myself like an anchoret' (cited in *Lost Property: The Woman Writer and English Literary History, 1380–1589* (Chicago: University of Chicago Press, 2000), p. 207). See further Margaret Cavendish, duchess of Newcastle, *The Convent of Pleasure and Other Plays*, ed. Anne Shaver (Baltimore: Johns Hopkins University Press, 1999). Cavendish's *The Female Academy*, not included in this anthology, is notably *not* infiltrated by masculine desire: as its frustrated First Gentleman laments in the last scene, the ladies 'will not permit us to come into their Company, but have barricadoed their Gats against us, and have incloystred themselves from us; besides, it is a dangerous example for all the rest of their Sex; for if all women should take a toy in their heads to incloyster themselves, there would be none left out to breed on' (The Lady Marchioness of Newcastle, *Playes* (London, 1662), p. 679).

vent dramas. As a landed gentry-class Elizabethan with aristocratic connections, Mary Ward received an excellent 'big house' education that
compares favourably with that of her dramatically-inclined peers: she
learned Italian and wrote Latin fluently, showing considerable 'flair for
the *colores* of classical rhetoric, poetry, and logic'.[35] Her ability to *play
herself out of* sticky situations, like a true stage heroine, was crucial to her
early development; her later vicarious appearances upon London stages
thus seem a fitting tribute.[36] The performing of plays, particularly comedies, was to form a distinctive part of her later teaching regimen. This
would much alarm Thomas Rant, agent of the English secular clergy in
Rome: 'the Jesuitesses (faeminae Jesuitissae) lead a loose life. They run
about all over England', he complains to the *curia* in 1624, 'and associate
with men. They refuse to pray in choir or to follow conventual practises
and, on the Continent, they train their pupils for just such a daring life
by the production of plays (ludis scenicis). In doing so they are a threat
to the women of England and a scandal to Catholics'.[37]

Not all English Catholics disapproved of Catholic dramatics: the
Jesuits were famed for their use of plays as educators.[38] Thomas Rant,
as champion of English secular clergy, saw himself *de facto* as enemy of
the Jesuits in England: such was the self-destructive logic within English Catholicism. Mary Ward, as *Jesuitessa,* was naturally associated with
the Jesuits; they certainly exerted significant influence upon her formation. The Jesuit confessor at the Babthorpe's manor of Osgodby,

---

35. James Walsh SJ, 'Introduction' to *Till God Will: Mary Ward through her Writings*, ed.
Emmanuel Orchard IBVM, foreword by Mother Teresa of Calcutta (London: Darton,
Longman and Todd, 1985), p. xviii. Ward remained dedicated to imparting Latin literacy to young girls (even poor ones) throughout her life: see Warnicke, *Women of the
English Renaissance*, pp. 174–5, 198–9. As Warnicke notes (p. 176), it was vital for Ward
and her companions to leave the cloister to properly serve the poor children they
proposed to teach, since these poor pupils could not observe the rule of enclosure
that the Council of Trent had recently imposed upon all female communities and
their students. On the high importance attached to rhetorical training for Jesuits, see
Grant Boswell, 'Letter Writing among the Jesuits: Antonio Possevino's Advice in the
Bibliotheca Selecta (1583)', *Huntington Library Quarterly*, 66.3–4 (2003), pp. 247–9.
36. See further below, p. 181–3.
37. Peters, *Mary Ward*, p. 389; *Mary Ward*, ed. Dirmeier, II, 63. For further play-related
activity, see below.
38. 'For more than two centuries', writes Paul V. Murphy, 'Jesuit drama in Milan and
elsewhere acted as a school of virtue and a method of teaching how to live actively in
the world' ('Jesuit Rome and Italy', in *The Cambridge Companion to the Jesuits*, ed.
Thomas Worcester (Cambridge: Cambridge University Press, 2008), p. 80).

where the young Mary spent some six and a half years (1599–1605), remarked that 'our house I might rather count as a religious house than otherwise'.[39] Yet this milieu, with its three knights and three ladies, plus extended family and domestic servants, still lived and functioned largely *as* a household in the Elizabethan–Jacobean mould. The sewing circle scene at Osgodby (*Painted Life*, 9; Figure 20), with its open workbasket and the lapdog curled up on a cushion, seems the epitome of contemporary country house living; even the painting of St George slaying his dragon seems unexceptionable. Such evocation of female companionship recalls a myriad of Elizabethan and Jacobean scenes, most memorably, perhaps, that recollected by Shakespeare's Helena, who recalls sharing childhood needlework with Hermia, 'sitting on one cushion'.[40]

The Protestant marriage imperative has already cast these two young women as rivals by this point of *A Midsommer nights dreame*.[41] Mary Ward and Osgodby's Barbara Babthorpe, however, will remain close (sharing exile together) for the rest of their lives. Mary Ward recognized herself 'apt for friendship', and in following the Ignatian Spiritual Exercises in 1619 resolved (under the subheading 'mortification') that 'I will sometimes...absent my self volluntarylie from the company of thos I more perticulerly affect'.[42] The powers of affect binding these women remained phenomenally strong. Only very occasionally, when

---

39. James Sharpe SJ, alias Pollard, as cited in Chambers, *Life*, I, 40; see further Littlehales, *Mary Ward*, p. 26; Peters, *Mary Ward*, pp. 44–49; McCoog, *English and Welsh Jesuits*, p. 292. Conditions for Catholics were easier in the south. Near Hastings, Magdalen Lady Montague, widowed in 1592, presided over a household of some eighty persons known locally as 'little Rome'; three priests, including the great-grandson of Thomas More, provided pre-Tridentine services. Elizabeth I actually came to visit in 1591; see Warnicke, *Women of the English Renaissance*, pp. 167–68.

40. *A Midsommer nights dreame*, in *Mr. William Shakespeares Comedies, Histories, & Tragedies* (London: Isaac Jaggard, 1623), p. 154.

41. 'Because in theory the place of married women was at home', writes Retha Warnicke of Protestant households, 'wives, too, were prevented from organizing together to accomplish social changes...By contrast, in convents and especially in teaching congregations, women were taught to work with one another for religious and sometimes for social endeavors' (*Women of the English Renaissance*, p. 179). In a letter to Jesuit General Mutius (Muzio) Vitelleschi at the beginning of 1622, Mary Ward argues elegantly and impeccably for a religious woman's right (and obligation) *not* to marry: she has already been spoken for by God, and 'yt must needs be fitt for princes to be ther owne chusers' (I, 604).

42. I, 471; see further Chambers, *Life*, I, 449–61; Littlehales, *Mary Ward*, pp. 67, 95.

Figure 20. *Painted Life*, 9: Mary Ward, aged fifteen, and the sewing circle at Osgodby.

persecuted by men who were supposedly their religious allies, did the pride or *disdegno* of lofty lineage peek through.[43] More often, however, we seem close to the plot of a country house drama as key moments of their evolving relationships are played out. The young Mary Poyntz, for example, finding herself under extreme pressure from the suit of a young cavalier, looks out of a window at Tockington Park to see Mary Ward walking in the pleasure garden: 'see, there she is', she exclaims, 'through whose instructions God will save me'. Pressured to give her gallant a portrait, she presents him with an image (still extant) that is true to life on one side of the face, and a worm-eaten death's head on the other. She becomes one of Mary's original group of seven; he joins a religious order.[44]

---

43. On Winefrid Wigmore's unfortunate outburst against a papal nuntius, see p. 183 below.
44. See Chambers, *Life*, I, 239–41, plus the alarming image at pp. 240–41; Gregory Kirkus CJ, *The Companions of Mary Ward* (Strasbourg: Éditions du Signe, 2009), pp. 39–41 (image, p. 40).

Mary Ward's early country house life might also be compared, in its more sober aspects, with that of Margaret, Lady Hoby, who kept a meticulous diary (1599–1605) while living in the same county of Yorkshire.[45] Margaret, who grew up in the household of the earl and countess of Huntingdon, made two quick and spectacular marriages: first to Walter Devereux, brother to the earl of Essex; and second to Thomas Sidney, brother to the sainted Philip and to Mary Herbert. Happily situated as a wealthy young double-widow in 1595, she endured an 'undignified treasure-hunt' of a courtship by Thomas Hoby but remained detached.[46] Hoby, however, was nephew to Lord Treasurer Burghley and the creature of Lord Huntingdon (charged with the suppression of Catholicism in the north). Margaret married, moved to Yorkshire, and began her remarkable journaling of events large and small. In Margaret's *Diary*, occasionally we glimpse Mr Hoby in pursuit of his religious quarry, as on Monday, 24 March 1600: 'Mr Hoby went that night to search a house for papests'.[47] Mostly, however, we see Margaret regulating her own great house and those who found their way to it. She gives basic instruction on the responsibilities of godfathers (p. 107); she is up 'in the granerie receiuing Corne' (p. 94); she marvels at a calf with two great heads and two ears (p. 171); she dresses 'apoore boies legge that Came to me' (p. 100). On Tuesday 25 August 1601, she is 'busie all the day' preparing her house to receive Thomas, Lord Burghley, her husband's cousin, lord president of the council of the north; the following day she performs major surgery on her kitchen table upon a local child born with no anus (p. 184). Margaret Hoby, while typically anxious to portray herself busy 'about som Huswiffrie', also finds 'that buseneses hindereth wanderinge Coggetation' (p. 109). She thus shared a rhythm of life with those other women in great houses who have left us literary remains—including those Catholic

---

45. *Diary of Lady Margaret Hoby, 1599–1605*, ed. Dorothy M. Meads (London: Routledge, 1930); all citations follow this edition.
46. The splendid phrase is that of Meads (ed.), *Diary*, p. 28.
47. *Diary*, ed. Meads, p. 110; see further pp. 261–62 for details of the activities that made Hoby unpopular in the district that, according to Meads, 'provided excellent lurking places for the priests of the old religion and their staunch adherents' (p. 261). Seventeen days after Mr Hoby's nocturnal Catholic-chasing, Margaret visited York Minster, 'wher I hard Mr Smith defend the truth against the papest' (p. 113).

families, such as the Wards, that her husband busily persecuted by night. Perhaps less obviously, she perpetuated the social function fulfilled by great houses of an earlier time, those convents and monasteries to which any child with a bad leg, or with 'no fundement', would be taken when all else failed.

Enfance religieuse: a Yorkshire childhood

According to the *Italian Life*, as adapted by the highly-pedigreed Mary Poyntz,[48] Mary Ward's paternal ancestors came over in 1066 with 'il duca Gugliemo (detto volgarmente il Conquistatore)'.[49] At that time the Ward family, so the *Italian Life* says, 'counted seven brothers of the Order of Golden Knights, a title in those days more highly regarded than is nowadays that of marquis (marchese)'.[50] Such embellishment of the Ward pedigree, and feudal romanticizing of England, reflects canny understanding of the Italian market. *Decameron* II, 3, for example, imagines far-off Britain as a playground of exotic, chivalric wonders: its young Florentine protagonist, who has prospered by mortgaging the castles of English barons, is seduced by an English abbot. She happily turns out to be the king of England's daughter; he becomes the first Italian earl of Cornwall and then, by right of conquest, king of Scotland.[51] Mary Ward's father is accordingly praised as a man much loved by his vassals, *vassalli;* his prowess in knightly arms, and his perfection in countenance, body, bearing, and manners is celebrated with a sequence of *–issimo* superlatives that Italian does best: 'bellissimo di volto, proportionatissimo di corpo, suavissimo nel tratto, compitissimo

---

48. Her ancestor Sir Robert Poyntz was knighted on Bosworth Field for valour by the new monarch, Henry VII, in 1485; his second son, John, was recipient of the famous epistolary poem by Sir Thomas Wyatt that bears his name. The family seat was long established at Iron Acton, Gloucestershire; the local parish church is full of Poyntz ancestors in medieval armour. See Kirkus, *Companions*, pp. 38–9.

49. *Breve relatione della santa vita, e felice morte della Signora Donna Maria della Guardia nostra Signora, e Madre*, in *Mary Ward*, ed. Dirmeier, IV, 100–145 (p. 101). Citations follow this edition; translations are mine. According to Kirkus, a Poyntz ancestor *did* come over with the Conqueror (*Companions*, p. 38).

50. '... e si contano sette fratelli dell'Ordine de Cavalieri Aurati, titolo in quei tempi più riguardevole che quello hoggidì di Marchese' (IV, 101).

51. *Decameron*, II, 3 in *Tutte le opere*, ed. Branca, vol. IV, pp. 108–118; Wallace, *Decameron*, p. 34.

nelle sue maniere, peritissimo ne'maneggi', and so on (IV, 101). The
English author of the *Italian Life* clearly knew that noble pedigree
counted for much with the families dominating the papal *curia*.
Mary Ward's surname suggests, however, modest ancestry: her forebears at
some point perhaps guarded piles of wood or of hay, as *haywards* or
woodwards.[52] In Italian, however, Mary Ward becomes Signora Donna
Maria della Guardia, when plain *Guardia* or *Guardi* might have served;
the *della* has something of the suggestive power of the *von* in von
Ashenbach.[53]

The *English Life*, devoting less space to Mary Ward's genealogy,
locates her not among the nobility, but the Yorkshire gentry: 'Our
dearest Mother of happy memory', it begins, 'was eldest Daughter
of Mister Marmaduke Ward of Ghendall, in the County of Yorke.
Mullwith and Newby were Maner houses of his' (p. 2). Marmaduke
(Marmaduca)[54] Ward was gentleman and bailiff to Henry Percy, ninth
earl of Northumberland; Ursula Wright, Mary's mother, was great-
granddaughter to Sir William Mallory, of Studley Royal (near Foun-
tains Abbey). Sir William, who died in 1547, had famously stood with
sword in hand for two days outside his parish church, 'to defend that
none should come in to abolish religion'.[55] The Wards thus belonged
to a well-rooted, highly interconnected community of Yorkshire Recusants of the gentry class; Mary passed her childhood living in, and
moving between, their large country houses. Such houses hosted,
when possible, the religious and educational work of the Jesuits. The
famous first *troika* of Robert Parsons, Edmund Campion, and Ralph
Emerson arrived in June 1580; numbers climbed as supported by the
foundation of new, English-focused seminaries at Valladolid (1589) and
Seville (1592), plus a school for English boys at St-Omer (1593). There
were eighteen Jesuits in England by 1598, forty in 1606, about one

---

52. See further Javierre, with Pablo-Romero, *La Jesuitessa*, p. 47.
53. Thomas Mann's novella famously opens 'Gustav Aschenbach oder von Aschenbach,
    wie seit seinem fünfzigsten Geburtstag amtlich sein Name lautete', *Der Tod in Venedig:
    Novelle* (Berlin: S. Fischer, 1922), p. 9.
54. The *Italian Life* finds this name especially felicitous, I would suggest, because it
    assonates nicely with the 'Duca Gugliemo' (William the Conqueror) just discussed;
    but Marmaduke was no duke.
55. Thus according to John Morris SJ, *The Troubles of Our Catholic Forefathers: Related by
    Themselves*, first series (London: Burns and Oates, 1872), p. 227.

hundred by the late 1610s, and double that number by 1639.[56] The Act against Jesuits, passed in 1585 (the year of Mary's birth), kept Jesuits— like men of Catholic persuasion more generally—on the move. Catholic country houses thus assumed something of a female-directed character; male religious depended upon women for sustenance and protection.[57] Much of the writing produced by women in seventeenth-century England, we have noted, was the fruit of country house education. It is perhaps unlikely that the 'Ursula Rudstone' who owned the University of Pennsylvania's copy of the 1542 Thynne Chaucer was Mary Ward's maternal grandmother, Ursula Rudstone.[58] It is likely, however, that the young Mary Ward, like the young Cavendishes, read or devised plays. Jesuit educationalists favoured teaching through drama; dramatic skills might help young Catholic women cover the tracks of their Jesuit teachers. When Mary planned on opening a school in London in 1639–40, she sent an oval-shaped embroidery pattern to her followers at Rome. The message inked upon it, having specified dimensions of 'the imbrothery', concludes: 'if don by Christmas, it will serve'. But this is a lemon juice letter: once held to the flame, the text is seen to appeal for 'plays', as many 'as can be had without notis or the leas suspect'.[59]

Ovid's poetry may be employed as a handbook to love, but also as a guide to extracting oneself from it;[60] and so too may plays involving amatory predicaments. It is clear that Mary Ward, one way or another,

56. See McCoog, *English and Welsh Jesuits*, pp. 10–11, 14; McCoog, 'The Society of Jesus in the Three Kingdoms', in *Companion to Jesuits*, ed. Worcester, p. 94; Geoffrey Holt, *St. Omers and Bruges Colleges, 1559–1773: A Biographical Dictionary*, CRS Publications (Records Series), 69 (London: CRS, 1979), p. 1.
57. See Walker, *Gender and Politics*, p. 11.
58. *The Workes of Geffray Chaucer newly printed* (London: Richard Grafton for Wyllyam Bonham, 1542), University of Pennsylvania Library, Folio PR 1850 (1542), fol. xci v. ('[Ur]sula Rudstone'); thanks to Megan Cook for this reference. Christina Kenworthy-Browne (private correspondence) thinks this signature likelier to be that of the Kent Ursula Rudstone (later Barnham).
59. *Mary Ward*, ed. Dirmeier, III, 520, 521 (dated 1639/40). While the old handlist to the Nymphenburg Archive dates this letter 'probably 1639', Wetter assigns it to 1641–42: see Immolata Wetter CJ, *Mary Ward in Her Own Words*, trans. Bernardette Ganne CJ (Roma: Istituto Beata Vergine Maria, 1999), p. 195. For an image of this letter, written in Mary Ward's own hand, see Littlehales, *Mary Ward*, p. 233.
60. See, for example, Brunetto Latini, *Tesoretto*, ed. and tr. Julia Bolton Holloway (New York: Garland, 1981), lines 2390–93.

learned to escape the clutches of eager young men: for between the ages of ten and twenty-one, she successfully resisted the wiles and entreaties of at least four suitors. These scenes are much to the liking of the *Painted Life*. At age ten we see her resisting a gartered gallant called Redshaw (*PL* 2) in that splendid, courtly, luxuriously long-sleeved dress that grows with her until she is twenty-one. At twelve, she rebuffs a young man named Shafto with whom her mother, in particular, seems quite enchanted (*PL* 5). In 1598, aged thirteen, she is pursued by a wide-sleeved, feather-hatted gallant called Eldrington; she escapes stage left with her father on a richly caparisoned white pony (*PL* 8; Figure 21). And at twenty-one, just as she is proposing to leave England, she is urged by her parents and her confessor to marry 'a young man named Neville' (so the *Painted Life* caption says), 'sole heir of a very ancient and noble (gräfflich) Westmoreland family' (*PL* 13). The cost of *this* last refusal is very high, for as the *English Life* says, this noble suitor has resolved 'never to marry if she would not have him; nor did he, but became a Religious Man and a Priest, and from

Figure 21. *Painted Life*, 8: Mary Ward, aged thirteen, wooed by Eldrington.

him the Title went to Heretikes, so as by his absence the Catholickes lost a great support' (p. 9). Suitor number four, Edmund (or Edward) Neville, in fact became—most appropriately—a Jesuit; he died on the English mission in 1646.[61]

An opening section of a romance that pertains to childhood, and childhood love, is called an *enfance*; the opening of the *English Life*, pitched somewhere between romance and hagiography, might be designated an *enfance religieuse*, or even an anti-*enfance:* for it shows the young Mary struggling to resist the unfolding of a conventional romance plot. But a tremendous amatory *agon* does in fact break out in the opening section of the *English Life*: a battle of fathers, earthly and heavenly, for the love and obedience of Mary Ward. Dorothea of Montau, Margery Kempe, and Elizabeth Cary, the other women considered in this book, must all break with an earthly husband in order to embrace a superior, heavenly spouse; Mary Ward, never to marry, must in effect renounce that earthly father, Marmaduke, established so strongly at the beginning of her English and Italian *lives*. God, as suitor, does not play fair; a jealous God, He proves a jealous and conniving lover. Mary Ward, aged ten, innocently assumes that she is to marry her first suitor: but 'the Devine Providence', the *English Life* tells us, 'would not let this Love, though so innocent, have longer place in her Hart reserved to himselfe' (p. 4). 'Devine Providence' thus fixes things so that 'this hopefull Youngman' has to rush to London on business; Mary Ward is thus weaned 'from this beginning Love by an apprehension of some Lacke of constancy and fervour in her pretended Spouse, his respects to her selfe, which yet really was not so, for he both loved and honored her till his Death, which [and here's the sinister part] in a few Monthes after happened' (p. 4). If Divine Providence knows all, foresees all, controls all, how convenient that this boy-suitor should disappear, and then die. But *Devine Providence* is only warming up; the next showdown sees Mary obliged to choose between obedience to her earthly and heavenly fathers. At age thirteen, she has been left with relatives to prepare for

---

61. In his early eighties: see McCoog, *English and Welsh Jesuits*, p. 251; Chambers, *Life*, I, 72–74, 96–7; *Mary Ward*, ed. Kenworthy-Browne, p. 9, n. 28. Sir William Babthorpe—son and heir to the Osgodby house where Mary Ward spent her most crucial, formative years—was so afflicted with fines and penalties that he sold up in 1633; he ended up serving as a simple soldier in the Spanish army in the Netherlands. See Dirmeier, *Mary Ward*, I, 34, n. 8.

her first communion, her parents having been driven to Northumberland by 'a great persecution' (p. 5). A 'Man on horsebake', supposedly from her father, arrives and reads her a letter, he 'on one side of the pale, and she on the other' (p. 5, a detail taken up by *PL* 6). Her father commands her 'on his blessing', the messenger says, not to communicate: 'for he had a match in hand for her, greatly advantageous, one of the Talbots of Graften' (p. 5). The horseman leaves, and Mary faces her dilemma: to obey 'her deare and deserving Father', or to live with 'a loving reproach from God Allmighty for her ingratitude' (pp. 5, 6).[62] She chooses God. The letter turns out to be a mysterious hoax but the choice, nonetheless, has been made.

Following this choosing of God's will above her father's ostensible veto, in the matter of first communion, Mary seeks a more reclusive life: 'she wou'd retyre herselfe alone in her Chamber, with an olde Catholicke Woman [du logis],[63] and heare her tell storyes of Religious Women' (p. 6). This would be *c.*1601, so an old woman would indeed *just* be able to recall nunneries as a feature of the English landscape. *Painted Life* 9, we have noted, firmly situates this scene within the comfortable milieu of the English country house, with St George attacking his dragon and the snoozing lapdog. Within this scene, the *Briefe Relation* tells us, the young Mary thrills to hear of a nun, 'who for having comitted a frailety, was severly punished for it' (p. 6). Such severity is greatly to her adolescent taste, inspiring her 'to spend much time in reading the Lifes of Saints, particularly Martyrs, which so enflammed her well prepared Hart, as nothing cou'd satisfy her but a Living or dying Martyrdome' (p. 7). This pleasing fantasy is pictured by the next canvass of the *Painted Life* sequence (10, Figure 22), where young Mary contemplates scenes of burning, beheading, and disemboweling while clutching an axe, a sword (for a noble beheading), and a portable mini-guillotine (handy for chopping off hands). Before her we see both a scimitar, presumably for the use of Saracens, and some stones (such as

62. Significantly, Mary chooses not to consult with anyone during this process of deliberation. This is ascribed both to a desire to protect 'the reputation of Catholick zeale her Father ever had fame of', and to 'a secrecy and closeness of nature' in herself; she makes up her own mind (p. 6).
63. The old woman 'of the lodge' (term supplied from the seventeenth-century French MS at York: cf. Kenworthy-Browne ed., p. 2) was Margaret Garrett at Osgodby, south of York (a Babthorpe house).

those which had crushed Margaret Clitheroe on Ouse Bridge, York, in 1586).[64] Fortunately, the *English Life* tells us, young Mary had 'a discreet Confessour': he resists her fervour for 'generall Confession' (an exhausting practise much loved by Margery Kempe) and provides her with more moderate spiritual reading.[65]

The lives of saints continued to shape Mary Ward's thinking throughout her life, proving fundamental to her mapping of both time and space. It mattered to her that she was born on 23 January, namely the feasts of Saints Emerentiana, John the Almoner, and Ildephonsus. From each of these, the *Italian Life* tells us, she received (as it were) hereditary predispositions (p. 101): from the first, 'the continual desire of martyrdom';

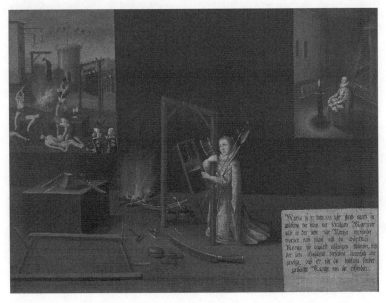

Figure 22. *Painted Life*, 10: Mary Ward, aged sixteen, inspired by reading the lives of martyrs, desires to emulate them.

64. Or perhaps those that stoned St Emerentiana, her birthday saint, to death at the tomb of St Agnes (see below).
65. On the function of martyr stories in English recusant households 'as comfort literature and conduct books', see Anne Dillon, *The Construction of Martyrdom in the English Catholic Community, 1535–1603* (Aldershot: Ashgate, 2002), p. 372.

from the second, charity to the poor, and from the third devotion to the Virgin.[66] Such devotions become almost traits of character: thus it was that, in later life, she came 'very neere the pinch' of giving her life for the faith in 'reprehending most undauntedly one of the Justices in Guildhall for blasphemy spoken against the sacred Virgin' (p. 95). Her journeyings, in later life, were made under the protection of various saints, including that saint whose day coincided with her departure. In her youth, in semi-reclusion, she associated each room in the house with devotion to a particular saint: a practise that formed a memory house in her mind that, Mary Ward tells us in her *Italian Autobiographical Fragment*, stayed with her for life.[67] Mary devised further spiritual exercises for herself, as a maturing girl, by devising what might be called class cross-dressing: for, having detected in herself 'great Love to her owne ranke and degree by birth' (p. 7), she 'would trusse up her Sleeves, put on an apron, take a broome in her hand, and so passe through the hall where the strangers were, that they might thinke she lived there in the nature of a Servant, which many did' (pp. 7–8). Such holy exhibitionism recalls Dorothea of Montau,[68] and so too the troubling of her own flesh: 'She being of herselfe in the highest degree neat and dainty', says the *English Life*, she 'thought necessary to curbe it, which she did by lying in Bed with one of the Maides that had the Itch, and gott it' (p. 8).[69] Chastity is something that a female religious can never flirt with: she must remain, in this particular, absolute—or all is lost. But class

---

66. Relics of John, Patriarch of Alexandria (606–16), were to be found in a chapel of St Martin's cathedral, Bratislava; Mary Ward might have visited them during her visit to the city in 1628. She could often have visited the tomb of St Emerentiana at Santa Agnese Fuori le Mura in Rome; the catachumen Emerentiana had been stoned to death by pagans while praying at the tomb of St Agnes (a rich Roman heiress). St Ildephonsus, archbishop of Toledo, died on 23 January 667; the Virgin Mary presented him with a priestly vestment by way of recognizing his devotion to her.

67. 'I applied myself so precisely to this practise', Mary Ward observes, 'that many years afterward returning to England for certain affairs, and coming to the said place to visit some relations etc., the house appeared to me like a paradise [la casa mi pareva uno certo paradiso], the same devotions and exercises presenting themselves at every step as I had before practised them, so that I had not freedom of mind sufficient to perform certain civilities and other things more fitting to that time and occasion' (*Mary Ward*, ed. Dirmeier, I, 32).

68. See above, p. 35.

69. *English Life*, p. 8; the *Italian Life* expands upon this episode (IV, 106).

identity can be toyed with, since—like the identity of young Gareth in King Arthur's kitchens—it really never is fungible.[70] Taking pride in rank and birth lineage, according to the *English Life*, is something that 'all noble harts naturally doe'.[71] As with strains of Franciscan theology,[72] where only the *voluntary* embrace of poverty counts (you get no spiritual credit for being born poor), so only a woman of pedigree wins kudos for embracing the servant state, or for lying with an itchy maid.

Following these six years of housebound or homemade religious apprenticeship, and approaching her twenty-first birthday, Mary Ward 'took opportunity to make knowne to her deare Father her great desire to be a Religious, and to have his permission, but he on noe tearmes wou'd hear of it' (p. 8). The last phase of the *agon* between fathers is thus set: but it really is no contest. Having now learned 'to follow councell of her heavenly Father', she has also learned 'as little to value the words before so deare and powerful', those of her natural father, 'that they not at all daunted her'; and so 'she resolved to embrace the first opportunity to passe the seas, and sayd in her selfe: "I will see him noe more", and that with joy, so as what had beene above thousands of Worlds deare to her, when in ballance with her best pleasing God, was as nothing' (p. 8). The absolute clarity of 'I will see him noe more' is terrible: but so too is the God envisioned by the young Mary Ward. Times are fraught: as Mary Ward travels south to London with her father the Gunpowder Plot is nearing completion; when the plot is discovered, Mary's father is arrested on the road as a suspect. Marmaduke is released, but the plot strikes close to home: all but two of the plotters are relatives; two of them are—like Mary Ward—great-great-grandchildren of the defiant Sir William Mallory.[73] 'Most of the unmarried women in the Gunpowder Plot families', Sophie Holroyd has recently written, 'left the country to seek

70. See 'The Tale of Sir Gareth of Orkney that was called Bewmaynes', in Sir Thomas Malory, *Works*, ed. Eugene Vinaver, 2nd edn (Oxford: Oxford University Press, 1971), pp. 175–226.
71. 'For example finding in her selfe (as all noble harts naturally doe) great Love to her owne ranke and degree by birth...' (p. 7). As noted above, Mary Poyntz, chief author of the *English Life*, was from a highly colourful and distinguished family.
72. See Janet Coleman, 'Property and Poverty', in *The Cambridge History of Medieval Political Thought, c.300–1450*, ed. J. H. Burns (Cambridge: Cambridge University Press, 1988), pp. 607–48.
73. See Chambers, *Life*, I, 86–90; Littlehales, *Mary Ward*, pp. 30–35.

refuge in the convents on the Continent'.[74] The early *lives* of Mary Ward make no mention of the Gunpowder Plot as possibly triggering her exile; their emphasis throughout, before and after 1605, is upon her long and slow process of discernment.[75]

When Mary gets to London more blood is spilt: this time from a chalice knocked over at mass by a priest. This priest, Fr Holtby, had been prevailed upon by Marmaduke Ward to try and talk his strong-willed daughter into marriage and out of religious life. As *Painted Life* 14 shows, Mary Ward is on hand after the unhappy mass with a towel. The priest weeps, 'then sighing sayd: "Shall I live to offend my God?" and to her: "I will never more hinder your Religious designe"' (p. 9). This takes place at 'Bawldwins Gardens in London', a street now between Gray's Inn Road and Hatton Garden, and half a mile northeast of Drury Lane. *Painted Life* 15 sees Mary bid farewell to her father, in the left panel; she then boards ship for Spanish Flanders and St-Omer. Mary's backward glance here is poignant. What she is bidding farewell to here is not England but her old life in England: the flowery dress will be seen no more.

'Not to be . . . some other thing': 'this holy Amazon', 1606–21

On arriving at St-Omer, Mary Ward heads straight for the English College, home to over one hundred English boys and their Jesuit teachers.[76] It should be remembered that towns such as St-Omer and Gravelines had once been held by the English, and that English claims to overlordship on this side of the Channel did not fade until 1558.[77] St-Omer is much closer to London than is York, and it is clear that Mary Ward

---

74. '"Rich Embroidered Churchstuffe": The Vestments of Helena Wintour', in *Catholic Culture in Early Modern England*, ed. Ronald Corthell, Frances E. Dolan, Christopher Highly, and Arthur F. Marotti (Notre Dame: University of Notre Dame Press, 2009), p. 109; see further p. 116, n. 47.

75. See however the account rendered by the Poor Clares of Gravelines: 'in 1606, at a time when all England was distracted on account of the Gun Powder Plot, Mary Ward of good family from near Repon in Yorkshire, left her home when she was 21 years of age, and came to St. Omer' (from the 'Map and Annuels' of the Poor Clares of Graveline as conserved in a copy of 1893 at St Clare's Abbey, Darlington; cited in *Mary Ward*, ed. Dirmeier, I, 149).

76. See Holt, *St. Omers*, p. 3. Numbers of English boys at St-Omer continued to rise, with 200 in 1635; a decade later the number had fallen to twenty-four.

77. See David Wallace, 'At Calais Gate', in *Premodern Places*, pp. 22–90.

(unlike Margery Kempe) continues to think of England throughout her continental travels. It thus dismayed her that her new father confessor, the moral theologian George Keynes SJ, could confidently announce that 'it was God's will she should be a Lay Sister amongst the french poore Clares in that Towne' (p. 10). This means that she is not to be enclosed herself, but to go begging through town and country for those who were. Since Mary Ward has spent the previous six years rehearsing a life of religious 'retyrement... in her Father's House', such a life on the streets is as welcome to her as immersion, she says, in 'a Caldron of boyling oyle': but she goes to it, since her confessor or 'ghostly Father' has insisted that 'it was God's will'. She thus, the *English Life* tells us, 'did exactly what the strongest and meanest borne amongst them did, carryed burthens, going into the Countrey to begg, faired rudely, and lodged worse, which though it could not master her heroicall and gallant mind, did in a few Monthes her young and delicate body'; she is soon limping along with 'a powltisse at her knee' (p. 10). Such a life for women on the streets has scant religious capital in this premodern period: it betokens low birth, poor education, and uncertain morals. The only undisputed sign of religious integrity for women was, as Margery Kempe could tell, enclosure. It was one thing for the well-born Mary Ward to play serving wench in her father's house; quite different to actually *be* one. Since she did finally embrace an apostolate of the streets, these early labours might have come to seem, in retrospect, Providential: indeed, the *English Life* tells us that the mature Mary Ward would 'speake of those times with great Content and satisfaction' (p. 10). But such a life beyond the cloister could only be validated by the kind of spiritual authority that the cloister alone could give. Mary Ward thus entered into a period of slow, evolutionary discernment that was to prove (so she later tells us) her most difficult decade.[78] From first to last, her thinking and visionary experience roots itself in thoughts of England, and of its peculiar religious situation.[79] Discernment evolves through negatives—*not this (way of life), not that*. Such progress along a *via negativa* has distinguished precedents in Catholic theology; yet there is something here, too, of the romance heroine who has yet to find her way.

---

78. Mary told the congregation of cardinals at Rome in 1629 that her '10 Yeares of Labours and sufferance to know God's will, was such as that once knowne, all her infirmytes and other suffrances seemed toyes' (*English Life*, p. 38).
79. H. J. Coleridge SJ, in the opening paragraph of his edition of the great work of Mary C. E. Chambers, characterizes Mary Ward as 'one who laboured so perseveringly for the love of her beloved country, in its darkest hours of religious revolution' (*Life*, I, vii).

The first step forward comes on 12 March 1607: that is, on the Feast of
St Gregory, the pope who sent Augustine from Rome to Canterbury.[80]
Mary has just offered up 'certaine devotions for the conversion of England' when she is summoned to attend a visit of the Spaniard Andreas de
Soto, the Franciscan Visitator General: 'my Child', he tells her, 'you are not
for this state of Life' (p. 11). Mary Ward, who 'allwayes had an unspeakable
Zeale for the good of England', ponders what might be done.[81] In April
1607 she leaves the Walloon Poor Clares, puts her idea to de Soto, then
travels on to the court of the Spanish princess Isabella Clara Eugenia, and
her husband the archduke, at Brussels. Isabella had received the Spanish
Netherlands as a wedding gift from her father, Philip II of Spain; de Soto
was her confessor. 'Who can heare expresse the courage', enthuses the
English Life, 'with which this holy Amazon...thus young and beautyfull
put her selfe to negotiate in the Arch-Duke his Court, for a Foundation
of a Monastery of Saint Clare's order for the English Nation' (p. 12).[82] The
English ambassador at Brussels wrote of Mary being urged on by the
Jesuits, adding that 'most of them that were dealers in the Gunpowder
Treason are, as your lordship knoweth, now resident here'.[83] This initiative
of a convent 'for the English Nation' develops rapidly; Mary looks forward to religious enclosure, a life (and here phrasing of the *English Life* is
quite splendid) 'out of the noyse and negotiation of the World' (p. 12).

80. 'Mio advocato perticolare', says Mary Ward in her *Italian Autobiographical Fragment*
     (I, 38).
81. Mary Ward is typical rather than exceptional among her female co-religionist con-
     temporaries in her patriotic zeal. Continental cloisters of English nuns, writes Claire
     Walker, 'were strikingly, even stridently, English in both orientation and composition';
     almost 94% of their inhabitants registered English (rather than Scottish, Irish, or
     Welsh) origins (*Gender and Politics*, p. 38).
82. The phrase 'la nostra Amazona' occurs in the *Italian Life* (IV, 110). A masque per-
     formed at Coleorton, Leicestershire, on 2 February 1618 speaks of 'brave Amazonian
     dames' (Sophie Tomlinson, *Women on Stage in Stuart Drama* (Cambridge: Cambridge
     University Press, 2005), p. 45). On the popularity of Amazons in period dramas and
     masquing, see further Tomlinson, pp. 30–33; on Henrietta Maria's strong encourage-
     ment of and investment in such iconography, see Tomlinson, pp. 115, 158; Rosalind K.
     Marshall, *Henrietta Maria: The Intrepid Queen* (London: HMSO, 1990), p. 82. The last
     masque of all, the extraordinary *Salmacida Spolia* (January 1640), saw Charles dancing
     as Philogenes (lover of the people) to Henrietta Maria's Amazonian queen. See
     Martin Butler, *The Stuart Court Masque and Political Culture* (Cambridge: Cambridge
     University Press, 2008), pp. 341–51.
83. Sir Thomas Edmondes to Robert Cecil, 1 June 1608 as cited in Chambers, *Life*, I, 169.
     Chambers transcribes the entire letter, of which this is the final sentence. Strangely,
     this last sentence does not appear in Dirmeier's edition (I, 129).

And yet, 'she had certain glimpses and hoverings in her mind that God would somewhat else with her' (p. 12). Things come to a head 'upon St Athanasius his day', 2 May 1609. As Mary sits engaged in buttonmaking, the *English Life* tells us, 'it occurred to her intellectually that that state of Life was not what she was to honour God by, but an other very much to Godes honour, and the good of others, particularly England' (pp. 13–14). In her *Italian Autobiographical Fragment*, Mary Ward remembers that it was not until the next day, the Feast of the Invention of the Holy Cross, that she reveals her intention to leave the English Poor Clares; the holy cross was, of course, discovered by an Englishwoman.[84] Mary further recalls making 'cords of St Francis' while reciting the litanies of Our Lady, *sotto voce*; plain buttonmaking, as in the *English Life*, hardly befits a major revelatory occasion.[85] Similarly, Mary recalls the divine intervention of 2 May 1609 not as a simple intellectual occurrence ('it occurred to her intellectually'), but rather as *Vernichtung,* an annihilation of the self that sees her possessed by God.[86] Her boldest step, which leads directly to the foundation of her Institute, is thus seen *not* to issue from a willful act: 'in me non era altra operatione', says Maria della Guardia, 'che quella che faceva Iddio' (I, 41).

As Mary Ward's proposal to leave her newly-founded English Poor Clares becomes widely known, 'glorious Hosanna' (as the *English Life* succinctly puts it) 'was turned to Crucifige: some said', it continues, 'she was left of God, and would dy in the Streets abandoned of all; others that pride and vanity had made her madd' (p. 14). Such outbursts *are* understandable: Mary Ward does leave frustrated suitors, disappointed families, and rudderless novices in her wake in adventuring forward to seek her particular calling. She is guided chiefly by a voice in her head that says, successively: *not this, not this.* Her female superior is thus moved to 'put her hand on her head and aske how she did'; to which the *mulier fortis*

---

84. See Antonina Harbus, *Helena of Britain in British Legend* (Cambridge: D. S. Brewer, 2002); Jacobus de Voragine, *Golden Legend*, tr. Ryan, I, 281.

85. In her 1621 letter to Antonio Albergati, papal nuncio at Cologne, Mary remembers making objects for the use of *female* religious: 'that she that should ware that I was then working might never commit mortall sin' (*Mary Ward*, ed. Kenworthy-Browne, p. 145; I, 538). This letter is an important source of both biographical detail and of the *agon* between the attractions of *vita activa* and 'abstraction from the world' (p. 144; I, 538).

86. 'Mi sopra venne cosa tale', Mary Ward explains, 'che non so, se mai sapevo esplicare, pareva totalmente divina, e venne con impeto tale, che m'annihilava à niente; la mia forza era istinta, et in me non era altra operatione, che quella che faceva Iddio' (I, 46); on *Vernichtung*, see Chapter 1 above.

replies, infuriatingly, 'with a cheerefull countenance, I am very well' (p. 14).

On leaving the Poor Clare house, Mary Ward changes clothes again, reassuming 'her secular habitt'; she resolves 'to labour in England in the good of her Neighbour' (p. 15). All is not quite as before, since on Palm Sunday 1609[87] she took a vow of chastity, and then later 'a vow of Obedience to her Ghostly Father', the Jesuit Roger Lee (p. 15; *PL* 16); she also promises, on her own initiative, to become a Carmelite nun, 'should he so command me'.[88] Mary Ward thus assumes a status somewhere between pious laywoman and dedicated religious. Such ambivalence, expressed by her mode of dress in England, is picked up by the *English Life*, which again seems caught generically between saint's life and fashionable romance: 'still retaining an extreame beauty, she went cloathed as became her birth for matter and manner, and woare underneath a most sharpe haircloath'; when occasion demanded, she would 'put on Servants' and 'meane Women's cloathes' (p. 15). Her wearing of fashionable clothes has now become a cross-dressing of almost Shakespearean complexity: she *is* of the rank she dresses, but has *crossed* to an illicit form of religious life, which is now disguised by wearing clothes of her own English rank; the flowery dress returns, but with a difference. All this is much to the liking of the *Painted Life* artists, who produce a sequence of canvasses with Mary Ward on active mission in a variety of disguises.[89] It also fed the lurid imaginings of her Catholic enemies: a document inscribed 'Godfathers information about the Jesuitrisses' tells of their living 'att Hungerfford howse in the Strand verye riotouse' (I, 763). Their dressing 'in the neewest and moste phantasticall maner' includes the wearing of 'jeolowe ruffes etc.'; their life on the Strand is such 'that they weare esteemed curtisans and suspected for hoores'.[90]

---

87. Such is her recollection in the *Italian Autobiographical Fragment*, I, 47; see further *Mary Ward*, ed. Kenworthy-Browne, p. 138, n. 29.
88. For this last detail see *Italian Autobiographical Fragment*, I, 48.
89. Some painted details find no counterpart in written records; too much written detail could, of course, endanger Catholic lives back in England.
90. The document, dating from March 1623, goes on to describe Mary Ward dressing 'her owne naturall sister Barbara Warde in a tufft taffeta gowne and riche peaticote etc. trymed of the neewest fashion in deape jeolowe ruffes etc. her breaste bare downe to the guirdell'; she and a companion are sent to an inn 'to gaine soules' (I, 763–4). The chief informant here is Mary Alcock, a disaffected follower of Mary Ward who was once her bursar at Liège but left the movement in 1619.

Painted Life 17 depicts Mary Ward, as the German caption says, at 'Coldam Hall in Engelandt'. This Suffolk residence of Gunpowder plotter Ambrose Rookwood, now owned by supermodel Claudia Schiffer, featured priest holes and a chapel in the attic.[91] The ailing, bedridden lady, who has resisted the ministrations of many learned men, is converted by the touch of Mary's hands; she confesses to the priest in the upper central quadrant before she dies. *Painted Life* 18 sees Mary exchanging her noble attire for that of her serving maid in order to meet with and convert her aunt, Miss Gray, in a London safe house. The next scene sees Miss Gray talking with a Jesuit while another woman on her deathbed, in the background, receives the Viaticum after meeting with Mary. *Painted Life* 20 sees Mary tempted by dainty food (sent by a noble admirer); she spends the night in prayer and penance. The next scene, *Painted Life* 21 (Figure 23), is truly remarkable. Both the English and Italian lives record this episode,[92] the *English Life* placing it precisely 'in her Lodgings in St Clement's Church-yard in the Strand' (p. 19): that is, at the heartland of the London Catholic community.[93] The fullest account, however, is provided by Mary Ward herself in her *Italian Autobiographical Fragment*. She has resolved, one morning, to help a person wishing to enter a convent, but who cannot afford the portion, or dowry. 'And then going to dress myself according to local custom', Mary tells us, 'while dressing up my head in the mirror, something very supernatural befell me, similar to that already mentioned on the day of St Athanasius, but more singular, and, as it appears to me, with greater force, if greater there could be'.[94] Mary is about to experience her climactic *not to be* vision: 'it was shown to me with clarity and unspeakable certainty that [I] was not to be of the Order of St Theresa, but that some other thing was

---

91. Staircases led from the room used as a chapel on the top floor to the roof; a high parapet on the roof could hide crouching figures. See Littlehales, *Mary Ward*, p. 57; Kirkus, *Companions*, p. 26.
92. *The English Life* incorrectly assigns this climactic vision to a later visit to England (1614–15; p. 19); the *Italian Life* abbreviates the scene but gets the chronology right (IV, 111).
93. See further Chapter 4 below.
94. 'E poi andando a vestirmi secondo l'uso del paese...mentre che mi conciavo la testa nel spechio mi veniva qualche cosa molto sopranaturale simile alla gia detta nell di di Sant'Athanasio, ma piu perticolare, et al mio parere con maggiore impeto—se maggiore poteva' (IV, 48). The *Italian Life* has Mary combing her hair and gazing at herself in the mirror ('pettinandosi, e mirandosi', IV, 111).

determined for me' (IV, 48). Once again, her autobiographical account is keen to emphasize that she in no way *authors* such a sudden, visionary moment ('fui astratta fuor d'ogni mio essere');[95] the *lives* written by her followers are more apt to accentuate her personal agency. Of the interior quality of this vision, Mary gives us nothing beyond a sound, 'il suono Gloria, Gloria, Gloria';[96] her autobiographical stream dries up soon after.

Mary Ward of the *lives* and paintings at once recognizes that she has, once again, reached a standoff between paternal authorities: between the will of her Jesuit Father Confessor and that of God, as expressed in this two-hour vision. The St Athanasius Day vision had occurred while she sat in a circle of women; this one comes as she sits alone at a mirror. Such tension between aloneness and sociality itself

Figure 23. *Painted Life*, 21: Mary Ward's 'Glory Vision', the Strand, London, 1609.

95. Literally, and gnomically, 'I was abstracted outside my every being' (IV, 48).
96. *Italian Autobiographical Fragment*, I, 48. Her letter to Albergati characterizes this incommunicable experience not as sound, but rather 'infused light' (*Mary Ward*, ed. Kenworthy-Browne, p. 145; I, 539).

seems Jesuitical, or Jesuit-like; the very next image in the *Painted Life* sequence (22; Figure 24) sees her sitting, again, in a circle of women. And *this* image in turn may recall Ignatius and his first circle of followers at Paris; among this 'first five' are Susan Rookwood, Barbara Ward, and the co-biographer and French translator Winefride Wigmore.[97] These well-born Englishwomen ('Hoch adelich Freylen') are shown setting off, in the right-hand panel, 'to serve God in the religious state' (as the *Painted Life* panel has it) 'under Mary Ward's direction'. These are still dangerous times. King James I dwells upon the evils of the Gunpowder Plot in his *Apologie* of 1608; in 1609 he adds

Figure 24. *Painted Life*, 22: Mary Ward and followers in London, and boarding ship for St-Omer, 1609.

97. According to Littlehales, 'the names of the first five, who became the foundation stones of the Institute, are Susan Rookwood, Catherine Smith, Joanna Browne, Mary Poyntz, and Winefride Wigmore' (*Mary Ward*, p. 57). Kenworthy-Browne, following an early eighteenth-century manuscript, includes Barbara Ward rather than Mary Poyntz (p. 16, n. 58). 'Since Mary Poyntz (1603/4–1667) was only six years old at the time', Kenworthy-Brown cogently argues, 'the traditional inclusion of her in this *Painted Life* picture is probably a courtesy'.

a preface to all Christian princes and sends copies to foreign courts.[98] On 14 May 1610, Henry IV of France—*le bon roi Henri*, father of Henrietta Maria—is assassinated in Paris in his coach by the Catholic zealot François Ravaillac. News reaches England with parliament in session; Jesuits are suspected, and there are further crackdowns on Catholic laity.[99]

On returning to St-Omer, Mary Ward buys a house and furnishes it 'so as to live a regular observance, and their cloaths conformable, very grave and retyred but not', the *English Life* insists, 'of the monasticall' (p. 16). A school soon flourishes; this serves both girls 'of our owne Nation (of which there were very many)', but also local girls, 'taught gratis' (p. 16). Mary's next visionary step brings her first thoroughly positive instruction. Its logic seems obvious, but its sensitivity is such that the crucial words do not appear in either the English or Italian life, nor in the panel of *Painted Life* 24 (although *Painted Life* 27 does see Mary meditating upon 'die Wort ET VOCABIS NOMEN JESUM').[100] These words are: 'take the same of the Society'; that is, establish an Institute for women modelled on, but not subjected to,[101] that founded by Ignatius Loyola.[102] This particular intellectual understanding, experienced in 1611, soon got Mary in trouble with her Jesuit confessor and with the Society of Jesus more generally. The Jesuits, jealous of their name, urged that 'we should take the name of some order confirmed,

98. *An Apologie for the Oath of Allegiance: Together, with a Premonition of his Majesties to all most mightie Monarches, Kings, free Princes and States of Christendome* (London: Robert Barker, 1609). The 'premonition' contains an attack upon the Jesuit Robert Parsons ('the perverse pamphleter Parsons', p. 5), associated with the abhorred Powder-treason (p. 6). It goes on to discuss the semi-complicity in the plot of 'my Popish Subjects, of all rankes and sexes, both men and women, as well within, *as without the Countrey*' (p. 7, emphasis added).

99. See Micheline Dupuy, *Henriette de France: Reine d'Angleterre* (Paris: Perrin, 1994), pp. 19–21; Alan Dures, *English Catholicism 1558–1642* (Harlow: Longman, 1983), pp. 44–9.

100. '[T]he words AND THOU SHALL CALL HIS NAME JESUS' (*Mary Ward*, ed. Dirmeier, IV, 300, Tafel 27).

101. While Mary Ward was convinced that 'the denomination' of her movement 'must be Jesus', she is equally mindful 'of the inconveniencies [that] would happen to both parties if ours should have any dependensy of the Fathers of the Society' (letter to Albergati, p. 147; I, 540); her women must have their own superior general. Mary Ward makes little reference to Ignatius in her writings, nor does she mention his canonization (confirmed while she was in Rome): see Gemma Simmonds CJ, 'Female Jesuits', in *Companion to Jesuits*, ed. Worcester, p. 126.

102. This imperative vision is recorded by just two surviving sources: Mary Ward's letter to John Gerard SJ of 1619, and her letter to papal nuncio Albergati (*Mary Ward*, ed. Kenworthy-Browne, pp. 141–3, 143–8, respectively; I, 436–7 and I, 536–42).

or some new one, or any we could think of, soe not that of Jesus'
(p. 146; I, 540). Despite such pleas, Mary Ward's Institute (Roman
branch) was officially renamed the Congregation of Jesus—but not
until January 2004.[103]

Mary Ward and her first followers had actually been living in accord-
ance with the Jesuit Constitutions almost from the beginning: they did
not meet together in choir, for example, but recited the Divine Office
alone. The real point of this way of life was not primarily the education
of girls, the activity to which the Institute would be chiefly restricted
in centuries to come, but rather to respond to the particular dangers of
the English situation. Mary Ward envisioned not competition with the
Jesuits, but rather complementarity: dedicated women could reach
people in England, particularly poor people, with whom the Jesuits
dared not dwell.[104] Mary Ward thus returned again to England in 1612,
in April 1614 for several months, and again from December 1614 until
c.September 1615. In England, so the *English Life* says, Mary Ward and
her followers are concerned

> especially [with] the poore, to whome Priests could not get but with great
> danger, and by Night, not having justifyable pretexts, as to those of quality
> they have, their Houses [those of the nobility] being frequented by all sorts. To
> remedy this want [this lack of ministry to the poor], our dearest Mother
> employed herselfe and hers; sometimes disguised, sometimes in her owne
> cloathes, using some times familiar conversation, other times authority
> amongst the common and poore sort... When it tooke, they instructed them
> how to make good Confessions, and so prepared them [so] as the priests had
> but to heare theire Confessions, and so avoid the danger which a long stay
> woud have brought them.
>
> (p. 20)

Catholic priests in England have been accused, by a modern historian,
of caring chiefly for Catholics found in or close to great houses, and of

---

103. Gemma Simmonds CJ, 'Recognition at Last', *The Tablet* (7 Feb. 2004): 'It took nearly
three hundred years to gain final Papal approval of Mary Ward's plan, but it was not
until 1979 that the Jesuit Constitutions could be adopted. Even then, reference to
women as spiritual directors, and the Jesuit characteristics of a vow of direct obedience to the Pope for the sake of mission and manifestation of conscience were not
permitted. Only last year (2004) did it become possible to adopt the full Constitutions
and with them a name close to that envisaged by Mary Ward' (p. 11).

104. The dangers run by the Jesuits in the earliest years of the English mission were so
extreme that their general contemplated suspension or cancellation: see McCoog,
English and Welsh Jesuits, p. 11.

evading 'the laxer observances of peasant religion'.[105] Mary Ward and
her followers here speak directly in matters of faith to the poor. In so
doing, however, they face the time-honored dictum from their own
side that women should not preach. Mary Ward might have resorted to
the Margery Kempe defence here: 'I preche nat, ser; I com in no
pulpytt' (4213). In the second St-Omer address, however, she develops
a more sophisticated position: that the words of every person, of whatever social class, should be respected *as if* possessed of sermon-like
authority; as something sacred: 'perhaps you thinke that weomen are
not to preach, therefore ther words are not to be much regarded. It is
certain that the words of everie one whoesoever, man or weoman, that
by ther place are to speake, are to be regarded . . . it is good to take
everie word and action that commeth from superiours, *or any who has
any cause to speake,* as from god'.[106] This catches the essence of Mary
Ward's distinctive ministry: that she is above all a superlative listener;
somebody who has evolved techniques of listening that, as we shall see,
would win the admiration of any modern therapist.

The *English Life* also emphasizes the adventurousness, and sometimes the recklessness, of Mary Ward's travels through England; here
again, we float between hagiography and romance. She is several times
captured, once in the Channel; she sings her way to jail with 'Our
blessed Lady her Litanyes'; she kisses the threshold of her jail as 'a place
sanctify'd by the cause' (p. 23). Her shadowy fame spreads, and the
archbishop of Canterbury is moved to say that 'she did more hurt than
6 Jesuits' (p. 21). Her friends, seeing her 'tyred out with mentall employ-
ments', urge her to take 'some recreation. At length yealding there-
unto', the *English Life* tells us,

she found out a very unexpected one, which was to give the Bishop of
Canterbury his wish of seeing her; and in effect, went to his House to
Lambeth with noe small apprehension to her companions, but to herselfe a
reall recreation. God permitted he was not at home, but she left her Name,
and that she had beene there to see him written in the glasse Window with
a Diamond.

(p. 22)

105. Christopher Haigh, 'From Monopoly to Minority: Catholicism in Early Modern
England', *Transactions of the Royal Historical Society*, 5th series, 31 (1981), p. 138; see
further Frances E. Dolan, *Whores of Babylon: Catholicism, Gender, and Seventeenth-
Century Print Culture* (Ithaca: Cornell UP, 1999), p. 88.
106. I, 361, emphasis added.

This bravura act is matched by others in the *English Life*, such as her showing 'a fine christall Riliquary' to a prison guard, her escape from 'a garden house neere London', ringed with 'spyes', or her 'reclayming of a Priest of a very good family' who now remembers 'neither Masse nor Office' (pp. 22–3). And such work continues once Mary Ward has returned to St-Omer through a network of her women in England leading secret, unrecorded lives. On 2 November 1622, notice passes from Douai to Rome of 'Jesuitresses' in England: 'in one house in Shoe-lane at London there live 14 of them'.[107] Beyond London, however, these women tended to live, again in Jesuit-like fashion, as single persons. One of them, known only as Sister Dorothea, gives a brief account of her life in the period 1621–3. She lives with a poor woman in a house close to Hintlesham Hall in Suffolk (another Elizabethan mansion, still in existence); her ministry, as she sees it, is primarily to the rural poor. 'I tend and serve poor people', she says,

in there sickness. I make salves to cure there sores, and endeavor to make peace between those at variance. In these works of charity I spend my time, not in one place, but in many … But it is much to be lamented, that when poor souls are come to that pass that they desire nothing more than to save there souls, by means of the Sacraments, it is incredible to say how hard a thing it is to gett a preist to reconcele them, partly through the scarsity of priests, and partly through the feare of those with whom they live.[108]

These priests who prove so scarce tend to live with the better off in larger country houses; in travelling into deep rural locations they render themselves more conspicuous, hence vulnerable. Dorothea thus provides vital linkage between the Catholic rural poor and the priesthood. Her efforts are much appreciated: a Jesuit and a Benedictine, talking together, 'wished that there were a thousand such as I in England' (I, 774); at the same time, not knowing Dorothea's affiliation with Mary Ward, they 'much oppose against Mistress Mary Ward and her companie' (I, 774). The Jesuit, however, is keen that Dorothea dedicate herself to the spiritual welfare of a single gentlewoman, a recent convert. This Dorothea refuses: 'I answered it was an unreasonable request, and that I would never forsake my poor freinds' (I, 775). Vilification

---

107. William Farrar to John Bennett (*Mary Ward*, ed. Dirmeier, I, 731). Although from a Catholic source, this is not a friendly witness (see further on Bennett below).

108. See *Mary Ward*, ed. Dirmeier, I, 773; further references to this account are given in the text. See further Chambers, *Life of Mary Ward*, II, pp. 27–39 (p. 28).

continues to flow from Dorothea's co-worker clergy: Mary Ward and her 'company' are called 'notable Goshops' (IV, 778), and Dorothea is asked if she 'would be a gallowping Nunn or a preacher, &c' (IV, 779). In travelling to London with Lady Timperley from Hintlesham Hall, Dorothea is able to reflect on the perennial genius of the Catholic Church for persecuting its own: 'soe long as I remayn unknown I have no enemys but heretiques [that is, Protestants], whom I fear not at all; but if once I be known, my lady bids me look for as many enemies of preists and Catholiques as I now have frinds of them' (I, 776). Dorothea's account ends with her Catholic tormentors passing on rumours concerning Mary Ward's Institute: 'they say she is gon to Rome to have it confirmed; but it will never be, without inclosure, and if it be not confirmed, it is noe Religion. I say litle to them', says Dorothea, 'but seeth much' (I, 778–9).

In fact, the rumours of Mary Ward's departure for Rome are true: she had set out from Liège on 21 October 1621, arriving on Christmas Eve. The *English Life* has her kneeling 'as soone as she beheld the Steeple of Saint Peeter's Church 16 Miles off Rome', rendering 'all submission to that holy seat and Chayre of his Successours' (p. 24); the *Italian Life* emphasizes her visiting, before finding lodging, 'the body of St Ignatius' (IV, 114). Her Institute Plan had been taken to Rome in November 1615, and Mary had meant to follow it there during the 'raigne' of Pope Paul V.[109] She had been frustrated in that design, however, by an illness that 'brought her to the last extreames'. Again, Providence works in unexpected ways, since 'the afore said Infirmity... had its begining by visiting two of her little ones who had the measells' (p. 18); two blotchy infants thus turned her back to further work in England and the Spanish Netherlands. But Mary Ward and her companions travelled hopefully in 1621; their London adherents back in Shoe Lane (according to one unfriendly Catholic witness) 'make themselves as sure of the confirmation of their order, as if they had it in their pocket'.[110]

The English and Italian lives fail to mention that Mary Ward's younger sister Barbara, with her from near the beginning, sickened

---

109. Papal approval was crucially important for Ward. Her movement was to be organized under a mother general, directly subordinate to the pope; this would free it from local ecclesiastical interference. See Ulrike Strasse, *State of Virginity: Gender, Religion, and Politics in an Early Modern Catholic State* (Ann Arbor: University of Michigan Press, 2004), p. 152.
110. Farrar to Bennett, as cited above (I, 731).

shortly after arriving at Rome and died on 25 January 1623; she was little more than thirty years old. Such an omission accentuates the strength of these *strong women* in ways that we moderns find terrible to contemplate: the female authors are writing *lives* of Mary Ward, and they will not be distracted. There is a document, however, that gives a most vivid account of Barbara's crucial participation in the 1621 'pilgrimage to Rome', her affliction with a disease 'not unlike to the small pox', and her slow and lingering death (I, 744, 745). This document has a strong sense of its own generic parameters, and is a text *between women*: it is, in short, a necrology, to be folded into the developing institutional history of the Institute. It begins with vivid recollection of Barbara as a member of the pilgrim *compagnye*: not, à la Margery Kempe, perennially serious towards her companions, but rather inclined 'to make them merry, especially when she came to the inne'.[111] The pains of incipient exile, of that homesickness which seemed to afflict early modern (rather than medieval) Englishwomen,[112] are then vividly remembered: 'we were in a strange country, farre from home, and little hope of humaine meanes, without language, acquaintance, provision, or mony' (IV, 744). 'The heavenly Bridgroome' then finds himself 'soe inamored' with Barbara, this 'odiferous and beautifull flower', that he sends sickness upon all the company and decides, 'being Lord of all...to have one' (I, 745). The long and lingering account of bodily sufferings that follows—the mouth-stopping 'fleame', the agues and 'continuall flux', the burning fevers—are really only for the eyes of professional religious (for whom the martyrdom of incipient death, and the moment of dying, form the climactic moments of a human *life*). The 'baroque' imaginings of the female author—writing just a few days after Barbara's demise—seem excessive even to the modern, German descendants of Barbara's movement.[113] 'Her feeble body', for example, is said to 'hast unto her Mother earth'; her body 'became a mere ottoma, nothinge left theron but skine and boanes' (I, 748). Her last words are said to be 'Jesus, Jesus, Je'; she dies 'not being able to

111. I, 744. 'Godfather's information' accuses Mary Ward of being a cheerful traveller: 'Item when shee travaileth shee ys extraordinarie joviall' (I, 763).
112. See further Wallace, 'Geneaologies of Homesickness: A Feminine Genre', in 'Periodizing Women', pp. 422–5.
113. 'Sie schöpfte aus eigener Kenntnis und persönlichen Beobachtungen, die sie in barocker Weise gestaltete' (*Mary Ward*, ed. Dirmeier, I, 743). This necrology (very unusually) survives in two distinct forms, A and B; Dirmeier prints only the shorter of the two, A.

pronounce the word sus' (I, 748). Mary Ward, here identified not as her
sister but as 'Mother Chief Superiour', is the vocal coach who 'bid[s]
her call upon Jesus' (I, 748). 'Jesus' recalls Mary Ward's famous first
word (as in *Painted Life* 1) and the 'Je', perhaps, the work of her Institute, not yet achieved.

'I have never seen so fine a death', says Margaret Horde, most likely
the author of this text,[114] 'nor ever expecte to see the like' (I, 749). She
clearly does not consider her own literary style to be culpable of baroque
('barocker') excess. Most memorably, she rejoices in authoring a text
between women, and for women; these highly literate English Catholics need no father confessor, she insists, to compose their accounts:

> Here are no exagerations, but a true relation, noe confessarious to declare
> what hath passed betwixt Christ, and her innocent soul, nor to garnish her out
> with a florishing stil.

(I, 750)

Apostolic Viragos in Rome, 1621–26

Mary Ward's arriving at Rome in pilgrim garb was colorfully reen-
acted at Rome on 5 October 2009, and at Westminster on 23 January
2010.[115] Her 1621 Christmas arrival was indeed an international sensation. The aspirations and assumptions of the 'Jesuitesses' (as they were
commonly known, even in the *curia*) were directly set forth by the
opening words of their *Memoriale*, addressed to the pope and dated 28
December 1621. Presenting Mary Ward's movement as a divinely-
sanctioned *fait accompli* is a bold opening move:

> Holy Father,
> Seeing by divine apointment we are to take upon us the same holy Institute
> and order of life already aproved by divers Popes of happie memory... to the
> Religious fathers of the Society of Jesus...[116]

114. *Nekrolog* B identifies Horde as author; Dirmeier thinks it probable that she also wrote
A (I, 743). Margaret Horde, who also copied the letter of Sister Dorothy cited above,
was effectively Mary's Ward's secretary at Rome in the period 1621–4 (I, 772).

115. There was also a celebratory Catholic eucharist at York Minster in Mary Ward's
honour on 29 January 2010.

116. *Mary Ward*, ed. Dirmeier, I, pp. 597–8. The text survives in both English and Latin.
Mary Ward's addresses to the papacy are usually framed in Latin (sometimes Italian).
Her correspondence with the archduchess Isabella Clara Eugenia, particularly inten-
sive at this period, is in French; others are addressed in Italian or English.

Sir Henry Wotton, later provost of Eton but then ambassador to Venice, wrote on 21 January with news of 'five English Gentlewoemen arrived at Rome', evincing 'much wonder at theire habits and heere at theire purpose'. Which, he gathers from an Italian source, is to 'catechize girles as fast as the masculine Jesuites doe boyes'.[117] A month later, John Bennett writes from Rome with his suspicions that the Jesuits are secretly in league with their female counterparts:

The Jesuitrices here follow there suite underhande; the Jesuites disclayme openly, but I knowe they assiste underhande what they can. But they will never in this courte gett other allowance but with clausure, as I am made assured.[118]

Lord Clarendon, writing of the court of Rome in 1650, observes 'so great a faccion amongst the seuerall distinctions of the Catholique Cleargy...that wee haue to great experience, how ready euery one is to pull downe what another of an order he is not kinde to desires to build'.[119] What seemed true in 1650 was never more true than in 1622: for English Catholicism was then consumed by a ferocious, self-destructive battle over whether to subject the island to the authority of a bishop, or not. Secular clergy were broadly in favour, and religious orders (above all, the Jesuits) not. John Bennett was in fact an agent in Rome of the English pro-bishop party; since Mary Ward was identified with the Jesuits his opposition to her was absolute. Within two months of her arrival at Rome, Catholic English seculars had sent the pope an *Informatio*, full of accusations concerning these 'Amazons' or 'Apostolic Viragos'; these 'chattering hussies' or 'Galloping Girls'.[120] Mary Ward's followers, Bennett insists, are 'a fullie [folly] to this towne'; their public appearances 'much impeached the opinion which was hold of the modesty and shamefastnesse of our country women' (I, 662). 'They are most ridiculous', he fumes in Italian, 'and people make fun of them

---

117. To Dudley Carleton, British ambassador to The Hague (*Mary Ward*, ed. Dirmeier, I, 619); a very similar text is sent on the same day to Sir George Calvert, 'Secretarie of Estate' to James I (I, 620–21).

118. To William Bishop from Rome, 22 February 1622 (I, 649).

119. Bodleian Library, Oxford, Clarendon MS 39, fol. 200, as edited in *Elizabeth Cary, Lady Falkland: Life and Letters*, ed. Heather Woolf, Renaissance Texts from Manuscript, 4 (Cambridge: RTM Publications, 2001), pp. 437–9 (p. 438).

120. Littlehales, *Mary Ward*, pp. 111, 135, 235. The English secular clergy, petitioning Pope Gregory XV in 1622, claimed that these women are called 'sometimes Galloping Girls, because they ride hither and thither, sometimes *Apostolicæ Viragines*' (Chambers, *Life*, II, 186).

when they see them going about the city squares, as if they were female
maestri, and they call them *the wives of the Jesuits*.[121] As 1622 wears on
Bennett positively gloats at the increasing poverty of the Englishwomen
in Rome: 'this wild company will come to desolation', he says on 31
July (I, 714); 'they goe about amongst the Cardinals here begging', he
writes on 15 August, 'for they are wholly spent' (I, 716).

As one who prides himself on knowing the mind of the *curia*, and
of the pope, John Bennett is stone cold certain that *clausura*, or enclosure, will be the sticking point to ruin Mary Ward's hopes: 'clausure
they must embrace', he insists on 18 March (I, 659); 'without clausure
they must dissolve', he reiterates one week later (I, 662). A laconic letter *between men,* sent from one Italian-speaking English Benedictine to
another, is also sceptical. According to a priest friend of his, writes
Dom Anselm Beech, 'le Jesuitesse Inglese' fear that he will write against
them from Monte Cassino to Rome. And that he will reveal to Rome
that blood and family ties bind the leaders of this movement to 'quelli
della coniuratione polveraria', the Gunpowder plotters. But, he
continues,

I had no inclination to involve myself with their affairs, since the great wisdom of that Court will never approve such an order of women: for in Italy,
doors, locks, ironworks and enclosure are never sufficient to keep nuns in
good order. How much danger and scandal there is to fear: that religious
women, dressed in silk and velvet, should traffic day and night with all kinds
of men, and with nothing but the spirit [il spirito] to keep them in order.[122]

How then are Mary Ward's biographers to represent her entry into this
murky masculine milieu, rife with misogynist fears, courtly dissem-
blings, and politic calculations? According to the *English Life*, she
presents the case for her Institute

with all simplicity and integrity, which many Polititians condemn'd her for,
pretending she might with more ease obtaine her ends by onely making

---

121. 'Sono ridicolosissime, et la gente sene burla del fatto loro quando le veggono andare
      intorno per le piazze, come se fossero huomini maestri, e le chiamano le moglie delli
      Giesuiti' (I, 737).
122. 'Ma io le resposi, che non havevi animo d'intricarmi con fatti loro, quantunque cre-
      devi certissamamente che la grand sapienza di quella Corte mai approverà una tale
      religion di donne, mentre che in Italia porte, serrature, ferrate e clausura non sono
      quasi bastante de tener molte monache in buon ordine, e quanto pericolo e scandalo
      à di temere, che donne religiose quà vestite di seta e veluto pratticano giorni e notte
      con ogni sorte de huomini et non è altro che il spirito per tenerli in ordine' (I,
      660–61; addressed to Anselm Beech OSB at Rome, dated 21 March 1622).

appeare what was more likely to be plausable, but she blessed herselfe at the name of Policy or double dealing in the wayes and cause of God: not that she was ignorant what force humane wayes had, but disdayned it should be thought so devine a worke shou'd either need cloake or patches, or that other then the candid truth should be treated betwixt her and his Holynes.

(p. 26)

Mary Ward is not quite the holy innocent here, the *ingénue*, because she *does* know how political rhetoric works, with its figurative cloaks and purple patches; her naivety consists, rather, in thinking that all can be worked out personally, one on one, between the pope and his loyal subject. This particular article of faith seems, again, most English: the belief that if only we can get to His Majesty, rather than those surrounding him, all will be well.

The odious John Bennett was right to harp on enclosure as a defining issue. On 18 March 1622 he mocks the notion that 'the Jesuitrices' would seek 'to be sent among Turkes and infideles to gayne soules' (I, 659). On 21 May he reports their petitioning the pope that, while respecting traditions of enclosure in Italy, 'they might beyond the mountaynes wander out of clausure' (I, 684). This notion of the Alps protecting the eyes of Rome from scandal, like a veil, recognizes that southern European *curial* males could not countenance women extending convent life and discipline to the streets. They would rather, so it seems, see the Catholic poor of rural England die alone without comfort or sacraments than have a woman minister to them or find them a priest. It is her grounding in the English situation, I would suggest, that makes Mary Ward so absolute in resisting enclosure. Early on in her first Roman sojourn, Cardinal Bandini offers her a very reasonable compromise. While reverencing the cardinal, the *English Life* nonetheless half-suggests reminiscence of *Matthew* 4, the third and final temptation of Christ.[123] The cardinal, who 'had duely the power of a meriting friend', urges Mary Ward to accept the mild form of enclosure applied to a group of wellborn female oblates in Rome,

the enclosure of Torre di Specchio (which in effect is lesse then in all our Houses was to be observed) on which condition she shou'd have freedome to

---

123.   See Matthew 4.1–11, especially verse 8: 'Next, taking him to a very high mountain, the devil showed him all the kingdoms of the world and their splendour. And he said to him, "I will give you all these, if you fall at my feet and do me homage"' (*The New Jerusalem Bible*, gen. ed. Henry Wansbrough (London: Darton, Longman and Todd, 1985), p. 1614).

sett up as many Houses all over the World as she wou'd. Which he thought was
noe litle offer, since those noble Ladyes have never beene able to procure the
begining of one more [house,] notwithstanding there being amongst them so
many Sisters and Allyes to Popes and Cardinalls. But to this faire offer our
dearest Mother gave for answer, that to obtain the foresaid grace of propagat-
ing, etc. she wou'd not admitt of two stakes putt in crosse in forme of
enclosure.[124]

The point that the enclosure imposed upon Mary Ward's women by
Mary Ward herself is actually stricter than the norm is made forcibly
elsewhere in the *lives*. 'In our houses', the *Italian Life* says, 'she made us
observe enclosure fully and exactly, not a formal but a real and substan-
tial enclosure' (IV, 135). The *English Life* speaks of 'the preventions
which she putt in all our Houses, even England itselfe'; these 'were
admirable for the efficaciousness of them and yet without certaine
restraints which have of the formall and affected' (p. 80). The crucial
point here is that a female community be allowed to impose and regulate *an enclosure of one's own*; if the world were *periculoso*, as the famous
enclosing bull surmised, it was for women to recognize the danger and
regulate themselves accordingly. It is further evident, from Mary Ward's
first St-Omer address, that she thought enclosure might give women a
false sense of security: 'many Religious after they have made their
wous [vows]', she says, 'thinke they are secure: with you it is not so' (I,
358). Insecurity, in fact, is the only security in matters of salvation; each
woman must work out *a salvation of her own*. The English and Italian
lives further record Mary Ward's charismatic transformations of a carriage, a bedroom, or alehouse lodgings into sanctified space, suggestive
of religious enclosure. 'Her presence', the *Italian Life* says, 'inspired an
indescribable sense of security, so that many persons of the one and the
other sex sought to stay with her during the times of greatest peril' (IV,
127): as when, for example, cannon balls and grenades rained down on
York during the English Civil War.

The sexual threat posed by Mary Ward and her followers, nowhere
acknowledged as an issue by her female-authored *lives*, emerges in the
dark corners of masculine correspondence. Thomas Rant, John

124. *Mary Ward*, ed. Kenworthy-Browne, p. 88; and see the associated letter of 1 July
     1622 from 'le Gentildonne Inglese' to Lorenzo Campeggi, Secretary of the
     Congregation for Bishops and Regulars (I, 698–9). Mary Ward's sister, Barbara, was
     sent to the Torre di Specchio convent to recuperate, and to learn Italian, following
     her sickness in 1622.

Bennett's successor at Rome, writes to Paul Overton of an attempt made by 'the Jesuitresses' to share the vast Palazzo Ferratini with bishop and diplomat of the Spanish Netherlands, Juan Batista Vives:

They asked a parte of his howse to dwelle in, alledging them selves to propagate the faithe. 'Nay', quoth hee, '*my* desighn is of propagatinge the faithe, and yf weomen were in my howse, yt might bee feared some *other* propagation might followe'.[125]

Juan Batista Vives had obtained the Palazzo Ferratini in 1613 with a view to filling it with foreign missionary students; in 1626 it became the Pontificio Collegio Urbano di Propaganda Fidei. The ultra-sexist *propagation* pun by the octogenarian Vives, looking forward to his own membership of Propaganda Fidei, augurs ill for what Mary Ward and company can expect from the newly-founded Inquisition.[126]

Mary Ward spent almost five years in Rome, from 1621 to 1626, while her proposal for an Institute was dissected by curial committees. In the summer of 1622 she opened a school. Within eight months 150 girls were being educated 'gratis' by the 'English Virgins': this 'produced such effects', the *English Life* notes, that 'the wicked sayd if this went on, the Stewes in Rome wou'd fayle'.[127] Journeys to Naples and Perugia lead to further Italian foundations; and a cardinal is cured by travel (as Mary Ward makes a pilgrimage to 'our Blessed Lady of Monte Giovino' in Umbria, p. 28; *PL* 36). All the while, however, poisonous reports continue to drip in from secular clergy in England, directed to Vives and his colleagues at Propaganda Fidei. In July 1624 Propaganda decrees closure or enclosure for the Institute. In April 1625 the three Italian houses are decreed suppressed; in June the school in Rome is closed, 'not without extream moaning and complaint of the Children's Parents, who, contrary to their wonted restraint, went in Troopes to the Cardinall Vicar his Palace' (p. 27). In 1626, Mary Ward reasoned 'there was not what needed her presence in Rome, and a necessity of it in the Low Countreyes and England' (p. 30). 1626, as we shall see in the next chapter, was a hopeful year for English Catholics: for it saw a young Catholic princess, Henrietta Maria of France, become queen of

---

125. II, 91 (thought to date from 1624/1625; emphasis added).
126. See *Mary Ward*, ed. Dirmeier, I, 568; II, 59; the Spaniard Juan Bautista Vives lived from 1542 to 1632.
127. Wetter, *In Her Own Words*, p. 95; *English Life*, p. 26.

England.[128] Charles I was crowned on 2 February (with Henrietta Maria refusing to attend the Protestant ceremony, even behind a specially devised screen); Mary Ward left Rome on 10 November.[129] Christmas Eve 1626 found her at a Capuchin church in the Austrian Alps, praying for 'the Conversion of England' (p. 31: *PL* 43).

The Ghibelline Mary Ward

The next two years, however, see Mary Ward deflected from her original intent of returning to England and the Low Countries into an ambitious programme of religious foundation: this leads her from Munich to Vienna to Prague to Bratislava. Here, 'upon the confines of the Turkes Dominion', she learns how the Hungarian Countess Mária Palffy, 'the Lady Palvy', gathers the poor into her castle 'when the Turke made his yearely incursions' (p. 35). Mary Ward has, in effect, exchanged Guelf for Ghibelline territory: finding her movement thwarted at Rome, she revels in the welcome accorded her by the elector Maximilian I[130] and the emperor Ferdinand II. She has found a space free both of the spy networks of Rome and the double persecutions of England (Catholic and Protestant). The new houses flourish; by 1628, 465 girls are attending the school in Vienna.[131] But a Bill of Suppression is already being prepared; in the early spring of 1629 Mary is back in Rome, making a last-ditch effort to save her Institute. On 25 March 1629, the Feast of the Annunciation, Maria della Guardia writes to Urban VIII, denying 'falcissimi rumori, dicendo tra l'altre cose, che

128. The recruitment of Englishwomen into continental religious communities reached an all-time high during the 1621–30 decade: see Walker, *Gender and Politics*, p. 20 (covering the period 1591–1710).

129. See Caroline M. Hibbard, 'Henrietta Maria', *Oxford Dictionary of National Biography*, ed. H. G. C. Matthew and Brian Harrison, 61 vols (Oxford: Oxford University Press, 2004) 26, p. 393b; Mark A. Kishlansky and John Morrill, 'Charles I', *ODNB*, 11, pp. 101a–103b; Michelle Anne White, *Henrietta Maria and the English Civil Wars* (Aldershot: Ashgate, 2006), p. 21. In refusing to accept her crown from the archbishop of Canterbury, Henrietta Maria became the first uncrowned English and Scottish queen consort.

130. On the peculiar, long-lived success of Mary Ward and her English Ladies at the Munich Paradeiserhaus, see the fine post-Weberian account of Strasser, *State of Virginity*, pp. 154–74.

131. According to the letter sent by Melchior Klesl, bishop of Vienna, to the Congregatio de Propaganda Fidei on 23 September 1628 (II, 381).

dette Inglesi predicavano in pulpiti, e piazze, e disputavano publica-
mente de rebus divinis'.[132] She is especially passionate about the new
work in Bratislava, perhaps because the educational fight against
Lutheranism may be analogized, in some respects, to conditions in
England. Since the governance of families is left to women in that part
of the world, she argues, Calvinists and Lutherans fear that the presence of the English Ladies might quickly lead to the extinction of
Protestantism ('si estinguerebbe presto', II, 430). Closure of houses and
confiscation of incomes, however, would be devastating, since 'this
Company consists of women from many homelands and nations, such
as Italian women, Spanish women, German women, Flemish women,
Bohemian women, Hungarian women, Frenchwomen, Irishwomen,
and Englishwomen'.[133] Many will be left far from home, and the English will suffer most: they are greatest in numbers, and they will not be
able to return to their heresy-ridden country without great danger.
Their relatives may not afford them house room, nor will they be able
(given the wretched state of English Catholics) to give them second
dowries. 'And in addition to this', she concludes, 'the imputation of
having lived a *vita scandalosa* will weigh them down beyond measure'
(I, 432). Rome is so keen to affirm enclosure for religious women that
it will evict religious women onto the streets, leaving them penniless,
far from home, and with scant prospects. The 'scandalous life' that
Rome supposes these women to lead might come closer to reality if
Rome shuts down their hard-won houses.[134]

Early in 1630 Mary Ward defended her Institute before a new Particular Congregation of Four Cardinals: 'there was nothing in it, nor
practised by her or hers', she says through the *English Life*, 'which had
not beene practised by Holy Woman [*sic*] and approved by the Holy
Church in particular Persons, but never practised by a community'
(p. 38). She here alludes to the conventional economy of thrift whereby
Rome manages extraordinary women: Bridget of Sweden and *then*

132. *Mary Ward*, ed. Dirmeier, II, 428 ('most false rumours, suggesting among other things
    that the said Englishwomen were preaching in pulpits and in piazzas and disputing
    points of divinity in public').
133. '[C]onsistendo detta Compagnia de piu paesi, e nationi, come d'Italiane, Spagnole,
    Alemagne, Fiamenghe, Boeme, Hongare, Francesi, Hibernosi, et Inglesi' (II, 431).
134. A point not lost on the Staffordshire Jesuit Robert Stanford (alias Stafford): see his
    compassionate letter from Liége addressed to Thomas Courtney SJ, dated 26 April
    1630 (II, 629).

Catherine of Siena, but never both at once: why not, she suggests, a communion or community of female saints? Soon after this she heads back to the northern European heartland of her communities, only to find that they are being suppressed. She then, on 6 April 1630, sends her followers a fateful letter. Such orders of suppression, she writes, 'are in no place to be accepted by Ours'; and, 'if it seems good to bishops or nuncios to proceed to a sentence of excommunication (which I would not believe), let it happen; a remedy will be found. It is for Ours to remain faithful to their Institute'.[135] Members of the Cologne community showed the letter to their confessor, the English Jesuit George Holtby (alias Duckett); a Latin copy reached the Inquisition in Rome on 15 June.[136] On 13 January 1631, Urban VIII signed the Bull of Suppression, *Pastoralis Romani Pontificis*. This begins by reporting that 'certain women or virgins, having taken the title of Jesuitesses, have lived together for some years without any particular approval of the Apostolic See . . . Free from the laws of enclosure', it continues, 'they wander about at will, and under the guise of promoting the salvation of souls, they have been accustomed to attempt and to employ themselves at many other works which are most unsuited to their weak sex and character [ingenii imbecillitati], to female modesty and particularly to maidenly reserve'.[137] The bull ends by affirming suppression in the most unambivalent terms:

Nulli ergo omnino hominum liceat hanc paginam nostrae suppressionis extinctionis subiectionis ablationis deletionis abrogationis decretorum privationis amotionis absolutionis liberationis praecepti declarationum permissionis

135. *Mary Ward*, ed. Dirmeier, II, 625 ('a nostris nullibi acceptandum est . . . si Episcopis aut Nuntiis visum fuerit, ad sententiam excommunicationis procedere (quod non crediderim) transeat, remedium bene invenietur'). This letter, sent to Mary Ward's followers at Trier, Cologne, and Liège, became (says Immolata Wetter CJ) 'a dark tunnel bringing her under the shadow of the Inquisition' (*Shadow*, p. 32).

136. The letter survives only in Latin; a copy of this Latin original describes it thus: 'copia della lettera della Generalessa delle Gesuitesse che le essorta à non ubbedir à decreti della Sacra Congregazione benche fosse loro imposto sotto pena di scomunica ecc' (II, 625). It is ironic (to use anaemic modern parlance) that Mary Ward should be betrayed by a Jesuit Holtby: she had arrived at the Jesuit College in St-Omer in 1606 armed with letters written by Richard Holtby SJ. This latter Jesuit is traditionally supposed to be the priest who spills the chalice (*English Life*, p. 9; *PL* 14); he was famed for his needlework.

137. Translation by Ganne and Harriss, in Wetter *Under the Shadow*, 213–18 (pp. 213–14); this is the first full English translation of this bull. For the Latin text, see *Mary Ward*, ed. Dirmeier, III, 121–7 (p. 122).

impartitionis monitionis hortationis voluntatum et mandatorum infringeret
vel ei ausu temerario contraire.

(III, 125–6)

Therefore, let it be permissible to no person whatsoever to infringe this page
of our suppression, extinction, subjection, removal, destruction, abrogation,
privation of decrees, withdrawal, disposal, liberation, precept, declarations,
permission, bestowal, warning, exhortation, of our will and our commands, or
rashly dare to go against it.

(p. 218)

This bull was fierce by the standards of its own time; it remained on the
books to block analogous female initiatives in years to come; it was
quoted back at Mary Ward's followers and admirers down the centuries.[138] Why then would somebody as astute as Mary Ward have defied
both the notice of suppression and the possibility of excommunication?
The answer again lies rooted, I would suggest, in the English situation.
Mary Ward attached great importance to her personal relationships
with popes: she sought to meet them one-on-one, and derived great
confidence from their words of encouragement. She thus failed to grasp
that in the curial division of labour it fell to the pope to meet, greet, and
be gracious; harsher aspects of policy were applied by committees of
cardinals. Decrees issued by 'nuncios or bishops' could not be dismissed
as unrepresentative of the will of the pope; papal authority attached to
them through the powers of cannon law. In attributing too much
importance to her direct dealings with popes, then, Mary Ward grossly
underestimated the powers of ecclesiastical hierarchy. And she was, it
must be said, especially deluded in believing Urban VIII to be a plain
dealer: his 'excellent parts and Qualityes befitting his devine call and
place', says the *English Life*, 'were ever inclining him to doe each one
right' (p. 37).[139] It was not until 1998, with the opening of Inquisition
archives at the Vatican, that the truth was laid bare: that Urban VIII had
become personally invested in suppressing Mary Ward's movement,
seeking language that achieved this with exceptional severity.

---

138. 'Anyone comparing suppression documents of earlier Popes with this bull is struck
by the vehemence of the language. Earlier papal documents might have been severe,
but still there was greater objectivity, and also here and there a milder word' (Wetter,
Under the Shadow, p. 135; and on the later effects of this bull, see pp. 137–40).

139. John Bennett, speaking of Gregory XV's view of the 'Jesuitrices', declares that 'I know
for certaiynty that he nor any can abide them. And from the first day he did utterly
mislike them' (letter to Edward Bennett from Rome, 18 December 1622: I, 736).

An English Catholic of the earlier seventeenth century had some grounds for thinking that she enjoyed a special and direct relationship with the pope: for in England there had been no hierarchy of bishops since 1558; the last of the old Marian bishops had died in 1585, the year of Mary's birth. This state of affairs was not uncontested: indeed, it was hotly topical at the time of Mary's travails with Rome. Members of religious orders in England, such as the Benedictines, Jesuits, and Dominicans, were happy enough without bishops, since they could regulate their own affairs without local interference. Ordinary, secular clergy, however, felt bereft of organizational clout. They thus petitioned for a bishop, and in 1623 Gregory XV gave them one. When he died, eight months later, he gave them another: Richard Smith, sometime tutor to Cardinal Richelieu. As we have noted, English Catholic seculars and regulars tended to fight with one another; the arrival of Richard Smith as so-called bishop of Chalcedon brought them to the brink of civil war. This strange saga of warfare within the persecuted minority of English Catholics is dramatized by an extraordinary play called *Hierarchomachia*.[140] It was composed between March 1629 and December 1630: that is, at the very period of Mary's climactic travails with Rome. In both Rome and London, then, questions of hierarchy and authority are the key issues of the day.

Hierarchomachia is very little known, but it is (given the circumstances) a very accomplished play. The text was discovered in the 1950s at the English College, Rome: an institution founded in 1579 and headed by Jesuits that trained priests for the English mission. There was an active theatrical life at the College, although *Hierarchomachia* was likely written by a secular priest in hiding in London.[141] It owes something to Shakespeare—there is a Constable Pumpkin, spouting malapropisms—but most to Ben Jonson's *Every Man Out of His Humour*. It also borrows from the black and white, allegorizing world of Thomas Middleton's *A Game at Chesse*. *Hierarchomachia*'s Catholic characters also divide into two camps: Guelfs and Ghibellines. Guelfs are those who support the papal initiative to reintroduce an episcopal hierarchy to England, headed by Richard Smith; the play's author is clearly on

140. *Hierarchomachia or The Anti–Bishop,* ed. Suzanne Gossett (East Brunswick: Associated University Presses, 1982).
141. See *Hierarchomachia,* ed. Gossett, pp. 7–11.

their side. The Ghibellines, opposing the bishop, are divided into three chivalric orders: the Knights of the Golden Fleece, also known as the Jesuits; the Knights of Malta, also known as Benedictines; the Knights of St James, *id est* the Dominicans. Many of the protagonists may be identified with living personages in the dispute, sometimes from anagrams or puns on their name. There are three female protagonists, Nivetta, Celia, and Valeria. Nivetta is a follower of the bishop, and therefore (according to the playwright) on the right side of the argument; she is acclaimed thus by Valeria:

> Thou art no woman, sure, of common strain,
> But some Athenian student, like Pope Joan,
> Brought in by head and shoulders to the world
> To countenance our modern spleen to popes;
> So thou to cross our women Ghibellines.   (2120–4)

Who are these 'women Ghibellines' that a follower of secular clergy in England might think 'to cross'? Suzanne Gossett, the editor of *Hierarchomachia*, thinks of Mary Ward and her followers (whom even the papacy now refers to as *Jesuitesses*).[142] The reference is timely: Mary Ward is demonstrating 'spleen to popes' in Rome even as this play is first being read in London Catholic circles (as the most closeted of closet dramas). This is not, however, Mary Ward's first surrogate appearance on the London stage. Six years earlier, as Prince Charles pondered a possible Spanish match,[143] she trods the boards in Middleton's *A Game at Chesse*. Charles is the White Knight of the play; Mary Ward is the Black Queen's pawn:

> I am my selfe a Secular Jesuite
> As many ladies are of wealth and Greatnes,
> A second sort are Jesuites in Voto,
> Giving theire Vowe in to the Father Generall
> That's the black Bishop of our house ....   (I.i.46–50)

The phrase 'secular Jesuit' brilliantly distills debate concerning the status of Mary Ward and her followers: were they, both Catholics and

---

142. See *Hierarchomachia*, ed. Gossett, note to line 2124.
143. See *The Spanish Match: Prince Charles's Journey to Madrid, 1623*, ed. Alexander Samson (Aldershot: Ashgate, 2006). Charles's return to London in October 1623 without the Infanta saw 'thousands of bonfires lit on the streets of London'; he was never more popular (Samson, 'Introduction', p. 1).

Protestants wondered, to be ceded *religious* status, or not? The play's fifth act sees the same Black Queen's pawn denounced as 'chiefe Agent for the Transportation / Of ladies daughters' (to Brussels and beyond, V.ii.108–9). *A Game at Chesse* was the most talked-about and most commercially successful drama of its time: the first single play to be printed with engraved title pages, it survives in more manuscript copies than any other play (Ben Jonson imagines it being used as toilet paper).[144] Even our man in Rome, Thomas Rant, heard news of 'a Comedie called "A game at chesses", acted 4 tymes or 5 tymes one day and thence forth a fortnight everie day'; it features, he learns, 'the Jesuitesses and in particular Mistress Twittie provincial of them'.[145] The mysterious provincial also appears in James Wadsworth's *The English Spanish Pilgrime, or A New Discoverie of Spanish Popery and Jesuitical Strategems*.[146] This work, published in London and exactly contemporary with *Hierarchomachia*, features Twitty as co-founder of the 'Iesuitrices or wandring Nuns':

> This Order of Nuns began some 12 yeeres since, by the means of Mistresse *Mary Ward*, and Mistresse *Twitty*, two *English* Gentlewomen, who observe the *Ignatian* habit, and goe clad very like to the Iesuites, in this onely differing from other Nunnes: They walke abroad in the world, and preach the Gospell to their sex in *England* and elsewhere.

(p. 30)

Wadsworth tells of 'no lesse then 200 *English* damsels, being most of them Ladies and Knights daughters', living at St-Omer, Liège, and Cologne; of Mary's negotiations with the pope in Rome, and of her recent work in Vienna (p. 31). Wadsworth is generally well informed, but such was his business. His father had turned Catholic while on embassy in Spain; young James studied with the Jesuits at St-Omer.[147]

---

144. See *A Game at Chesse*, ed. Bald, pp. 1–25; Gary Taylor, 'Middleton, Thomas', *ODNB* 38, 79a–85a. Jonson's 'toilet paper' remark appears in *The Staple of News*, III.ii; reports of the play were dispatched to Brussels, The Hague, Madrid, Florence, Rome, and Venice (Taylor, 80b, 84a).

145. *Mary Ward*, ed. Dirmeier, II, 77.

146. *The English Spanish Pilgrime, or A New Discoverie of Spanish Popery and Jesuitical Strategems. With the Estate of the English Pentioners and Fugitives under the King of Spaines Dominions, and else where at this present. Also laying open the new Order of the Iesuitrices and preaching Nunnes* (London: T.C. for Michael Sparke, 1630).

147. See A. J. Loomie, 'Wadsworth, James, *pseud.* Diego de Vadesfoote (b. 1604)', *ODNB* online (2004); G. Martin Murphy, 'Wadsworth, James (*c.*1572–1623)', *ODNB* online (2004).

One of his sisters, Katherine, joined the exiled Bridgetines of Syon at Lisbon. The other, Mary, joined the Benedictines at Cambrai: that brilliant intellectual community supplied with medieval English spiritual texts by the Welsh Benedictine, and sometime avid playgoer, Augustine Baker.[148] James Wadsworth, having been captured by Moroccan pirates, and having then served as interpreter for the Spanish-marriage-seeking Prince Charles in Madrid, returned to England, denounced popery, and spied for the privy council. He later translated a treatise on chocolate. He chiefly earned his living, however, as a *pursuivant*: those agents of the privy council who, armed with warrants, rampage their way through the pages of *Hierarchomachia* in search of priests and those who shelter them. His account of Mary Ward ends with notice of what should afford him further profitable labour: 'she is daily expected in *England*, to take account of her she-Apostles labours' (p. 31). Mary Ward clearly continued to haunt English imaginaries, both Catholic and Protestant, during her longest period of continental exile.

Incarceration, suppression, romance

As the 'Guelf/Ghibelline' conflict neared its climax in England, Mary Ward returned to her own Ghibelline heartland, travelling in the summer of 1630 from Munich to Vienna. Her close companion, Winefrid Wigmore, was dispatched to try and revive the repressed houses at Liège. Unfortunately, having made some extravagant claims for Mary Ward's authority, she got into warm debate with the papal nuncio, Pier Luigi Carafa, on the subject of social pedigree (that topic of the utmost delicacy to the *Italian Life*). Discussion comes to that heated point

wherin the Nuntio had sayd that Mary Ward was scarse or no gentelwoman; Mistress Winefrid replyed before them all, that he was a basse companion or fellow, she being more noble then himself as being nobly borne, wheras the

148. It was the failure of the 'Spanish match' in 1624 that drove sometime playgoer Augustine Baker OSB to the English nuns at Cambrai: see further Ch. 4 below. Baker's playgoing dates to 1596–98, his years as a law student at the Inner Temple (a heady period for Shakespearean drama). Baker's London residencies (1607–24, 1638–41) overlap with Mary Ward's known visits (1609, 1614, 1617, 1618–19, 1639–42).

Nuntio had *bought* his nobility, and that she well knew his frinds and family in Italy. O tempora! O mores!¹⁴⁹

The expressions of horror here, clearly more darkly masculine *jouissance,* come from the mouth of George Holtby, also known as Duckett: that same Jesuit who, some months before, had hotwired Rome notice of Mary's defying the papal bull. The emperor Ferdinand was determined to protect Mary Ward, since she had travelled to Vienna at his invitation; but, having consulted with the local cardinal, Mary elected to return to Munich.¹⁵⁰ On 28 November she dispatched a final, last-ditch appeal to Urban VIII, still hoping to save her Institute, her life's work. It is telling that even *in extremis,* Mary Ward inclines to life narrative. In necessarily highly compressed compass, she tells her life story in Italian: 'it was twenty-five [years] ago that I left my homeland and my family...'¹⁵¹ No response was made to this letter; she was arrested at Munich on 7 February 1631.

Mary Ward's prison was the Angerkloster, a community (surprise, surprise) of strictly-enclosed nuns: or, more precisely, an airless cell whose walls were speckled with the blood of a nun who had died recently from tuberculosis or lung cancer. Such scenes, although enacted on German soil, find no place in the *Painted Life* at Augsburg: but they do form the imaginative and dramatic heart of the *English Life.* Mary Ward initiates the drama herself and chooses the appropriate saint's day for it. And so 'on Saint Sebastian his Day in the morning', she decides to 'goe abroad that they may see I am not afrayd' (p. 46); she is then arrested by the reading of a letter, 'to this tenour: "Take Mary Ward for an Hereticke, Schismatike and Rebell to the Holy Church"' (p. 47). With one of her forty companions, she is locked up 'in the Roome that had beene used for all desperate and infectious diseases' (p. 48); the two little windows look out on graves. Some extraordinary passages of feminine romance follow, as not one but two communities of women attempt to communicate with her. Her own followers do this through lemon juice letters, written on the wrapping

---

149. George Ducket SJ to Michael Freeman SJ from Liège, 8 September 1630 (III, 23); emphasis added. This intemperate outburst might be contrasted with the letter of Mary Ward to Winefrid Bedingfield which speaks of the visit of 'a poor man but a great servant of God almights'. He teaches her humility: 'let this his lesson serve for us both' (7 Feb. 1637; III, 489).
150. See Chambers, *Life of Mary Ward,* II, pp. 332–3.
151. 'Venti cinque [anni] dà che lasciai Patria, e Parenti...' (III, 105; my translation. See also *Mary Ward,* ed. Kenworthy-Browne, pp. 155–7).

paper of her laundry.[152] The nuns within the *Kloster,* expecting to find
a 'monstruous Heretike, found themselves in a strange surprise of rev-
erence and devotion' (p. 48). One of them, 'an auncient Religious',
begs her mother abbess for 'the happyness at the Doore to see her,
though I speake not'. Mary Ward is thus surprised 'to see that dumb
shew, a venerable Religious Women in the Doore on her knees, with
her hands up, not knowing what it meaned' (p. 48); she must have
looked like Chaucer's flood-apprehending Nicholas, who 'evere caped
upward into the eir'.[153]

The Angerkloster at Munich was in fact a community of Poor
Clares; Mary Ward thus comes full circle in reembracing the regimen
of enclosed life for which she first left England, en route to St-Omer,
in 1606. And at first this makes her happy, knowing that she might
finally escape what she earlier memorably called 'the noyse and negotiation of the World' (p. 12). But her content, in this brilliant passage of
The English Life, is short-lived; her mind moves forward through a
typical process of restless discernment:

Making an act of resignation and oblation of herselfe to God, finding an
unspeakable content, peace and joy of mind in the hope she had that now was
come that long wished for Time wherein she might have nothing to doe but
to thinke of God, love him and depend upon him, with confidence he wou'd
take care of hers. In this disposition she went to her Bed, hoping to rest very
quietly, all Labours being now taken out of her hands. But in all these her
contents, she found, as it were, a suspension of the graunt from above and
rather something that had of the checke: that she shou'd thinke it enough to
suffer, and not labour. She did not murmurre, but had a little inclination to
dispute, but resolved to doe neither then but sleepe, and this notwithstanding
the condition of her mind, and the extreame smell the Bedsteed and Walls had
of spitt, and such like as contagious and dying People doe ordinarily leave. The
exteriour she soone overcame, but in her mind grew a strong force and threate
if she did not resolve to labour in the defence of her owne and hers their
innocency, and consequently her own delivery, which at Length she promised
to doe and so fell a sleep which till this resolution made, she by noe meenes
cou'd doe, so slept well according to her slepes.

(pp. 48–9)

152. *Zitronensaft* letters written by her followers to Mary Ward do not survive, but a good
     number of missives *from* Mary Ward are extant. Many are now indecipherable, but
     happily Mary Ward's secretary, Elizabeth Cotton, made copies. See Littlehales, *Mary
     Ward,* p. 206, and *Mary Ward,* ed, Dirmeier, III, 149ff.
153. See 'The Miller's Tale', in *The Riverside Chaucer,* ed. Benson, I, 3473.

This turbulent and then triumphant moment of intellectual resolve is immediately matched by the author of the *Life* as she relives *her* emotional experience at this point (as Mary Ward is locked away). In short, she (rather like Winefrid in Liège) has an *I hate men* moment: 'I confes my wickednes', she says, 'it was growne a horrour to me to see Priest or Fryer but at the Altar, and in the Confession Seate' (p. 49). She soon recovers, rebuked by recollection of Mary Ward's teachings; she goes on to tell of Mary Ward's further Sebastian-like sufferings at the Kloster. Mary falls into a 'violent Feaver', and is thought likely to die. The 'good Deane' denies her Viaticum until she signs a statement; she refuses to sign, prepares to die, and asks that she be carried to the grate to bid farewell to her companions. The Poor Clares thus carry her, and 'had not other word to say but, "oh, what love, o what Love!"' (p. 52). She gets better the very next day. On the Friday before Palm Sunday, after ten weeks, her release is ordered.[154] Her followers are overjoyed, but Mary elects 'to passe her Palme-Sunday with those good Religious' (p. 52). As the *English Life* recalls, and as she recalls herself in the *Italian Autobiographical Fragment*, Palm Sunday was the day 'I made a vow of chastity'.[155] With this small delay, Mary Ward relives both her commitment to enclosure and her passing beyond it. At this powerfully limenal moment of liturgical time, she knits together the enclosed and the unenclosed: the two communities of women with whom she has shared her life.[156]

The Bull of Suppression, published on 31 May 1631, had been posted in Rome at St Peter's and the Lateran, in the Chancellery and in the flower market, the Campo dei Fiore, where malefactors were put to death.[157] Mary Ward's 'adversaryes' thus report 'that were she in Rome, she wou'd have beene burnt alive in Campo Fiore' (p. 53). But when Mary Ward met with Urban VIII in Rome on 4 March 1632, she was warmly received: on her declaring herself not to be a heretic he

---

154. There are some discrepancies with dates here: see *Mary Ward*, ed. Kenworthy-Browne, p. 53.

155. 'Facevo nella Domenica delle Palme voto di Castita' (I, 47); 'a Day whereunto she bore great devotion, having on it made her first vow of Chastity' (pp. 52–3).

156. Mary Ward's Munich foundation was the only house to escape the suppression of 1631. It was to play a vital role in Bavarian female education for centuries to come, although its educational mission drifted from instruction in Latin—the language of law, liturgy, and power—to fashionable French. See Strasser, *State of Virginity*, pp. 154–72.

157. Wetter, *Under the Shadow*, p. 136.

reportedly says: 'we believe it, we believe it, we neede no other proofe, we and the Cardinalls all' (p. 53). Mary Ward is free to move about the environs of Rome, and to go on local pilgrimages; the pope supplies her with coaches from the papal stables, papal wine, and papal medicine. 'She had a most devine art in making this Life happy', says the *English Life*: 'it was ordinary to say her Presence made each place a court' (p. 56). She is, nonetheless, subjected to the religious equivalent of electronic tagging; undercover inquisitors await her arrival in every town. This goes on for five years. She has long suffered from stones of both kidney and bladder; in the summer of 1637 she falls sick and is expected to die. On 10 August, however, she makes an extraordinary declaration to her attendants: 'I will goe to the Spaw' (p. 59). Spa is the health resort thirty miles south-east of Liège, that sometime stronghold of Mary Ward's movement; Mary had visited the town to drink the waters in 1616.[158] What then are we to make of this revelation, that she is to rise from her sickbed in Rome, once again cross the Alps, and return to the heartland of her Institute? It seems, on the face of it, a convenient way for her to escape perennial surveillance. On the other hand, mental clarifications do strike her with a force felt as powerfully objective, as if from the will of another. Her realization here is straightforward: 'heere I must dy, there I may recover' (p. 59). And so one month later she sets off in a litter, accompanied by Mary Poyntz and Winefrid Wigmore—her two closest companions, and authors of her *English Life*—plus four servants. 'This was the beginning', the *English Life* recalls, 'of her last carreere, of her great if not greatest sufferaunce' (p. 60). As with the *Book of Margery Kempe*, Book II, the later travels of the ageing, semi-invalid Mary Ward are seen as something, in themselves, near miraculous. But as with Margery Kempe, there is also something romance-like in these travels: the *English Life* becomes a strange romance, with God (again) as enigmatic author.

A sure sign of romance, in English texts, is the appearance of a dog: in the Middle English *Tristan*, but only in that version, a dog called Hodain appears and laps up the love potion.[159] In November 1637, on

158. See Chambers, *Life*, I, 395.

159. 'An hounde ther was biside / That was yclepede Hodain; / The coupe he licked that tide / Tho doun it sett Bringwain' (*Sir Tristrem*, in *Lancelot of the Laik and Sir Tristrem*, ed. Alan Lupack (Kalamazoo, Michigan: Medieval Institute Publications, 1994), lines 1673–6). See further the small dog that 'koude no good', yet performs a vital linking and guiding function, in Chaucer's *Book of the Duchess* (line 390).

St Martin's Day, Mary Ward and company are trapped on the Alps by a terrible snowstorm; four people die. But then the remaining travellers are saved by 'the instinct of a little dogg, which served through God's providence to bring us safe' (p. 61).When Mary reaches Paris she lies sick until May. These are 'desperate times for Souldiers and robbing' (p. 62), with the Thirty Years War in full spate, and her companions urge her to travel no further. But, she says, 'her busines was to the Spaw. What God wou'd with her, she confessed she cou'd not tell, *whither her cure or what*. But thither she must goe' (p. 62; emphasis added). She hires a boat, giving three poor people free passage. Fifteen soldiers 'with barbarous and horridd aspects' board her vessel; on seeing Mary Ward they scramble rapidly out again, seized with 'dread and feare' (p. 62). And so she comes to Liège.[160] Here she is soon sent for by 'a certaine Lady of greate note and fame in eminent danger of her Life with a Cancer in her breast' (p. 63). Mary Ward visits and, 'after once or twice seeing the soare, she told her opinion'. When they finally travel to Spa the woman moves in with Mary Ward; her husband, mightily relieved, says that in Mary Ward he seemed to see 'an Angell from Heaven sent to take all weight and anxiety from his hart' (p. 63). As the limenal drama of death approaches, however, the woman grows terrified:

The lady coming neere her End, none but this true and disinterested friend durst propose her preparing for that last passage, which was putt off with a strange and unexpected unwillingnes, not enclining to confesse or communicate... She now grew awfull [*terrified*], which did not serve to lessen the fidelity of this Friend and Servant of God, who by her importune and opportune means gained her to receave the Sacraments with much satisfaction, and at the last dyed with great peace and quiet.

(p. 64)

In dedicating all her time and care to this woman, Mary Ward forfeits the chance of her own cure at Spa. And when, Poyntz and Wigmore say through the *English Life*, 'we murmured at it she wou'd smile and say: "So I doe what my Master sent me for, what imports it whither I recover?"' (p. 64). Earlier, you will recall, Mary had wondered 'what God wou'd with her' at Spa, 'whither her cure or what' (p. 62). The answer is now plain: she has been sent to Spa not to be cured, but

160. The site of Winifrid's unhappy embassy and outburst in 1630; but the text, concentrating only upon Mary Ward, makes no mention of this.

rather to attend a woman with terminal breast cancer; a woman terrified at the thought of dying. God romances her back across the Alps from Rome to perform the kind of ministry she once practiced in England, the site of many lonely Catholic deaths. Hence, perhaps, her smile.

ReCatholicizing English space, 1639–45

Mary Ward returned to England in May 1639 after an absence of twenty years. Inigo Jones had completed Henrietta Maria's Catholic chapel at Somerset House three years earlier; Mary Ward visited Henrietta Maria with a letter of commendation from Rome.[161] Richard Smith, the second so-called Bishop of Chalcedon, had left England in 1631, never to return: the Ghibelline side of *Hierarchomachia* had won the argument, and English Catholics again lived without episcopal hierarchy. But the pursuivants or priest hunters, deemed 'the bugbears of the time' or 'hounds of state' by *Hierarchomachia* (809, 1027), continued to swarm through Catholic houses. Mary Ward's London dwelling, where 'she kept a great Family and a Chappell standing', could be raided up to four times a day. But, says the *English Life*, no soldier or pursuivant dared enter her private spaces: 'her Chamber was still as a sanctuary' (p. 66). Mary Ward's charismatic ability to create the sanctified *effect* of enclosure within public space is much accentuated by the later part of the *English Life*; so too her *reCatholicizing* of English space as she moves through it. As civil war looms, Mary Ward is forced to abandon plans for opening a school in London; she heads north, to her native Yorkshire. Before embarking on a journey, we are told, Mary Ward 'comm[e]nded it to some one Saint her Patron, as also to the Saint or Protector of the place wither her journey tended'; the *Itinerarium* is then said, plus prayers to 'the Angell of her voyages', to St Ignatius, and to other saints (pp. 97–8). Her Catholicism is thus spatialized onto the landscape of her journey before she even sets out. In

---

161. Written in Italian by Cardinal Francesco Barberini and dispatched on 28 August 1638 (III, 500–501); Mary Ward writes to Urban VIII to thank him for the letter on 19 November (III, 502–3). Barberini understands that Mary Ward is to visit her homeland with her companions ('con la sua comitava à rivedere la Patria') before returning to Rome; he affirms her to be much esteemed in these parts ('molto stimata in queste parti', III, 500).

1642 she heads north to Yorkshire with '3 Coachfulls'; one of these contains a priest 'with Church-stuffe, and all convenient to say Masse by the way' (p. 66).[162] She travels, in short, in a moving chapel. This brings her, first, to 'a most obscure and solitary place, formerly belonging to the Carthusians of that most famous place of Mount Grace' (pp. 66–7). She arrives 'at the Exaltation of the Holy Crose, 1642' (p. 67): the very ceremony that Margery Kempe had witnessed in Norway, halfway to Danzig, in 1433. She sets up 'a Chappell where the blessed Sacrament was kept continually with a Light burning'; this proves 'an exceeding consolation to all the poore Catholikes about' (p. 67). Mount Grace is a place 'so destroyed and defaced', the *English Life* says, that 'onely the bare 4 walls remaine, without roofe or cover'; and 'yet shall you find Catholickes praying there howers together'. Mount Grace is the place where *The Book of Margery Kempe* had been conserved, annotated, and read; it was most likely then, in the early 1640s, being conserved by Catholics elsewhere in the north of England.[163]

Mary Ward and company moved to Heworth, one mile from York, early in 1643. When York comes to be besieged, in April 1644, Mary Ward simply continues her Catholic remapping of English space. 'Feare not', she says, 'we will have our recourse to God and his Angells and Saints; they will helpe us. We will place St. Michael at one end of the Village and St Joseph at the other, and put the power of the great Canons and Peeces on the sacred name of JESUS, which will keepe them from hurting' (p. 69). Eventually they shelter within York itself, returning to Heworth only 'when Yorke was taken by the Parlamentarys' (p. 70). Her house at Heworth is in an appalling state, with 'all the Leadd off the House, all the Iron from the Windowes and Doores, full of stinck and vermine, 400 Soldiers beseides the sicke having lodged therein' (p. 71); many soldiers lie buried in the garden. But once again, sustaining a theme seen throughout the *English Life*, Poyntz and Wigmore emphasize that all spaces associated with their wandering 'Mother' retain a cleanliness and sanctity suggestive of enclosure:

But what was very remarquable, was that God shou'd please to put, as it were, a defence so powerfull, that the Roomes that had beene employed for the

---

162. Another coach, unmentioned in the text, contains her closest companions, Wigmore and Poyntz.
163. On the reappearance of the *Book* from a house of Lancastrian Catholic provenance in 1934, see above Chapter 1.

Chappell and our dear Mother her Chamber were left neate and cleane, not so much as the matts on the floore hurt.

(p. 71)

The end of life, and *life* writing

Mary Ward dies on 20 January 1645, according to the Julian calendar ('style veteri', p. 73) and 30 January according to the Gregorian. The *English Life* remains, to the end, romance-like in tone; the Italian seems more Jesuitical. In the *English Life*, Mary Ward feels her last illness coming over her 'on St Thomas of Canterbury his Day' (p. 72). Seeing 'signes of sadnes' in her companions, she urges them to sing 'and actually sung herselfe, truly like the Swanne dying within les than 24 howers after it' (p. 73). The exact moment of death inspires a preliminary bout of *life* writing in her biographers. This shares something of the necrological impulse that followed the death of her sister, Barbara, almost exactly twenty-two years earlier. But remarkably, this recording of life stages unfolds not just into a history of a body, but of a body in motion:

At about a quarter before eleaven the same morning gave up her blessed Soule to its Creatour having lived 60 Yeares and 8 Dayes: From thirteene Yeares without dispute resolved to serve God in a consecrated state. At 16 vowed Chastity, at 20 left England, at 21 laboured in the beginning of the poore Claires, at 25 began our Course of Life. From 26 never had perfect health, at 36 went on foot from Trevers[164] to Rome in the hart of Winter. From 40 Yeares never lay downe in her Bedd.

(p. 73)

The morning after her death she seems more beautiful than ever, 'her veynes a perfect and lively azure, her Lipps a lovely but fading redd as when in Life, the dy of her skinne as when in Life not as a sicke or dead body, without the least offence rather gra[c]efull and inviting. All these did continue with encrease to the last moment that her coffin was shut up' (p. 75). The *Italian Life* adds that her last word is 'Giesù' (so her last word is her first), and that she dies in the octave of her birth saint, the Roman Emerentiana (IV, 131); this is all very tidy. It also sharpens the final scene of *Abschied,* gathering and departure, played

164. Trèves / Trier / Treviso, site of the *faux*-miraculous cure of *Decameron* II, i.

out between Mary, her closest companions, and her jealous God. As in the *English Life*, the later Italian text has Mary Ward exclaim 'I wou'd all were heere'; she then embraces her remaining companions 'one by one'.[165] And then: she forgets all about them. This last transition captures the core dialectic of Mary Ward's life, lived out between love of human society and private affection for God; between work in the world and a kind of spiritual enclosure:

Poi con segni di grandissimo affetto abbracciandoci ad una ad una ci diede la sua benedittione, et ultimo Adio, ne parlò più, *ne mostrò d'haver più pensiero di noi*, mà con volto sereno, e tutto divino diede segni di suavi, et internii affetti verso Dio, e così passò quello, che gli restò di vita, che fù 4 hore in circa con perfetto conoscimento, e memoria sino all'ultimo.

(IV, 130; emphasis added)

Then with signs of the greatest affection, embracing us one by one, she gave us her blessing and final farewell: spoke no more, *nor seemed to have any further thought of us*, but with a countenance serene and wholly divine, she gave signs of sweet and interior affections towards God. And thus she passed what remained to her of life, which was about four hours, in perfect consciousness and memory to the end.

Both Italian and English *lives* continue beyond the moment of death to evoke the personal qualities, inclinations, virtues, and practices of their subject. The founder's death, according to Max Weber, poses the greatest challenge to any religious movement, precipitating transition from its charismatic origins (associated with the physical presence of the founder) to the routinization of charisma and thence, finally, to bureaucracy.[166] These women, given the assault on their houses by the institutional church, run no immediate risk of bureaucratizing their movement; but they do strive to define and retain the physical and spiritual *charism* of Mary Ward. Her allure was, and continues to be, palpable. Mary Poyntz, the *English Life*'s chief author, first fell for Mary Ward by glimpsing her through a window. Helena Catesby and Elisabeth Rookwood, both related to Gunpowder plotters, became deeply

---

165. 'I wou'd all were heere' (*English Life*, p. 73); 'che vi fussero tutte (intendendo delle assenti)' (*Italian Life*, IV, 130).

166. See Max Weber, 'Charisma and its Transformation', in *Reason and Society*, ed. Guenther Roth and Claus Wittich (Berkeley: University of California Press, 1978), 2 vols with continuous pagination, 1111–57, esp. p. 1113 ('bureaucracy depends upon continuous income, at least *a potiori* on a money economy and tax money, but charisma lives in, not off, this world').

attached to the elderly Mary Ward and vowed never to leave: Helena died serving Mary's movement at seventy, and Elisabeth at fourteen.[167] There are many other examples. Among the numerous personal gifts recorded by her *lives*, Mary Ward evidently possessed one highly prized, if rarely found, by moderns: that of listening. Her resolve not to act out emotions, or to react prematurely, when listening, was hard-won: she knows herself to be 'sanguine' and thus 'cholerike' by temperament— but where she finds in herself 'an inclination of speaking quicke… she made stoppe till that kind of eagerness was over'. Thus when someone who owes much to her chooses to 'vente herselfe' at her, she 'resolved not onely not to answer but with an inward and outward peace and silence to heare all she would say' (p. 58). This, what Mary Ward called a 'manner of practise', is far different from the Ann Widdecombe method.[168] Listening was not Margery Kempe's strong suit either: her gift was a cry that could empty whole churches. But then poor Margery fails to make a single disciple, excepting her sickly son; women and young girls flock to Mary Ward.

Comparisons of Mary Ward to Margery, as to Ann, are uncharitable. But the two premodern women are comparably determined to travel: indeed, their texts accentuate the pains and travails of their late-life journeying, almost as if this amounted to a species of martyrdom. But more particularly, each attempts to marry the intensity of religious enclosure with travel. This attempt famously irritates Margery Kempe's fellow pilgrims: a religiously intense Margery, sustaining her intensity mile by mile, is more than a *compagnye* can bear. But Margery's praxis does intuit something that Mary Ward's travelling realizes more fully: that a woman simply cannot be identified as religious, within a specific locus, and then just *leave the house*. That privilege falls only to men. Chaucer, in opening the feminist fable of *The Wife of Bath's Tale*, grasps this brilliantly. His foundational myth for a post-feminist age proposes that itinerant male religious, friars or *lymytours*, desacralize and disenchant every space—every barn, dairy, and stables—into which they intrude (3.857–81). A woman in open space, *au contraire*, must bring the charge of sanctified religious space with her. Even so, she may fall foul

---

167. See Chambers, *Life*, II, pp. 463–5.
168. It might be compared with the 'maner of practise' advocated by Aquinas in *Paradiso* 13.112–20; see further Robin Kirkpatrick, *Dante's Paradiso and the Limitations of Modern Criticism: A Study of Style and Poetic Theory* (Cambridge: Cambridge University Press, 1978), pp. 28–32.

of masculine violence ('masculine desire' being an inadequate term here) like the poor nameless *mayde* at the beginning of Chaucer's *Tale*. For the threat of 'Galloping Girls' is all, of course, in the masculine mind: a murky place, to judge from the mind of Thomas Rant, or of Inquisitor Vives. Much is at stake here: for should women gain the right to traverse public space, sustaining their integrity as private religious individuals, they might come to have some say in how that space is regulated.[169]

The *English Life* was carried to Paris in 1650 and translated into French within an extraordinarily rich English Parisian Catholic milieu.[170] Catherina Henriqueta de Bragança, queen to Charles II, supported the English Ladies at Hammersmith, and in 1686 the Bar Convent was founded at York (just outside Micklegate, where the royalist city had surrendered in 1644; Figure 25). Hopes for Catholic restoration rose rapidly,[171] then nosedived precipitately, in 1688. In Augsburg the pictures of the *Painted Life* remained on view until 1745, went into the attic until 1773, came out until 1844, and so on as Mary Ward's fortunes waxed and waned. Village priest Marcus Fridl's pioneering study of Mary Ward, published at Augsburg in 1732, remained on the Index Librorum Prohibitorum until the Index was abolished in 1966.[172] In England the Bar Convent provided a refuge for priests fleeing the French Revolution; these same priests, however, managed to force the women into a life of deeper enclosure. By the time that Mary Ward's name could legitimately be spoken in her schools, 1909, these schools had spread (chiefly via Ireland) around the globe; her followers reached India as early as 1841. In 1944, a member of the Loreto branch in India was moved, like her founder, to develop an apostolate of the streets for a nation in crisis: this she was able to do, when Rome gave her permission, four years later.

The relationship of Agnesë Gonxhe Bojaxhiu of Skopje to Mary Ward of Yorkshire must be a complex one; it has yet to be written. It

169. See 'Introduction' above, p. xxxi.
170. See further Chapter 4 below. Margaret Lucas had accompanied Henrietta Maria to Paris in 1644. Having met the marquis of Newcastle at court, she became Margaret Cavendish in 1645; they were based in Antwerp during the 1650s.
171. In 1685, according to Steve Pincus, the new Catholic monarch 'could count on political adulation. James appeared the perfect king for the moment' (*1688: The First Modern Revolution* (New Haven: Yale University Press, 2009), p. 118).
172. *Englishe Tugend–Schul . . . Maria Ward*, 2 vols (Augsburg, 1732).

Figure 25. Bar Convent and Mickelgate Bar, York.

might be thought that in Teresa of Calcutta, Weberian hermeneutics come full circle as a new charismatic figure emerges from a thoroughly routinized, bureaucratic structure (a Loreto convent school) to initiate, once again, an apostolate of the streets. This, however, would be to ignore the diverse ways in which Mary Ward's followers elsewhere have continued to develop their own ways of extending her mission. One striking point of similarity, however, concerns issues of enclosure and public engagement: of extending dedicated religious sacrality into unvisited spaces of the poor. Here, for example, is a visionary call to mission spoken by Jesus to Mother Teresa and recorded by her own text in 1947:

My little one—come—come—carry me into the holes of the poor.—Come be My light—I cannot go alone—they don't know Me—so they don't want Me. You come—go amongst them, carry Me with you into them.—How I long to enter their holes—their dark unhappy homes.[173]

173. *Mother Teresa: Come Be My Light. The Private Writings of the 'Saint of Calcutta'*, ed. and with commentary by Brian Kolodiejchuk (New York: Doubleday, 2007), p. 98.

Mary Ward's God, as we have seen, is ruthless and jealous; Mother Teresa's, if anything, is harsher. For as long as she is petitioning ecclesiastical authorities to pursue an apostolate of the streets, she is buoyed by positive and hopeful desire. Once granted, however, this collapses into a grim, seemingly interminable bleakness. The cosmic irony emerging from her writings is that God grants her wish. In entering into 'the holes of the poor' she enters into a state of spiritual destitution that matches theirs: a state of perfect empathy.'How cold', she writes in 1965

—how empty—how painful is my heart.—Holy Communion—Holy Mass—
all the holy things of spiritual life—of the life of Christ in me—are all so
empty—so cold—so unwanted.[174]

It is not so much the contents of such passages, for the purposes of this book, that form the most instructive point of comparison with Mary Ward, but their mediation. For, as with Mary Ward's literary corpus until 2007, Mother Teresa's textual legacy is under tight control. The excerpts above come from a volume edited by a priest who writes both as 'Postulator, Cause of Canonization of Blessed Teresa of Calcutta' and as 'Director, Mother Teresa Centre' (p. xii). Aware that full and proper editing of Teresa's letters and papers might make the faithful jittery at an inopportune time,[175] Brian Kolodiejchuk has embedded his extracts in life narrative and directive commentary. While not as all-controlling as John of Marienwerder's *Leben der Heiligen Dorothea*,[176] his book nonetheless defers the day when we will be able to read Teresa of Calcutta's writings for ourselves. It rather replicates the format in which Mary Ward was read for several decades, by means of the volume *Till God Will* (1985). This prints extracts from her writings in modernized English, plus biographical details; it features a long introduction by a Jesuit priest and a foreword, a very short one, by Mother Teresa of Calcutta.[177]

174. To Father Joseph Neuner, in *Mother Teresa*, ed. Kolodiejchuk, p. 232.
175. Witness the uneasy opening sentence of a review in the *National Catholic Register* of Kolodiejchuk's book, entitled 'Mother's Darkness', that runs as follows: 'It should be no surprise that a *Time* magazine story is using the 10th anniversary of the death of Mother Teresa to suggest she doubted whether or not God existed' (2 September 2007). The article in question is David Van Biema, 'Mother Teresa's Crisis of Faith', *Time* (23 August, 2007).
176. See Chapter 1 above.
177. See *Till God Will*, ed. Orchard.

The sudden release of almost all Mary Ward-related writings is a dizzying prospect, given the paucity of access to them over the last four centuries. H. J. Coleridge, in attempting to edit *The Life of Mary Ward* by Mary Catherine Elizabeth Chambers, experienced the utmost difficulty in gaining access to vital materials in the 1880s.[178] Fifty years later, Ida Goerres Coudenhove 'met with disaster' (her words) in attempting to obtain access to archival materials for her own biography.[179] Rebuffed but unbowed, she fell back upon the Chambers *Life* and proceeded to write her own spiced-up version. The young Mary Ward, according to Coudenhove, is a worry to her mother from the start:

In the great four-poster bed, Lady Ursula, slender and transparent as the single taper burning beside her, awaited her husband's return with a fast-beating heart and wide haunted eyes.

(p. 4)

Elsie Codd's translation, prepared for the Catholic Book Club in 1938, gets into high gear as the teenage Mary Ward struggles with her suitors, or at least with their olfactory traces:

Every night now she dreamt of the tall flaxen-haired lad. Often, when she knew herself unobserved, she would steal into his room, which smelt of riding boots and leather doublets, and would stand there surrounded by a welter of masculine disorder, not daring to touch a thing.

(p. 17)

Such prose leads one to sympathize with, even applaud, the English Ladies of Augsburg for *not* granting Ida Goeres Coudenhove, clearly a forerunner of Barbara Taylor Bradford, free run of their archives. But perhaps the chiefest pleasure of the new, four volume *Ausgabe* is its releasing us from the strict generic and teleological constraints of *life* writing. True, the material is arranged chronologically—but in a way suggestive of experiential latitude, of words and details relished and enjoyed, of the texture of everyday life. The charismatic energy of

---

178. Chambers' book, published in 2 volumes in 1882 and 1885, remains indispensable. The original *Dictionary of National Biography*, edited by Leslie Stephen (Virginia Woolf's father), omits Mary Ward; but Sidney Lee's 1901 supplement, deriving almost everything from Chambers, finds room for her.

179. Ida Goerres Coudenhove, *Mary Ward*, tr. Elsie Codd (London: Longmans, Green and Co., 1939), vii (first issued by the Catholic Book Club, Dec. 1938).

Mary Ward shines through her English letters, even in her consistent idiosyncracies of spelling ('cheif', 'begg'), her fondness for Italianate and Latinate constructions, and her occasional drifting into Italian ('the preti they come in troups') and even Anglo–Dutch/Deutsch ('my Youngfraw all').[180] Some of the more sensitive letters resort to code or nicknames that make them both comic and semi-scrutable: a letter of 11 December 1632 telling 'Ned' (Mary Poyntz) that 'all knows the woulf ys gone towards the west Indies' encodes the Electress of Bavaria as 'Billingsgate' (III, 398); a letter of 30 July 1633 makes reference to the elector Maximilian and his spouse as 'the miller and his mate' and to Prince Albrecht and his wife as 'Hue and Sue' (III, 418). The pope, in the next letter, figures as 'the Scoof' (III, 421); Cardinal Barberini appears, delightfully, as 'Antony the loome-maker' (IV, 426). Reference to 'Shimill his ould Mister' in the 11 December letter thus decodes as 'the husband of the she-miller', namely the elector Maximilian of Bavaria. Writing from Rome on 19 February 1633, Mary Ward confides to Mary Poyntz that

Fillice in that time will see the utmost what and wheather or no ought wilbe done in Turkish affairs, and ys resolved not to loos time to her so pretious, the service of Pan ys dear to her.

(III, 410)

Fillice is here Mary Ward, Turkish is English, and Pan Charles I; Henrietta Maria features later in the letter as the mother of the young Prince Charles, 'Benigno his Mother' (III, 410). Much has not survived; another missive to Mary Poyntz concludes 'Now I will end. Burn all mine' (III, 424). This letter's very survival attests to the strong attachments linking these women across dispersed locales of European exile. Mary Ward's strength of feeling is plentifully evident: 'how happie a thinge ys yt to love God and serve and seeke him da vero', she tells Winefrid Bedingfield on 29 October 1633. 'I ever loved much more then ordenarie, but I shall fear to love you too much yf your proceedings be still such as I verily thinke they will' (III, 438). Earlier that same year we find Mary chafing for news from Mary Poyntz: 'I have nothinge from you this poste which gos somewhat hard, but patience for

---

180. To Elisabetta Chesia (Elizabeth Keyes) at Rome, from London, in 1642 (III, 528); to Winefrid Bedingfield at Munich, 1634 (III, 452). Dirmeier edits the 1642 letter as 'the prete—they come in troups; I must end...' (suggesting that the letter was abruptly concluded).

remedy'.[181] Such fretful notes might encourage us to associate this correspondence with female epistolary exchanges of the eighteenth and
nineteenth centuries (up to Jane Austen). Mary Ward, however, is running an international network of schools and religious houses in the
context of incipient English civil war; her communications thus compare more closely with those of Margaret Paston. Such combining of
affectionate familiarity with worldly sense is beautifully exemplified by
a letter sent to Winefrid Bedingfield at Munich on 26 July 1627. Mary,
writing from Vienna, offers congratulations on the progress of her 'lattin Schools', and especially on the accomplishments of 'tow towardly
girels', star pupils who have dazzled the priests:

Thes [words] are indeed cheifly to congratulate the unexpected progress of
your lattin Schools. You cannot easily beleeve the content I tooke in the
theames of those tow towardly girels. You will worke much to your owne
happines by advanceinge them a pace in that learninge, and god will concurr
with you, becaus his honore and service so requirs. All such as are capable,
invite them to yt. And for such as desirs to be of ours, noe tallant ys to be so
much regardded in them as the lattin tounge. The lattin hand Maria Mich.
wrote her theam in, ys hear by thes fathers much comm[e]nded, though I
thinke yt ys farr short of what yt wil be.

(II, 233)

At this point in the letter, a light pops on in Mary's mind: not one of her
major visions, but rather a more worldly thought about how those Latin
'theames' or exercises got quite so good. Since the English Ladies were
not an enclosed order, their pupils were not enclosed either; homework
was done offsite, and perhaps Maria Mich's handwriting was just *too*
good. 'I fear thes subtill wenches', Mary continues, 'hadde some help at
home to make ther Theames: but you will looke to them for that'.

Understanding the wiles of 'towardly girels', of course, is essential to
Mary's *rôle* as leader and educator of young women. It thus seems
appropriate to end as we began, with a single woman addressing a
female assembly: over four hundred years before Virginia Woolf at
Cambridge, we have Mary Ward at St-Omer. She muses in her first
'spech' on a priest's scorn for female experience; she ends by locating

181. III, 422 (27 August 1633; similarly anxious sentiments are expressed a week later, III,
   423). Ignatius Loyola did accept that the regular exchanging of letters, once his
   movement had lost the small-scale intimacy of its earliest years, was needful for
   fostering an 'apostolic community of love' (cited in Boswell, 'Letter Writing among
   the Jesuits', p. 257).

such experience beyond masculine reach. In between she shows her sixty women how the full range of classical rhetorical technique, *ars dicendi et tacendi*, might fruitfully align with Vulgate wisdom:[182]

> Ther was a father that lately came into England whom I hard say, that he would not for a 10.000 of worlds be a woaman, because he thought a woaman could not apprehend god. I answered nothing but only smyled, allthough I *could* have answered him by the experience I have of the contrarie. I could have been sorry for his want of iudgement: I mene not *want of iudgment*, nor to condem his iudgement, for he is a man of a *verie* good iudgment; *his* want is in experience.

(I, 359; emphases added)

King-Kok Cheung, mindful that minority women are thought to dwell under a *uniform* veil of silence, has more recently shown that 'silence, too, can speak many tongues'.[183] Mary Ward models earlier, equally nuanced strategies of feminine speaking and silence. Words wasted on masculine scepticism, Ward demonstrates, may be saved and carried forward to international assemblies and networks of women; the 'man of verie good judgment', excluded from such alternative public spheres, is left only with the ghostly memory of an enigmatic, feminine smile. Happily, the absolute silence of textual oblivion has not befallen Mary Ward. Her writings, now properly edited, now form a major addition to the canon of premodern women's texts.

---

182. *Ecclesiastes* 3:7: 'tempus tacendi et tempus loquendi'. On feminine practise of *ars dicendi et tacendi*, see Wallace, *Chaucerian Polity*, pp. 212–46.
183. King-Kok Cheung, *Articulate Silences: Hisaye Yamamoto, Maxine Hong Kingston, Joy Kogawa* (Ithaca, NY: Cornell University Press, 1993). Cheung's three chief analytical categories are rhetorical silence, provocative silence, and attentive silence. See further, more generally, Tillie Olsen, *Silences* (London: Virago, 1980), esp. p. 151 (Olive Schreiner's 1883 anticipation of the 'Shakespeare's sister' motif from Woolf, *A Room of One's Own*).

4

Vice Queen of Ireland: Elizabeth Cary of Drury Lane, *c*. 1585–1639

In May 1639, when Mary Ward visited Henrietta Maria with letters of recommendation from Rome,[1] the queen consort's new Roman Catholic chapel at Somerset House was a national sensation. The queen had laid the foundation stone herself, before more than two thousand people, in September 1632; in 1638 she had celebrated the birth of the Dauphin by processing through the streets of London to Somerset House, singing *Te Deum Laudamus*.[2] Her new chapel, designed by Inigo Jones, was opened on the Feast of the Immaculate Conception (8 December) 1636 with much ceremony and an eight-part sung pontifical mass.[3] The chapel was manned by newly-imported Capuchin friars who, the queen's Capuchin confessor declared, were visited by 'people of all conditions...as one goes to see Indians, Malays,

1. See Ch. 3 above, p. 189. While such letters formed part of diplomatic protocol, the circulation of letters between women had come to form a new and distinctive aspect of life at the English court. Jacques du Bosque's *The Secretary of Ladies. Or, a New Collection of Letters and Answers Composed by Moderne Ladies and Gentlewomen* had been translated from the French and published in 1638; it was dedicated to Mary Sackville, countess of Dorset, a member of the queen's household. See Diana Barnes, '*The Secretary of Ladies* and Feminine Friendship at the Court of Henrietta Maria', in *Henrietta Maria: Piety, Politics, and Patronage*, ed. Erin Griffey (Aldershot: Ashgate, 2008), pp. 39–56.
2. See Erica Veevers, *Images of Love and Religion: Queen Henrietta Maria and Court Entertainments* (Cambridge: Cambridge University Press, 1989), p. 136; Kevin Sharpe, *The Personal Rule of Charles I* (New Haven: Yale University Press, 1992), p. 305.
3. See Jonathan P. Wainwright, 'Sounds of Piety and Devotion: Music in the Queen's Chapel', in *Henrietta Maria*, ed. Griffey, pp. 198–9. Richard Dering, formerly organist to a community of English Benedictine nuns in Brussels, followed Henrietta Maria to London; for text and music of his 'Sancta et immaculata virginitas', see Wainwright, pp. 207–8.

Figure 26. Elizabeth Cary, Tanfield Tomb, Burford parish church (St John the Baptist).

Savages, and men from the extremes of the earth'; they offered cate-
chesis and preaching in French on Thursdays and in English on
Wednesdays and Saturdays.[4] A sculptor was brought in from Rome to
create a scenic machine, forty feet high, to display the Blessed Sacrament, resplendent in a glorious Paradise: a twenty-foot crucifixion
scene by Rubens, his only such painting, was soon added.[5] The chapel

4. Fr. Cyprien Gamache, '*Memoirs of the Mission in England of the Capuchin Friars of the Province of Paris, from the Year 1630 to 1669*', in *The Court and Times of Charles the First*, ed. Thomas Birch, 2 vols (London: Henry Colburn, 1848), II, 309, 315; Dolan, *Whores of Babylon*, p. 42.
5. See Gamache, II, 311–13; Veevers, p. 165–7. The Rubens was destroyed on 30 March (Holy Thursday) 1643 by 'the half-mad Ulsterman John Clotworthy'; surviving shreds and fragments were thrown into the Thames (Diane Purkiss, *The English Civil War: Papists, Gentlewomen, Soldiers, and Witchfinders in the Birth of Modern Britain* (New York: Basic Books, 2006), p. 244).

survived, amazingly, until Somerset House was itself demolished to make way for the administration buildings of Sir William Chambers, which survive today. In October 1639, later in the year of Mary Ward's royal visit, this royal English Catholic chapel at Somerset House became the last resting place of Elizabeth Cary, née Tanfield, the fourth and last of the *strong women* in this book.[6]

Between two tombs

Just ninety years earlier, in 1549, Somerset House had been conceived in the spirit of a newly triumphal, state-driven Protestantism. The duke of Somerset, Lord Protector, had torn down a parish church and the inns of bishops to make room for the building that bears his name. Further building materials were freed up by demolishing a chapel in the north cloister of St Paul's; verses of John Lydgate, and a painted dance of death, disappeared into the rubble. Elizabeth Tanfield lived out her life in places marked by abrupt changes of fortune and architectural style, beginning with her childhood home. She was born in or c.1585—the same year as Mary Ward—in a large country house that had once been Catholic: Burford Priory, some eighteen miles from Oxford (Figure 27). A community of hospitallers, following the Augustinian Rule and dedicated to St John, is first recorded there in 1226; some fine medieval arcading was moved to its current, rather eccentric position inside the main entrance in 1908 (Figure 28). In 1543, Henry VIII granted Burford Priory to his barber surgeon Edmund Harman; one of the two figures above the main door puns doubly on his name (Figure 29). The priory was purchased by Lawrence Tanfield some time before 1580. Admitted to the Inner Temple in 1569, Tanfield was created serjeant-at-law at Easter 1603; September of that year saw the royal progress of King James stop at Burford Priory. In 1607 Tanfield became chief baron of the exchequer, a lucrative post that he retained until his death in 1625. He married Elizabeth Symonds, from

6. 'She was buryed by her Maiesty's permission in her chaple, where the office was performed for her by the charity of the Capuchin Fathers (who were in her life euer ready to doe her any courtesy...)' (*The Lady Faulkland Her Life*, in Cary, *Life and Letters*, ed. Wolfe, p. 221). This 'chaple' was almost certainly that of Somerset House (rather than of St James' Palace); Somerset House was just a few hundred yards from Drury Lane. See Cary, *Life and Letters*, ed. Woolf, p. 25; Dolan, *Whores of Babylon*, pp. 150–51.

a Norfolk family; their daughter, Elizabeth, was also their only child; she was thus sole heir to a comfortable fortune.[7]

Sir Henry Cary, knighted at Dublin in 1599, married Elizabeth Tanfield at Burford Church on 27 June 1602. 'He married her only for being an heir', one of her daughters later observed, 'for he had no acqvaintance with her (she scarce euer hauing spoke to him) and she was nothing handsome though then very faire'.[8] Henry then left to pursue his career; the young Elizabeth was thus on hand to help host the Jacobean progress on 9–11 September 1603. Elizabeth was to have no children until 1609; in 1625 she described herself as having 'nine children not unhopeful' (p. 249); two more by then had died. Burford church, where Elizabeth Tanfield became Elizabeth Cary, contains an extraordinary funeral monument that lays out her family fortunes in arresting fashion. The ambitious *Tanfield Tomb,* commissioned by

Figure 27. East front, Burford Priory, Oxfordshire.

7. See E. I. Carlyle, rev. David Ibbetson, 'Tanfield, Sir Lawrence (*c.*1551–1625)', *ODNB*, 53, 760a–761a.
8. *Life,* in *Life and Letters,* ed. Wolfe, p. 108.

Figure 28. Medieval arcading at Burford Priory.

Elizabeth's mother after Sir Lawrence's death in 1625, was apparently conceived for a berth in Westminster Abbey; it sits rather oddly in an Oxfordshire parish church. The style is fashionably Italianate (Figure 30), although the *transi* skeleton contrasts shockingly with the ornateness above. Sir Lawrence gazes up at a canopy supporting ten figures; they represent his virtues in allegorical form. Lady Tanfield lies by him (Figure 31), with some bad, self-composed verses on her side of the monument: 'Love made me poet / And this I writt'. At their feet kneels Lucius (Figure 32), their first-born grandchild; he was to be feted as one of the great martyr-heroes of the English Civil War by Edward Hyde, Lord Clarendon.[9] By 1624, Lucius was sole heir to the Tanfield fortune; Elizabeth Cary had alienated her father by selling or mortgaging part of her jointure to help pay for her husband's lord deputyship of Ireland. In 1626, Elizabeth alienated her husband, and her long-suffering mother, by performing an unspeakable act in the stables of Lord Ormond in Drury Lane: conversion to Roman Catholicism.

9. Hyde was advanced to the earldom of Clarendon in April 1661: see Paul Seaward, 'Hyde, Edward, first earl of Clarendon (1609–1674)', *ODNB* 29, p. 132a–b.

Figure 29. Double *rebus* for Barber Surgeon Edmund Harman, Burford Priory.

This, her mother asserted, would prove catastrophic for her husband's career, for her children's future, and for her own peace and quiet in old age. In a passionate, semi-literate letter, Elizabeth senior berates her daughter 'Bes' in ways that measure the full cost of a *mulier fortis* following her own mind: 'bes', she exclaims,

all your resons ar grovnded ovt of your own will and your fanteses I prays my god I never dyd that thing, to ofend my father, my mother my Der, I [my] most Dere hvsband your most loving father for whych I fynd now my conchence cler and wish with my sowll that you had taken such example by your hart greved mother but your hart is to hard, to giue me content, where only your willful ways, forbeds all your chyldren, comforts, bredyng or my menes herafter to lyue.

(p. 280)

Elizabeth senior signs herself off as 'your dyscomforted pore mother'; her death on 21 July 1629 spared her from learning of further daughterly outrages. These included the conversion of four Cary daughters to

Roman Catholicism in 1634 and, most spectacularly, the kidnapping of Patrick and Henry Cary from Oxfordshire in 1636. This last, bold move—that saw Elizabeth's two youngest sons translated from the Anglicanism of Great Tew to the Benedictine educational regime of St Edmund's, Paris—provoked a national scandal and landed their mother in Star Chamber.[10] It seems fitting that Elizabeth Cary should appear on the Tansfield tomb (Figure 33) facing away from her mother, her father, and her son Lucius; while they all face the church's altar, she looks back down the aisle. This serves to remind us that her body was never fated to rest in that church; it lies in, perhaps somewhere now below, Somerset House.

Figure 30. Tanfield Tomb, Burford parish church (St John the Baptist).

10. A colourful account of Elizabeth's 'stealing away her little sonnes' and its aftermath is offered in *Life*, ed. Wolfe, pp. 194–207 (p. 207).

Figure 31. Lady Tanfield above *transi* skeleton, Tanfield Tomb.

'Publike language': *Mariam* and Anne Boleyn, Salome and Isabel

While Elizabeth Cary was converting to Roman Catholicism in Drury Lane, Henry Cary was putting Roman Catholic priests to the rack in Dublin castle. In writing to Charles I, Henry speaks of his wife's 'apostasy', and of his desire to protect 'my Innocent child hir Daughter', Victoria, 'from the perill of that most leperous Infection... For howe cann your Throne be long well established', he continues, 'or your sacred Person safe in it, whilest these Locusts of Rome, whose doctrines are full of horrid treasons... be permitted to passe at liberty' (pp. 268–9). The 'liberty' that his wife enjoys in Drury Lane, so close to the court and Somerset House, is intolerable: she must be rusticated, sent forcibly back to live with her mother in Burford. On 18 May

Figure 32. Lucius Cary, Tanfield Tomb.

1627, however, Elizabeth herself writes to Charles I, assuring him that this is not practical: her mother is away, visiting the baths at Bath, and in any case refuses to have anything to do with her (pp. 282–5). Elizabeth writes from Drury Lane, and it is to Drury Lane—the urban heartland of English Catholic life, well known to Mary Ward—that she forever conspires to return.[11]

In writing to her monarch, Elizabeth Cary is anxious to dispel one rumour: 'that your maiesty was pleased to beleeue, that I altred my profession of religion, upon some court hopes'; she would never, she

11. On the growth of the 'ragtaggle collection of Catholic intelligentsia, discontented courtiers, and ambitious Platonists' associated with Henrietta Maria and with this area of London (extending north to Holborn), see Jerome de Groot, 'Coteries, Complications and the Question of Female Agency', in *The 1630s: Interdisciplinary Essays on Culture and Politics in the Caroline Era*, ed. Ian Atherton and Julie Sanders (Manchester: Manchester University Press, 2006), pp. 189–90.

Figure 33. Elizabeth Cary, Tanfield Tomb.

says, 'make religion, a ladder to clime by' (p. 283). Elizabeth was compelled to say this because the year of her conversion, 1626, was also the year of Henrietta Maria's arrival in England. It was also the year, we have noted, that Mary Ward planned on returning from Rome; 1626 seemed auspicious for English Catholics, and there *were* some fashionable conversions. Henry Cary lamented that he had, as the king's deputy in Ireland, 'become notorious ouer all the Christian world for this defection of his Wiues'; the king should do nothing for her or 'hir Popelinges' (pp. 293-4). But he was on delicate ground here, for through her conversion, Elizabeth Cary had actually made him a more perfect royal vicar, or deputy: for, as with the royal household, the husband is Protestant and his wife Catholic. This mirroring of the Cary and Stuart households was later exploited by Sir Kenelm Digby in writing to Pope Innocent X: Elizabeth Cary is dubbed not just Viscountess Falkland, but 'Vice Regina d'hibernia' (Vice Queen of Ireland).[12]

Such elevation to royalty may remind us of Elizabeth Cary's most famous composition: *The Tragedy of Mariam, the Fair Queen of Jewry*. Its heroine, conscious of the impeccable lineage of her 'high blood', derides the pretensions of her husband's family: her sister-in-law Salome, and her husband's discarded wife, Doris. Mariam's husband is Herod, the stage villain par excellence of medieval drama. But the play's most striking aspect is the variety, vigour, and inventiveness of female speech. Elizabeth Cary has clearly mastered antifeminism as a genre, understanding its utility to male bonding: 'You creatures made to be the humane curse', says Constabarus, on his way to death with the sons of Babas; 'you giddy creatures, sowers of debate' (4.315, 329).[13] The chorus censures Mariam's public speaking, 'publike language' (3.240), as something best left to her husband: but even husband Herod recognizes her 'world amazing wit' (4.428). Salome, too, has some original ideas—such as a woman's right to divorce: 'Ile be the custome-breaker', she says, 'and beginne/ To shew my Sexe the way to freedomes doore' (1.309–10). Mariam is warned that her strong-headedness could prove disastrous for her children: 'yet for your issues sake', an advisor urges her, 'more temp'rate bee' (3.149–50). But Mariam refuses to compromise her speaking of truth to power: 'I would not that my spirit were impure' (3.178); her children do indeed perish in her downfall.

The life and death of Anne Boleyn, and the tortuous outworking of her public reputation in England, colours or shadows *The Tragedy of Mariam*. As early as 1549, Jane Lumley's Englishing of the Euripedian *Iphigenia at Aulis* suggested how the sacrificing of noblewomen in

12. This phrase occurs in a letter written on 20 November 1647 to promote the career of Patrick Cary. Eleven years earlier, on 25 May 1636, Digby had been interrogated in Star Chamber for sending his sons Kenelm and John 'into forreigne parts' for a Catholic education. Elizabeth Cary was similarly examined in Star Chamber on the very same day for abducting her two sons, Henry and Patrick, for the exact same purpose. See Cary, *Life and Letters*, ed. Wolfe, pp. 420, 397; on Digby's reconversion to Catholicism in 1635, see R. T. Petersson, *Sir Kenelm Digby: The Ornament of England, 1603–1665* (Cambridge, MA: Harvard University Press, 1956), pp. 109–112.

13. Line numbers follow Elizabeth Cary, Lady Falkland, *The Tragedy of Mariam the Fair Queen of Jewry with The Lady Falkland her Life by one of her Daughters*, ed. Barry Weller and Maureen Ferguson (Berkeley: University of California Press, 1994). I have restored the spellings of the 1613 edition, as presented in *Works By and Attributed to Elizabeth Cary*, ed. Margaret W. Ferguson, The Early Modern Englishwoman: A Facsimile Library of Essential Works, vol. 2 (Aldershot: Scolar Press, 1996).

affairs of state proved newly haunting.[14] Anne Boleyn was little mentioned after her death in Henrician England, vilified during the five years of Mary, then gently rehabilitated with the accession of her mother, Elizabeth I. But a new and vibrantly negative portrayal appeared in 1585 with Nicholas Sander's *De origine ac progressu schismatis anglicani*.[15] Sander, a sometime fellow of New College, Oxford, was ordained in Rome in 1561. He spent six years in Spain and died attempting to raise rebellion in Ireland in 1581; two of his sisters were nuns of Syon.[16] His *De origine*, reprinted four times by 1610 and at least fourteen times by 1700, appeared in French (1587) and German (1594) versions; three Italian works had cannibalized it by 1602. The work of Dr Sander, thus influential, was widely resented in England; Elizabeth Cary's illustrious neighbour at Burford, Peter Heylyn, was later to rename him 'Dr Slander'—chiefly for his characterization of Anne Boleyn.[17] Sander's most egregious claim was that Anne was actually the king's daughter: Henry had Sir Thomas Boleyn sent to France on royal affairs so that he might sleep with his wife. Sander also spread the story that Anne was born with six fingers on her right hand, had a large wen or cyst under her chin (hence her high-necked dresses), and a sallow, jaundiced complexion ('colore subflavo'); she was nonetheless (says Sander, a little implausibly), 'handsome to look at', a skilled lutanist, and 'a good dancer'.[18] This last detail is elaborated by Nicholas Harpsfield, author of *The Life and Death of Sr Thomas Moore*, who

14. See *Iphigenia at Aulis, Translated by Lady Lumley*, ed. Harold H. Child and W. W. Greg, Malone Society Reprint Series (London: Charles Whittingham, 1909); *Mariam*, ed. Weller and Ferguson, pp. 26–7.

15. While the title page claims Cologne as place of publication, it was actually produced at Rheims by Jean Foigny: see T. F. Mayer, 'Sander, Nicholas (*c.*1530–1581)', *ODNB* online (Oct. 2007). For a colourful translation and partisan preface, attesting to the work's long-lived influence, see Nicolas Sander D.D., *Rise and Growth of the Anglican Schism*, tr. and intr. David Lewis (London: Burns and Oates, 1877). On the uses of Catholic imagery and poetics within Protestantism in the gentler, pre-Sander period, see Stephen Hamrick, *The Catholic Imaginary and the Cult of Elizabeth, 1558–1582* (Farnham: Ashgate, 2009).

16. Sir William Cecil imagines that Sander, 'wandering in the mountains in Ireland without succor, died raving in a frenzy' (Mayer, 'Sander'). Margaret Sander, sister of Nicholas, was prioress under abbess Katherine Palmer during the return of the Syon community to England during the reign of Mary: see Sander, *Anglican Schism*, tr. Lewis, pp. xvii–xviii; Duffy, *Fires of Faith*, p. 191.

17. See Mayer, 'Sander'; Anthony Milton, 'Heylyn, Peter (1599–1662)', *ODNB* online (Jan. 2008); Sander, *Rise and Growth*, tr. Lewis, p. xxii.

18. Sander, *Anglican Schism*, tr. Lewis, p. 25.

pictures Anne Boleyn dancing like a new Salome for the heads of More and Fisher.[19]

Harpsfield's association of Queen Anne with Salome, 'this dancing, devilish damsel', is colourful, explicit, and ingenious.[20] This particular figuration may not have reached the young Elizabeth Cary,[21] but anything pertaining to Anne would have piqued her interest: for she was related to the Boleyns by marriage. Mary Boleyn, Anne's older sister, married William Carey on 4 February 1520 and very likely accompanied him, along with 6,000 other men and women, to the Field of Cloth of Gold in June of that year. She was perhaps the king's mistress by 2 March 1522, when Henry jousted on a horse embroidered with a wounded heart; on the Shrove Tuesday following, in a related spectacle, Mary stormed the Château Vert as *Kindness* (with Anne as *Perseverance*). Royal grants were made to William Carey during the period of Mary's involvement with the king; this ended with the birth of her son Henry Carey on 4 March 1526. William Carey was the great-uncle of the Henry Cary who married Elizabeth Tanfield (at the church of St John the Baptist) in 1602.[22]

Cary's *Mariam*, like Anne Boleyn, is a second wife put to death as an adulteress by a tyrannical, all-powerful husband; the first wife is on hand to vilify her and denounce her offspring as 'bastards' (2.256). But identifications need not be pressed too hard: some commentators, we

---

19. Harpsfield, another sometime New College man, was a close associate of the More circle and of Cardinal Pole; his life of More was presented to William Roper as a New Year's gift in 1557. The association between Anne Boleyn and Salome is made in the course of his *Treatise on the Pretended Divorce between Henry VIII and Catherine of Aragon*. See Sander, *Anglican Schism*, tr. Lewis, p. 121 n. 2; Duffy, *Fires*, pp. 181–5; Cary, *Tragedy of Mariam*, ed. Weller and Ferguson, p. 32.

20. Harpsfield has her fall through a frozen river. As her neck becomes trapped by ice, 'her body beneath in the water, wagging to and fro, did represent and exhibit a marvellous spectacle and a strange kind of dancing' (*A Treatise on the Pretended Divorce between Henry VIII and Catherine of Aragon*, ed. Nicholas Pocock, Camden Society, NS 21 (London: Camden Society, 1878), p. 251).

21. Neither Harpsfield's *Life of Moore* nor his *Treatise*, both written in Mary's reign, was published, although much of the latter fed into Sander's *De origine*. See Duffy, *Fires*, p. 185; Thomas S. Freeman, 'Harpsfield, Nicholas (1519–1575)', *ODNB* online (2004).

22. On the 'various Henry Carys, Careys, and Caryes in the late Elizabethan and early Jacobean period', see Sean Kelsey, 'Cary, Henry, first Viscount Falkland (c.1575–1633)', *ODNB* online (Jan. 2008). See further Jonathan Hughes, 'Mary Stafford, née Boleyn, *other married name* Carey (c.1499–1543)', *ODNB* online (Jan. 2009); David Grummitt, 'Participants in the Field of Cloth of Gold (act. 1520)', *ODNB* online (Sept. 2009); Cary, *Mariam*, ed. Weller and Ferguson, p. 153, n. 27; Wallace, *Premodern Places*, pp. 25, 34, 67–8.

have noted, were likelier to remember Anne as a Salome, than as Mariam. Remarkably, Herod himself at one point conflates or confuses the names of the two female protagonists: 'I will requite/ Thee, gentle *Mariam. Salom* I mean'.[23] An invitation to consider the sisters-in-law as practitioners of a single female art, employed to good and bad ends, is offered elsewhere in the play. Pheroras, Herod's brother, here speaks of Mariam's *wit,* or verbal facility:

> *Pheroras*   Her wit exceeds her beautie.
> *Salome*   Wit may show
> The way to ill, as well as good you know.[24]

Salome here rehearses a great classical and premodern commonplace: that *Rettorica*, Lady Rhetoric, is amoral; that her tropes and terms of intensified language, *parole ornate*, may equally be applied to good or evil ends.[25] Mariam, shortly after this, acknowledges both her own rhetorical powers (bodily, as well as verbal) while refusing to employ them in pleasing Herod:

> I know I could inchaine him with a smile:
> And lead him captive with a gentle word,
> I scorn my looke should ever man beguile,
> Or other speech, th[a]n meaning to afford.   (3.163–6)

Mariam's belief that what she says should express directly what she means, ostensibly a refusal of rhetorical arts *tout court,* is then refined as a belief in 'mine innocence' (3.171). In the context of an absolutist court, such as Herod's, this is a perilous creed: a blue-blooded faith that

---

23. This enigmatic moment at 4.84 is rationalized, but not explained away, by the couplet following: 'The thought of *Mariam* doth so steale my spirit, / My mouth from speech of her I cannot weane' (4.83–6).

24. *Mariam*, ed. Weller and Ferguson, 3.1.23–4. The understanding of *wit* as verbal facility is sustained by the lines spoken by Pheroras, immediately following: 'But wisedome is the porter of her head, / And bares all wicked words from issuing thence' (3.1.25–6).

25. Beatrice dispatches Vergil to save Dante 'con la tua parola ornata' (*Inferno* 2.67); Jason deceives Hypsipyle 'con segni e con parole ornate' (*Inferno* 18.91); Brunetto Latini defines *rettorica* as 'una scienzia di bene dire, ciò è rettorica quella scienzia per la quale noi sapemo ornatamente dire e dittare' (*La Rettorica*, ed. Francesco Maggini (Florence: Galletti and Cocci, 1915), p. 4; *Medieval Grammar and Rhetoric: Language Arts and Literary Theory, AD 300–1475*, ed. Rita Copeland and Ineke Sluiter (Oxford: Oxford University Press, 2009), p. 758). See further and more capaciously Teodolinda Barolini, *The Undivine Comedy: Detheologizing Dante* (Princeton: Princeton University Press, 1992), p. 77; Rita Copeland, 'Chaucer and Rhetoric', in *The Yale Companion to Chaucer*, ed. Seth Lerer (New Haven: Yale University Press, 2006), esp. p. 125.

one's personal speech need not accommodate to circumstances, nor to any particular person. Sohemus, Herod's counsellor, sees the danger as Mariam, repeating her claim, leaves the stage:

> Mine innocence is hope enough for mee. *Exit.*
> Sohemus   Poore guiltles Queene! Oh, that my wish might place
> A little temper now about thy heart:
> Unbridled speech is *Mariams* worst disgrace.   (3.180–83)

The phrase 'a little temper' points here to the cardinal virtue (like rhetoric, gendered feminine) of *temperantia*: the exercise of a practical wisdom that, in this context, would regulate powers of speech to achieve the happiest of outcomes.[26] But in her great showdown with Herod, Mariam still affects to abstain from prudent self-regulation in matters of speech and expression:

> I cannot frame disguise, nor never taught
> My face a looke dissenting from my thought.   (4.145–6)

Again, this amounts to abstention from the courtly world, from court-liness, itself.[27] It is only after her fall, on her way to death, that Mariam concedes 'that I improvidently wrought' (4.553); that she was deluded in thinking that 'one vertue for a woman might suffice' (4.562). If only, she muses, she had 'with humilitie bene grac'te', had thus allowed 'humilitie *and* chastitie' to govern her (4.564; emphasis added). Mariam is on the way to discovering the truth of her own condition, as that *and* suggests: one virtue or principle of action is never enough. Premodern rhetoricians, such as the widely-diffused Albertanus of Brescia, taught the art of speaking *and* of keeping quiet: *Ars dicendi et tacendi*.[28] Mariam is routinely castigated for saying too much in public, but sometimes she says too little. Her very first words to Herod, for example, are but a single couplet that, closing in on itself, quite shuts him out. The *circumstantiae* to which her speech adapts here are not those of Herod's homecoming (and his expectation of welcome), but those of her own mental processes. Cary's use of *colour* here slyly nods to the rhetorical *colores* that Mariam will *not* be unpacking for Herod's benefit:

---

26. *Temperantia* thus relates, in this verbal context, to *prudentia*.
27. Thoughts, feelings, and faces align in the fabliaux world (as Chaucer's Nicholas grabs at Alisoun), but not in the *Knight's Tale* (as ruled by that supreme rhetor, Theseus).
28. See Wallace, *Chaucerian Polity*, pp. 212–23.

> My Lord, I suit my garment to my minde,
> And there no cheerfull colours can I finde.   (4.91)

Mariam goes on to die, unhappily, without ever quite grasping the *ars agendi* so brilliantly enacted by her sister-in-law. Life in a public sphere dominated by masculine tyranny requires flexible adaptation of verbal strategy to contingent circumstances: 'for my will', Salome succinctly has it, 'I will imploy my wits' (1.296). In doing so she manages not only to survive her brother's violent fits, but to orchestrate them. The play ends with Herod alone on stage: we see him, as the concluding *Chorus* speech has it, 'strangely, lunatickly rave' (5.287). He thus aligns both with the ranting Herods of the Mystery plays,[29] and the newer kind of stage tyrant described by Rebecca W. Bushnell.[30] Such performative indulgence inevitably stirs comparisons between Herod and Henry VIII. Each shows particular fascination with technologies of execution: Henry contemplates flames for Anne, but brings in a swordsman from Calais;[31] Herod contemplates (at some length) beheading, drowning, and death by fire (4.357–80). Each condemns his queen to a very public death (Cary speaks of 'the curious gazing troope', 5.21) that he does not trouble to attend. Each performs grief over this death in maudlin fashion; each understands himself to be the true protagonist of every scene, even when the queen is at the block:

Nuntio	'Tell thou my lord', said she—
Herod	'Mee, ment she mee?' (5.67–8)

This single line captures succinctly the dilemma of any premodern *mulier fortis* seeking to narrate her own *life*. Her words are here reported by one man and interrupted, through self-referential excitement, by another; we are already at two removes from the woman ending her

---

29. The roles of Herod and Pilate offered much scope for debased, amateur ranting. In Chaucer's *Miller's Tale*, Absolon 'pleyeth Herodes upon a scaffold hye' by way of impressing Alisoun (1.3384); the drunken Miller cries out, unstoppably, 'in Pilates voys' (1.3124).
30. See *Tragedies of Tyrants: Political Thought and Theater in the English Renaissance* (Ithaca: Cornell UP, 1990). Bushnell's book concludes, with its last sentence, as if observing the end of Cary's play: 'the theater locates the tyrant at centre stage, even though he was meant to be pushed to the margins of political life and of humanity' (p. 187).
31. 'One can only wonder', says Eric W. Ives, 'at a psychology which transmutes doubt about the guilt of a loved one into a loving concern about how to kill her' (*Anne Boleyn* (Oxford: Basil Blackwell, 1986), p. 401).

life at the royal block. Quite what Anne Boleyn said on 19 May 1536 will never be known.[32] Elizabeth Cary's *History of the Life, Reign, and Death of Edward II*, composed 1626–8,[33] continues *Mariam's* exploration of the courtly dynamics of one historical period through the shifts and scandals of another. Edward II and his favourites Gaveston and Spenser clearly invite comparisons with James I and his favourite George Villiers, first duke of Buckingham. Once again, there are kinship connections: Frances Cary, sister to Elizabeth Cary's husband Henry, had married Buckingham's uncle in 1605.[34] On 17 November 1626, just three days after her conversion, Elizabeth Cary was said to be 'newly banished the Court, for lately going to Masse with the Queene';[35] among the women permitted to attend Mass with Henrietta Maria was Katherine Villiers, the duchess of Buckingham. Elizabeth exploited her Buckingham connections to the full in advancing her children at court, both before and after the duke's assassination in 1628. After Buckingham's fatal stabbing, Cary composed an elegy that lets him plead his case from beyond the grave.[36] All this confirms a fascination with intrigues of court entirely undiminished by her religious conversion: Elizabeth Cary felt no impulse, on becoming Roman Catholic, to retreat from the world. Her conversion did indeed force her, temporarily, away from London. But while the duchess of Buckingham pleaded for her with Viscount Edward Conway, secretary of state to Charles I,[37] Elizabeth alleviated her rusticated tedium by refining and retouching her account of Edward II. This text 'is everywhere eager', Curtis Perry remarks, 'to engage, invoke, parallel, and comment upon key issues—favouritism, its corruption, the monarch's culpability,

---

32. See 'Introduction' above, p. xxi.
33. Two fair copies of Cary's *Edward II*, of differing lengths, were discovered by Jeremy Maule in the mid-1990s. Both in the same scribal hand, one is dated 7 January 1626/7 and the other 2 February 1627/8; there is a printed folio edition from 1680. See Heather Wolfe, 'Introduction' to *The Literary Career and Legacy of Elizabeth Cary, 1613– 1680*, ed. Heather Wolfe (New York: Palgrave Macmillan, 2007), 1–13 (pp. 2, 6–7).
34. See Nadine N. W. Akkerman, ' "Reader, Stand Still and Look, Lo Here I Am": Elizabeth Cary's Funeral Elegy "On the Duke of Buckingham" ', in *Career*, ed. Wolfe, pp. 183–200.
35. BL Harleian MS 390, fol. 161, a letter from Reverend Joseph Mead to Sir Martin Stuteville (cited in Cary, *Life and Letters*, ed. Wolfe, p. 1).
36. See Ackerman, 'Reader', p. 185.
37. See the letter of 24 March 1627 in Cary, *Life and Letters*, ed. Wolfe, p. 276.

resistance, and rebellion';[38] it is not a work from the cell of a penitent Magdalene.

The 'Author's Preface to the Reader' in the 1680 edition, dated 20 February 1627 and signed 'E.F.' (Elizabeth Falkland),[39] declares 'I have not herein followed the dull Character of our Historians': rather than imitating the likes of Stow, Speed, and Holinshed,[40] Cary develops a neo-classicism essayed as early as *Mariam*. The publisher's preface insists that it was a 'Gentleman that wrote this History':'we are apt to believe', it continues, that 'those days [i.e. *c*.1627] produced very few who were able to express their Conceptions in so Masculine a Stile' (A2). But the sympathetic drift of identification in this text runs increasingly in favour of Isabel, Edward II's neglected queen. Spencer, Edward's favourite, 'sings the right Night-crow's tune of upstart Greatness', and 'understands the plain-Song of the state' (p. 51); even he knows the queen 'to be a Woman of a strong Brain, and stout Stomack' (p. 86). Spencer devises a strategy that would dispatch Queen Isabel, daughter of the French king, on embassy to France; when things go badly, Isabel can take the fall. Getting wind of this, Isabel proves herself all Salome and no part Mariam: 'she *seem'd* wondrously well-pleas'd, and offers to undertake, and to assure the business' (p. 88; emphasis added). Once committed to the journey, she seeks 'a fit subject' for the expression of her jealousy, rage, and sexual frustration:

She saw the King a stranger to her bed, and revelling in the wanton embraces of his stoln pleasures, without a glance on her deserving Beauty. This contempt had begot a like change in her, though in a more modest nature, her youthful Affections wanting a fit subject to work on, and being debarr'd of that warmth that should have still preserv'd their temper, she had cast her wandering eye upon the gallant *Mortimer*, a piece of masculine Bravery without exception; had those his inward Gifts been like his outside, he had not been behinde-hand in

38. '"Royal Fever" and "The Giddy Commons"': Cary's *History of the Life, Reign, and Death of Edward II* and The Buckingham Phenomenon', in *Career*, ed. Wolfe, p. 77.
39. *The History of the Life, Reign, and Death of Edward II King of England, and Lord of Ireland . . . Written by E.F. in the year 1627* (London: J.C. for Charles Harper, 1680). The Huntington Library exemplar has the 'E' of 'E.F.' erased by an early hand, with 'Henry Cary Lord Viscount Falkland' written above: see the facsimile provided in *Works by Cary*, ed. Ferguson. Page numbers in the text refer to this edition; some useful annotation is provided by *Women Writers in Renaissance England*, ed. Randall Martin (London: Longman, 1997), pp. 164–87.
40. See Barbara Kiefer Lewalski, *Writing Women in Jacobean England* (Cambridge, MA: Harvard University Press, 1993), p. 203.

reception, but with a Courtly, brave respect, full meets her Glances. A silent Rhetorick, sparkling Love, findes quick admittance.

(p. 89)

Isabel hatches a plot to escape to France with Mortimer, now in the Tower, while still courting her adversary, Spencer, 'with all the shews of perfect reconcilement' (p. 90). The strategy of Edward and his favourite now shifts: Isabel should not 'be a gadding' (p. 90); 'if Spencer once more seiz'd her in his clutches', she realizes, 'she should be surely mew'd, and kept from Gadding' (p. 104). But it is Spencer who eventually falls into *her* clutches; she then parades him all the way from Hereford to London 'behind the Carriage, with Reeds and Pipes that sound the summons to call the wondering Crue together [that] might abuse him' (p. 128). Spencer, at journey's end, is hanged; Queen Isabel 'comes to *London*, where she hath all the Royal Entertainment due to her Greatness' (p. 130). Getting to and staying in London, in close contact with the royal court, was to remain one of Elizabeth Cary's dearest objects for the rest of her life.

The Lady Faulkland: Her Life

The most extraordinary thing about *The Tragedy of Mariam* (to drop back two decades) is its author's youth: Cary was about twenty when she wrote it, *c*.1605.[41] The play thus predicts, rather than draws upon, the extraordinary course of her life. Her spouse, like Herod in her tragedy, was indeed absent when she began writing: he was in fact a prisoner in the Spanish Netherlands. This husband, whom she hardly yet knew, became famed for his volcanic, Herod-like temper: 'advise him to a more Temperate course', wrote one lord to another, 'or... assuage him at the Boorde in these furyes against those he loves not in this kyngdome'.[42] Elizabeth, as a brilliantly intellectual young woman (and sole heir to a considerable fortune) might have discerned

41. Richard Hawkins entered the play in the Register of the Stationers' Company on 17 December 1612; it was printed in quarto for him by Thomas Creede in 1613. There are signs that the play, which had circulated in manuscript, was disowned in print (perhaps by Henry or Elizabeth Cary); it remains, nonetheless, 'the first original drama by a woman to be printed in England' (*Works by Cary*, ed. Ferguson, p. ix).
42. Lord Wilmot to Lord Dorchester, 9 June 1630 (p. 362).

Mariam-like qualities in herself, as well as in historical surrogates. But her authorship of a tragedy at twenty should be set in a wider family culture of courtly masquing and playgoing: Henry Cary danced in two masques by Thomas Campion and tilted for Ben Jonson; their daughter Victoria appeared in Townshend's *Tempe Restored*, Inigo Jones's *The Temple of Love*, and Wat Montagu's *Shepheard's Paradise*. Even Lucius Cary, Elizabeth's resolutely Protestant son, enthused about Montagu's pioneering[43] pastoral drama (at Somerset House), and Henrietta Maria's central role in it.[44] Elizabeth Cary's deep grounding in the protocols of courtly play-acting remained with her all her life;[45] her close association with Henrietta Maria made her seem a natural defender of 'Playes in generall'.[46] Even in the immediate aftermath of her conversion scandal, she interpellates Viscount Conway, secretary of state, as Lancelot to her Guenevere: 'that my lord Conway', she writes to him in June 1627, 'was both a gentleman, a souldier, and a courtier, made well for mee, since all those, haue either inclination, or obligation, to succor, distressed ladyes' (p. 291). Two months later she writes again: 'I beseech your lordship now, show, the diffrence betweene a gentleman, and none, in neuer leauinge, till you find meanes, to get mee, my right' (p. 300). She did try to cut down on play-going after converting, and again after Henry's death in 1633, but with less than complete success: 'After her Lords death she never went to Maskes, nor Plays not so much as att the Court, though she loved them very much especially the last extreamely . . . yet she continved to goe very much abroad to court and other places about her busynesses' (pp. 155–6).

43. This is 'the first English play known to have been acted by women' (Sarah Poynting, ' "The Rare and Excellent Partes of Mr Walter Montague": Henrietta Maria and her Playwright', in *Henrietta Maria*, ed. Griffey, p. 73.

44. 'I must say this', says Lucius, 'both of it and the great actresse of it, that her action was worthy of it, and it was worthy of her action, and I beleeue the world can fitt nether of them, but with one another' (Walter Montagu, *The Shepherd's Paradise*, ed. Sarah Poynting, Malone Society Reprints, 159 (Oxford: Oxford University Press for the Malone Society, 1998), p. xiii. Lucius here writes in hope of obtaining a copy of the play. Henrietta Maria's pastoral dramas, unlike her court masques, were habitually performed at Somerset House: see Karen Britland, *Drama at the Courts of Queen Henrietta Maria* (Cambridge: Cambridge University Press, 2006), p. 111.

45. Even in penning her *Edward II*, Cary sometimes visualizes scenes as if for performance: 'This Act ended, *Baldocke* the Chorus, who equally hated the Queen, seconds it with a learned approbation' (p. 88).

46. In collecting the works of John Marston in 1633, the printer appeals to Cary as one who will defend 'Playes in generall' from the 'Many opprobies and aspersions [that] have not long since been cast upon [them]' (cited in Britland, *Drama at the Courts*, p. 113).

This last quotation is from *The Lady Faulkland: Her Life*, written and annotated by three of her 'popelinges', her Catholic children, between 1645 and 1649. The *Life*, magnificently edited by Heather Wolfe, survives in one manuscript now at Lille.[47] Four of Elizabeth Cary's daughters became Benedictine nuns at Cambrai, an enclosed community founded in 1623 by the great-great-grandaughter of Sir Thomas More. As part of the group of six that formed the brilliant 'class of 1640', they proved prolific in producing original poems, prose, and sermons and in translating and transcribing texts.[48] The Benedictine Augustine Baker, an avid playgoer in younger years, supplied this group with works of medieval English spirituality, much of it excavated from Sir Robert Cotton's library in London, such as *The Cloud of Unknowing* and the works of Walter Hilton.[49] The two most important Julian of Norwich manuscripts are associated with this milieu. The 'old manuscript book' described by Baker at Cambrai may have been the immediate exemplar of the Paris manuscript (Watson and Jenkins' base manuscript). The Sloane manuscript (Vincent Gillespie's favourite) was likely written by the founder of the English Benedictine convent in Paris: that is, by Dame Clementina Cary, formerly Anne Cary, Elizabeth's oldest surviving daughter.[50] *The Lady Faulkland: Her Life* thus issues from a milieu far different from the one embraced and sustained by Elizabeth Cary at Drury Lane. She loved plays, controversialism, conversation with friends, and could never stop going to court; the *Life*'s authors chose to live as enclosed contemplatives. The *agon* at the heart of *The Lady Faulkland: Her Life* is all the more fascinating in pitting disciplined daughters against a headstrong mother: daughters who know that their own lives of English-speaking exile are underpinned, if not entirely determined, by their mother's life decisions.

The unique manuscript of the *Life* was discovered in the 1850s by Richard Simpson, a sometime Anglican clergyman who had converted

47. Archives Départementales du Norde, Lille, France, MS 20H9: see Cary, *Life and Letters*, ed. Wolfe, pp. 86–9.
48. See 'Introduction' in Cary, *Life and Letters*, ed. Wolfe, pp. 45–8.
49. Placid Spearritt, OSB, 'The Survival of Mediaeval Spirituality among the Exiled English Black Monks', in *That Mysterious Man: Essays on Augustine Baker OSB, 1575–1641*, ed. Michael Woodward, intr. Rowan Williams (Abergavenny, Wales: Three Peaks Press, 2001), pp. 19–21; *Sir Robert Cotton as Collector: Essays on an Early Stuart Courtier and his Legacy*, ed. C. J. Wright (London: British Library, 1997); and see above, p. 183.
50. *Writings of Julian of Norwich*, ed. Watson and Jenkins, pp. 14b–15a, 40a–b; Vincent Gillespie, private conversation.

to Roman Catholicism on 1 August 1846, aged twenty-five. Having married his cousin two years earlier, Simpson could not assume Catholic holy orders; he thus became an historian of English Catholicism and wrote for the *Rambler*, a liberal Catholic monthly founded by converts. His edition of the *Life*, published in 1857 as 'A Conversion from the Time of Charles I', filleted out reference to Cary's breadth of reading, learned writing, and much else besides; a full transcription was published in book form four years later.[51] Simpson's intellectual outlook, later much admired by Matthew Arnold, got him fired as *Rambler* editor by English Catholic authorities. Having found the 1870 definition of papal infallibility hard to swallow, he turned increasingly to Shakespeare Studies and advised Gladstone on his tract *Vaticanism* in 1874.[52] In 1883 Lady Georgiana Fullerton's *The Life of Elizabeth Lady Falkland 1585–1639* was published by Burns and Oates, the Catholic publishing house that published *The Life of Mary Ward* by Mary C. E. Chambers IBVM in 1882 and 1885. Fullerton had converted to Roman Catholicism in 1846, the same year as Simpson; her *Life* does little more than fashion Simpson's various materials into a continuous narrative. Eschewing Chambers' commitment to the archive, Fullerton relies upon the imaginative flair that inspired her eight religious-themed novels.[53]

The religious preoccupations of these Victorian convert-editors are not shared by the next *Life* edition, that of Barry Weller and Margaret W. Ferguson (1994). No new edition of *Mariam* appeared between 1613 and 1914,[54] but by 1994 the play represented Cary's chief claim

51. See, respectively, 'A Conversion from the Time of Charles I', *Rambler*, 8 (1857), pp. 173–89, 258–72; *The Lady Falkland, Her Life, from a Manuscript in the Imperial Archives at Lille* (London: Catholic Publishing and Bookselling Company, 1861). See further Josef L. Altholz, 'Simpson, Richard (1820–1876)', *ODNB* online (2004); Cary, *Life and Writings*, ed. Wolfe, pp. 89–94.

52. Simpson was among the first to propose that Shakespeare was a Roman Catholic: see Altholz, 'Simpson'. The Shakespearean interests of this first *Life* editor are shared by the last: Heather Wolfe is Curator of Manuscripts, Folger Shakespeare Library.

53. Her novels, said to have inspired Catholic conversions, were written between 1844 and 1881. Novel writing helped finance the work of the Sisters of St Vincent de Paul, whom she helped bring to England; she later co-founded a religious community for women whose families could not afford dowries. Her life of Louisa de Carvajal dates from 1873: see Solveig C. Robinson, 'Fullerton, Lady Georgiana Charlotte (1812–1885)', *ODNB* online (Sept. 2004); Cary, *Life and Letters*, ed. Wolfe, pp. 94–6.

54. See *The Tragedie of Mariam, Faire Queen of Jewry*, ed. A. C. Dunstan and W. W. Greg (London: Oxford University Press for the Malone Society, 1914). And this can hardly be classed as a 'new edition', since it presents a facsimile of the 1613 edition, with a list of textual variants; the Weller and Ferguson edition is thus really the first new text.

to fame; Weller and Ferguson offer their modernized *Life* as 'an ancillary text to *Mariam*' (p. 50). Finally and definitively, in 2001, Heather Wolfe produced an edition of *The Lady Faulkland: Her Life* as part of the Renaissance Texts from Manuscripts series. The aim here is to present the *Life* as 'a manuscript in revision' (p. 98). Marginal comments thus remain in the margins (rather than being relegated to footnotes); erasures and double erasures are reproduced; hesitations, false starts and second thoughts are all preserved. Lucy Cary (Dame Magdalena) is identified as the main scribe; she also annotates the manuscript, along with sister Mary (Dame Maria), brother Patrick, and an unidentified Benedictine. Wolfe's painstaking editorial work wins us unprecedented possibilities to grasp the extreme difficulties of this particular *life* undertaking.[55] Four daughters, who have willingly embraced the discipline of religious enclosure, are attempting to narrate the life of a mother who, like her heroine Isabel, wishes never to be 'mew'd, and kept from Gadding' (p. 104). The observant Benedictines of Cambrai must come to terms with the unruly spirit of Drury Lane.

'Little Rome': life in Drury Lane

The daughters knew of Elizabeth Cary's turbulent life in Drury Lane because they had been part of it. Attachment to this part of London dated back to Lawrence Tanfield's leasing of part of Drury House in the financial year 1615–16. John Donne was a near neighbour until he left to become dean of St Paul's in 1621; his house abutted the Tanfield kitchen.[56] Drury House, at the far southern end of Drury Lane, was swallowed up by the widening of Aldwich; its foundations lie now below the BBC's Bush House. But originally, Drury Lane intersected

---

55. Wolfe's edition of the *Life* is buttressed not by an edition of *Mariam*, but by some 137 letters and documents; her book is hence entitled *Life and Letters*. Interpretation of Cary is thus tilted away from narrowly religious or purely literary concerns towards understanding within a greater public sphere.

56. See R. C. Bald, *Donne and the Drurys* (Cambridge: Cambridge University Press, 1959), pp. 119–120. This information derives from the Redgrave Muniments, some of which (fifty deed boxes) were bought and taken to the University of Chicago in 1925 and 1929. They were painstakingly catalogued by Edith Rickert on Saturday afternoons (by way of resting from her monumental labours with Manly on *The Text of the Canterbury Tales*).

with the Strand: an intersection that formed one of the Catholic hotspots of Stuart London. Mary Ward, you will recall, experienced her 'Glory vision' in the Strand.[57] On 2 June 1628 it was observed that 'in Drury Lane, there are three families of Papists there residing for one of Protestants; insomuch that it may well be called Little Rome'; a list of 'Middlesex Recusants Lodgers' from *c.*1632 features 'the Ladie Falkland' among many other ladies, gents, and servants.[58] This was a fashionable and dynamic area of London, the cutting edge of westward expansion that found its 'decisive moment' in the 1630s.[59] Somerset House lay just a few hundred yards away; post-Great Fire construction would push further west down the Strand, allowing linkups down alleyways with Covent Garden. The most evocative such alleyway is Bull Inn Court, featuring a pubsite frequented by Nell Gwynne and now earmarked for office development (Figure 34). When Victoria Cary danced in *The Temple of Love* in 1635 the composer–architect of this masque, Inigo Jones, was busy building another temple for his Catholic queen; when it opened at Somerset House, Londoners were dazzled by its theatrical effects.[60] Elizabeth Cary's daughter-biographers make much of the fact that their mother, at a difficult moment of her life, 'left of [stopped wearing] chopins, which she had euer worne, being very low, and a long time very fatte' (p. 186). *Chopines* are shoes with high platform soles: Hamlet greets one of the actors to Elsinore by remarking 'By'r Lady, your ladyship is nearer to heaven than when I saw you last by the altitude of a chopine'.[61] 'Your ladyship' is of course a young boy actor. It is thus commendable, to her Benedictine daughters, that Elizabeth Cary should renounce *chopines*: but it is worth noting that her renunciation of her worldly ambition to walk 'nearer to heaven' must wait until she is fifty years old.

The 1630s was an exceptional decade both for court theatre and for the private theatre of religious controversy. Debaters at places like Great Tew, presided over by Lucius Cary, could maintain Catholic positions just for the sake of argument; Erasmians imagined

57. In her lodgings close by St Clement's churchyard: see Chapter 3 above, p. 161.
58. See Cary, *Life and Letters*, ed. Woolf, p. 382 and n.219.
59. Peter Whitfield, *London: A Life in Maps* (London: British Library, 2006), p. 51a.
60. See Veevers, *Images of Love and Religion*, pp. 7, 136.
61. *Hamlet*, ed. Ann Thompson and Neil Taylor (London: Arden Shakespeare, 2006), 2.2.363–4.

Figure 34. The Nell Gwynne, Bull Inn Court, Covent Garden, London.

Christian reunion; Arminians hosted intellectual games of chicken or 'how far can you go' (towards the abyss of Catholic conversion) that could never have been imagined in the sixteenth century.[62] In the year of their conversion, the four Catholic Cary daughters were treated to a theological dispute that rolled on for days (with their allegiance as motivation and prize). In one corner was William

62. Lucius, according to the *Life*, was accustomed to make arguments on the Catholic side against his fellow Protestants: a practise that Lucius himself affirms in a tract entitled *Of the Infallibilitie of the Church of Rome* (1645). Edward Hyde, the best friend of Lucius, was at the heart of the Great Tew circle, along with William Chillingworth; frequent visitors included Ben Jonson, Thomas Hobbes, and the poets Sidney Godolphin, Sir John Suckling, and Edmund Waller. Elizabeth Cary's conversion was seen as damaging to the Arminian cause. See Cary, *Life and Letters*, ed. Woolf, pp. 5–6 and 264–5; 156–7 and n.149 (on Lucius); David L. Smith, 'Cary, Lucius', *ODNB* 10, 440a–445a (p. 441a).

Chillingworth, a flip-flopping Protestant who had converted to Catholicism in 1628 and then back again in 1631. Chillingworth is the panto villain of the *Life*, a character of sleights and deceptions—an Anglican Archimago.[63] In the other corner was a Mr Chaperlin, 'a zealous catholike and a very good man', the *Life* says, 'but somwhat violent... that the vttermost of what he could doe was to keepe his hands from having their part in the dispute' (p. 177). Chillingworth receives all Chaperlin's arguments 'with so calme a serenity as if his peace and patience, were immouable'. He calls upon the daughters to observe his mild demeanour, and 'their esteeme was much increased' (p. 177). But when the Jesuit Guy Holland steps into the ring,[64] Chillingworth 'lost all his pretended serenity, as to be so vncivil as to call the other foole and knave', preferring now 'instead of proofes to thunder out threats, with a confused heape of dreadfull words, as hell damnation and divells etc., as dreadfully spoken, seeking to frighten them whom he knew enough inclined to feare' (pp. 179–80). Chillingworth is banned from the house, 'with the consent and good will of all' (p. 180).

This milieu of impassioned theological debate recalls the similarly impassioned, inter-Catholic polemics of *Hierarchomachia*: that extraordinary play sparked by the attempt to reestablish a Catholic hierarchy in England, headed by Richard Smith as bishop of Chalcedon. Remarkably, Richard Smith is reported in 1630 as living 'in the Chamber iust ouer my lady Faulklands besides diuers Jesuitts more'.[65] It was 'my Lord of Calcedon', the *Life* tells us, who confirmed Elizabeth with the name of Maria (p. 141); from June 1632 onwards her signature appears as 'E. M. Falkland'. Mary Ward, we have noted, ghosts across *Hierachomachia* as a *woman Ghibelline*, a figure associated with the Jesuits. Elizabeth Cary seemed to transcend these Guelf and Ghibelline

63. At one point in the *Life* Chillingworth is represented as a religious rapist, forcing himself upon a young maid called Camilla: 'and to a young Catholike... daring to doe more, he would make her heare him by force, holding her a spite of her teeth when she offred to goe, and keeping downe her hands when she would stopp her eares, into which he would ball his blasphemys' (p. 189).
64. Holland, born in Lincoln *c.*1585 and ordained in Valladolid (1613), took his final vows on 14 June 1628 in the Gatehouse Prison, London (McCoog, *English and Welsh Jesuits*, p. 209).
65. This according to a deposition of 'Benedicto Rollini, Master Gardner to the French Ambassodor' (Cary, *Life and Letters*, ed. Wolfe, pp. 365–6).

divides: she was confirmed by Smith himself, but converted or recon-ciled by a Benedictine,[66] represented in the play by Spirius, a Knight of Malta. Lady Falkland, a woman at the heart of London Catholic court and intellectual life, seemingly offends nobody in this Catholic play-world. She is, *au contraire,* commended as 'Falconia', a woman admired by another woman, Nivetta, for her 'style'.[67]

Elizabeth Cary understands 'style' not just in the attenuated mod-ern sense of writing well, or even dressing well, but in the capacious premodern sense of rhetorical *ars agendi*: negotiating specific situa-tions through appropriate use of language and gesture, of topical inventiveness and social connectedness. Her daughters might be trou-bled by her personal deportment, but her understanding of *style* determining public affairs pervades both *Mariam* and *Edward II*. But what *style* were the daughters to adapt in narrating their mother's life? The obvious genre was one in which they were well schooled at Cambrai, with Augustine Baker leaving illustrious examples: saint's life. Elizabeth Cary was herself prolific in this genre: 'she writ the liues of St Mary Magdalene, St Agnes Martir, and st Elizabeth of Portingall in verse', the *Life* tells us, 'and of many other saints' (p. 141). St Eliza-beth of Portugal (1271–1336), canonized in 1625, was a fashionable choice, and topical: a woman of spirit who had attempted to reform her dissolute husband and then prevented civil war by riding between

66. According to the *Life*, this was 'black Father Dunstan'; the 'Benedictine' marginal hand identifies him as 'Pettenger' (p. 130). Dunstan Pettenger OSB was confessor to the English Benedictine nuns at Paris in 1653–6 (while both Anne and Mary Cary were resident there). There is perhaps some confusion between the 'Fathers Dunstans' in the *Life* (p. 128); Dunstan Everard OSB also played some part in Elizabeth Cary's conversion. He was attached to the English Benedictine house at Paris known as St Edmund's (from Bury St Edmund's); it was this community that provided aid to Mary Ward, Mary Poyntz, and Winefrid Wigmore after their epic wintertime crossing of the Alps in 1637. See *Life*, ed. Kenworthy-Browne, p. 61; Stephen Marron OSB, 'Annals of our Monastery in Paris', *Douai Magazine* 5.3 (1929), pp. 202–7. On Everard's per-sonal acquaintance with Charles I, see Marron, 'The English Benedictines and the Stuarts', *Douai Magazine* 1.4 (1921), pp. 249–59.

67. Nivetta's admiration for 'Falconia' is intuited by the play's best-developed character: 'Bitomattus', *id est* Sir Tobie Matthew, son of the archbishop of York albeit—beneath gaudy clothes and extravagant courtly mannerisms—a Jesuit in disguise. See *Hierarchomachia*, ed. Gossett, p. 17. Bittomattus remarks: 'It seems my mistress lately is inspired / With Odoena and Falconia's style, / And like another Sappho can enchant / The hearer's sense with raptures of her wit' (2010–13). Nivetta's response, beginning 'Nay, jest not', raises the possibility that either Matthew or Cary might have written a version of 'Count Troilus' legend' (2016), now lost.

the armies of father and son.[68] The chief difficulty for the Cary daughters in contemplating their mother within the saint's life framework is that she is clearly no saint. This realization finds expression through erasures that run through the manuscript, some of them functioning as wry commentaries on the mother/daughter *agon*. 'She allways much esteemed and loved order', proclaims the *Life*—but then adding, under erasure, 'when she remembred there was such a thinge' (p. 144). The contemplative daughters could not help but notice that their mother was absent-minded, sometimes to the point of social insult: 'her fashion was in nothinge gracefull', says the *Life*, not under erasure; 'her neglect, through forgettfullnesse, of all customary civilitys, was so noatable, that it was passed into a privilege' (p. 215). Some of Cary's reading choices, such as 'French Mountaine, and English Bacon' (p. 212), are also subjected to heavy Benedictine erasure. In pursuing such an imperfect heroine, the narrative is nudged away from simple hagiography. The basic Providential framework, furnished by Catholic conversion and a good death, is secure. But marginal glosses, nonetheless, pop up to point the way like hermits in a Vulgate romance.

Reading, Ireland, Benedictine death

This book has come gradually to realize that for a strong woman to emerge, and get her story written, a man must die. Another man then comes to take his place: a divine spouse of the woman's choosing and, we may say, imagining. In the case of Dorothea and Margery the obstructive living male was the husband; in the case of Mary Ward, her father. Elizabeth Cary battles with both father and husband; their deaths are of great significance in her *Life*. But scenes of death absorb an exceptional amount of narrative energy in this text: more, certainly,

---

68. See François Paludanus, *A Short Relation of the Life, Virtues, and Miracles of S. Elizabeth called the Peacemaker. Queen of Portugall*, translated out of Dutch by Sister Catherine Francis, Abbess of the English Monasterie of S. Francis third Rule, in Bruxelles (Brussells: John Morris, 1628), esp. pp. 18–21. Catherine Francis's chaplain, Francis Bell, speaks of a French version of this widely-diffused text in his dedicatory preface to the work (A2); Cary might have translated from this source. Francis, in her own preface, speaks warmly of Archduchess Isabella Clara Eugenia; Mary Ward enjoyed the archduchess's strong support in the early 1620s and exchanged letters in French with her.

than in any of the previous three. Its daughter-authors write from a space of enclosure that is dead to the world. This is not the living death of the anchoress, but a space that holds the *limen* of life and death steadily in view as part of Benedictine formation. 'Death comes to be seen', Basil Hume observed, 'as the way that leads us to God'.[69] This explains the cheery handshake and 'Congratulations!' from a fellow Benedictine that so baffled the world when Hume announced his terminal cancer in 1999. It is chiefly by focusing upon such limenal moments of death, I am suggesting, that *Lady Faulkland: Her Life* seeks to arrest a narrative stream that might otherwise run to romance, or the picaresque.

One of the most arresting death scenes in this text actually folds into the narrative moment of conversion; the path to this climactic moment must be told in some detail. This path is long, *un chemin de longue étude*, since Elizabeth Cary begins reading herself towards conversion almost in exiting the baptismal font: 'she was their only child', says the *Life*. 'She was christened Elizabeth. She learnt to read very soone and loved it much' (p. 105). It is as a lonely and precocious *reader*, above all, that the *Life* characterizes its heroine in its *enfance*: 'she having nether brother nor sister', it relates, 'nor other companion of her age, spent her whole time in reading, to which she gave herself so much that she freqvently redd all night' (p. 108). Such nocturnal study requires candles, which she purchases from her servants; by the time she is twelve she is £100 in debt. At twelve her father presents her with Calvin's *The Institution of Christian Religion*; her critiques are extensive, and Sir Lawrence deduces that 'this girle hath a spirit averse from Calvin' (p. 108). She is delighted by Augustine, but underwhelmed by the wishy-washiness of Hooker's *Ecclesiastical Polity*. As she cogitates, her serving women pursue her around the room, attempting to pin on jewellery; when she sits to read or write they 'curle her haire and dreess her head' (p. 116). She reads deeply into other languages, teaching herself French, Spanish, Italian, Latin, and Hebrew. She translated copiously; her most famous such work, which translates Cardinal du Perron's polemical exchange with King James I of England from the French, was

---

69. In the 1930s, Father Paul Nevil OSB was told by a fellow headmaster that the purpose of his school was ' "to equip our boys for life". *Sotto voce*, Father Nevil was heard to murmur: "How fascinating! You see, at Ampleforth we always seek to prepare our boys for death" ' (Anthony Howard, *Basil Hume: The Monk Cardinal* (London: Headline Nook Publishing, 2005), p. 293.

commended at Rome in Latin and Italian.[70] She was moved to make this translation, the *Life* tells us, 'for the sakes of the scholers of Oxford and Cambridge (who doe not generally vnderstand french)' (pp. 131–2). She composed a good deal of verse: a 'life of Tamberlaine' and, just possibly, 'Count Troilus' legend'.[71] But it is above all as a mighty *reader* that she is commemorated by the *Life*; as a woman reading her way out of one belief and into another. It perhaps seems counter-intuitive to find a premodern woman exiting Protestantism by diligent reading, centred on the study of Scripture. But this is exactly how Elizabeth Cary represents herself shortly after her conversion: 'I must onely bee guided by illumination', she tells Lady Denbigh in December 1626, 'and not beleeve the church of england, as it is the church of england, but as I am instructed, out of the scripture' (p. 267).

Elizabeth Cary arrived in Ireland with seven children on 6 September 1622. 'Being there', the *Life* immediately states, 'she had much affection to that nation, and was very desirous to haue made vse of what power she had on any occasion, in their behalfe' (p. 119). Not surprisingly, her first initiative to help 'that nation' is made as a reader: 'she there learnt to read Irish in an Irish Bible' (p. 119). The learning of Bible Irish proves difficult: but she assuredly enjoyed more success by direct oral method, since she had earlier learned 'of a transilvanian, his language' (p. 106). The *Life* goes on to say that she forgot her Transilvanian 'intirely', on account of 'never finding any vse of it' (p. 106). But she soon found use for the Irish she had learned by hitting upon her 'great designe' (p. 120); this was

> to bring vp the vse of all trades in that country, which is faine to be beholding to others for the smalest comoditys; to this end she ~~preur~~ procured some of each kind, to come from those other places where those trades are exersised, as severall sorts of linnen and wolen weauers, dyers, all sorts of spinners, and knitters, hatters, lace makers, and many other trades att the very begining; and for this purpose she tooke of beggar children (with which that country swarmes) more than 8 score prentices, refusing none aboue seven yeare old, and taking some lesse; these were disposed to their severall masters and mistresses, to learn those trads they were thought most fitt for, the least amoungst them being set to somthinge, as making points, tags, buttons, or lace, or some other thinge; they were parted in their severall romes or houses where they

70. See Cary, *Life and Letters*, ed. Woolf, pp. 405, 412–14.
71. See note 67 above.

exersised their trades, many romes being filled with little boys or girles, sitting all round att work; besids those that were bigger for trads needing more vnderstanding and strengthe; she brought it to that passe that they there made broad cloath, so fine and good (of Irish woole, and spunne and weaved and died and dressed there) that her Lord being Debuty wore it.

(p. 120)

This is an extraordinary enterprise. For centuries, England had resented exporting its own raw materials of wool and cloth to Flanders and Tuscany (where it would be developed—through complex divisions of labour—into a superior product). Why, Richard Hakluyt had asked Elizabeth I, should the English not take raw materials, manufacture finished products in England, and then dump them onto the Irish market? Do unto the Irish as the Flemish do to us.[72] Here, *au contraire*, Elizabeth Cary envisions importing the infrastructure of a complex cloth industry to Dublin so that the Irish themselves can generate superior manufactured products. Her large-scale cottage industry, run by child apprentices, seems strangely to combine Sunday School and factory piecework: but it does respond to abject poverty and seems, for a while, to work. Ultimately, however, 'it came to nothinge': for two chief reasons, according to the *Life* authors. Firstly, these Catholic children are forced to attend Protestant services by their overseers: God is not pleased, and there are 'great losses by fire and watter' (p. 120). Secondly, their good-hearted mother is easily cheated and has no head for accounts, 'having the worst memory, in such thinges, in the world' (p. 121). The business continues under her direction for two years, but collapses shortly after she leaves Ireland in July 1625. There is little doubt, I think, that her Irish experiences helped accelerate Elizabeth Cary's conversion. She became Catholic in Drury Lane in Irish stables: those of the earl of Ormond, a peer who had spent seven years in the Fleet prison. And the first of the two sons she had in Ireland was named Patrick, 'the great patron of the Country' (p. 125). She must also have seen things in and from Dublin castle that confirmed 'affection to that nation'. Her husband, the king's deputy, was starved of supply by his monarch: when a Spanish man-of-war landed at Drogheda in 1627, and then Dublin, 'it committed many spoiles and outrages' that Cary was powerless to prevent.[73] The search for

<hr />

72. See Wallace, *Premodern Places*, p. 120.
73. Letter of Lord Falkland and the Irish Privy Council to Charles I, 2 August 1627 (Cary, *Life and Letters*, ed. Wolfe, p. 296).

income led the desperate deputy to imprison Phelim McFieugh Byrne and his six sons in Dublin castle the following year, accused of treason; the supposition was made that Lord Falkland wished to confiscate Byrne's estates. He was recalled from Ireland in semi-disgrace in 1629; his successor, the earl of Strafford, fared worse.[74]

In her final years, approaching death, Elizabeth Cary confined herself to two forms of activity. Firstly, she 'imployed herself in setting poore folks on worke with yarn and woole, for the entertainment of her thoughts and time' (p. 207). Finally, a 'coffe cough of the lungs' appears: 'from which time', the *Life* tells us, 'her whole imployment was writting and reading; renewing somewhat her Hebrew, and her Latin' (p. 207). 'She died', the *Life* reports, 'about the begining of these trowbles of England'; she was thus spared knowing that her two Protestant sons soon died in the civil war 'without any signe of hope' (p. 212). The *Life's* first posthumous thought of Elizabeth Cary is that 'she had read very exceeding much' (p. 212); an extraordinary list of authors then stretches on for two pages. The Benedictine daughters are pleased to report that she was received into the Confraternity of St Benedict 'a little more than a yeare before her death' (p. 217); masses could thus be said for her at the convents of Douai and Cambrai (p. 222). It is worth noting, however, that while she chose to live with the Benedictine 'scapular' for one year (p. 217), she lived without it for fifty-two. And that her path to dying reprises the two main forces that powered her to conversion in 1626: incessant reading and, through this late-life experience of 'setting poore folks on work with yarn and woole, for the entertainment of her thoughts and time' (p. 207), her years among the poor Catholics of Ireland.

Fabricating Catholic dying: the husband and the best of daughters

Elizabeth Cary contemplated death intensively long before her final year; like most premodern women, like Dorothea of Montau and

74. Cary's *Edward II* astutely evaluates being 'sent to an *Irish* or *Welsh* Employment' by English governing powers as a form of silencing and political ostracism; this remained true down to Margaret Thatcher's dispatching of Jim Prior to Belfast in 1981. Charles I signed Strafford's death warrant on 10 May 1641.

Margery Kempe, she faced serial childbirth. The Benedictine daughters struggle with this. 'While she was with child of her 2^d and 4th child', they tell us, 'she lost the perfect vse of her reason' (p. 118): but then they change their minds, putting this passage under not single but double erasure. The passage following speculates that such 'plaine distractednesse' was a bid to win her husband's attention that got out of hand; but the daughters think again, and this passage too is erased. A few pages earlier they tell how their mother, 'whilest she had but tow or 3 children', had decided to write them a letter so that 'her care of them, might not dye with her' (p. 114). This text represents a genre much favoured by Protestant women. The most famous exemplar is *The Mothers Legacie, to her Unborn Childe*, written by Elizabeth Jocelin (1596–1622) and published a dozen times by 1674; comparable texts were written by Frances Aburgavennie, Elizabeth Crashawe, Elizabeth Grymeston, Dorothy Leigh, Elizabeth Richardson, and Elizabeth Cooke Russell.[75] In writing while pregnant, addressing a child yet unborn, a woman occupied an immensely powerful site; a limenal space between life and death. Elizabeth Jocelin, who died nine days after giving birth to her daughter, became a Protestant saint, a martyr to the Protestant imperative to bring forth children.[76] In premodern Catholic culture, wifehood ranks lowest in rate of spiritual return; widowhood ranks second, and virginity comes top.[77] The female religious, however, ranks even higher in choosing to live between life and death: she becomes dead to the world (as the door of enclosure shuts behind her); she looks to the next world (in gazing at the altar). This finds heroic expression in the burial service with which the anchoress is walled away, and in her life as a living death: she is up there continually, says *Ancrene*

75. See Wendy Wall, *The Imprint of Gender: Authorship and Publication in the English Renaissance* (Ithaca, NY: Cornell University Press, 1993), pp. 283–96; *Women Writers*, ed. Martin, pp. 97–125; Wallace, 'Periodizing Women', pp. 400–01. The 'Approbation' that prefaces the pocket-sized 1624 edition of Jocelin, by Thomas Goad, begins as follows: 'Our lawes disable those, that are vnder *Couert-baron*, from disposing by Will and Testament any temporall estate. But no law prohibiteth any possessor of morall and spirituall riches, to impart them vnto others, either in life by communicating, or in death by bequeathing' (Elizabeth Jocelin, *The Mothers Legacie, to her Vnborne Childe*, second impression (London: John Haviland for William Barrett, 1624), A3).

76. Her *Mothers Legacie* was reproduced more widely than any other original composition by a Renaissance Englishwoman (excepting Elizabeth I); it was, says Randall Martin, 'reissued eleven times between 1622 and 1674, translated into Dutch in 1699, and reprinted in the eighteenth and nineteenth centuries' (*Women Writers*, p. 34).

77. See Chapter 1 above, p. 81 and n. 54.

Wisse, with Christ on the cross.[78] Her active suspension between living and dying, like that of every enclosed female religious, brings limenal power, a mysterious authority analogous to that of pregnancy. This strangely displaced continuity between Catholic and Protestant cultures further connects with yet longer traditions of fear and awe attaching to women as bearers of life.

The text of 'morall precepts' written by Elizabeth Cary as she was 'like to dye' is taken most to heart by Katherine, 'the most dutyfull and best loving of all her children' (p. 114). Katherine herself dies, the *Life* tells us, 'betweene sixten and seventen yeare old, in child bed of her first child' (p. 114); it is discovered by 'her owne mother' that she has always most carefully observed 'the rule she had given her' (p. 115). The death of Katherine recurs later in the *Life* in a highly charged context: between Elizabeth's return from Ireland and her conversion in the stable:

> After arriuing safe, and having first kissed her Maiestys hands (who was not long before come into England) she retired to her mothers for feare of the plague (then very hott) carrying with her (besids the rest) her maried daughter, great with child; who in the iourny, being carryed ouer a narrow bridge by a gentleman of her mothers (who out of particular care desired to carry her) his foot sliping, fell into the watter; but he in the fall (taking only care of her) cast himself so along in the watter, that she fell vpright with her feet on his brest; and she seeing them all trowbled for feare of her, and he especially (who had long serued her father and mother) much afflicted att it, she would not acknowledge feeling any hurt nor being frightened, but att the end of her iourny the same night fell sike, and within a weeke died, being first deliverd, allmost three mounths afore her time, of a daughter, which lived three howers and was christened. had it lived, the mother was resolved, to haue nursed her daughters child together with her owne, not yet weaned. her daughter died in her armes.
>
> (pp. 125–6)

This is limenal drama, par excellence: a pregnant woman falls from a 'narrow bridge', a limenal site, as her mother passes from the hands of a Catholic queen to her own conversion. Originally, the *Life* simply moved on from this point by resuming Elizabeth Cary's journey to the

---

78. 'All you endure is penance', says the opening of Part VI, 'and hard penance, my dear sisters; all the good you ever do, all you suffer, is martyrdom for you in the most severe of orders, for night and day you are up on God's cross' (*Anchoritic Spirituality: Ancrene Wisse and Associated Works*, tr. and intr. Anne Savage and Nicholas Watson (New York: Paulist Press, 1991), p. 176. The translation of *Ancrene Wisse* here is from British Library, MS Cotton Titus D.xviii.

stables ('She coming againe to London...', p. 127). But their elder sister's death clearly haunted the authors as an episode entirely undigested by the greater narrative: and so they returned to it, tipping in a new leaf. The suggestion that a sibling should die in agony and without Catholic comfort was clearly hard to take. By that part of the *Life* which tells of their brothers dying in the civil war,[79] Patrick added a marginal annotation, expressing 'some...hopes they died cath[olic]'; this Mary rewrote, changing Patrick's 'some' to 'great' (p. 212). Their sister requires an equivalent intervention, but her last recorded words are not encouraging: 'she often repeated with a sadd lamentable mournfull voice, "Wo is me, is there no remedy[?]"' (p. 126). These are understandable sentiments from a teenager about to die. Her sister-authors respond, first, with strong narrative intervention: Katherine sees 'by her bed a bright woman cloathed in white having a crown on he[r] head'; this must be, the mother persuades her dying daughter, 'our Blessed Lady'. Secondly, the mother 'did persawd herself' that her daughter's cries of 'Wo is me, is there no remedy[?]' do not show fear of death; they reflect apprehension 'of what she was to suffer (as she hoped) in purgatory' (p. 126). Maternal hermeneutics, exercised just *before* Catholic conversion, thus seek to save the daughter who loved her best, and who followed her precepts.

The *Life*'s account of the twinned figures that Elizabeth Cary must overcome, her father and husband, also resorts to preemptive or speculative Catholicization. These figures of masculine authority are twinned not through actual alliance—the father actively disapproves of the husband—but because Elizabeth is passed from one to the other: 'att fifteene yeare olde', the *Life* says, 'her father maried her to one Sir Harry Cary' (p. 108). Father and husband thus represent a continuum of paternal, Protestant authority that our Catholic heroine must be shown to respect and yet, ultimately, to disavow. Such a narrative trajectory begins with childhood and ends, again, in death; from first to last, paternal authority is continuously diminished by feminine access to a higher truth.

The first wonder recounted by the *Life* features a rebellious horse (p. 105): a creature that might have wandered in from the opening

79. 'Lorenzo Cary, 'a very hopeful gentleman', was on 13 January 1642 reported 'shot of a musket bullet in his head' while campaigning in Ireland (p. 416); Lucius died at the Battle of Newbury, 20 September 1643.

pages of the *Book of Margery Kempe* (290–310). Elizabeth's father, when a young lawyer, encounters a judge on circuit who demands the summary execution of a Catholic priest. The priest is despatched and the judge takes horse: 'he was no sooner vp', the *Life* tells us, 'but his horse, att all other times most gentle (as those, of Judges commonly are) began to curvet, threw him of of his backe, casting his head against a stone, where his braines were dasht out. this same thinge, it may be, might incline him [Elizabeth's father] to be lesse forward to persecute catholiks' (p. 105). The second such exemplary tale of the *Life* takes us to imaginative territory familiar from *A Pistil of Susan*,[80] the oft-painted tale of Susannah and the elders; in this variant, 'about ten yeare old' Elizabeth Cary plays the part of young Daniel (p. 106). An old woman is brought before her father, accused of being a witch and of 'having bewitched tow or 3 to death' (p. 106). 'Did not you', asks an accuser in court, 'send your familiar in the shap of a blake blacke dogg, a hare, or a <f…d> catt,[81] and he finding him a sleep, licked his hand, or breathed on him, or stept over him, and he presently came home sicke and languished away?' This, the old woman says, is all true. 'But the child', the *Life* continues, 'thought feare had made her idle, and so she whispered her father' (p. 107). What Elizabeth 'whispers' to her father is a winning strategy for cross-examination; the old lady is cleared, and truth prevails.

Judge Tanfield fades from the narrative at this point and is 'dead', as the *Life* summarily puts it, 'before her coming backe into England' (p. 139). Attention now shifts from father to husband, and great pains are taken to emphasize how hard Elizabeth tries to be a good Mrs Cary: 'He was very absolute', the *Life* says, 'and though she had a strong will, she had learnt to make it obey his' (p. 115). To please him she takes up things in which she has no interest whatsoever: such as housework, and horseriding. She fell from a horse once in jumping a hedge, while pregnant, and almost lost her fourth baby—just 'to see him pleased' (p. 116). This episode occasioned second thoughts in the daughter-authors, and

---

80. This stanzaic alliterative text survives in five copies. One once formed part of the famous London library of Sir Robert Cotton (1571–1631); see now British Library, Cotton Caligula Aii (late fifteenth century, lacking the first eight stanzas).

81. The term under erasure 'f…d' is damaged (as indicated by the diamond brackets); the word 'catt' is an interlinear insertion.

went under erasure,[82] as did a number of marginal comments.[83] This attempt to convince us of Elizabeth's extreme fidelity to husbandly and fatherly rule is delicate: had she not rebelled against both, this text could not have been written. Henry Cary's death, as the *Life* tells it, finesses this paradox most ingeniously.

On first returning from Ireland in 1629, Henry Cary was furiously angry with his newly-Catholic wife and had nothing to do with her. By the summer of 1632, however, some degree of reconciliation had been achieved: one letter sees Lady Falkland writing as 'it hath pleased my lord', and another sees them sharing the same sheet of paper (pp. 378–9, 381). The following year, however, Henry Cary suffers an appalling accident. While 'waiting on the King' at Theobalds Park, the royal hunting ground in Hertfordshire, he falls from a stand and breaks his leg. The king comes to him, and Henry breaks his leg again in attempting to rise in the royal presence. The text is then immediately revised: Henry 'brock his legg, and instantly brocke it in a secound and a thirde ~~third~~ place, with ~~t~~ standing vp vpon it att the Kings coming to him' (pp. 147–8). The phrase 'and a thirde' is here added as an interlinear gloss: three breaks in the leg, more closely aligning with the three wounds favoured by saints' legends, is more tidily Trinitarian.

King Charles sends for Elizabeth Cary. She, of course, is in London—although the couple had spent time together that summer, and Henry had spoken 'of both their coming to liue at home together... designing a place for her chaple, and for her Priest to liue in' (p. 148). Such an arrangement would align Elizabeth yet more closely with Henrietta Maria, making the Carys a couple to mirror the Stuarts. Elizabeth comes to Henry's sickbed, and 'left him not till his death' (p.148). This takes just a week, but this time is long and highly charged, in narrative terms. Henry's leg is badly set, and 'it Gangrend'; consultants resolve that 'the legg was to be cutt of iust aboue his knee' (p. 149). 'Whilest they cutt if of', the *Life* assures us,

---

82. So too did the comment originally appended to this episode: 'she being continvually after as long as she lived with him ether with child or giuing suck' (p. 116). This form of life might have seemed, to the Benedictine daughters, a life of perpetual penance comparable with that of *Ancrene Wisse*, VII; but they thought better of this remark.

83. See especially Lucy's three attempts to exonerate her grandfather Tanfield from charges of anti-Catholicism, bribery, and corruption on folio 2r. (p. 105).

he never changed his countenance, nor made any shew of paine, no more he had nott att the breaking of it...nor all the time of the dressing of it, only when they went to search how farre it was gangrend he once frowned and cryd oh softly. she was allso present; and in the very time it was a cutting, his daughters from home and his tow younger sonnes from schole coming to see him...

(p. 149)

This bringing in of the children during amputation is a desperate moment: but the moment is prolonged, since from now on the leg never ceases to bleed. So we enter not just another limenal scene, played out between life and death, but one reminiscent of martyrdom or saint's life: Saint Cecelia, perhaps most famously, bleeds to death for three days while continuing to teach and comfort.[84] Henry wins much sympathy in the *Life* by comforting his children, the *Life*'s future authors. His physicians, negligent and incompetent, decide finally 'to lett him bleed to death' (p. 150). The narrative now enters a kind of inner sanctum, shared only by husband and wife: a transition marked by their speaking in French, the language of Henrietta Maria and of Cardinal Perron. Having given his wife instructions, Henry asks

(still in french, which he spoke ill enough) if her man were there, calling it homme; which she tooke only for and ill phrase, but having told him, he that vsed to waite on her abroad was there; and that he sayd he ment not him; she saw he ment her pre Priest.

(p. 150)

No priest being available, Elizabeth herself 'told him the best she could how to dispose him self interiorly'; which is to say, like Mary Ward and her followers in similar circumstances, she performs the office of a priest. 'He seemed to harken to all she sayd', the *Life* says, 'but spoke no more; he was bleeding to death more then three howers': the husband sheds the blood, and the wife imitates St Cecelia.[85] The suggestion is made, gilding the lily of this story, that his wife's French translating 'might haue cheifly inclined him to haue a desire of being a Catholike': for 'her translation of Perone', we are told, 'was found in his clossett after his death, all noated by him' (p. 151). This daughterly wish

84. 'Thre dayes lyved she', says Chaucer's Second Nun of St Cecelia, 'in this torment' (8.537); she has been semi-decapitated by 'thre strokes in the nekke' (8.526).
85. Chaucer's Cecelia bleeds as she teaches and preaches for three days; her supporters staunch the blood 'with sheetes' (8.536).

might actually be true: for the copy of Elizabeth Cary's Perron translation in the Queen's College, Oxford, 61.B.11, is heavily annotated in a hand 'similar to that of Henry, Lord Falkland'.[86]

Mother trouble

Anne, Elizabeth, Lucy, and Mary Cary converted to Catholicism just six months after their father's death. In describing his passing they assign to their mother, *faut de mieux*, a priestly role; in the matter of their own conversion, however, they carefully try to keep their mother out of it. They tread delicate theological ground here: as Benedictine nuns, they need to accentuate both their own powers of volition and the decisiveness of priestly mediation; maternal influence must be deemphasized. And so once again, the *Life* finds a limenal figure to carry its narrative: a young man living between life and death who dies, like Christ, at 'about 33' (p. 160). This Benedictine priest lives between life and death not through anchoritic enclosure, but by 'being ever sickly' (p. 161). Although affirming himself to be 'an owle out of his Monastery', he was 'sent into England for his health' (p. 160); he appears, the *Life* says, 'not to be of the world' (p. 161). Lusting for martyrdom, he seeks permission to assist 'those sicke of the Plague (which was then in London)' (p. 162). Refused this option, he sickens anyway: 'coming to dye', the *Life* says, 'he did earnestly desire death' (p. 162). News of his converting the daughters comes to their mother, as the *Life* tells it, immediately following notice of his last suffering. 'After a strong Agony of 3 howers', the same timespan allotted to Henry Cary's last struggle, 'his sences and devotion continuing to the last, he died happyly by the grace of God. She was most exceedingly ioyed att the resolution of her daughters', continues the *Life*, directly,

when she was made acqvainted with it which yet they kept from her, till by their forbearing to goe to church, it was suspected by their protestant frinds, and that they had as good as acknowledged it to them, they then profest it to her too, who ether knewe nothinge afore or durst not take any notice of it, for feare of hindering it ~~(but though she might have some glimpse of hope it is like she did not know any thinge, for she could very hardly conceale what she knew)~~.

(p. 163)

---

86. Heather Wolfe's note at *Life and Letters*, ed. Woolf, p. 151, n.139.

This attempt to build a firewall between Elizabeth Cary's conversion and that of her four daughters reads awkwardly, and for good reasons. The saintly young Benedictine converter in question, Cuthbert Fursden, actually served as Elizabeth Cary's chaplain until he died in 1638; he was said to live 'in great abstraction'.[87] The *Life* pictures the daughters speaking with him 'by accident, or rather Gods especiall providence' (p. 161): but given such close links to their mother's household, such meetings were hardly surprising. Fursden's dying is narrated as if it were the springboard to the daughters' conversions: but they had already been Catholic for four years by then. Speculation on *what mother knew when* leads the daughters into difficulties and ultimately, in the passage just cited, erasure. The last part of the passage above might be paraphrased thus: 'Anything that Mama knew, she'd be sure to talk about'. Narrating a life within traditional hagiographical parameters proves tricky when the saint is someone you know too well: your mother.

Violence and economy on Drury Lane

Elizabeth Cary, according to her daughters, 'conversed ~~very~~ much...the conversation of her frinds, being the greatest delight of her life' (p. 214). The next page of the *Life* affirms that 'she spoke very much' (and this time the 'very' does not come under erasure). She was a creature, the *Life* implicitly acknowledges, better suited to Drury Lane than to Cambrai. Her absent-mindedness could not easily be glossed as mystical abstraction; her pregnancy-related depressions were alien to convent life. Her answers in Star Chamber, following her kidnapping of Patrick and Henry from Great Tew in 1636, were reportedly 'vncertaine and illusory'.[88] In 1637 she planned transferring herself and all six children to Rome so that the Holy See

---

87. Cuthbert Fursden, alias John Breton, dedicated his translation of the Benedictine Rule to Anne Cary; it was most likely used at Cambrai. See Wolfe, 'Introduction' to *Life and Letters*, p. 46, n.95. Much influenced, as a young man, by Augustine Baker, he was said to live 'in great abstraction and endeavoured the conversion of souls more by good example and prayer than by disputing': see 'An Account of the Life of the Venerable Fr. Augustine Baker', *Ampleforth Journal*, 4 (1898), p. 199.
88. See 'King's Bench Examination of Lady Falkland', in Cary, *Life and Letters*, ed. Wolfe, pp. 395–6 (p. 396).

could support them: she must be 'lunatica', writes Cardinal Barberini's secretary, 'a bear of little brain' ('di poco cervello').[89] George Con, the papal agent in England, wrote back to explain that she was driven by fear of poverty and to affirm her serious academic credentials.[90] But even her own daughters admitted that Elizabeth Cary was, once committed to a project, a woman of *violence*. The seventeenth-century resonances of this term are worth pondering. Elizabeth Cary, the *Life* relates, was unwilling to see how she was 'cosened', cheated,

in all things on which she was sett with such violence (as she was on all the things she vndertooke, which were many) which violence in all occasions, made her ever subiect to nessessitys...and made her continvually pawne and sell any thinge she had (though it were a thinge she should need (allmost) within an hower after) to procure what she had a mind to at the present: the same violence made her subiect to make greate promises...which being many, could not allways be performed.

(p. 121)

These usages of *violence* have been glossed to mean, following OED, *excessive fervour*.[91] This helpfully pinpoints *fervour* as a defining characteristic of seventeenth-century *mulieres fortes*. The women following Mary Ward, we have noted, were commended for their fervour and assured, by a Yorkshire Jesuit, that it could not last: 'fervour will decay, and when all is done they are but wemen'.[92] This exemplifies a perennial dilemma for premodern women: that they will always be judged as being too little or too much by the standard of masculine middleness.[93] But a *mulier fortis* must always be too much; were she not, her life would never be written. Elizabeth Cary's daughters thus acknowledge their mother's *violence* as a quality essential to a life begetting a *Life*. The necessary excess of the *mulier fortis* has led contemporary critics, however, to pathologize her: this is especially true for Dorothea of

89. Secretary Ferragalli to George Con, 12 March 1637, pp. 404–5 (p. 405).
90. George Con to Secretary Ferragalli, 9 April 1637, 405. Con believes that 'la sua intenzione di peregrinare nasca dalla pouertà'; he identifies Elizabeth Cary with her translation of 'le opere del Cardinale Duperone'.
91. VIOLENCE, *OED sb, 5*; *Life and Letters*, ed. Woolf, p. 121.
92. *Mary Ward*, ed. Dirmeier I, 357; and see Chapter 3 above, p. 138.
93. 'Female', Caroline Bynum has written, 'was seen as below and above reason—as witch or saintly visionary—whereas male was seen as a rather pedestrian middle, incapable of direct contact either with angelic or demonic power' ('Why All the Fuss', p. 17).

Montau, Margery Kempe, and for Cary.[94] But in all cases, behaviours judged idiosyncratic might symptomatize disturbances in the greater world: social, political, and economic. Discussion of Cary's *violence* is actually framed, by her *Life*, in economic terms: she pawns and sells to procure her objects; she binds herself in pledges of credit-worthiness that she cannot always perform or redeem.[95]

Four models of economy might quickly be spotted in Cary's *Life*; they are shadowed by a fifth. The first is that of the *oikos*, or household, where a mother makes her children 'her busyness' (p. 115); Cary struggles to affirm credentials here, but admits that, for 'taking care of her house', she has 'no inclination' (p. 116). The first 'macro' model is Providence-minded prodigality: all may be given away, or spent on candles, because God will provide. Margery Kempe incenses her travelling companion, the broken-backed Richard, by giving away all their money (3012–18); Mary Ward also honours such impulses.[96] Elizabeth Cary reembraces this attitude late in life by resolving to live from 'charity and assistance', and not 'by borrowing' (p. 186): an upscale, urban variant of religious mendicancy. 'Borrowing' locates her within a different economic model: that of business-like accountability. Her 'greate design' (p. 120) in Dublin, the creation of an Irish finished cloth industry, foundered chiefly because of 'the ill order she tooke for paying mony' (p. 121). Her taste for business did not diminish during her Drury Lane years: like Margery Kempe, she happily traversed earthly and heavenly economies.[97] The *Life* is censorious: when 'her hopes… were built on

---

94. See, for example, Heather Woolf, 'Introduction' to *Life and Letters*, pp. 74–7. 'Manic behaviour', writes Woolf, 'leads to grandiose plans, poor memory, and over-spending'. Wolfe surmises that 'there may have been a family history of manic-depression' (pp. 76–7).

95. The passage quoted above, as it continues, melds moral and economic terms of censure. In modern terms, which also moralize the economic, Elizabeth Cary would be termed less than credit-worthy: 'it made her too, to acknowledge, smale thinges, done att the instants she desired them, so greate (and without regarding to whom it was) that if it chanced to be to such, as would claime a reqvitall according to the acknowledgment (and not the worth of the thing) att a greater distance, looking on it with truer eyes, *what she had sayd could not allways be stood to*' (pp. 121–2, emphasis added).

96. 'She gave it as for a Rule to us, that Charity shou'd still preceade, and Prudence follow' (*English Life*, ed. Kenworthy-Browne, p. 83).

97. For her entanglements with Philip Burlamachi, financier to the crown, see letters 25 (p. 294), 87 (p. 391), and 105 (p. 411); for her attempt to access funds deriving from Henry's license for transportation of pipe staves (used primarily for cask making), see 28–9 (pp. 297–9). On Margery Kempe's late-life induction into the Trinity Guild, see above, p. 129.

humaine policys and industrys they did infailably deceave her'; only when entrusting herself 'to the service of God' did she 'withoute faile experience his mercy to goe beyond her hopes' (p. 153). Even in pointing to divine prodigality, however, Cary's daughters themselves sustain yet another economic model: that of patronage networks and royal largesse. The dower of a Cambrai nun was £450; such a sum could not be raised without the good offices of Lucius, the Protestant heir, and of Henrietta Maria.[98] Elizabeth Cary was a tireless worker of patronage networks: she wrote endlessly, seeking preferment for and from the widest range of acquaintance. In 1636, for example, she wrote a note to Sir Edward Nicholas, carried by a poor man: 'this poore man desires to bee swabber of a ship that is a bildinge at woolwich'; and, she takes the opportunity to remind him, 'my wants are extreme'.[99]

The final economic model, shadowing all these others, is slavery. In 1605, white noblewomen blacked up to dance at Ben Jonson's (and Inigo Jones's) *Masque of Blackness*; and Elizabeth Cary's *Tragedy of Mariam*, very likely dating from the same year, differentiates a queen of true title and notable whiteness from 'brown' or 'mongrel' competition.[100] The language of slavery pervades even Mary Ward's circle. All this helps prepare the way for one of the first acts of the Restoration: the foundation of the Royal African Adventurers in 1660. Leading investors in this slaving enterprise were to include four members of the royal family, two dukes, a marquis, and five earls; Henrietta Maria, as queen mother, joined them three years later.[101]

The proliferation of economic models to be discerned in Cary's *Life*, then, testifies not so much to her own pathology as to that of the greater polity: the incompatibility of divine prodigality, royal largesse and aristocratic patronage, on the one hand, with realistic accounting and sober-suited business, on the other. Such differences would be fought out after her death on 19 October 1639: 'about the begining', as her *Life* has it, 'of these trowbles of England' (p. 212).

98. See *Life and Letters*, ed. Wolfe, pp. 218–19; Walker, *Gender and Politics*, p. 32.
99. 4 February 1636: Cary, *Life and Letters*, ed. Wolfe, 394–5 (pp. 394, 395).
100. See Wallace, *Premodern Places*, p. 250; *Mariam*, ed. Weller and Ferguson, on 'the browne Egyptian' (Cleopatra, 1.190) and 'thou Mongrel: issu'd from reiected race' (Salome, 1.236). Herod later apostrophizes Mariam as 'thou white Inchantres' (4.176), with Salome 'to her a Sun burnt Blackamore' (4.462). Such discourse intensifies in the latter part of the play: see further 4.576; 5.150–51; 5.195–6; 5.239.
101. See Wallace, *Premodern Places*, p. 249.

A mother's legacy: her children's *lives*

Walter Montagu, writing in 1638, recommends Patrick Cary to Cardinal Barberini at Rome by virtue of his mother:'la mere est une catolique fort virtuesse...la piete et le zêle de la mere est fort notable et de grand example' (p. 407). Montagu here envisions a *mulier fortis*'s power extending beyond her own life to play out through the lives of her children. The four Catholic daughters struggle throughout the *Life* with this proposition but, as Benedictine nuns, can hardly deny it. What of the other Cary offspring? Katherine marries an earl, lives 'amongst most earnest scotch puritans' (p. 127), and dies in her mother's arms. The *Life* attempts to bring Katherine into the Catholic fold, but Victoria is untouchable. She remains Protestant, dances at court, and plans on marrying William Uvedale, the younger; when he dies in Venice she marries William Uvedale the elder, his father.[102] She outlives all her siblings, dies in 1694, and lies buried in St James, Westminster as 'Lady Victory Udall'. Sir Lorenzo Cary, the second son, dies Protestant fighting 'rebels' with the royalist army in Ireland (p. 416). Lucius, the second Viscount Falkland, a man of great skill and learning, was deeply depressed by the war. Dying near-suicidally at the battle of Newbury, he was lamented by his intimate friend, Lord Clarendon, as perhaps the greatest 'single loss' of 'this odious and accursed civil war'.[103] It seems, from these very different trajectories, that Elizabeth Cary's children chose highly individuated life courses, like upper class siblings of more recent times: the

102. And when Uvedale senior died, she married 'a blinde man that lived in the house with her...[who] has bin in loue with her seuenteen year':so says Dorothy Osborne, offering an account of Victoria's marital adventures worthy of Dorothy Parker. 'She was handsom Enough once', she continues, 'or Else som Pictur's that I haue seen of her flatterd her very much, that, and her witt together, gott her soe many servant's, that they hindered one another and her too I think. Sir William Udall and his sonn were Rivalls and (which was stranger) she pleased them both, the son thought himself sure of her as longe as hee lived, and the Father knew hee might have her when his son was dead' (extract from a letter to William Temple, in *Life and Letters*, ed. Wolfe, p. 469; the 'blinde man' who succeeds Uvedale senior is Sir Bartholomew Price).

103. Edward [Hyde], Earl of Clarendon, *The History of the Rebellion and Civil Wars in England begun in the Year 1641*, ed. W. Dunn McCray, XVI books in 6 vols (Oxford: Clarendon Press, 1888), vol. 3, p. 179; see further Smith, 'Cary, Lucius', p. 444b. Clarendon's tribute to Lucius is extensive (vol. 3, pp. 178–90); 'his mother' is briefly noted as 'a lady of another persuasion in religion, and of a most masculine understanding, allayed with the passion and infirmities of her own sex' (vol. 3, p. 180).

Mitfords of the past century, or the Hitchens of our own.[104] But the maternal impress may be seen most clearly in the lives of the two boys she had kidnapped from Oxfordshire in 1636 and sent to Paris for a Catholic education: Patrick and Henry.

In 1638, the year after Elizabeth Cary considered taking her six Catholic children to Rome, Patrick Cary arrived there from Paris, aged just fourteen; on 30 October he dined with John Milton at the English College. For years, enjoying some Barberini patronage, he lived at the edge of the curia. When Urban VIII died and Barberini support evaporated he found all doors closed to him: 'si consola pero con le muse', Cardinal Barberini was informed in 1646, 'essendo riuscito uno de' primi Poeti Italiani della Città. E ha fatta una comedia pastorale tutta in verso, di argomento ben si profano ma modestissima, che in giudizio di quelli che l'hanno letta non cede punto alle prime compositioni uscite in stampe'.[105] [He consoles himself with the Muses, having become one of the leading Italian poets of the city. And he has written a pastoral comedy, all in verse. Its argument is profane, but only moderately so, and in the judgment of those who have read it is no way inferior to the finest compositions that have appeared in print.] This pastoral comedy is not known to exist, but the British Library does contain a volume of Patrick's Italian songs, 'messe in Musica da Diversi Autori'.[106] This curious small book, BL Add. MS 58853, is 25cm long and just 10cm high; it contains eleven songs, all set to music. They sing of betrayal in love, jealousy, and disappointed hopes: 'Di' mio cor è ver', the first song begins, 'che tù hai tradito non sò chi' (f.2a). 'Non replicarmi Amor', begins the second, 'Io son tradito, non è vano il sospetto' (f. 8a). 'Con lusinghe di Sirena', the last song begins, 'un pensier nel sen mi dice' (78a). Such language indicates how easily a young man seeking patronage and advancement at the Roman curia could let his feelings flow into the conventional channels of courtly love. Despairing, finally, of advancement in Rome he returns to France, becoming a Benedictine novice at Douai in May 1650.

104. See Mary S. Lovell, *The Mitford Girls: The Biography of an Extraordinary Family* (London: Little, Brown, 2001); Christopher Hitchens, *Hitch-22: A Memoir* (London: Atlantic Books, 2010).
105. Dom Wilfred Selby to Cardinal Barberini (1646) in *Life and Letters*, ed. Wolfe, p. 419.
106. *Parole di Gio. Patrizio Carey messe in musica da Diversi Autori*, BL Additional MS 58853.

The true hero of Patrick Cary's life is Edward Hyde, first earl of Clarendon and chancellor of Oxford University. In July 1649 he actually visited the Cary sisters at Cambrai, en route to Madrid; he subsequently interpreted his extreme love of Lucius as obligation to Patrick.[107] This encouraged Patrick to write Clarendon two remarkable letters that, read together, themselves comprise something of a *Life*. 'I doe thus', he tells Clarendon, 'to make my selfe lesse a stranger to you, to entertayne you with a kind of Romance' (p. 428). Less than a year before, Patrick had read *The Lady Faulkland: Her Life* at Cambrai. He was moved to annotate most intensively at that point in the *Life* where his mother engineers his fateful abduction from Oxfordshire. Where his mother's *Life* tells how the watermen hired for the kidnapping were drunk, he writes 'true' (p. 198); where it tells of an escape from soldiers in a wood near Rouen, he writes 'these were all visions' (which is to say: my sister has made this up, p. 205). This section of the *Life* certainly reads like romance, although the Benedictine sisters take care to emphasize that the successful abduction is blessed by Providence. But Patrick, in the second part of his own 'life' letter to Clarendon, is less certain of the providential framing of his own, unfinished *vita*: 'such contrary chances', he laments, 'such extrauagant miscariages of Letters and Papers of necessary buisnesse... Many such particulars could I relate', he continues, 'which would make any one beleeue that I were the Unfortunate Spanyard translated in to English; and indeed by that name I used to stile my selfe' (p. 450). Patrick here most likely refers to *Gerardo the Unfortunate Spaniard*, a volume published in London in 1622.[108] Its subtitle is *A Patterne for Lascivious Lovers. Containing severall strange miseries of loose Affection*: a strange text for a Benedictine novice to contemplate, although Patrick's Italian verse does testify to

---

107. Anne Cary writes to Clarendon on 4 March 1650, grateful 'at your beeing heere'; the visit took place between 21 and 31 July 1649 (letter 114, *Life and Letters*, ed. Wolfe, pp. 423–7 (p. 424)). See further Clarendon's letter to Patrick of 25 April 1650: 'since the unspeakable losse of your excellent Brother, I haue rarely felt soe great a pleasure as the first sight of your Name in a Letter, gaue me' (*Life and Letters*, ed. Wolfe, 432–5 (p. 432); and see pp. 436–42. On the dynamics and symbolic forms of male–male (mostly) friendships in this premodern period, see Alan Bray, *The Friend* (Chicago: University of Chicago Press, 2003).

108. *Gerardo the Unfortunate Spaniard, or A Patterne for Lascivious Lovers. Containing severall strange miseries of loose Affection. Written by an ingenious Spanish Gentleman, Don Gonçalo de Cespedes, and Meneçes, in the time of his five yeeres Imprisonment. Originally in Spanish, and made English by L.D.* [Leonard Digges] (London: printed for Ed. Blount, 1622); BL 12489 bb.39.

mini-tragedies of 'loose affection'. Its hero is a 'dismayed Youth' (p. 2). After almost five hundred adventurous pages, in which the heroine shows 'Masculine' bravery (p. 473), Leontio thinks to marry Nise. But she has come to reinterpret the seeming accidents of the plot: 'All this (beleeue me)', she implores him, 'was not without some mysterie, or gouernment of Gods most liberall hand' (p. 472). She thus resolves upon 'this wholesome remedy of holy retirement' (p. 474), namely, to become a nun. And so the heroine, like Patrick's sisters, retires 'into her cell' (p. 475); 'the unfortunate Spaniard' is left to go his way.

Patrick Cary did not persist with his Benedictine novitiate: in September 1650 he returned to England to live with his sister Victoria; in March 1651 he converted to Protestantism and in September married a niece of Victoria's husband. Some thirty English poems or songs survive from this period, written in Patrick's neat hand: 'Triviall Ballades', each matched with a designated 'tune', followed by religious poems illustrated by pen-and-ink emblems.[109] In 1653 he held office at Drogheda and Trim, and in 1654 at County Louth. In 1655, while justice of the peace for County Meath and clerk of the pells (an exchequer office), he is said to be living 'an vnhansome rambling life, some times in Ireland and sometimes in England';[110] he dies in Dublin, the city of his birth, two years later, aged thirty-four. The difference between hagiography and romance is essentially a matter of hermeneutics: do accidents of plot reveal 'Gods most liberall hand', or are they—in the modern sense—accidental? While his sisters might have imparted providential shaping to their mother's *Life*, Patrick's own life genre turns out to be not hagiography, nor even romance, but rather the picaresque.[111]

---

109. The *ballade* beginning 'Fayre Beautyes! If I doe confesse / My selfe inconstant in my drincke', for example, is to be performed 'To the tune of *Troy–towne*' (*The Poems of Patrick Cary*, ed. Sister Veronica Delany (Oxford: Clarendon Press, 1978), pp. 9–10). The song-book portion of the manuscript shows signs of heavy use. Emblems include a two-tailed mermaid, a fool on a pedestal, and a winepress. This unique text was acquired by Walter Scott and published by John Murray in 1819; the disguised Charles II speaks of 'Pat Cary' in Scott's *Woodstock* (*Poems*, ed. Delany, pp. xiii, lxxxviii, xc–xci).

110. Percy Church to Sir Edward Nicholas, 29 October 1655, in Cary, *Life and Letters*, ed. Wolfe, 473–5 (p. 475); *Poems*, ed. Delany, p. lx–iii.

111. His sole-surviving son Edward, born at Dublin in 1656, became MP for Colchester at the time of the 1688 'Glorious Revolution', and High Bailiff of Westminster; he was thus near-neighbour to his long-lived aunt, Victoria. See *Poems*, ed. Delany, pp. lxii, lxvii.

Patrick Cary abandoned Benedictine life because, he said, he loved the quiet but hated the fish.[112] His brother Henry, the youngest son, was made of sterner stuff: he was professed Dom Placid at St Edmund's, Paris, in 1641. The highpoint of his public career as Benedictine priest came on 23 April 1651, when he preached in Paris before Henrietta Maria. Yet he too left Paris, converted to Protestantism, and (like Patrick) was admitted to Lincoln's Inn. In 1655 he sailed on the Cromwellian expedition to the West Indies as secretary to General Robert Venables. This was a catastrophe: by July, thousands of men lay dying off the coast of Jamaica. Henry was induced to frame two depositions, to the effect that Venables was not to blame: 'Mr Henry Cary', the second of them declares, 'is ready to depose upon Oath, being the expressions of a dying man'.[113] Historicist criticism, now a sickly patient, believed one sure thing: that a simple sentence, without intrinsic literary merit, may move as much as any line of poetry if its resonances be fully heard. Scenes of death, we have noted, supply the most vital nodes of narrative energy in *Lady Faulkland: Her Life*. The authors of this text are Benedictine; for them, the whole of life prepares for death. Henry, too, is a Benedictine; four years after preaching in Paris, however, he is 'a dying man' off Jamaica, forced to concentrate his last mortal thoughts, and literary endeavours, on a cheesy memo of exculpation.

How to live

Preparation for death shapes *Lady Faulkland: Her Life* from beginning to end: such was the training of its Benedictine authors. But such was not the chief life-aim of Lady Falkland herself: what she contrived to do was to live on Drury Lane. And to totter on stacked heels from Drury Lane to the high theatre of mass at Somerset House; to seek out entertaining religious controversialists; to read voraciously and to translate; to engage in speculative business ventures; to network with the high and mighty and to seek employment for a dancing daughter, or for a poor, would-be ship-swabber. Like Virginia Woolf, she preferred London life to Oxford, or Oxfordshire (although she happily

---

112. See his long letter to Clarendon, p. 450.
113. 'Deposition of Henry Cary', in *Life and Letters*, ed. Wolfe, pp. 471–3 (p. 471).

caters to Oxford's scholarly deficiencies by translating from the French). She goes on pilgrimage, twice, to St Winefride's Well in north Wales (Treffynnon): the most fashionable of high society Catholic excursions.[114] In short, she evolves a style of life for herself far different[115] from the life of enclosure chosen for *them*selves by her Benedictine daughters.

Enclosure has emerged as the single most powerful question for women in this book. Enclosure, enforced more severely upon Catholic women in the Renaissance than in the Middle Ages, guaranteed elite spiritual standing. It also diminished the chances of women's lives being written: like Chaucer's Second Nun, such women write the lives of others while remaining, themselves, unknown. We have no writing in Middle English known with certainty to be the work of a nun. The four *mulieres fortes* considered here live lives worth recording by borrowing something of the sanctity and seriousness of female enclosure, but then taking it on the road. All four, by way of modern comparison, are not film stars but stage actors, catching the eye with large gestures. Their choice between lives of secure and respected enclosure or of insecure public exposure is not, one would think, of concern to women of later times. The Protestant family, however, might be considered a form of female enclosure, since it proves exceptionally jealous of women's time; those Catholic occasions for getting out of the house enumerated by the Wife of Bath—vigils, processions, preachings, pilgrimages, miracle plays, and marriages (3.556-8)—have diminished.

114. Elizabeth Cary makes her November 1629 pilgrimage to St Winefride's Well, or Holywell (Welsh Treffynnon), accompanied by 'divers other knights, ladies, gentlemen and gentlewomen of diverse Cuntries to the number of fowerteene or fifteene hundreth', plus some 150 priests (*Life and Letters*, p. 342). Archbishop Laud's register, in Lambeth Palace Library, reports on 21 February 1637 'great resorte of Recusants to Holywell. And that this Summer the lady Falkland and her Company came as Pilgrimes thither, who were the more observed, because they travayled on foot, and *dissembled neither their qualitie* nor their Errand' (p. 404, emphasis added).
115. It was in summertime (August) that at St Winefride's Well, 'popular festivity prevailed over the spirit of Counter-Reformation restraint' (Michael A. Mullett, *Catholics in Britain and Ireland, 1558–1829* (New York: St Martin's Press, 1998), p. 31. On the positive encouragement of old pastimes under James I and Charles I, see Leah S. Marcus, *The Politics of Mirth: Jonson, Herrick, Milton, Marvell, and the Defense of Old Holiday Pastimes* (Chicago: University of Chicago Press, 1986), esp. pp. 3–6. The legendary Winefride, dating from the seventh century, miraculously survived decapitation by a would-be rapist and then lived as a nun; the exterior of the shrine, a highly sophisticated building, dates from the early sixteenth century.

It is perhaps in the contemporary university that the spirit of enclosure lives on, most powerfully: for in this (protected, if now only semi-
protected) environment, women may achieve stability of employment,
perform brilliantly, and so win fame within the academic world. It is
becoming commonplace not to notice that your chair, your dean, or
your university president are women.[116] It remains difficult, however,
to translate such accomplishment, and such favourable models of
employment, to the greater public sphere. Hopefully, as this work
approaches historical realization, there will continue to be differing
ways of living a life, leaving a *life*, as exemplified by the brilliant daughters, and brilliant mother, of *The Lady Faulkland: Her Life*.

116. As this book appears these positions at the University of Pennsylvania are held,
respectively, by Nancy Bentley, Rebecca Bushnell, and Amy Gutmann. It should be
noted that the work of university deans and presidents is performed (like that of a
premodern abbess) in an expanded public sphere; Judith Rodin, Amy Gutmann's
predecessor as Penn's president, likened herself to the CEO of a midsized
corporation.

Bibliography

'An Account of the Life of the Venerable Fr. Augustine Baker', *Ampleforth Journal*, 4 (1898), 59–74, 196–213.

Agamben, Giorgio, *Homo Sacer: Sovereign Power and Mere Life*, tr. Daniel Heller-Roazen (Stanford: Stanford University Press, 1998).

Akkerman, Nadine N. W., ' "Reader, Stand Still and Look, Lo Here I Am": Elizabeth Cary's Funeral Elegy "On the Duke of Buckingham"', in *Career*, ed. Wolfe, 183–200.

Allen, Hope Emily, 'Some Fourteenth Century Borrowings from *Ancrene Riwle*', *Modern Language Review*, 18 (1923), 1–8.

——'Further Borrowings from *Ancrene Riwle*', *MLR*, 24 (1929), 1–15.

Allen, Jr., John L., *Cardinal Ratzinger: The Vatican's Enforcer of the Faith* (NY: Continuum, 2000).

Altholz, Josef L., 'Simpson, Richard (1820–1876)', *ODNB* online (2004).

Ancrene Wisse, tr. Hugh White (London: Penguin, 1993).

Archibald, Elizabeth and A. S. G. Edwards, eds, *A Companion to Malory* (Cambridge: D.S. Brewer, 1996).

Argyle, Gisela., *German Elements in the Fiction of George Eliot, Gissing, and Meredith* (Frankfurt am Main: Peter Lang, 1979).

Arnold, John H. and Katherine J. Lewis, eds, *A Companion to The Book of Margery Kempe* (Cambridge: D.S. Brewer, 2004).

Atherton, Ian and Julie Sanders, eds, *The 1630s: Interdisciplinary Essays on Culture and Politics in the Caroline Era* (Manchester: Manchester University Press, 2006).

Atkinson, Clarissa W., *Mystic and Pilgrim: The Book and the World of Margery Kempe* (Ithaca: Cornell University Press, 1983).

Aubin, Herman, 'The Lands East of the Elbe and German Colonisation Eastwards', in *Cambridge Economic History of Europe*, 1, ed. Postan, 449–86.

Bald, R. C., *Donne and the Drurys* (Cambridge: Cambridge University Press, 1959).

Barber, Richard, 'The Round Table Feast of 1344', in *Round Table*, ed. Munby et al., 38–43.

Barnes, Diana, '*The Secretary of Ladies* and Feminine Friendship at the Court of Henrietta Maria', in *Henrietta Maria*, ed. Griffey, 39–56.

Barolini, Teodolinda, *The Undivine Comedy: Detheologizing Dante* (Princeton: Princeton University Press, 1992).

Barron, Caroline M., 'Pilgrim Souls: Margery Kempe and other Women Pilgrims', Confraternity of Saint James Occasional Paper no. 6 (London: Confraternity of St James, 2004).

Bartlett, Robert, *The Making of Europe: Conquest, Colonization and Cultural Change, 950–1350* (London: Allen Lane, 1993).

Barton, John and John Muddiman, eds, *The Oxford Bible Commentary* (Oxford: Oxford University Press, 2001).

Bartoš, F. M., *The Hussite Revolution 1424–1437*, tr. John M. Klassen (Boulder: East European Monographs, 1986).

Behn, Manfred, ed., *Wirkungsgeschichte von Christa Wolfs Nachdenken über Christa T.* (Königstein: Athenäum, 1978).

Beilin, Elaine V., ed., *The Examinations of Anne Askew* (New York: Oxford University Press, 1996).

Bell, H. I., 'Kenyon, Frederick George (1863–1952)', *ODNB* 31, 341a–343a.

Benedict XVI, Pope, see Ratzinger, Josef.

Bennett, J. A. W., ed., *Essays on Malory* (Oxford: Clarendon Press, 1963).

——rev. Emma Plaskitt, 'Lewis, Clive Staples (1898–1963)', *ODNB* 33, 593b–596a.

Bennett, Philip E., 'Vinaver, Eugène [Yevgeny Maksimovich Vinaver] (1899–1979)', *ODNB* 56, 528a–529a.

Bible, *Biblia Sacra iuxta Vulgatam Versionem*, ed. Robert Weber, 2 vols (Stuttgart: Württembergische Bibelanstalt, 1969).

——*The Holie Bible faithfully translated into English out of the authentical Latin*, tr. Cardinal Allen, Gregory Martin, and Richard Bristow, 2 vols (Douai: The English College, 1609).

——*The New Jerusalem Bible*, gen. ed. Henry Wansbrough (London: Darton, Longman and Todd, 1985).

Birch, Thomas, ed., *The Court and Times of Charles the First*, 2 vols (London: Henry Colburn, 1848).

Bloch, Howard, '842: The First Document and the Birth of Medieval Studies', in *French Literature*, ed. Hollier, 6–13.

Boccaccio, Giovanni, *Tutte le opere di Giovanni Boccaccio*, ed. Vittore Branca, 10 vols (Milan: Mondadori, 1964–98).

——*The Decameron*, tr. G. H. McWilliam, 2nd edn (London: Penguin, 1995).

Böthig, Peter, ed., *Christa Wolf: Eine Biografie in Bildern und Texten* (Munich: Luchterhand, 2004).

Boffey, Julia, '"Many grete myraclys...in divers contrys of the eest": The Reading and Circulation of the Middle English Prose *Three Kings of Cologne*', in *Medieval Women*, ed. Wogan-Browne et al., 35–47.

——and Pamela King, eds, *London and Europe in the Later Middle Ages* (London: Centre for Medieval and Renaissance Studies, Queen Mary and Westfield College, University of London, 1995).

Bogdanowicz, Stanisław, *The Basilica of St. Mary's Church in Gdańsk* (Dülmen: Edition Laumann, 1995).

Bonfil, Roberto, *Jewish Life in Renaissance Italy*, tr. Anthony Oldcorn (Berkeley: University of California Press, 1994).

Bordo, Susan, *Unbearable Weight: Feminism, Western Culture, and the Body*, 10th anniversary edn (Berkeley: University of California Press, 2003).

Boswell, A. Bruce, 'Jagiełło's Successors: The Thirteen Years' War with the Knights, 1434–66', in *History of Poland*, ed. Reddaway et al., 232–49.

Boswell, Grant, 'Letter Writing Among the Jesuits: Antonio Possevino's Advice in the *Bibliotheca Selecta* (1583)', *Huntington Library Quarterly*, 66.3–4 (2003), 247–262.

Bourdieu, Pierre, *La domination masculine* (Paris: Seuil, 1998).

—— *Masculine Domination*, tr. Richard Nice (Stanford: Stanford University Press, 2001).

Brady, Philip, Timothy Mcfarland, and John J. White, eds, *Günter Grass's Der Butt: Sexual Politics and the Male Myth of History* (Oxford: Clarendon Press, 1990).

Bray, Alan, *The Friend* (Chicago: University of Chicago Press, 2003).

Bridget of Sweden, *The Liber Celestis of St Bridget of Sweden*, ed. Roger Ellis, vol. I (Text), EETS, 291 (Oxford: Oxford University Press for EETS, 1987).

—— *Birgitta of Sweden: Life and Selected Revelations*, ed. Marguerite Tjader Harris, tr. Albert Ryle Kezel (New York: Paulist Press, 1989).

—— *Sancta Birgitta: Revelaciones*, Lib. VII, ed. Birger Bergh (Uppsala: Almqvist & Wiksells Boktryckeri, 1967).

Britland, Karen, *Drama at the Courts of Queen Henrietta Maria* (Cambridge: Cambridge University Press, 2006).

Brown, Sylvia, ed., *Women, Gender, and Radical Religion in Early Modern Europe* (Leiden: Brill, 2007).

Bruch, Hilde, *The Golden Cage: The Enigma of Anorexia Nervosa* (New York: Vintage, 1979).

Brückner, Undine and Regula Forster, 'Die Herzenserneuerung bei Dorothea von Montau, Katharina von Siena und Muhummad', *Oxford German Studies*, 39.2 (2010), 198-212.

Bryan, W. F. and Germaine Dempster, eds, *Sources and Analogues of Chaucer's Canterbury Tales* (New York: Humanities Press, 1958).

Burleigh, Michael, *Prussian Society and the German Order: An Aristocratic Corporation in Crisis, c.1410–1466* (Cambridge: Cambridge University Press, 1984).

Burns, George, 'Margery Kempe Reviewed', *The Month*, vol. 171 (March, 1938), 238–44.

Burns, J. H., ed., *The Cambridge History of Medieval Political Thought, c.300–1450* (Cambridge: Cambridge University Press, 1988).

Bushnell, Rebecca W., *Tragedies of Tyrants: Political Thought and Theater in the English Renaissance* (Ithaca: Cornell UP, 1990).

Butler, Martin, *The Stuart Court Masque and Political Culture* (Cambridge: Cambridge University Press, 2008).

Bynum, Caroline Walker, 'Why All the Fuss about the Body?: A Medievalist's Perspective', *Critical Inquiry*, 22 (Autumn 1995), 1–33.

—— *Wonderful Blood: Theology and Practise in Late Medieval Northern Germany and Beyond* (Philadelphia: University of Pennsylvania Press, 2006).

Caesarius Of Heisterbach, *The Dialogue on Miracles*, tr. H. von E. Scott and C. C. Swinton Bland, intr. G. G. Coulton, 2 vols (London: Routledge, 1929).

Cameron, Jennifer J. IBVM, *A Dangerous Innovator: Mary Ward, 1585-1645* (Strathfield, New South Wales: St. Pauls, 2000).

Camp, Claudia V., *Wisdom and the Feminine in the Book of Proverbs* (Sheffield: Almond, 1985).

Carlyle, E. I., rev. David Ibbetson, 'Tanfield, Sir Lawrence (*c.* 1551–1625)', *ODNB* 53, 760a–761a.

Carruthers, Mary, *The Book of Memory: A Study of Memory in Medieval Culture* (Cambridge: Cambridge University Press, 1990).

Carter, Francis W., *Trade and Urban Development in Poland: An Economic Geography of Cracow, from its Origins to 1795* (Cambridge: Cambridge University Press, 1994).

Carus-Wilson, Eleanora Mary, *Medieval Merchant Venturers: Collected Studies* (London: Methuen, 1954).

—— 'The Overseas Trade of Bristol', in *English Trade*, ed. Power and Postan, 183–246.

Carver, Martin, 'The Future of Sutton Hoo', in *Voyage to the Other World*, ed. Kendall and Wells, 183–200.

Cary, Elizabeth, 'A Conversion from the Time of Charles I', ed. Richard Simpson, *Rambler*, 8 (1857), 173–89, 258–72.

—— *Elizabeth Cary, Lady Falkland: Life and Letters*, ed. Heather Woolf, Renaissance Texts from Manuscript, 4 (Cambridge: RTM Publications, 2001).

—— *The History of the Life, Reign, and Death of Edward II King of England, and Lord of Ireland ... Written by E. F. in the year 1627* (London: J.C. for Charles Harper, 1680).

—— *The Lady Falkland, Her Life, from a Manuscript in the Imperial Archives at Lille*, ed. Richard Simpson (London: Catholic Publishing and Bookselling Company, 1861).

—— *The Tragedie of Mariam, Faire Queen of Jewry*, ed. A. C. Dunstan and W. W. Greg (London: Oxford University Press for the Malone Society, 1914).

—— *The Tragedy of Mariam the Fair Queen of Jewry with The Lady Falkland her Life by one of her Daughters*, ed. Barry Weller and Maureen Ferguson (Berkeley: University of California Press, 1994).

—— *Works By and Attributed to Elizabeth Cary*, ed. Margaret W. Ferguson, The Early Modern Englishwoman: A Facsimile Library of Essential Works, vol. 2 (Aldershot: Scolar Press, 1996).

Cary, Patrick, *Parole di Gio. Patrizio Carey messe in musica da Diversi Autori*, BL Additional MS 58853.

—— *The Poems of Patrick Cary*, ed. SisterVeronica Delany (Oxford: Clarendon Press, 1978).

Castle, Terry, *The Professor and Other Writings* (New York: Harper Collins, 2010).

Castree, Noel, 'Differential Geographies: Place, Indigenous Rights and "Local" Resources', *Political Geography*, 23 (Feb. 2004), 133–67.

Cavendish, Elizabeth and Jane, ed. Nathan Comfort Starr, '*The Concealed Fancies*: A Play by Lady Elizabeth Cavendish and Lady Elizabeth Brackley', *Publications of the Modern Language Association*, 46 (1931), 802–38.

Cavendish, Margaret, Duchess of Newcastle, *The Convent of Pleasure and Other Plays*, ed. Anne Shaver (Baltimore: Johns Hopkins University Press, 1999).

—— *Paper Bodies: A Margaret Cavendish Reader*, ed. Sylvia Bowerbank and Sara Mendelson (Peterborough, Ontario: Broadview, 2000).

—— *Playes* (London: A. Warren for J. Martyn, J. Allestry and T. Dicas, 1662).

Cerasano, S. P. and Marion Wynne-Davies, eds, *Renaissance Drama by Women: Texts and Documents* (London: Routledge, 1996).

Chambers IBVM, Mary C. E., *The Life of Mary Ward*, ed. H. J. Coleridge SJ, 2 vols (London: Burns and Oates, 1882–5).

Chambers, R. W., *On the Continuity of English Prose from Alfred to More and his School* (London: EETS, 1932).

Chaucer, Geoffrey, *The Riverside Chaucer*, ed. Larry D. Benson (Boston: Houghton Mifflin, 1987).

—— *The Workes of Geffray Chaucer newly printed* (London: Richard Grafton for Wyllyam Bonham, 1542).

Cherry, John, 'King John's Cup', in *King's Lynn and the Fens*, ed. McNeill, 1–16.

Cheung, King–Kok, *Articulate Silences: Hisaye Yamamoto, Maxine Hong Kingston, Joy Kogawa* (Ithaca, N.Y.: Cornell University Press, 1993).

Choudhury, Mita, *Convents and Nuns in Eighteenth-Century French Politics and Culture* (Ithaca: Cornell University Press, 2004).

Christiansen, Eric, *The Northern Crusades: The Baltic and the Catholic Frontier, 1100–1525* (London: Macmillan, 1980).

Cieślak, Edmund, ed., *Historia Gdańska*, 5 vols, incomplete (Gdańsk: Wydawnictwo Morskie, 1978–).

—— and Czesław Biernat, *History of Gdańsk*, tr. Bożenna Blaim and George M. Hyde (Gdańsk: Fundacji Biblioteki Gdnańskiej, 1995).

Clarendon, Edward [Hyde], Earl of, *The History of the Rebellion and Civil Wars in England begun in the Year 1641*, ed. W. Dunn McCray, XVI books in 6 vols (Oxford: Clarendon Press, 1888).

Clarke, K. P., *Chaucer and Italian Textuality* (Oxford: Clarendon Press, 2011).

Coleman, Janet, 'Property and Poverty', in *Medieval Political Thought*, ed. Burns, 607–48.

Conrad Of Heisterbach, *The Dialogue on Miracles*, 2 vols, tr. H. Von E. Scott and C. C. Swinton Bland, intr. G. G. Coulton (London: Routledge, 1929).

Cooper, Helen, *The English Romance in Time: Transforming Motifs from Geoffrey of Monmouth to the Death of Shakespeare* (Oxford: Oxford University Press, 2004).

Copeland, Rita, 'Chaucer and Rhetoric', in *Yale Companion*, ed. Lerer, 122–43.

——'Why Women Can't Read: Medieval Hermeneutics, Statutory Law, and the Lollard Heresy Trials', in *Representing Women*, ed. Heinzelman and Wiseman, 252–86.

——and Ineke Sluite, eds, *Medieval Grammar and Rhetoric: Language Arts and Literary Theory, AD 300–1475* (Oxford: Oxford University Press, 2009).

Correale, Robert M. and Mary Hamel, eds, *Sources and Analogues of the Canterbury Tales*, vol. I (Cambridge: D.S. Brewer, 2002).

Corthell, Ronald, Frances E. Dolan, Christopher Highly, and Arthur F. Marotti, eds, *Catholic Culture in Early Modern England* (Notre Dame: University of Notre Dame Press, 2009).

Coudenhove, Ida Goerres, *Mary Ward*, tr. Elsie Codd (London: Longmans, Green and Co., 1939).

Cox, Virginia, *Women's Writing in Italy, 1400–1650* (Baltimore: Johns Hopkins University Press, 2008).

Cross, John W., *George Eliot's Life, as Related in Her Letters and Journals*, 3 vols (Edinburgh and London: Blackwood, 1886).

Cummings, Brian, *The Literary Culture of the Reformation: Grammar and Grace* (Oxford: Oxford University Press, 2002).

——and James Simpson, eds, *Cultural Reformations: Medieval and Renaissance in Literary History* (Oxford: Oxford University Press, 2010).

——'Reformed Literature and Literature Reformed', in *Cambridge History*, ed. Wallace, 821–51.

Dalrymple, Roger, '"Evele knowen 3e Merlyne, in certeyn": Henry Lovelich's *Merlin*', in *Medieval Insular Romance*, ed. Weiss et al., 155–67.

Dante Alighieri, *The Divine Comedy*, tr. and ed. Robin Kirkpatrick, 3 vols (London: Penguin, 2006–7).

De Certeau, Michel, *The Writing of History*, tr. Tom Conley (New York: Columbia University Press, 1988).

De Cespedes Y Meneçes, Don Gonçalo, *Gerardo the Unfortunate Spaniard, or A Patterne for Lascivious Lovers. Containing severall strange miseries of loose Affection. Written by an ingenious Spanish Gentleman, Don Gonçalo de Cespedes, and Meneçes, in the time of his five yeeres Imprisonment. Originally in Spanish, and made English by L.D.* [Leonard Digges] (London: printed for Ed. Blount, 1622).

The deceyte of women. To the instruction and ensample of all men, yonge and olde, newly corrected (London: Abraham Vele, c. 1560).

De Groot, Jerome, 'Coteries, Complications and the Question of Female Agency', in *The 1630s*, ed. Atherton and Sanders, 189–209.

Devries, Kelly, *Joan of Arc: A Military Leader* (Thrupp: Sutton, 1999).

Diderot, Denis, *La Religieuse*, ed. Heather Lloyd (London: Bristol Classical Press, 2000).

—— *The Nun*, tr. and intr. Leonard Tancock, lithographs by Charles Mozley (London: Folio Society, 1972).

Dillon, Anne, *The Construction of Martyrdom in the English Catholic Community, 1535–1603* (Aldershot: Ashgate, 2002).

Dinshaw, Carolyn, *Getting Medieval: Sexualities and Communities, Pre- and Postmodern* (Durham, NC: Duke University Press, 1999).

——'Margery Kempe', in *Women's Writing*, ed. Dinshaw and Wallace, 222–39.

——'Temporalities', in *Middle English*, ed. Strohm, 107–23.

—— and David Wallace, eds, *The Cambridge Companion to Medieval Women's Writing* (Cambridge: Cambridge University Press, 2003).

Dolan, Frances E., *Whores of Babylon: Catholicism, Gender, and Seventeenth-Century Print Culture* (Ithaca: Cornell UP, 1999).

Donoghue, Daniel, *Lady Godiva: A Literary History of the Legend* (Oxford: Blackwell, 2003).

Drescher, Angela, ed., *Dokumentation zu Christa Wolf, Nachdenken über Christa T.* (Hamburg: Luchterhand, 1991).

Drost, Willi, *Die Marienkirche in Danzig und ihre Kunstschätze* (Stuttgart: W. Kohlhammer Verlag, 1963).

—— and Franz Swoboda, *Kunstdenkmäler der Stadt Danzig*, vol. 5, *St. Trinitatis, St. Peter und Paul, St Bartholomäi, St. Barbara, St. Elisabeth, Heilig Geist, Englische Kapelle, St. Brigitten* (Stuttgart: W. Kohlhammer Verlag, 1972).

Du Bosque, Jacques, *The Secretary of Ladies. Or, a New Collection of Letters and Answers Composed by Moderne Ladies and Gentlewomen*, tr. Jerome Hainhofer (London: Thomas Cotes for William Hope, 1638).

Du Castel, Étienne, *Ma Grand-Mère Christine de Pizan* (Paris: Hachette, 1936).

Du Castel, Françoise, *Damoiselle Christine de Pizan: Veuve de Madame Étienne de Castel, 1364–1431* (Paris: Éditions A., et J. Picard, 1972).

Duffy, Eamon, *Faith of Our Fathers: Reflections on Catholic Tradition* (London: Continuum, 2004).

—— *Fires of Faith: Catholic England under Mary Tudor* (New Haven: Yale University Press, 2009).

—— *The Stripping of the Altars: Traditional Religion in England, 1400–1580*, 2nd edn (New Haven: Yale University Press, 2005).

Dupuy, Micheline, *Henriette de France: Reine d'Angleterre* (Paris: Perrin, 1994).

Dures, Alan, *English Catholicism 1558–1642* (Harlow: Longman, 1983).

'Editorial Comments', *The Month*, 172 (July 1938), 3–4.

Edwards, A. S. G., ed., *A Companion to Middle English Prose* (Cambridge: D.S. Brewer, 2004).

——'The Reception of Malory's *Morte Darthur*', in *Companion to Malory*, ed. Archibald and Edwards, 241–52.

Eliot, George, *Middlemarch*, ed. Rosemary Ashton (London: Penguin Classics, 1994).

Elizabeth I, *Autograph Compositions and Foreign Language Originals*, ed. Janel Mueller and Leah S. Marcus (Chicago: University of Chicago Press, 2003).

—— *Collected Works*, ed. Leah S. Marcus, Janel Mueller, and Mary Beth Rose (Chicago: University of Chicago Press, 2000).

Elliott, Dyan, 'Authorizing a Life: The Collaboration of Dorothea of Montau and John Marienwerder', in *Gendered Voices*, ed. Mooney, 168–91.

Ellis, Pamela. '"They are but Women": Mary Ward, 1585–1645', in *Radical Religion*, ed. Brown, 243–63.

Ev. Kirche St. Nikolai, Bad Wilsnack (Regensburg: Verlag Schnell & Steiner, 1994).

Evans, Angela Care, *The Sutton Hoo Ship Burial*, revised edition (London: British Museum Press, 1994).

Fein, Susanna and David Raybin, eds, *Chaucer: Contemporary Approaches* (University Park: Pennsylvania State University Press, 2010).

Feistner, Edith, Michael Neecke, and Gisela Vollmann–Profe, *Krieg im Visier: Bibelepik und Chronistik im Deutschen Orden als Modell korporativer Identitätsbildung* (Tübingen: Max Niemeyer Verlag, 2007).

Fellows, Otis, *Diderot*, 2nd edn (Boston: Twayne, 1989).

Finney, Gail, *Christa Wolf* (New York: Twayne, 1999).

Flandreau, Annie, 'Du Nouveau sur Marguerite Delamarre et "La Religieuse" de Diderot', *Dix–Huitième Siècle*, 24 (1992), 410–19.

Ford, Aleksander, *Krzyżacy* (TVP S.A./ Pegaz, 1960).

Foster, Allyson, 'A Short Treatyse of Contemplacyon: *The Book of Margery Kempe* in its Early Print Contexts', in *Companion*, ed. Arnold and Lewis, 95–112.

Foxe, John, *Actes and Monuments* (London: John Day, 1563).

Freeman, Thomas S., 'Harpsfield, Nicholas (1519–1575)', *ODNB* online (2004).

Fridl, Marcus, *Englishe Tugend–Schul…Maria Ward*, 2 vols (Augsburg, 1732).

Gamache, Cyprien, 'Memoirs of the Mission in England of the Capuchin Friars of the Province of Paris, from the Year 1630 to 1669', in *Court and Times*, ed. Birch, II, 289–501.

Gardner, Edmund G., ed., *The Cell of Self–Knowledge: Seven Early English Mystical Treatises Printed by Henry Pepwell in 1521* (London: Chatto and Windus, 1910).

Gillespie, Vincent, 'Vernacular Books of Religion', in *Book Production*, ed. Griffiths and Pearsall, 317–44.

Gillis, Stacey, Gillian Howie, and Rebecca Munford, eds, *Third Wave Feminism: A Critical Exploration* (Basingstoke: Palgrave Macmillan, 2004).

Gizzi, Corrado, ed., *Giovanni Stradano e Dante* (Milano: Electa, 1994).

Goebel, Ulrich and David Lee, eds, *Interpreting Texts from the Middle Ages: The Ring of Words in Medieval Literature* (Lewiston, NY: Edwin Mellen Press, 1994).

Goenner, Mary Ellen, *Mary-Verse of the Teutonic Knights* (Washington: Catholic University of America Press, 1943).

Goodman, Anthony, *Margery Kempe and Her World* (London: Longman, 2002).

Gower, John, *Complete Works*, ed. G. C. Macaulay, 4 vols (Oxford: Clarendon Press, 1899–1902).

Gransden, Antonia, *Historical Writing in England, II: c. 1307 to the Early Sixteenth Century* (Ithaca: Cornell University Press, 1982).

Grass, Günter, *Beim Häuten der Zwiebel* (Göttingen: Steidl, 2006).

——*Peeling the Onion*, tr. Michael Henry Heim (London: Harvill Secker, 2007).

——*Die Blechtrommel: Roman* (Darmstadt: Luchterhand, 1959).

——*The Tin Drum*, tr. Ralph Manheim (London: Secker and Warburg, 1970).

——*Der Butt: Roman* (Darmstadt: Hermann Luchterhand Verlag, 1997).

——*The Flounder*, tr. Ralph Manheim (Brooklyn, New York: Fawcett Crest, 1979).

Greene, Graham, *Articles of Faith: The Collected Tablet Journalism of Graham Greene*, ed. Ian Thomson (Oxford: Signal Books, 2006).

Greene, Roland, *Unrequited Conquests: Love and Empire in the Colonial Americas* (Chicago: University of Chicago Press, 1999).

Griffey, Erin, ed., *Henrietta Maria: Piety, Politics, and Patronage* (Aldershot: Ashgate, 2008).

Griffiths, Jeremy and Derek Pearsall, eds, *Book Production and Publishing in Britain, 1375–1475* (Cambridge: Cambridge University Press, 1989).

Grimme, Ernst Günther, *Der Aachener Domschatz* (Düsseldorf: Verlag L. Schwann, 1972).

Grisar SJ, Josef, *Die ersten Anklagen in Rom gegen das Institut Maria Wards, 1622* (Rome: Pontificia Università Gregoriana, 1959).

Grummitt, David, 'Participants in the Field of Cloth of Gold (*act.* 1520)', *ODNB* online (Sept 2009).

Gumbrecht, Hans Ulrich, '"Un Souffle d'Allemagne Ayant Passé": Friedrich Dietz, Gaston Paris, and the Genesis of National Philologies', *Romance Philology*, 40 (1986), 1–37.

Gunn, Cate, *Ancrene Wisse: From Pastoral Literature to Vernacular Spirituality* (Cardiff: University of Wales Press, 2008).

Haeberli, Simone. '*Manchirley groz bitter und lang liden*: Herkunft, Zweck und theologische Rechtfertigung der Leiden Dorotheas von Montau in der deutschen Vita des Johannes Marienwerder', *Oxford German Studies*, 39.2 (2010), 124–37.

Haigh, Christopher, 'From Monopoly to Minority: Catholicism in Early Modern England', *Transactions of the Royal Historical Society*, 5th series, 31 (1981), 129–47.

Haight, Gordon S., *George Eliot: A Biography* (New York: Viking Penguin, 1985).

Hakluyt, Richard, *Voyages, Navigations, Traffiques, and Discoueries of the English Nation*, 3 vols (London: George Bishop, Ralf Newberie, and Robert Barker, 1598–1600).

Halecki, O., 'Problems of the New Monarchy: Jagiełło and Vitold, 1400–34', in *Cambridge History of Poland*, ed. Reddaway et al., 210–31.

Hamrick, Nicholas, *The Catholic Imaginary and the Cult of Elizabeth, 1558–1582* (Farnham: Ashgate, 2009).

Hanawalt, Barbara A., *'Of Good and Ill Repute': Gender and Social Control in Medieval England* (New York: Oxford University Press, 1998).

Harbus, Antonina, *Helena of Britain in British Legend* (Cambridge: D.S. Brewer, 2002).

Harpsfield, Nicholas, *A Treatise on the Pretended Divorce between Henry VIII and Catherine of Aragon*, ed. Nicholas Pocock, Camden Society, NS 21 (London: Camden Society, 1878).

Harvey, Margaret, *The English in Rome, 1362–1420: Portrait of an Expatriate Community* (Cambridge: Cambridge University Press, 1999).

Heinzelman, Susan Sage and Zipporah Batshaw Wiseman, eds, *Representing Women: Law, Literature, and Feminism* (Durham: Duke University Press, 1994), 252–86.

Helm, Karl and Walter Ziesemer, *Die Literatur des Deutschen Ritterordens* (Giessen: Wilhelm Schmitz Verlag, 1951).

Henry, Astrid, *Not My Mother's Sister: Generational Conflict and Third-Wave Feminism* (Bloomington: Indiana University Press, 2004).

Hess, Cordelia, *Heilige machen im spätmittelalterlichen Ostseeraum: Die Kanonisationsprozesse von Birgitta von Schweden, Nikolaus von Linköping und Dorothea von Montau* (Berlin: Akadamie Verlag, 2008).

Hibbard, Caroline M., 'Henrietta Maria', *ODNB* 26, 392a–406a.

Hierarchomachia or The Anti–Bishop, ed. Suzanne Gossett (East Brunswick: Associated University Presses, 1982).

Higden, Ranulph, *Polychronicon*, ed. Churchill Babington (vols 1–2) and Joseph R. Lumby (vols 3–9), Rolls Series (London: Longman etc., 1865–86).

Hilzinger, Sonja, *Christa Wolf*, Suhrkampf BasisBiographie, 24 (Frankfurt am Main: Suhrkamp, 2007).

Hipler, Franz, rev. Hans Westpfahl, 'Johannes Marienwerder, der Beichtvater der seligen Dorothea von Montau', *Zeitschrift für die Geschichte und Altertumskunde Ermlands*, 29 (1954), 1–92.

Hirsch, John C., *Hope Emily Allen: Medieval Scholarship and Feminism* (Norman, Oklahoma: Pilgrim Books, 1988).

Hirsch, Theodor, Max Töppen, and Ernst Strehlke, eds, *Scriptores rerum Prussicarum*, 5 vols (Leipzig: S. Hirzel, 1861–74).

Hitchens, Christopher, *Hitch-22: A Memoir* (London: Atlantic Books, 2010).

Hoby, Margaret, *Diary of Lady Margaret Hoby, 1599–1605*, ed. Dorothy M. Meads (London: Routledge, 1930).

Hodges, Kenneth, 'Wounded Masculinity: Injury and Gender in Sir Thomas Malory's *Le Morte Darthur*', *Studies in Philology*, 106.1 (2009), 14–31.

Hörner, Petra, *Dorothea von Montau. Überlieferung-Interpretation; Dorothea und die osteuropäische Mystik* (Frankfurt am Main: Peter Lang, 1993).

Hollier, Denis, ed., *A New History of French Literature* (Cambridge, MA: Harvard University Press, 1989).

Hollington, Michael, *Günter Grass: The Writer in a Pluralist Society* (London: Marion Boyars, 1980).

Hollywood, Amy, *Sensible Ecstasy: Mysticism, Sexual Difference, and the Demands of History* (Chicago: University of Chicago Press, 1992).

Holroyd, Sophie, '"Rich Embroidered Churchstuffe": The Vestments of Helena Wintour', in *Catholic Culture*, ed. Corthell et al., 73–116.

Holt, Geoffrey, *St. Omers and Bruges Colleges, 1559–1773: A Biographical Dictionary*, CRS Publications (Records Series), 69 (London: CRS, 1979).

Horrox, Rosemary, ed. and tr., *The Black Death* (Manchester: Manchester University Press, 1994).

Horstmann, C., ed., *The Three Kings of Cologne: An Early English Translation of the Historia Trium Regum by John of Hildesheim*, EETS OS 85 (London: EETS, 1886).

Howard, Anthony, *Basil Hume: The Monk Cardinal* (London: Headline Nook Publishing, 2005).

Huber, Augustinus Kurt, ed., *Sacrum Pragense Millennium, 973–1973* (Königstein: Königsteiner Institut für Kirchen- und Geistesgeschichte der Südetenländer, 1973).

Hughes, Jonathan, 'Mary Stafford, *née* Boleyn, *other married name* Carey (*c.*1499–1543)', *ODNB* online (Jan 2009).

Hulme, Peter, *Colonial Encounters: Europe and the Native Caribbean 1492–1797* (London: Methuen, 1986).

Humphreys, C. C., *The French Executioner* (London: Orion, 2002).

Innes-Parker, Catherine, 'The Legacy of *Ancrene Wisse*: Translations, Adaptations, Influences, and Audience, with Special Attention to Women Readers', in *Companion*, ed. Wada, 145–73.

Ives, Eric W., *Anne Boleyn* (Oxford: Basil Blackwell, 1986).

Jacobus De Voragine, *The Golden Legend*, tr. William Granger Ryan, 2 vols (Princeton: Princeton University Press, 1993).

James I & VI, King of England and Scotland, *An Apologie for the Oath of Allegiance: Together, with a Premonition of his Majesties to all most mightie Monarches, Kings, free Princes and States of Christendome* (London: Robert Barker, 1609).

Javierre, José Maria with Maria De Pablo–Romero IBVM, *La Jesuitessa Mary Ward: Mujer rebelde que rompió moldes en la Europa del XVII* (Madrid: Libros Libres, 2002).

Jocelin, Elizabeth, *The Mothers Legacie, to her Unborne Childe*, second impression (London: John Haviland for William Barrett, 1624).

Johannes Von Marienwerder, *Des Leben der zeligen frawen Dorothee clewsenerynne yn der thumkyrchen czu Marienwerdir des landes czu Prewszen*, ed. Max Toepen, in *Scriptores rerum Prussicarum*, ed. Hirsch, Töppen, and Strehlke, II, 197–350.

Johannes Von Marienwerder, *The Life of Dorothea von Montau, a Fourteenth-Century Recluse*, tr. Ute Stargardt, Studies in Women and Religion, 39 (Lewiston, NY: Edwin Mellen Press, 1997).

——*Septililium Beatae Dorotheae Montoviensis*, ed. Franz Hipler (Brussels: Polleunis, Ceuterick and Lefébure, 1885).

Jones, Michael, ed., *The New Cambridge Medieval History, vol. VI, c.1300–c.1415* (Cambridge: Cambridge University Press, 2000).

Jones, Terry, *Chaucer's Knight: The Portrait of a Medieval Mercenary*, rev. edn (London: Methuen, 1985).

Jones, Trevor, ed., *The Oxford–Harrap Standard German–English Dictionary*, 4 vols (Oxford: Clarendon Press, 1977).

Julian of Norwich, *The Writings of Julian of Norwich*, ed. Nicholas Watson and Jacqueline Jenkins (University Park: Penn State University Press, 2006).

Justice, Steven, 'Literary History', in *Chaucer*, ed. Fein and Raybin, 199–214.

Keen, M. H., 'Oakeshott, Sir Walter Fraser (1903–1987)', *ODNB* 41, 322a–323a.

Kelly, Joan, *Women, History, and Theory* (Chicago: University of Chicago Press, 1984).

Kelsey, Sean, 'Cary, Henry, first Viscount Falkland (c.1575–1633)', *ODNB* online (Jan. 2008).

Kempe, Dorothy, *The Legend of the Holy Grail, its Sources, Character, and Development. The Introduction to, and Part V of, Henry Lovelich's Verse 'History of the Holy Grail'*, EETS ES 95 (London: N. Trübner for EETS, 1905).

Kempe, Margery, *The Book of Margery Kempe*, ed. Sanford Brown Meech with prefatory note by Hope Emily Allen and notes and appendices by Sanford Brown Meech and Hope Emily Allen, EETS OS 212 (Oxford: Oxford University Press for EETS, 1940).

—— *The Book of Margery Kempe 1436: A Modern Version*, tr. W. Butler-Bowdon, with an introduction by R. W. Chambers (London: Jonathan Cape, 1936).

—— *The Book of Margery Kempe*, ed. Barry Windeatt (Cambridge: D.S. Brewer, 2004).

Kendall, Calvin B. and Peter S. Wells, eds, *Voyage to the Other World: The Legacy of Sutton Hoo* (Minneapolis: University of Minnesota Press, 1992).

Kendrick, T. D., ed., *The Sutton Hoo Ship Burial: A Provisional Guide* (London: British Museum, 1947).

Kieckhefer, Richard, *Unquiet Souls: Fourteenth-Century Saints and Their Religious Milieu* (Chicago: University of Chicago Press, 1984).

Kingsford, Charles Lethbridge, ed., *Chronicles of London* (Oxford: Clarendon Press, 1905).

Kinoshita, Sharon, '"Pagans are Wrong and Christians are Right": Alterity, Gender, and Nation in the *Chanson de Roland*', *Journal of Medieval and Early Modern Studies*, 31:1 (2001), 79–111.

Kipling, Gordon, 'Wriothesley, Charles (1508–1562)', *ODNB* online (2004).

Kirkham, Victoria and Armando Maggi, eds, *Petrarch: A Critical Guide to the Complete Works* (Chicago: University of Chicago Press, 2009).

Kirkus CJ, Gregory, *The Companions of Mary Ward* (Strasbourg: Éditions du Signe, 2009).

Kirkpatrick, Robin, *Dante's Paradiso and the Limitations of Modern Criticism: A Study of Style and Poetic Theory* (Cambridge: Cambridge University Press, 1978).

Kishlansky, Mark A. and John Morrill, 'Charles I', *ODNB* 11, 96a–122b.

Klapisch-Zuber, Christiane, *Women, Family, and Ritual in Renaissance Italy*, tr. Linda Cochrane (Chicago: University of Chicago Press, 1985).

Kölbel, Martin, ed., *Ein Buch, Ein Bekenntnis: Die Debatte um Günter Grass' Beim Häuten der Zwiebel* (Göttingen: Steidl, 2007).

Kolve, V. A., *Chaucer and the Imagery of Narrative: The First Five Canterbury Tales* (London: Edward Arnold, 1984).

Krug, Roberta, 'Margery Kempe', in *Medieval English Literature*, ed. Scanlon, 217–28.

Kuhn, Anna K., 'Rewriting GDR History: The Christa Wolf Controversy', *GDR Bulletin*, 17 (Spring 1991), 7–11.

Lancelot of the Laik and Sir Tristrem, ed. Alan Lupack (Kalamazoo, Michigan: Medieval Institute Publications, 1994).

Lanyer, Aemelia, *The Poems of Aemelia Lanyer*, ed. Susanne Woods (New York: Oxford University Press, 1993).

Latini, Brunetto, *La Rettorica*, ed. Francesco Maggini (Florence: Galletti and Cocci, 1915).

——— *Tesoretto*, ed. and tr. Julia Bolton Holloway (New York: Garland, 1981).

Lerer, Seth, ed., *The Yale Companion to Chaucer* (New Haven: Yale University Press, 2006).

Lewalski, Barbara Kiefer, *Writing Women in Jacobean England* (Cambridge, MA: Harvard University Press, 1993).

Lewis, C. S., 'What Chaucer Really Did to Il Filostrato', *Essays and Studies*, 17 (1932), 56–75.

The Libelle of Englyshe Polycye: a poem (attributed to A. Molyneux) on the use of sea-power, 1436, ed. Sir George Frederic Warner (Oxford: Clarendon, 1926).

Littlehales CJ, Margaret Mary, *Mary Ward: Pilgrim and Mystic, 1585–1645* (Tunbridge Wells: Burns and Oates, 1998).

Litwin, Jerzy, 'Boat and Ship Archaeology in Poland', in *Down the River to the Sea: Eighth International Symposium on Boat and Ship Archaeology, Gdańsk, 1997*, ed. Litwin (Gdańsk: Polish Maritime Museum, 2000), 7–10.

Livländische Reimchronik, ed. Leo Meyer (Paderborn: Ferdinand Schöningh, 1876).

The Livonian Rhymed Chronicle, tr. Jerry C. Smith and William L. Urban (Bloomington: Indiana University, 1977).

Lloyd, T. H., *England and the German Hanse, 1157–1611* (Cambridge: Cambridge University Press, 1991).

Lochrie, Karma, *Margery Kempe and Translations of the Flesh* (Philadelphia: University of Pennsylvania Press, 1991).

Löffler, Anette, 'Das sogenannte deutschsprachige Stundenbuch', in *Deutschsprachige Literatur*, ed. Päsler and Schmidtke, 95–106.

Lonelich, Herry, see Lovelich, Henry.

Loomie, A. J., 'Wadsworth, James, *pseud*. Diego de Vadesfoote (b. 1604)', *ODNB* online (2004).

Lovelich, Henry [Herry Lonelich]. *The History of the Holy Grail*, ed. Frederick J. Furnivall, EETS ES 20, 24, 28, 30, 95 Part I (London: N. Trübner for EETS, 1874–1905).

——*Merlin*, ed. Ernst A. Kock, EETS ES 93, 112, OS 185 (London: Oxford University Press for EETS, 1904–32).

Lovell, Mary S., *The Mitford Girls: The Biography of an Extraordinary Family* (London: Little, Brown, 2001).

Lowes, John Livingston, *The Road to Xanadu: A Study in the Ways of the Imagination* (Boston: Houghton Mifflin, 1927).

Lützow, Franz Heinrich Hieronymus Valentin, *The Hussite Wars* (London: J. M. Dent, 1914).

Lukowski, Jerzy and Hubert Zawadzki, *A Concise History of Poland* (Cambridge: Cambridge University Press, 2001).

Lumley, Jane, *Iphigenia at Aulis, Translated by Lady Lumley*, ed. Harold H. Child and W. W. Greg, Malone Society Reprint Series (London: Charles Whittingham, 1909).

Makowski, Elizabeth, *Canon Law and Cloistered Women: Periculoso and its Commentators, 1298–1545* (Washington DC: Catholic University of America Press, 1997).

Malory, Sir Thomas, *Works*, ed. Eugene Vinaver, 2nd edn (Oxford: Oxford University Press, 1971).

Mann, Jill, *Chaucer and Medieval Estates Satire* (Cambridge: Cambridge University Press, 1973).

Mann, Thomas, *Der Tod in Venedig: Novelle* (Berlin: S. Fischer, 1922).

Marcus, Leah S., *The Politics of Mirth: Jonson, Herrick, Milton, Marvell, and the Defense of Old Holiday Pastimes* (Chicago: University of Chicago Press, 1986).

Marron, Stephen OSB, 'Annals of our Monastery in Paris', *Douai Magazine*, 5.3 (1929), 202–7.

——'The English Benedictines and the Stuarts', *Douai Magazine*, 1.4 (1921), 249–59.

Marshall, Rosalind K., *Henrietta Maria: The Intrepid Queen* (London: HMSO, 1990).

Martin, Randall, ed., *Women Writers in Renaissance England* (London: Longman, 1997).

Mayer, T. F., 'Sander, Nicholas (c. 1530–1581)', *ODNB* online (Oct. 2007).

McCobb, Anthony, *George Eliot's Knowledge of German Life and Letters* (Salzburg: Institut für Anglistik und Americanistik, 1982).

McConica, James Kelsey, *English Humanists and Reformation Politics under Henry VIII and Edward VI* (Oxford: Clarendon Press, 1965).

McCoog, Thomas M., *English and Welsh Jesuits 1555–1650*, 2 vols, Catholic Record Society Publications (Records Series), 74–5 (CRS, 1994–5).

——'The Society of Jesus in the Three Kingdoms', in *Companion to Jesuits*, ed. Worcester, 88–103.

McCullough, Diarmid, *Reformation: Europe's House Divided 1490–1700* (London: Penguin/Allen Lane, 2003).

—— *Tudor Church Militant: Edward VI and the Protestant Reformation* (London: Penguin/Allen Lane, 1999).

McFarland, Thomas, 'The Transformation of Historical Material: The Case of Dorothea von Montau', in Brady, McFarland, and White, eds, *Günter Grass's Der Butt*, 69–96.

McGrath, Patrick, *The Merchant Venturers of Bristol* (Bristol: Society of the Merchant Venturers of the City of Bristol, 1975).

McLaren, Mary-Rose, *The London Chronicles of the Fifteenth Century: A Revolution in English Writing* (Cambridge: D.S. Brewer, 2002).

McMullan, Gordon and David Matthews, eds, *Reading the Medieval in Early Modern England* (Cambridge: Cambridge University Press, 2007).

McNeill, John, ed., *King's Lynn and the Fens: Medieval Art, Architecture and Archaeology*, The British Archaeological Association Conference Transactions, 31 (2008) (Leeds: Maney, 2008), 1–16.

Meale, Carol M., '*The Libelle of Englyshe Polycye* and Mercantile Literary Culture in Late-Medieval London', in *London and Europe*, ed. Boffey and King, 181–228.

Medioli, Francesca, 'An Unequal Law: The Enforcement of *Clausura* before and after the Council of Trent', in *Women*, ed. Meek, 136–52.

Meek, Christine, ed., *Women in Renaissance and Early Modern Europe* (Dublin: Four Courts Press, 2000), 136–52.

Meltzer, Françoise, *For Fear of the Fire: Joan of Arc and the Limits of Subjectivity* (Chicago: University of Chicago Press, 2001).

Mentzel-Reuters, Arno, 'Das pomesanische Domkapitel als literarisches Zentrum: Der Fall des Prager Magisters Johannes Marienwerder', in *Deutschsprachige Literatur*, ed. Päsler and Schmidtke, 157–75.

Middle English Dictionary, ed. Hans Kurath, Sherman M. Kuhn (G–P), and Robert E. Lewis (Q–Z), 20 vols (Ann Arbor: University of Michigan Press, 1952–2001).

Middleton, Thomas, *A Game at Chess*, ed. R. C. Bald (Cambridge: Cambridge University Press, 1929).

Milton, Anthony, 'Heylyn, Peter (1599–1662)', *ODNB* online (Jan. 2008).

Montagu, Walter, *The Shepherd's Paradise*, ed. Sarah Poynting, Malone Society Reprints, 159 (Oxford: Oxford University Press for the Malone Society, 1998).

Mooney, Catherine M., ed., *Gendered Voices: Medieval Saints and Their Interpreters* (Philadelphia: University of Pennsylvania Press, 1999).

Morris, Bridget, *St Birgitta of Sweden* (Woodbridge, Suffolk: The Boydell Press, 1999).

Morris SJ, John, *The Troubles of Our Catholic Forefathers: Related by Themselves*, first series (London: Burns and Oates, 1872).

Morse, Charlotte C., 'Exemplary Griselde', *Studies in the Age of Chaucer*, 7 (1985), 51–86.

Mossman, Stephen, 'Dorothea von Montau and the Masters of Prague', *Oxford German Studies*, 39.2 (2010), 106–23.

Mountney, Hugh, *The Three Holy Kings of Cologne: How They Journeyed to Cologne and Their Veneration in England* (Leominster: Gracewing, 2003).

Mueller, Janel, 'Katherine Parr and Her Circle', in *Tudor Literature*, ed. Pincombe and Shrank, 222–37.

Mullett, Michael A., *Catholics in Britain and Ireland, 1558–1829* (New York: St Martin's Press, 1998).

Munby, Julian, Richard Barber, and Richard Brown, *Edward III's Round Table at Westminster: The House of the Round Table and the Windsor Festival of 1344* (Woodbridge: Boydell Press, 2007).

Murphy, G. Martin, 'Wadsworth, James (c.1572–1623)', *ODNB* online (2004).

Murphy, Paul V., 'Jesuit Rome and Italy', in *Cambridge Companion to Jesuits*, ed. Worcester, 71–87.

Nashe, Thomas, *The Works of Thomas Nashe*, ed. Ronald B. McKerrow, with corrections and supplementary notes by F. P. Wilson, 5 vols (Oxford: Basil Blackwell, 1958).

Neame, Alan, *The Holy Maid of Kent: The Life of Elizabeth Barton, 1506–1534* (London: Hodder and Stoughton, 1971).

Newman, Barbara, *From Virile Woman to Woman Christ* (Philadelphia: University of Pennsylvania Press, 1995).

—— *Sister of Wisdom: St Hildegard's Theology of the Feminine* (Aldershot: Scolar Press, 1987).

Nicholson, Helen, *Love, War, and the Grail* (Leiden: Brill, 2001).

Nieborowski, Paul, *Die selige Dorothea von Preussen: Ihr Heiligsprechungsprozess und ihre Verehrung bis in unsere Zeiten* (Breslau: Ostdeutsche Verlagsanstalt, 1933).

Nolan, Maura, *John Lydgate and the Making of Public Culture* (Cambridge: Cambridge University Press, 2005).

Normington, Katie, *Medieval English Drama: Performance and Spectatorship* (Cambridge: Polity Press, 2009).

Nuttall, A. D., *Dead from the Waist Down: Scholars and Scholarship in Literature and the Popular Imagination* (New Haven: Yale University Press, 2003).

Oakshott, W. F., 'The Finding of the Manuscript', in *Essays on Malory*, ed. Bennett, 1–6.

Olsen, Tillie, *Silences* (London: Virago, 1980).

O'Neill, Rosemary, *Accounting for Salvation in Middle English Literature*, Ph.D. Dissertation (2009), University of Pennsylvania.

Ormond, Leonée, *St Joan by George Bernard Shaw* (London: Macmillan, 1986).

Overy, Richard, *The Morbid Age: Britain Between the Wars* (London: Allen Lane, 2009).

Oxford Dictionary Of National Biography, ed. H. G. C. Matthew and Brian Harrison, 61 vols (Oxford: Oxford University Press, 2004), plus online supplements.

Oxford–Harrap Standard German–English Dictionary, ed. Trevor Jones, 4 vols (Oxford: Clarendon Press, 1977).

Päsler, Ralf G. and Dietrich Schmidtke, eds, *Deutschsprachige Literatur des Mittelalters in östlichen Europa* (Heidelberg: Universitätsverlag Winter, 2006).

Paley, Grace, 'Introduction' to Wolf, *Writer's Dimension*, ed. Stephan, vii–xii.

Paludanus, François, *A Short Relation of the Life, Virtues, and Miracles of S. Elizabeth called the Peacemaker. Queen of Portugall, translated out of Dutch by Sister Catherine Francis, Abbess of the English Monasterie of S. Francis third Rule, in Bruxelles* (Brussells: John Morris, 1628).

Parker, Kate, 'Lynn and the Making of a Mystic', in *Companion*, ed. Arnold and Lewis, 55–73.

Perry, Curtis, '"Royal Fever" and "The Giddy Commons": Cary's *History of the Life, Reign, and Death of Edward II* and The Buckingham Phenomenon', in *Career*, ed. Wolfe, 71–88.

Peters CJ, Henriette, *Mary Ward: A World in Contemplation*, tr. Helen Butterworth CJ (Leominster: Gracewing, 1995).

Petersson, R. T., *Sir Kenelm Digby: The Ornament of England, 1603–1665* (Cambridge, MA: Harvard University Press, 1956).

Petrarca, Francesco, *Seniles* 17.3, ed. J. Burke Severs (from Biblioteca Apostolica Vaticana, Rome, MS Vat. Lat. 1666) in *Sources and Analogues*, ed. Bryan and Dempster, 288–331.

—— *Seniles* 17.3, ed. Thomas J. Farrell (from Peterhouse, Cambridge, MS 81, collated with eight other manuscripts) in *Sources and Analogues*, ed. Correale and Hamel, 108–29.

Phillimore, J. S., 'Blessed Thomas More and the Arrest of Humanism in England', *Dublin Review*, 153 (1913), 1–26.

Pincombe, Mike and Cathy Shrank, eds, *The Oxford Handbook of Tudor Literature, 1485–1603* (Oxford: Oxford University Press, 2009).

Pincus, Steve, *1688: The First Modern Revolution* (New Haven: Yale University Press, 2009).

Postan, M. M., ed., *The Cambridge Economic History of Europe*, vol. 1, *The Agrarian Life of the Middle Ages*, 2nd edn (Cambridge: Cambridge University Press, 1966).

—— *Medieval Trade and Finance* (Cambridge: Cambridge University Press, 1973).

Postan, M. M., 'The Trade of Medieval Europe: The North', in *Trade and History*, ed. Postan and Miller, 168–305.

——and Edward Miller, eds, *The Cambridge Economic History of Europe*, vol. 2, *Trade and History in the Middle Ages*, 2nd edn (Cambridge: Cambridge University Press, 1987).

Power, Eileen and M. M. Postan, eds, *Studies in English Trade in the Fifteenth Century* (London: George Routledge, 1933).

Poynting, Sarah, ' "The Rare and Excellent Partes of Mr Walter Montague": Henrietta Maria and her Playwright', in *Henrietta Maria*, ed. Griffey, 73–88.

Purkiss, Diane, *The English Civil War: Papists, Gentlewomen, Soldiers, and Witchfinders in the Birth of Modern Britain* (New York: Basic Books, 2006).

Quarrie, Bruce, *Hitler's Teutonic Knights: SS Panzers in Action* (Wellingborough: Patrick Stevens, 1986).

Rabasa, José, *Inventing A–m–e–r–i–c–a* (Norman: University of Oklahoma Press, 1993).

Ratzinger, Josef, *Die Christliche Brüderlichkeit* (Munich: Kösel Verlag, 1960).

——*The Meaning of Christian Brotherhood* (San Francisco: Ignatius Press, 1993).

——*Christlicher Glaube und Europa. 12 Predigten* (Munich: Erzdiözese München und Freiin, 1981).

——Interview with *Le Figaro* as reported by CWNews.com, Paris, 11 August 2004.

——'The Spiritual Roots of Europe: Yesterday, Today, and Tomorrow', in Ratzinger and Marcello Pera, *Without Roots: The West, Relativism, Christianity, Islam*, foreword by George Wiegel, tr. Michael F. Moore (New York: Basic Books, 2007), 51–80.

——<www.ratzingerfanclub.com> 2000-2005; see now www.popebenedictxvi fanclub.com.

——<www.thepapalvisit.com> Address to Teachers and Religious, Chapel of St Mary's College, Twickenham, Friday, 17 September 2010.

Reddaway, W. F., J. H. Penson, O. Halecki, and R. Dybowski, eds, *The Cambridge History of Poland: From the Origins to Sobieski (to 1696)* (Cambridge: Cambridge University Press, 1950).

Rex, Richard, *Henry VIII and the English Reformation*, 2nd edn (Basingstoke: Palgrave Macmillan, 2006).

Robinson, Solveig C., 'Fullerton, Lady Georgiana Charlotte (1812–1885)', *ODNB* online (Sept. 2004).

Röder–Bolton, Gerlinde, *George Eliot in Germany, 1854–55: 'Cherished Memories'* (Aldershot: Ashgate, 2006).

Rogers, Nicholas, ed., *England in the Fifteenth Century: Proceedings of the 1992 Harlaxton Symposium*, ed. Nicholas Rogers (Stamford: Paul Watkins, 1994).

Rossman, Heribert, 'Johannes Marienwerder OT, ein ostdeutscher Theologe des späten Mittelalters', in *Sacrum Pragense*, ed. Huber, 221–33.

Rowell, S. C., 'Baltic Europe', in *New Cambridge Medieval History, VI*, ed. Jones, 699–734.

Rubin, Miri, *Mother of God: A History of the Virgin Mary* (London: Allen Lane, 2009).

Rühle, Siegfried, 'Dorothea von Montau. Das Lebensbild einer Danziger Bürgerin des XV. Jahrhunderts', *Altpreussiche Forschungen*, 2 (1925), 59–101.

Samson, Alexander, ed., *The Spanish Match: Prince Charles's Journey to Madrid, 1623* (Aldershot: Ashgate, 2006).

Sandberger, Dietrich, *Studien über das Rittertum in England, vornehmlich während des 14. Jahrhunderts* (Berlin: Verlag Dr. Emil Ebering, 1937).

Sander, Nicolas, *Rise and Growth of the Anglican Schism*, tr. and intr. David Lewis (London: Burns and Oates, 1877).

Sanok, Catherine, *Her Life Historical: Exemplarity and Female Saints' Lives in Late Medieval England* (Philadelphia: University of Pennsylvania Press, 2007).

Savage, Anne and Nicholas Watson, tr. and intr., *Anchoritic Spirituality: Ancrene Wisse and Associated Works* (New York: Paulist Press, 1991).

Scala, Elizabeth, 'The Gender of Historicism', in *The Post-Historical Middle Ages*, ed. Scala and Sylvia Federico (New York: Palgrave Macmillan, 2009), 191–214.

Scanlon, Larry, ed., *The Cambridge Companion to Medieval English Literature 1100–1500* (Cambridge: Cambridge University Press, 2009).

Scheper-Hughes, Nancy, *Child Survival: Anthropological Perspectives on the Treatment and Maltreatment of Children*, ed. Scheper-Hughes (Dordrecht: D. Reidel, 1987).

——*Death Without Weeping: The Violence of Everyday Life in Brazil* (Berkeley: University of California Press, 1992).

Schlauch, Margaret, 'King Arthur in the Baltic Towns', *Bulletin Bibliographique de la Société Internationale Arthurienne*, 11 (1959), 75–80.

——'A Sixteenth-Century English Satirical Tale about Gdańsk', *Kwartalnik Neofilologiczny*, 4 (1957), 95–120.

Schlöndorff, Volker, *Die Blechtrommel* (1979).

——*Der Unhold* (1996).

Seaward, Paul, 'Hyde, Edward, first earl of Clarendon (1609–1674)', *ODNB* 29, 120a–138a.

Shahar, Shulamith, *Growing Old in the Middle Ages*, tr. Jael Lotan (London: Routledge, 1997).

Shakespeare, William, *Hamlet*, ed. Ann Thompson and Neil Taylor (London: Arden Shakespeare, 2006).

——*Mr. William Shakespeares Comedies, Histories, & Tragedies* (London: Isaac Jaggard, 1623).

Sharpe, Kevin, *The Personal Rule of Charles I* (New Haven: Yale University Press, 1992).

Shaw, Bernard, *The Complete Plays of Bernard Shaw* (London: Constable, 1931).

Sheehan, Jonathan, 'Sacred and Profane: Idolatry, Antiquarianism, and the Polemics of Distinction in the Seventeenth Century', *Past and Present, 192* (August 2006), 35–66.

Simmonds CJ, Gemma, 'Female Jesuits', in *Companion to Jesuits*, ed. Worcester, 120–35.

——'Recognition at Last', *The Tablet* (7 Feb. 2004), 11.

Simpson, James, *Reform and Cultural Revolution*, The Oxford English Literary History, 2, *1350–1547* (Oxford: Oxford University Press, 2002).

Simson, Paul, *Der Artushof in Danzig und seine Brüderschaften, die Banken* (Danzig: T. Bertling, 1900).

Smith, D. Vance, *Arts of Possession: The Middle English Household Imaginary* (Minneapolis: University of Minnesota Press, 2003).

Smith, David L., 'Cary, Lucius', *ODNB* 10, 440a–445a.

Smith, Lucy Toulmin, ed., *Expeditions to Prussia and the Holy Land made by Henry Earl of Derby (afterwards King Henry IV) in the Years 1390–1 and 1392–3. Being the Accounts kept by his Treasurer during two years* (London: Camden Society, 1894).

Sobecki, Sebastian I. *The Sea and Medieval English Literature* (Cambridge: D.S. Brewer, 2008).

Spearing, A. C., 'Margery Kempe', in *Companion*, ed. Edwards, 83–97.

—— *Textual Subjectivity: The Encoding of Subjectivity in Medieval Narratives and Lyrics* (Oxford: Oxford University Press, 2005).

Spearritt OSB, Placid, 'The Survival of Mediaeval Spirituality among the Exiled English Black Monks', in *Mysterious Man*, ed. Woodward, 42–56.

Spengler, Oswald, *The Decline of the West*, tr. C. F. Atkinson, 2 vols (London: Allen and Unwin, 1926–8).

Spencer, Brian, *Pilgrim Souvenirs and Secular Badges*, Medieval Finds from Excavations in London, 7 (London: Stationery Office, 1998).

Spurling, Hilary, *The Girl from the Fiction Department: A Portrait of Sonia Orwell* (London: Hamish Hamilton, 2002).

Stachnik, Richard, ed., *Die Akten des Kanonisationsprozesses Dorotheas von Montau von 1394 bis 1521*, ed. Richard Stachnik (Cologne: Böhlau Verlag, 1978).

Staley, Lynn, *Margery Kempe's Dissenting Fictions* (University Park: Pennsylvania State University Press, 1994).

Stargardt, Ute, 'Dorothea von Montau, the Language of Love, and Jacop Karweysze, "Goldsmyd"', in *Interpreting Texts*, ed. Goebel and Lee, 305–21.

——'Political and Social Backgrounds of the Canonization of Dorothea von Montau', *Mystics Quarterly*, 11 (1985), 107–22.

Stephan, Alexander, ed., *The Writer's Dimension: Selected Essays*, tr. Jan van Heurck (London: Virago, 1993).

Stephen, Sir Leslie and Sir Stephen Lee, eds, *The Dictionary of National Biography: From the Earliest Times to 1900* (London: Oxford University Press, 1973).

Strasse, Ulrike, *State of Virginity: Gender, Religion, and Politics in an Early Modern Catholic State* (Ann Arbor: University of Michigan Press, 2004).

Stratford, Jenny, 'John, duke of Bedford (1389–1435)', *ODNB* 30, 183b–190a.

Strohm, Paul, *England's Empty Throne: Usurpation and the Language of Legitimation, 1399–1422* (New Haven: Yale University Press, 1998).

——ed., *Middle English*, Oxford Twenty-First Century Approaches to Literature (Oxford: Oxford University Press, 2007).

Suerbaum, Almut, '"O wie gar wunderlich ist die wibes sterke!": Discourses of Sex, Gender, and Desire in Johannes Marienwerder's Life of Dorothea von Montau', *Oxford German Studies,* 39.2 (2010), 181–97

——and Annette Volfing, eds, *Oxford German Studies,* 39.2 (2010), a special issue dedicated to Dorothea von Montau.

Summit, Jennifer, *Lost Property: The Woman Writer and English Literary History, 1380–1589* (Chicago: University of Chicago Press, 2000).

Sutton, Anne F., 'Caxton was a Mercer: His Social Milieu and Friends', in *England in the Fifteenth Century*, ed. Rogers, 118–48.

Szpakiewicz, Alina, *The Artus Court*, tr. Danuta Gumowska (Gdańsk: Museum of the History of Gdańsk, 1996).

Talbot, C. H., ed. and tr., *The Life of Christina of Markyate: A Twelfth Century Recluse* (Oxford: Clarendon Press, 1959).

Taylor, Gary, 'Middleton, Thomas', *ODNB* 38, 79a–85a.

Terdiman, Richard, *Body and Story: The Ethics and Practise of Theoretical Conflict* (Baltimore: Johns Hopkins University Press, 2005).

Teresa Of Calcutta, Blessed Mother, *Mother Teresa: Come Be My Light. The Private Writings of the 'Saint of Calcutta'*, ed. and with commentary by Brian Kolodiejchuk (New York: Doubleday, 2007).

Thomas, R. S., *Poems of R. S. Thomas* (Fayetteville: University of Arkansas Press, 1985).

Times, The, http://archive.timesonline.co.uk/tol/archive/

Times Literary Supplement, The, *http://entertainment.timesonline.co.uk/tol/arts_ and_entertainment/the_tls/*

Thrupp, Sylvia L., *The Merchant Class of Medieval London (1300–1500)* (Ann Arbor: University of Michigan Press, 1948).

Tilbury, Jasper and Paweł Turnau, *Blue Guide to Poland* (London: A & C Black, 2000).

Tillotson, John, 'Visitation and Reform of the Yorkshire Nunneries in the Fourteenth Centuries', *Northern History*, 30 (1994), 1–21.

Tomlinson, Sophie, *Women on Stage in Stuart Drama* (Cambridge: Cambridge University Press, 2005).

Toomaspoeg, Kristjan, *Histoire des Chevaliers Teutoniques* (Paris: Flammarion, 2001).

Tournier, Michel, *Le Roi des Aulnes* (Paris: Gallimard, 1970).

Trigg, Stephanie, 'The Vulgar History of the Order of the Garter', in *Reading the Medieval*, ed. McMullan and Matthews, 91–105.

Urban, William, *The Teutonic Knights: A Military History* (London: Greenhill Books, 2003).

Van Biema, David, 'Mother Teresa's Crisis of Faith', *Time* (23 August, 2007).

Vauchez, André, *Sainthood in the Later Middle Ages*, tr. Jean Birrell (Cambridge: Cambridge University Press, 1997).

Veale, Elspeth, 'Gregory, William (d. 1467)', *ODNB* 23, 685a–b.

Veevers, Erica, *Images of Love and Religion: Queen Henrietta Maria and Court Entertainments* (Cambridge: Cambridge University Press, 1989).

Vinaver, Elizabeth, 'Eugène Vinaver', in *The Winawer Saga*, ed. Winawer, 166–93.

Vinaver, Eugène, Letter to Kenneth Sisam, 30 June 1934, Oxford University Press Archives, 917.16.

Volfing, Annette, '"Du bist selben eyn himmel": Textualization and Transformation in the "Life" of Dorothea von Montau', *Oxford German Studies*, 39.2 (2010), 147–59.

Von Bülow, W., *Heinrich von Plauen: Des deutschen Ritterordens letzter Held* (Leipzig: Verlag für Literatur, Kunst und Musik, 1911).

Wada, Yoko, ed., *A Companion to Ancrene Wisse* (Cambridge: D.S. Brewer, 2003).

——'What is *Ancrene Wisse*', in *Companion*, ed. Wada, 1–28.

Wadsworth, James, *The English Spanish Pilgrime, or A New Discoverie of Spanish Popery and Jesuitical Strategems. With the Estate of the English Pentioners and Fugitives under the King of Spaines Dominions, and else where at this present. Also laying open the new Order of the Iesuitrices and preaching Nunnes* (London: T.C. for Michael Sparke, 1630).

Wainwright, Jonathan P., 'Sounds of Piety and Devotion: Music in the Queen's Chapel', in *Henrietta Maria*, ed. Griffey, 195–213.

Walker, Claire, *Gender and Politics in Early Modern Europe: English Convents in France and the Low Countries* (Basingstoke: Palgrave Macmillan, 2003).

Wall, Wendy, *The Imprint of Gender: Authorship and Publication in the English Renaissance* (Ithaca, NY: Cornell University Press, 1993).

Wallace, David, ed., *The Cambridge History of Medieval English Literature* (Cambridge: Cambridge University Press, 1999).

Chaucerian Polity: Absolutist Lineages and Associational Forms (Stanford: Stanford University Press, 1997).

—— *Giovanni Boccaccio: Decameron* (Cambridge: Cambridge University Press, 1991).

——'Inside East Germany', *The Tablet*, 231 (1977), 859–60, 884–5.

——'*Letters of Old Age*: Love between Men, Griselda, and Farewell to Letters', in *Petrarch*, ed. Kirkham and Maggi, 321–30.

——'Nuns', in *Cultural Reformations*, ed. Cummings and Simpson, 502–23.

——'Periodizing Women: Mary Ward (1585–1645) and the Premodern Canon', *Journal of Medieval and Early Modern Studies*, 36.2 (Spring 2006), 395–451.

—— *Premodern Places: Calais to Surinam, Chaucer to Aphra Behn* (Oxford: Blackwell, 2004).

Walsingham,Thomas, *Historia Anglicana 1272–1422*, ed. H.T. Riley, 2 vols, Rolls Series (1863–4).

Ward, Mary, The Venerable. *Mary Ward und ihre Gründung: Die Quellentexte bis 1645*, ed. Ursula Dirmeier CJ, 4 vols, Corpus Catholicorum 45–8 (Münster: Aschendorff Verlag, 2007).

——*Mary Ward (1585–1645): A Briefe Relation …with Autobiographical Fragments and a Selection of Letters*, ed. Christina Kenworthy-Browne CJ (Woodbridge: Boydell Press for the Catholic Record Society, 2008).

——*Till God Will: Mary Ward through her Writings*, ed. Emmanuel Orchard IBVM, intr. James Walsh SJ, foreword by Mother Teresa of Calcutta (London: Darton, Longman and Todd, 1985).

Warnicke, Retha M., *Women of the English Renaissance and Reformation* (Westport, CT: Greenwood Press, 1983).

Warren, Michelle R., *History on the Edge: Excalibur and the Borders of Britain 1100–1300* (Minneapolis: University of Minnesota Press, 2000).

——'Translation', in *Middle English*, ed. Strohm, 51–67.

Warren, Nancy Bradley, *Spiritual Economies: Female Monasticism in Later Medieval England* (Philadelphia: University of Pennsylvania Press, 2001).

——*Women of God and Arms: Female Spirituality and Political Conflict, 1380–1600* (Philadelphia: University of Pennsylvania Press, 2005).

Watson, Nicholas, '*Ancrene Wisse*, Religious Reform, and the Late Middle Ages', in *Companion*, ed. Wada, 197–226.

Weber, Max, *Reason and Society*, ed. Guenther Roth and Claus Wittich, 2 vols (Berkeley: University of California Press, 1978).

Weir, Alison, *The Lady in the Tower: The Fall of Anne Boleyn* (New York: Ballantine Books, 2010).

Weiss, Judith, Jennifer Fellows, and Morgan Dickson, eds, *Medieval Insular Romance* (Cambridge: D.S. Brewer, 2000).

Wetter CJ, Immolata, *Maria Ward: Misverständnisse und Klärung* (Augsburg: Augsburger Universität, 1993).

——*Mary Ward in Her Own Words*, trans. Bernadette Ganne CJ (Rome: Istituto Beata Vergine Maria, 1999).

——*Mary Ward under the Shadow of the Inquisition*, tr. Bernadette Ganne CJ and Patricia Harriss CJ (Oxford: Way Books, 2006).

White, Michelle Anne, *Henrietta Maria and the English Civil Wars* (Aldershot: Ashgate, 2006).

Whitfield, Peter, *London: A Life in Maps* (London: British Library, 2006).

Whitman, Walt, *Leaves of Grass*, ed. Jerome Loving (Oxford: Oxford University Press, 1990).

Wildhagen, Harald and Torsten Buchholz, *Der Lettner im Dom zu Havelberg* (Halle-Zürich: Verlag Janos Stekovics, 1995).

Winawer, Herman Marjan, ed., *The Winawer Saga* (London: H. M. Winawer, 1994).

Windeatt, B. A., 'Introduction: Reading and Re-reading *The Book of Margery Kempe*', in *Companion*, ed. Arnold and Lewis, 1–16.

Wisłoujście Fortress: History, Present, Future (Gdańsk: Muzeum Historii Miasta Gdańska, 2000).

Wittig, Susan, *Stylistic and Narrative Structures in the Middle English Romances* (Austin: University of Texas Press, 1978).

Wogan-Browne, Jocelyn, Rosalynn Voaden, Arlyn Diamond, Ann Hutchison, Carol M. Meale, and Lesley Johnson, eds, *Medieval Women: Texts and Contexts in Late Medieval Britain: Essays for Felicity Riddy* (Turnhout: Brepols, 2000).

Wolf, Christa, *Nachdenken über Christa T.*, ed. Sonja Hilzinger (Munich: Luchterhand, 1999).

—— *The Quest for Christa T.*, tr. Christopher Middleton (New York: Farrar, Straus and Giroux, 1970).

—— *Was bleibt: Erzählung* (Frankfurt am Main: Luchterhand, 1990).

—— *What Remains and Other Stories*, tr. Heike Schwarzbauer and Rick Takvorian (New York: Farrar, Strauss and Giroux, 1993).

Wolfe, Heather, ed., *The Literary Career and Legacy of Elizabeth Cary, 1613–1680* (New York: Palgrave Macmillan, 2007).

Wolfrum, Heinrich, *Die Marienburg: Das Haupthaus des Deutschen Ritterordens und seine Geschichte* (Leer, Ostfriedland: Verlag Gerhard Rautenberg, 1972).

Woodward, Michael, ed., *That Mysterious Man: Essays on Augustine Baker OSB, 1575–1641*, intr. Rowan Williams (Abergavenny, Wales: Three Peaks Press, 2001).

Woolf, Virginia, *Between the Acts*, ed. Frank Kermode (Oxford: Oxford University Press, 1992).

—— *The Diary of Virginia Woolf*, ed. Anne Olivier Bell, assisted by Andrew McNeillie, 5 vols (London: Hogarth Press, 1977–84).

Worcester, Thomas, ed., *The Cambridge Companion to the Jesuits* (Cambridge: Cambridge University Press, 2008).

Wright, C.J., ed., *Sir Robert Cotton as Collector: Essays on an Early Stuart Courtier and his Legacy* (London: British Library, 1997).

Wriothesley, Charles, Windsor Herald, *A Chronicle of England during the Reigns of the Tudors*, ed. William Douglas Hamilton, 2 vols, Camden Society NS 11, 20 (London: Camden Society, 1875–77).

Yoshikawa, Naoë Kukita, *Margery Kempe's Meditations: The Context of Medieval Devotional Literature, Liturgy, and Iconography* (Cardiff: University of Wales Press, 2007).

Zbierski, Andrej, 'The Maritime Fortress of Wisłoujście as seen in the Complex Research by the Department of Archaeology of IHKM PAN and the Central Maritime Museum', in *Wisłoujście Fortress*, 29–49.

Zehm, Günter, 'Nachdenken über Christa W.', in *Wirkungsgeschichte*, ed. Behn, 38–9.

Index

University of 246
Oxfordshire xxx, 248

Painted Life (Das Gemalte Leben)
141, *145*, 150, *150*, 152, *153*,
156, 160–1, *162*, 163, 164, 170,
184, 194
Palestine 58
Palffy, Mária, Countess 176
Palmer, Katherine 212*n*
papacy, role of 37, 170, 181
Paris xx, 63, 245
St Edmund's 207, 227*n*
University of 38
Parker, Kate 85
Parsons, Robert 148
Particular Congregation of Four
Cardinals 177
Paston, Margaret 199
Paston family 76
Pastoralis Romanis Pontifici (Bull of
Suppression) xxxi, 134, 139,
178, 178–9, 184, 186
Paul V, Pope 168
Paul VI, Pope 48
Payne, Peter 114
Pennsylvania, University of 250*n*
Pepwell, Henry 65
Periculoso 137
Perron, Cardinal Jacques-Davy du
229, 238–9
Perry, Curtis 217–18
Perugia 139
Petrarch xviii, 135
Seniles 10–11, 20–1
Pettenger, Dunstan 227*n*
Philip II, King of Spain 158
pilgrimage 3, 24, 78, 82–3, 86–7,
170, 249
A Pistil of Susan 236
Pius V, Pope 137
Pius XII, Pope 138*n*
Pleasington Old Hall, Lancashire 70
Poland 28, 37, 39, 47*n*
Poor Clares 156*n*, 158, 159–60, 185,
186

Postan, Maurice 98, 114, 115
Poyntz, Mary 140, 141, 145, 147,
163*n*, 187, 188, 190, 192, 198,
227*n*
Poyntz, Sir Robert 147*n*
Prague 17, 139, 176
archbishop of 120*n*
Price, Sir Bartholomew 244*n*
Prior, Jim 232*n*
Propaganda Fidei 175
Prussia 2, 4, 13–14, 16, 24, 39, 41, 54,
58, 101–2
Punch 43*n*

Radcliffe College 65
The Rambler 222
Rant, Thomas 143, 174–5, 182, 194
Ratzinger, Josef (later Pope Benedict
XVI) xviii, xxxi, 48, 53, 61,
135, 136, 138*n*
Die Christliche Brüderlichkeit 58–9
Christlicher Glaube und Europa 58
Ravaillac, François 164
Recusants 148, 224
Redshaw, Mr 150
Reformation, English xxi, xxii–xxiii
Reformation Studies xxvi
Reineke Fuchs 44*n*
religious, as category xxvi
Rex, Richard xxv
Reymann, Johannes 26
Richard II, King xx, 91*n*, 102
Richardson, Elizabeth 233
Richelieu, Armand-Jean, Cardinal 180
Robert of Avesbury 30
Robinson, F. N. 68
Rodin, Judith 250*n*
Rolle, Richard 65, 67, 70*n*
romance, and hagiography xxvii,
140, 151, 247
Rome 2, 3, 34, 82, 86, 119, 138, 139,
140, 141, 168–76, 187, 189, 240
Campo dei Fiori 186
Chancellery 186
hospice of St Thomas, later English
College xxvi*n*, 180, 245

Printed and bound by CPI Group (UK) Ltd, Croydon, CR0 4YY